The Cloth of Many Colored Silks

Northwestern University Press

Series in Islam and Society in Africa

The Cloth of Many Colored Silks *Papers on History and Society Ghanaian and Islamic in Honor of Ivor Wilks*

EDITED BY JOHN HUNWICK AND NANCY LAWLER

Northwestern University Press
EVANSTON, ILLINOIS

Northwestern University Press
Evanston, Illinois 60208-4210

Printed in the United States of America

ISBN: 0-8101-1299-X

Library of Congress Cataloging-in-Publication Data

The cloth of many colored silks : papers on history and society, Ghanaian and Islamic in honor of Ivor Wilks / edited by John Hunwick and Nancy Lawler.
p. cm. — (Series in Islam and society in Africa)
Includes bibliographical references (p.).
ISBN 0-8101-1299-X (cloth : alk. paper)
1. Ghana—History. 2. Islam—Africa, West—History. 3. Africa, West—Religion. I. Hunwick, John O. II. Lawler, Nancy Ellen. III. Wilks, Ivor. IV. Series.
DT510.5.C56 1997
966.7—dc21 96-47480
CIP

The paper used in this publication meets the minimum requirements of the American National Standard for Information Sciences—Permanence of Paper for Printed Library Materials, ANSI Z39.48-1984.

Contents

CONTENTS

Introduction

It is an unusual pleasure to write an introduction to a volume of essays dedicated to a colleague whose work I have admired and whose friendship I have enjoyed for more than thirty years. I first met Ivor Wilks when I visited the University of Ghana in December 1962 for a conference of the Historical Society of Ghana, at a time when I was teaching at the University of Ibadan. I was already familiar with his ground-breaking *The Northern Factor in Ashanti History,* and drew on it in the paper I presented there. Over the coming few years I got to know him better as I visited Ghana for conferences and as external examiner for M.A. theses in African Studies.

The theses were among the early fruits of a graduate training program at the Institute of African Studies. Thomas Hodgkin, a close friend of Ivor's, had taken over directorship of the institute in 1961, and had inspired a rich program of research and teaching. The institute provided an intellectual home for a distinguished group of scholars—Peter Shinnie, Polly Hill, Bradford Martin, Greville Freeman-Grenville, Kwabena Nketia, Yaw Andoh, Salah Ibrahim, and of course Ivor Wilks—and research training for younger scholars, such as Charles Stewart and Paulo de Moraes Farias, who would later become authorities in their own fields. Among the many initiatives of this period of the early 1960s for which Ivor and Thomas Hodgkin were primarily responsible was the photocopying of close to five hundred local manuscripts in Arabic, Hausa, and, in a few cases, Ghanaian languages in the Arabic script. None of this would have been possible without the dedicated collaboration of a Ghanaian Muslim scholar and imam, Alhaji Osmanu Esaka Boyo, whose patience, goodwill, and multilingual talents persuaded owners of private collections to open up their treasures. Ivor enjoyed an especially close relationship with Alhaji Osmanu, who as senior research assistant accompanied him on many of his field trips.

After Ivor left Ghana in 1966 I kept in touch with him, at least sporadically, and always read with deep interest his publications on the Dyula Muslim tradition in West Africa. Fifteen years later our paths came together again, and on a closer and more enduring basis, when I took up an appointment in the Department of History at Northwestern University, where Ivor had been a tenured professor since 1966. Over the next twelve years, from 1981 until Ivor's retirement in 1993, we saw each other on an almost daily basis, and although our different research agendas and the demands of teaching and administration prevented us from undertaking much joint work of substance, the period was one of continual intellectual stimulation and maturing friendship.

When he announced his impending retirement I made it my pleasant duty to organize a presentation volume for him with the help of Nancy Lawler, whom he had married in 1989. Keeping this a secret from Ivor until the appropriate time required some diplomacy, and there must have been times when our coded telephone conversations and whispered asides in Ivor's company caused puzzlement—if nothing more. The response to our call for contributions was overwhelming, and we were able to put together a rich and varied Festschrift comprising contributions by many of Ivor's former graduate students and a wide spectrum of friends and colleagues. Altogether thirty-two contributions were received and were handsomely bound in two volumes, with an addendum containing two that arrived at the last minute. A second set was made and is now housed in the Melville J. Herskovits Library of Africana at Northwestern University. The essays were presented to Ivor during the course of an unforgettable farewell reception in his honor on 22 May 1993, attended by colleagues and friends as well as many former students now teaching at various universities.

It was hard to establish a principle for selection of essays for a published volume, since it inevitably meant excluding many excellent contributions from old friends and former students. In the end we decided that the focus would be on the two themes that have dominated Ivor's African research: Ghanaian history and Muslim communities of West Africa. Regretfully we had to ask many authors to find other publishing venues, though their contributions are permanently incorporated in the library copy of the Festschrift. A list of such papers is given below.

I had at first thought that I would write a long and learned introduction to this published volume. On reflection it became clear that I lacked the learning—certainly as far as Ghanaian history is concerned—that might have made such an introduction of any value. Nor yet did it seem worthwhile, in the manner of many such introductions, merely to summarize the content of some or all of the papers and pour praise on their authors. Good wine needs no bush! In this spirit, then, I decided simply to let the contributors speak for themselves, and this they do with both eloquence and learning.

This volume would not have been possible without the dedicated assistance of many persons: the contributors who not only wrote the essays but responded with unsurpassed alacrity to the demands made of them by the editors; Nancy Lawler and Roberta Zimmerman, who performed miracles of formatting and computer translation for the original presentation volumes; Ray Kea, who took the initiative, and the Department of History and the dean of the Faculty of Arts and Sciences at the University of California, Riverside, who provided publication subventions; also the Department of History, Northwestern University, which hosted Ivor's farewell party jointly with the Northwestern Program of African Studies, and contributed toward the publication subvention; and Nicholas Weir-Williams, director of the Northwestern University Press, who recognized that this was, indeed, an exceptional volume honoring an exceptional scholar.

John Hunwick
June 1995

JOHN HUNWICK

List of Additional Papers in the Original Festschrift

A. I. Asiwaju: Borderlands in Africa: A Comparative Research Perspective with Particular Reference to Western Europe

Hamidu Bobboyi: The *'Ulamā'* and the State in Sayfawa Bornu: the Role of the Mahrams (published in *Sudanic Africa* 4 [1993]: 175–204)

Daniel Britz: Bibliography of Nineteenth-Century European Travellers to Asante

Lisa Brock: The Molungu Cometh: Capital, Class and "Being Shangaan" in Late Nineteenth-Century Gaza

David W. Cohen: Men in Power . . . Men of Wealth: Investigations into the Death of The Honourable Minister John Robert Ouko in Kenya, February, 1990

Ronald Cohen: Individualism and Collectivism in African Political Culture: A Revisionist Perspective

Jonathon Glassman: Stolen Knowledge: Struggles for Popular Islam in Nineteenth-Century East Africa

Karen Tranberg Hansen: Local Court, Custom, and Gender Relations in Post-Colonial Lusaka

John O. Hunwick: A Historical Whodunit: The So-Called Kano Chronicle and Its Place in the Historiography of Kano (published in *History in Africa* 21 [1994]: 127–46)

Cheryl Johnson-Odim: The Lioness of Lisabi: The Fall of a Ruler

Nehemiah Levtzion: Eighteenth-Century Renewal and Reform in Islam: The Role of the Sufi *Ṭuruq* in West Africa

Gregory Maddox and Pamela A. Maack: Land, Labor, and Capital in East Africa: How Traditional Is Tradition?

Carl F. Petry: From Slaves to Benefactors: The Ḥabashīs of Cairo (published in *Sudanic Africa* 5 [1994]: 57–66)

John Rowe: Muslim Historical Memoirs from Buganda

Charles C. Stewart: Colonial Justice and the Resurgence of Islam in Twentieth-Century West Africa

Ibrahim Sundiata: Trade and State Formation Revisited: The Rise and Fall of the Bubi Polity, c. 1840–1910

Timothy Welliver: Observations on the Mwinyi Mkuu of Unguja

Ivor Wilks: A Biographical Note

Ivor Wilks was born in England in 1928. His father's family had farmed for centuries on the Warwickshire and Gloucestershire border; his mother's had its roots near Wrexham in North Wales. Both parents were teachers. His father had a deep interest in local history, and many weekends and holidays were spent poring over parish registers and the like, and in exploring the sites of prehistoric settlements and medieval abandoned villages. This was to be the basis of Ivor's abiding interest in history, although it was to be many years before he was to make it his profession.

After completing elementary and junior school, in 1938 Ivor won a scholarship to Bablake, in Coventry. He was to spend only two years there; the school had to be closed as a result of the massive German air raid of 14–15 November 1940. Evacuated to Lincoln, he attended its grammar school for several months, and then his parents were transferred to the southern Warwickshire village of Warmington, in order to supplement local teaching resources hard-pressed by the influx of evacuees from the towns. Ivor joined them there, and continued his secondary school education first at Banbury County School and then at Leamington College.

Country life suited Ivor. He became skilled in farm practices now virtually extinct: mowing by scythe, building haystacks, laying hedges, and so forth. He decided to become a veterinarian. Accordingly he pursued scientific subjects in the sixth form. This career choice, however, was abruptly abandoned in 1945, during his final year at Leamington College, when a much-beribboned brigadier, recruiting for the Indian Army, talked to the sixth formers on the glory and romance of soldiering in far-flung parts of the Empire. The idea of assisting cows and sheep to reproduce

Ivor Wilks.

immediately lost its appeal, and Ivor decided to dedicate his life to the Raj. He informed the brigadier accordingly. It remained to convince his bemused parents of the wisdom of his choice. Reluctantly, they gave their approval.

As an Indian Army cadet attached to the Queen's Royal Regiment, Ivor underwent a long and grueling training at the Guards Depot, Caterham. He should have completed the remaining courses in India, but this was not to be. The end of the Raj was imminent, and the services of new British officers were no longer required. Ivor was transferred to the British Army, and given the choice of remaining as a regular or returning to civilian life under general demobilization, whenever that might be. He took the second option, and was duly commissioned as a second lieutenant at Mons Barracks, Aldershot. Posted now to the Royal Army Service Corps, he underwent specialized training in amphibious operations. He came to know the Irish Sea very well, but it was a far cry from his dreams of soldiering on India's Northwest Frontier! He requested an overseas posting. He arrived in Palestine in December 1947. In its infinite wisdom the War Office decided that, on the strength of his higher school certificate in the sciences, he had the qualifications of a technical officer. He joined 376 Petrol Platoon at Nesher Camp, near Haifa.

At that time the platoon's function was to maintain supplies of petrol for the Sixth Airborne Division in Northern Palestine. Ivor found himself responsible, among other things, for liaison with the Arab workers' unions on the installations, and this was much to his liking. He acquired a rudimentary knowledge of Arabic, having to do principally with such things as opening and closing taps on the pipelines and dispensing fuel into jerricans. He little dreamed that the language would come to play such an important part in his future research; otherwise he might have endeavored somewhat to extend the range of his vocabulary. In the first half of 1948, as the British Mandate drew to its chaotic close, Ivor came to work closely with the Haganah upon which, increasingly, the security of 376 Petrol Platoon depended. With the birth of Israel on 15 May, most British forces were evacuated, but Ivor's platoon remained in Nesher for a further six weeks, in effect under the protection of the new Israeli army.

Throughout his service in Palestine, Ivor kept a diary. This is the basis of his memoirs, *Unholy Months in a Holy Land*, at present being prepared for publication. He left Israel on 30 June 1948, and was posted to the Suez Canal Zone where he joined a waterborne unit—finally—on the Great Bitter Lake. But the amphibious landing craft floated unused on the water, and Ivor found himself assigned to escorting an assortment of cabinet ministers, members of Parliament, and mandarins from the remoter depths of Whitehall, between Cairo Airport and Canal Zone headquarters.

Ivor left the army under general demobilization in September 1948; he remained, however, on Z-Reserve and was twice recalled for brief periods. He had decided to continue his education, and thought that forestry might open up interesting prospects for the future. He was admitted to the University College of North Wales at Bangor. In the event, his foray into forestry proved abortive. In a recent talk, Ivor described what happened: "I had a few beers at lunchtime with a number of fellow ex-servicemen, and then we went along to register. When I reached the front of the queue I was asked what I was studying. I said 'Forestry,' but perhaps I had had more than a few beers, because the clerks wrote it down as 'Philosophy.'" Deciding on the spot that philosophy, whatever precisely that was, sounded fascinating, Ivor nodded assent, and soon found himself dealing with Socrates and Plato rather than with hardwoods and softwoods. By such quirks of fate are lives changed.

In Bangor, Ivor shared lodgings with a Ghanaian, a Gold Coaster at that time of course. This was Britton Spio-Garbrah. They became very close friends. Spio-Garbrah was a strong supporter of Kwame Nkrumah and the new Convention Peoples' Party, and over the months patiently initiated Ivor into the intricacies of Gold Coast politics. Their university years completed, they parted. Again, in Ivor's own words:

> The time came when both Spio-Garbrah and I received our degrees. This was in 1951. He was returning home to the Gold Coast, and I was moving to Oxford to do postgraduate work [in philosophy]. Sadly and solemnly, we shook hands. "You must come to my country one day," he said. "I will," I replied, but we both knew how very unlikely that was!

Ivor was in residence at University College, Oxford, for two years. In the second, he was summoned to see Professor Gilbert Ryle in his rooms in Magdalen College. Having been wondering what transgression he had committed, Ivor was astonished to be offered a position at the University College of the Gold Coast, to teach philosophy there on a two-year exchange. It was a welcome offer, for at the time Ivor was editing the monthly paper of the secessionist Welsh Republican Movement, then the subject of intense scrutiny by British police and security organizations. Feeling that, in the circumstances, discretion might be the better part of valor, he accepted Ryle's offer with alacrity. He arrived in Accra in September 1953.

Little of the present Legon campus had yet been built, and Ivor found himself teaching at Achimota in one of the small round huts built by the army during the war, when General Headquarters, West Africa, had been located there. He had five students that year. Two of them, W. E. Abraham and Kwesi Wiredu, now enjoy international academic reputations as philosophers. In 1954, Ivor also accepted a position as tutor in the university's Department of Extra-Mural Studies. This involved teaching weekly classes in Big Ada and Ada Foah, towns near the mouth of the Volta. It was this experience that first led him to an active interest in Ghana's past. He began to work on the history of the Ada people, and by a natural progression, on that of the Akwamu kingdom that had once been dominant in the region.

In 1955, at the expiration of the two-year contract, Ivor decided not to return to Oxford but to stay on in the Gold Coast. He was offered a full-time position in Extra-Mural Studies, as resident tutor for the Northern Territories. Based in Tamale, he traveled constantly and extensively, and became familiar with virtually every part of that huge protectorate. Although he began working upon the history of the northern peoples, who were to remain an abiding interest, he used what little free time he had to write his master's thesis on Akwamu. It was accepted by the University of Wales in 1958. Such was the infancy of the discipline of African history at this time that Ivor's principal examiner was Professor S. T. Bindoff, a London University specialist in British Tudor history.

After three years in the Northern Territories, Ivor was transferred to Kumase in 1958, to become resident tutor for the Ashanti and Brong-Ahafo Regions. Again, he had to travel extensively, and in doing so developed a deep interest in the history of the Akan, and particularly of the Asante. He carried out much of the basic research that would eventually be the foundation for his classic *Asante in the Nineteenth Century.*

In 1961, Ivor was appointed senior research fellow at the newly created Institute of African Studies at the University of Ghana, Legon. There he was to work closely with Thomas Hodgkin, who was appointed director of the institute in 1962. Ivor had responsibility for the development of historical and social science studies within the institute, and his colleague, Kwabena Nketia, for music and the arts. Ivor initiated a number of projects. One of these had to do with the history of the many, but virtually unstudied, Muslim communities in Ghana. In this venture, he secured the invaluable cooperation of a scholar he had first met in Bonduku in December 1959; this was Alhaji Osmanu Esaka Boyo, who was subsequently recruited to the institute. In this period Ivor also worked closely with Joseph Agyeman-Duah, a royal of Mampon and a senior official in the Kumase traditional administration. Agyeman-Duah began the compilation of basic data on Asante stools, many of which had never previously been studied. His three hundred or so "stool histories" have proved an invaluable resource to scholars in the field, some of whom, much to Ivor's distress, have used them without any appreciation of the pioneering nature of Agyeman-Duah's work. At the same time Ivor, in cooperation with Agyeman-Duah and Edmund Collins, began to make a series of transcripts of the records of the Kumase courts, then stored in the Ahenfie, the Asantehene's palace. Subsequently, the original records have been rehoused in the new Manhyia Record Office in Kumase, where they are now available for consultation.

In 1964, Ivor was made research professor in African history in the Institute of African Studies, and in the following year became its deputy director. He continued to carry out further fieldwork in northern Ghana and in Asante, but was also able to write up much of the data he had accumulated over the preceding years. The first monograph to appear was *The Northern Factor in Ashanti History*, which Ivor now insists on regarding as "juvenilia" though it is widely regarded as a seminal contribution to Ghanaian historiography. During his years in Ghana from 1953 to 1966, Ivor wrote two short monographs, some twenty-eight journal articles, nine chapters in edited works, and numerous book reviews. He also had amassed a large amount of unused data that he would continue to work on in the coming years.

In 1965, Ivor made his first visit to the United States, to spend a semester as visiting professor in the Department of History at Indiana University. He turned down offers of professorships there and at Northwestern University, and returned to Ghana in January 1966. However, the February 1966 coup that toppled Kwame Nkrumah, and the resulting uncertainty in the political situation, led him to review his position, and he decided to accept the offer from Northwestern. He negotiated, however, a leave of absence for his first year, to enable him to take up a one-year Simon Senior Research Fellowship in the Department of Anthropology and Sociology at Manchester University. During this year he wrote a first draft of what was later to appear as *Wa and the Wala.*

Ivor arrived in Evanston in the fall of 1967. His first stint at Northwestern was, however, to be a short one: another opportunity arose, this time at Cambridge, where he was offered the position of assistant director of research in the Faculty of History, and a Senior Research Fellowship at Churchill College. He resigned from Northwestern and took up his duties at Cambridge in the autumn of 1968. He was charmed by his new academic environment, although he rapidly came to realize that Cambridge offered less opportunity for serious work in African history than had Northwestern. Its graduate program became a source of frustration rather than of accomplishment. Few students chose to work in the field, and funding for research in Africa was difficult to find. His reservations were strengthened by his experiences during the summer of 1968 when he ran the joint Northwestern and University of Ghana Interdisciplinary Seminar in Field Methods. Funded by the U.S. Department of Health, Education, and Welfare, the purpose of the seminar was to train Northwestern graduate students, paired with Ghanaian opposite numbers, in the theory and practice of field research. Work was carried out in Yendi and Kumase, and the results were compiled into fourteen volumes of texts made widely available to Africana libraries. Ivor found the seminar invigorating. Having carried out so much fieldwork himself, it gave him the opportunity to pass his skills and enthusiasm on to others. It was the sort of experience that he found lacking at Cambridge. In 1970, Northwestern University asked Ivor if he would consider returning there. It was an extremely difficult decision to make, but he decided to accept, and took up his professorship again in January 1971.

Ivor was to spend twenty-three more years with Northwestern's Department of History. He was also very active in its Program of African Studies, although the year he spent as its acting associate director convinced him that academic administration was not his forte. During these years he was the adviser of twenty-eight students who completed Ph.D.s in African history, and he served on the committees of thirty-five others. He also developed a hitherto unsuspected interest in undergraduate teaching, and offered a wide range of courses from the annual "Background to African Civilization and Culture" to such occasional offerings as "Arthur, King of the Britons: Fact or Fiction." In 1984, Ivor was appointed Melville J. Herskovits Professor of African Studies. He continued to pursue his research and writing. His first major book, *Asante in the Nineteenth Century,* won the 1976 African Studies Association Herskovits Award. In the early 1980s he took some time off from African history to return to a long-standing interest in Wales. This resulted in the publication of *South Wales and the Rising of 1839. Class Struggle as Armed Struggle,* which received the 1985 Welsh Arts Council Prize for Non-Fiction. In 1986, another long-standing project was completed with the publication of *Chronicles from Gonja: A West African Tradition of Muslim Historiography,* written in collaboration with Nehemia Levtzion and Bruce Haight. *Wa and the Wala* appeared in 1989. In 1993, a collection of essays on the Akan and Asante was published under the title *Forests of Gold.* All of Ivor's Africa writings depended heavily upon his fieldwork, and the texts of his interviews, "Conversations about the Past," conducted principally in Ghana, Burkina Faso, and the Ivory Coast, are now on deposit at the African Library at Northwestern University. In 1992, Ivor received the Distinguished Teaching Award of the College of Arts and Sciences.

Ivor took his retirement from Northwestern University at the end of 1993 and was named professor emeritus. A party given in his honor, at which he was presented with the collection of essays from which the present volume has been crafted, was a truly festive occasion. Some two hundred people, including former graduate students, many of whom had themselves become university teachers of African history, came to celebrate and wish him well. To the gratification of the organizers, a senior colleague in American history was overheard muttering, "Only the Africanists can put on a do like this!"

Coincident with his retirement, Ivor was appointed to honorary professorships in history at both the University of Wales, Aberystwyth, and the University of Wales, Lampeter. In March 1995, he delivered—to more than a thousand people each evening for a week—the prestigious Aggrey-Fraser-Guggisberg Memorial Lectures at the University of Ghana. They are published under the title *Ghana Past and Present: One Nation, Many Histories.* Ivor continues both to research and write. Among his current projects are a study of Asante under colonial administration, an Asante biographical dictionary, a life of Abu Bakr al-Siddiq of Timbuktu, and an essay on Islam in Juula society. Retirement, he grumbles, is an awfully busy time, for one can no longer use teaching and committee work as excuses for not getting on with things.

Nancy Lawler

Toward a Historiography of Renewal

BASIL DAVIDSON

That the writing of African history can and even should be aimed at assisting to give depth of scale and clarity of focus to the interests and concerns of the writer's own world, the reader's world of "today," tends nowadays to look like a funny old Whiggish notion bereft of serious historiographic value. The past has no lessons for the present, let alone the future; and this being so, none should be sought. In my otherwise blameless youth I used to share this view of the matter, and I can still recall my surprise when first going to the Gold Coast (not then quite Ghana) in search of what seemed to count in the field of unfolding history—the nascent record, in other words, of anticolonial nationalism—to meet Ivor Wilks and find him enwrapped most Wilksishly in no such record but, stubbornly and passionately (but with unvarying courtesy), in the interests and concerns of the Asante empire. These interests and concerns, he gave you to understand, were no mere antiquarian distraction from tomorrow's Ghana, no bland scholarly withdrawal from the arguments and abrasions of Nkrumahist action: far from that, they were centered upon the very soil and substance out of which the viable culture of tomorrow's Ghana, or much of it, would have to be built. The conclusion, this being the case, was that yesterday's history was going to be useful history. That was in 1952 and it became for me, concerning the difficult business of understanding Africa, a large and practical part of the beginning of wisdom, or, at least, of such wisdom as I have managed to acquire.

There was already in those distant days, of course, a certain blaring and airing of "drum and trumpet history" amid enthusiasm, among the nationalists, for the "glories" (a term then much in use) of otherwise neglected empires, forgotten battles, antiquated kings—yes, and even queens. All such were politically helpful in rejecting the imperialist racism which held, almost universally held, that Africa possessed no past, could display no record of its own development, and knew no sense of indigenous achievement. Yet the archival credentials of these "glories" tended to seem weak, or worse than weak, while their generally polemical context sent them, academically speaking, to the bottom of the class with a stern warning of imminent dismissal. But then there came the rise of what a notable pioneer of far more effective purpose, the late Father Gervase Mathew, used to call "intuitive history" (Melville Herskovits, I recall, preferred to call it "ethnohistory"), and this in those still early days represented what rapidly grew into a multidisciplinary process of giving our historiography a broad base in practical and demonstrable research. Archaeological as much as archival in those times, this process was of course the formative matrix from which so much has since and so fruitfully derived. All the same, it has to be admitted that the same dismissive attitude as had greeted the "glories of the past" was not therefore removed from the scene; it is indeed still to be found to repeat itself among those who, never having learned any African history, continue to suppose that there is none to be learned. Such persons are still to be heard expatiating, usually at a high level of self-assurance (at least this is so in Britain), in prominent journals or newspapers. They do this with little nods and winks in the direction of a profound respect for Africa and All That. But they do not believe for a moment that serious claims for self-civilizing achievement in the African past are to be taken seriously.

Only the other day an otherwise approving reviewer, American this time, of a recent work of my own (but the case is barely personal, and the reviewer had no doubt the best of intentions) arrived at passages concerned with precolonial civic achievement in parts of tropical Africa, and felt in conscience bound to write them off as "hopelessly sentimental." I had written cautiously, being less reckless than I used to be, that the political cultures of those parts of Africa, say over several centuries into the precolonial past, should be studied for their ancestral bearing on the political cultures of this postcolonial present where, the evidence now suggests, all is crisis or confusion. And the question that should then be asked, I went on to suggest, is what was so crucially different in a formative sense between then and now? If peoples such as the Yoruba—in one prominent example among many—could and did govern themselves over a very long period without inviting any crisis of structure and morality on the scale of the 1990s, then this success must be in some way relevant to current concerns and conceivable structures of today. If Africa, generally, was able through centuries to develop from its own potentials and within its own history, how had it come to pass that this development had ceased to be thinkable, and that any such thinking of it must be "hopelessly sentimental"?

Within our disciplines the answer may be said to have been long settled. The colonial dispossessions either stopped all that development stone-dead, or else gravely disturbed and dislocated it. Furthermore, the modern world, *sensu lato,* has hugely understated or essentially ignored the enormously destructive consequences of those dispossessions, above all in their psychological and sociological dimensions: consequences for the moral and social securities of the dispossessed, one should add, as for the civilizing potentials of the dispossessors. Making this point is not to do with any vulgar issue of "apportioning degrees of blame" for the troubles of today, but of tracing links between the history of then and the history of now. Yet the dispossessions were so invasive and so prolonged, however unevenly in their impact, that no such links were agreed to have any developmental meaning: the very concept of precolonial development, meaning self-development, came to seem unreal to the dispossessors and, at least among the educated elites, sadly often to the dispossessed as well. I go back again to Herskovits, whose chair Wilks has so brilliantly occupied. Even if it was little noticed at the time, Herskovits wrote presciently about this psychological dispossession in his *Human Factor in Changing Africa* (1958): it carried with it, he said, an acute mental displacement. "The result, as one African put it, was that: 'We see the peoples of independent African states for the most part tormented by a basic cultural discomfort: they have not . . . recovered the spiritual basis for re-establishing their unsettled societies, they have not recovered their cultural independence.'"[1]

There were Africans, as we know, who measured this result in cultural dispossession even before that dispossession was made complete or even threatened to become complete. Did the constitutional framers of the Fanti Bond of 1867 know anything of what was happening in Japan? It seems unlikely, but not for those who immediately followed them. The Fanti of the 1870s were well enough aware of the Meiji reformation of those same years and of what had begun to flow from those reforms. West African nationalists certainly pondered on the painful contrast with their own dispossessed situation, as their journalism bore witness. In a Japan that had remained uninvaded and undispossessed, the Meiji emperor and his henchmen were able to carry through their great project of modernization without loss of their culture. They were able to recover control of their treaty ports. In 1904 they were even able to sink an aggressive fleet of Russian warships. How different was the African case! "Fanti patriots, and the Japanese emperor with his statesmen," Mensah Sarbah could write in 1910, when the facts of dispossession were burning in memory, "were both striving to raise up their respective countries by the proper education and efficient training of their people." But "the African's attempt was ruthlessly crushed and his plan frustrated."[2]

What the Fanti reformers of the 1860s had in mind was not the import, wholesale or retail, of a modernization based on reproducing British political institutions, but one that should enable a Fanti state to build an independence, as they hoped, workable in the world of the 1870s and after. They could never have succeeded? But who knows: what actually happened was the freezing to subzero of any further process of self-development, and the imposition of a direct colonial rule meant to endure for any then forseeable future. The reforming relevance of Asante after the 1880s, as Wilks has taught us, is even closer to the argument: an argument, today, that is really a "debate that has long been waiting to be born," and one that surely merits promotion in a Festschrift for Ivor, the words I have just quoted in this same context being his own. For with the dispossession of the independent talents of the dispossessed, even more than of their material resources, it came to be accepted and proclaimed, *urbi et orbi,* that a hitherto missing history could now at last begin; and the great problem of the postcolonial future, as it loomed in the wake of the Second World War, would no longer be the reform or modernization of indigenous institutions, such as these had evolved over centuries, but the installation of nonindigenous institutions derived from an absolutely nonindigenous history. And with this, as Herskovits was among the first to insist, the achievement of a cultural independence passed beyond reach.[3] Between the realities of precolonial culture and the permissible options of "today and tomorrow" there now stood, and would continue to stand, an unconnectable disjunction. The study of the past would be gradually degraded to the study of the ornamental even while this study acquired a new and even clamant life of its own. The contradiction would become notable. "It seems to me," an Africanist historian could say with authority in 1975, that "African historiography has been important in Africa for reasons of pride because"—and he emphasised these words—"it could not possibly have been useful for anything else."[4] What had developed in the past, in other words, was shut off from any useful bearing on what may develop in the present. An irreversible alienation had occurred.

Dispossession always means alienation: of course, and yet what may still remain surprising in an Africanist context is that this truly enormous alienation, imposed by the dispossessors, should be so easily accepted as right and natural. Have the politics of independence proved a failure over several decades? Then the answer must be to try out the failed models, the imported models, all over again, and hope, this time, that they can be made to work. So that, for one excoriating example among many, the solution in the vast land of Zaire, after 1990, must be to revert to the textbook prescriptions of European parliamentary rule in substitution for the Mobutist dictatorship. Whereupon no fewer than 230 "political parties" are heard to proclaim themselves even while their more or less complete incompetence to operate on the parliamentary model is plain to all, and even to themselves. Yet no alternative, it appears, was to be considered: disjuncture from the political culture of the precolonial past was irreversible as it was functionally imposed.

However you look at it, this conclusion does indeed seem strange. Peoples in Africa do not prosper when severed from their own historical roots any more than peoples anywhere else: any more (in what seems to me a reasonable comparison) than one can suppose that the English democracy of the later nineteenth century, if severed from the consequences of the Civil War of the 1640s and all that then ensued, could have reached the urbane stability of the Victorian era. Can we imagine modern France without the revolution of the 1790s, or the United States of America without the endowment of its republican struggles? The argument for colonialism in Africa used to be that dispossession equaled or would develop into modernizing revolution; but I doubt if anyone will care to stand firm for that case today. Rafts of prescriptive analysis and structural readjustment, programs of reconstruction of great or little ingenuity, much else to the same effect, have continued to emerge from non-African sources. All of them have taken the disjunction from Africa's past as granted and necessary. They have taken it for granted, and the modernizing revolution still fails to arrive.

That there could be no realistic alternative to this disjunction was rather easily argued so long as imperialist dominance remained intact; alienation was and had to be the core and ideological drive of the whole system of dispossession. Would this still be so, once dominance were removed? The case for thinking that the disjunction then becomes removable is certainly, today, one that now begins to be heard, at any rate outside the confines of the neocolonial orthodoxy. This argument, at least as I myself repeatedly hear it, is not that the institutions of the precolonial past can be revived and reinstalled. In Yorubaland, for an obvious example, the Ogboni may well have acted as a viable and even vital check on autocratic greed or aristocratic self-inflation. But the Ogboni are no more recoverable today than the Oyo Mesi and the Alafin whom they were called upon to influence or control, even if such persons still have presence on the social scene. The Asantemanhyiamu certainly set itself to guarantee public participation in the politics of Asante. But not even the most historically minded person in Asante today seems likely to think that the Asantemanhyiamu, as such, can be launched into the twenty-first century.

Yet this is different, even very different, from affirming that the example and precedent of those old institutions—their ancestral inspiration, their mode of moral self-conception, above all their weight of historical presence—do not have value for the further development of postcolonial politics. I ask to be allowed another English reference. "I think, " argued Thomas Rainborough during the Putney Debates of 1647, when the winners of the Civil War were met to think about the further development of English politics after dethronement of the divine right of kings, a victory for liberty those stern Roundheads were there to defend: "I think that the poorest he in England hath a right to live, as the greatest he and therefore, truly sir, I think it's clear, that every man who is to live under a government ought first by his own consent to put himself under that government." The meaning of his words, whatever their fate at this time or at that, have echoed down the years of England's politics ever since. Not even the Thatcherite years have availed to silence Rainborough. No disjunction here; none even thinkable.

It was in reflecting on this kind of contrast that I found myself returning to the wonderful lucidity of *Asante in the Nineteenth Century* and its investigation of the circumstances whereby Asante was brought to accept the dispossessions after 1900. This investigation was not of course unfolded with a view to showing that the *asikafo* and their kind elsewhere had their hands firmly and consciously upon the keys to a revolutionary future: no one reading Wilks will be forgiven for thinking that history is about what might or should happen, or has happened, if the intrusions of the present were absent. History is there to explain that Asante in the 1890s had within itself, actually existing and beginning to operate, at least some of the potentials for a postcolonial development that need not remain a neocolonial development. If Ivor will overlook a gloss for which he is in no way responsible, the investigation is to suggest that a nondispossessed Asante had begun to have "Meiji potentials" in the general sense that Mensah Sarbah was writing about in 1910. Nondispossession, in short, would be nonalienation without presuming stagnation. It would be historical process in an indigenous but no longer isolated dimension.

This kind of view is, at the moment, gravely unfashionable; and proposing it is what most easily gets oneself accused of gilding precolonial lilies. That may be barely surprising: so many generations of "Westerners" (Africans often included) have been fed on tales of cannibal chaos that any notion of precolonial civilizing order has come to be seen as absurd. Eighty-one years have passed, after all, since the Reverend Attoh Ahuma dismissed the African past as a "savage backwoods" whence no light would ever come; and Ahuma's view, broadly put, has long become a truism. And such has been the power of this truism that our respectable tribunes, holding forth from the top to the bottom of their columns, or beyond whenever necessary, have managed to bury a good half of the findings of the scholarship that has sought to tell how Africans lived and governed themselves before the dispossessions. I mean especially in this context here the findings of ethnography and social anthropology in the wake of Evans-Pritchard and the 1940s. I think, for a few random examples, of Godfrey Lienhardt on Dinka thought and belief, of John Middleton on Lugbara lineage and its meanings, or, in the matter of due legal process, of Max Gluckman on Barotse jurisprudence. The idea that such peoples as these lived customarily in Stygian darkness is what then becomes truly absurd.

Everyone will have preferences in the lists of ethnographic excellence, but if these I have named were all male I do not mean to suggest that the female names in those lists deserve any less respect; very much, indeed, to the contrary. I mean only to note that the years of postcolonial independence have not been good for their successors. And in terms of the great disjunction I have been writing about here the difference has evidently lain in the contemporary rise of different methodologies of primarily political analysis. This was altogether expectable in a situation, after the 1950s, and even a little before, when Africa was thought to have entered the realms of modernity, and when the pressing need was to understand and explain how this modernity, duly blessed and prompted by the ancestors of Westminster and the Palais Bourbon, was working out or should be working out: when historical process in Africa, above all in tropical Africa, had been severed from its past and joined by remote affiliation to an altogether different past. This particular (and, as it seems to me, critically influential) aspect of the disjunction was already well advanced by the outset of the 1960s, along with advances in the number of colonial states promoted to be nation-states. One saw it then, for a notable example, in the work of another valiant pioneer, David Apter, when writing of the Gold Coast become Ghana and of an emergently independent Uganda.[5] It has seemed to me that Apter is particularly interesting in this context. That is partly because of his analytical dynamism but, even more, because of his particular concern with the consequences of colonial intrusion on preexisting structures. Apter was careful to insist upon the need to keep shrewd account of traditional systems of authority, as for example in Buganda. It remained, however, that "it was not our purpose to delve into the mysteries of African history."[6]

With less genial analysts this disregard tended to merge with another attitude: with an attitude which could take it for granted that "the mysteries of African history," insofar as these were more than "drum and trumpet" propaganda, had very little real relevance. More and more, the task of the 1960s and later became a question of unraveling the complexities of newborn constitutional politics: yet not so as to measure their success against whatever had preceded them in precolonial times, but against the pristine beauties of the Westminsterial model. It could seem as though the living springs of political behavior, the moral and social values from which this behavior had flowed wherever it had acquired a mandatory power, had lost all useful significance.

If this has been the case, as I believe, then it becomes easy to see why the findings of African historiography, as these have evolved in practice and as "solution-seekers" have generally received them, have run into some pretty rough criticism. It has been complained that this historiography does not teach how to make Africa prosper, how to safeguard civil society, how to find alternatives to violence and tyranny, even how to grow more food. This is where the absence of the insights of ethnography, using a wide sense of that term, again reveals the disjunction which through the wear and tear of life leads down to the suspicion, more often the conviction, that the African past has never been more than a dismal failure. Terence Ranger has written challengingly on all this; and one of his papers has quoted a Kenyan critic who felt able to assert, even in 1974, that any such few "glittering achievements like the Zimbabwe architecture, the primitive peasant empires of the Sudan and the Makonde sculptures"—truly a curious selection that speaks for itself—were no more than "flashes within a background of utter stagnation." But supposing this critic had absorbed the implications of, for example, Gluckman's findings on Barotse checks and balances against the abuse of delegated power? Then he would have known that the Barotse (not exceptionally, however) well understood that delegated power was bound to become abused by those to whom it was delegated, unless it were embraced by effective safeguards against this all-too-certain attempt at abuse. The Barotse in their historical institutions have been, "apparently terrified of giving away power, even power to protect, for once a man is elevated, it is feared he will stand against those he ought to care for. They think always of the dual pressures of the ambivalence of power on an individual," and their political arrangements were organized to provide appropriate safeguards. "Barotse law embodies an elaboration of their theory that power may corrupt and that those in power must be restrained from abusing it."[7] This and the way it was done appear to me as far more interesting and instructive of precolonial culture than any quantity of Zimbabwe architecture; and subsequent inquiry into these arrangements, so far as I have read the evidence, has not questioned the general validity of what Gluckman was able to report.[8]

Such findings have of course been replicated many times over, and in numberless variations of context or detail, in the literature of sociological analysis ever since Evans-Pritchard called upon his colleagues to accept that "social anthropology is a kind of historiography";[9] and these findings do regularly insist upon the reality of power-control in all those systems that were able to master their environnment at a level of progressive self-survival. As against the suffocating and self-defeating centralism of colonial and neocolonial systems, the successful ones relied, precisely, upon mechanisms of sociopolitical participation; and it was above all from a devolutionary panoply of such controls that moral creativeness became operative, and frustration could be held in check.

It is in any case in these regards and connections that I offer this necessarily modest because personal tribute to Wilks and Wilksism: to the study of precolonial African history *wie es eigentlich gewesen:* of course, because that is how Wilksist history is written, but above all in its implications for those who prescribe or wish to prescribe solutions for today's problems of African community. These solutions will have to lie, if our historiography can be a true teacher, along the pathways to consistent and courageous power devolution. Today, whenever one puts one's ear closely to the ground of actual and present experience and debate in perhaps a very large number of African communities, there does indeed arrive the waft and whisper of a well-nigh countless quantity of initiatives "at the base"—whether in peasant associations, in cooperative enterprises, in community self-reappraisals, or in *amicales* of one sort or another—that tell of endeavors to recover the power of local self-administration that centralizing bureaucracy has wrested from these communities.

How far then does all this striving draw inspiration, however indirectly and in whatever number of languages or idioms of thought, from sources of ancestral precedent? From that terror of giving away power, so vividly portrayed in the ethnographic literature of half a century ago and more? I await instruction on this and a thousand other things. But it is surely in response to questions such as these, and to the issues that derive from the answers and from the implications of those answers, that there can arise a historiography of renewal. Which, no doubt, is what is needed most of all.

Notes

1. M. J. Herskovits, *The Human Factor in Changing Africa* (London, 1958), 465.

2. M. J. Sampson, *Gold Coast Men of Affairs* (1937; London, 1969), quoting J. M. Sarbah, 221.

3. Among many aspects of this necessarily controversial debate—as to how far there was scope for constitutional change derived from existing precolonial systems and ideas—the case of Abeokuta is of much interest. See Agneta Pallinder-Law, "Aborted Modernization in West Africa? The Case of Abeokuta," *Journal of African History* 15, no. 1 (1974): 65–82. But whether the Saro could ever have carried through a modernizing revolution is what others have strongly questioned, given the distrust or worse in which they were held in the African communities to which they emigrated. See E. A. Ayandele's blistering conclusions in his *The Educated Elite in The Nigerian Society* (Ibadan, 1974), passim but especially 42, where he explains that, from the standpoint of the existing elites (and not only in Abeokuta), the Saro "were culturally, and in their disposition, fifth columnists who would mentally and ideologically team up with the British invaders rather than sympathize with the unlettered masses" and were barely tolerated. The Saro, after all, stood on the invaders' side of the disjunction, and could look across it only in embarrassment or dismay.

4. T. O. Ranger, "Towards a Usable African History," in *African Studies since 1945*, ed. C. Fyfe (London, 1976), 23.

5. D. E. Apter, *The Political Kingdom in Uganda* (Princeton, 1961).

6. Ibid., 85.

7. M. Gluckman, *The Ideas in Barotse Jurisprudence* (New Haven, 1965), 40, and more generally throughout his second chapter, "The Theory of Power."

8. G. Prins, *The Hidden Hippopotamus: Reappraisal in African History: Colonial Experience in Western Zambia* (Cambridge, 1980), passim.

9. E. E. Evans-Pritchard, *Essays in Social Anthropology* (London, 1962), 26, drawn here from his Marett Lecture of 1950: "Social Anthropology: Past and Present," and firmly repeated in his "Anthropology and History," 1961.

Adultery and the State in Asante: Reflections on Gender, Class, and Power from 1800 to 1950

JEAN ALLMAN

Introduction

In 1866, an adultery case came before the king of Asante, Kwaku Dua Panin, involving the son of the Asantehene's barber, who was accused of committing adultery with a wife of Sanaahene Sanaa Poku, the chief in charge of the Asantehene's household treasury. The son was found guilty and his father was made to pay damages to Sanaa Poku of "more than 24 ounces of gold." Before the same court in the following year, an "unnamed man was executed for impregnating a wife of Bantamahene Adu Gyawu [and] . . . the woman was placed under arrest, having been sentenced to execution following childbirth."[1] On 31 January 1911, Edwesohene Yaw Awyah charged Kwaku Wie for having had a sexual connection with his wife, Abina Kobi. The case was heard before the British chief magistrate in Kumasi and the Edwesohene was awarded £100 in compensation. On 17 January 1927, Ama Kyirewo appeared before the native tribunal of the Kumasihene, accusing Akwasi Poku of having seduced her daughter. In an adultery claim based on subrogation (Ama Kyirewo's son-in-law was in debt to her), Ama Kyirewo sought to collect the damages herself. The Kumasihene's tribunal ruled against Ama Kyirewo, assessing her with costs and a fine of £2.2.0 "for trying to extort."[2]

On 14 February 1936, Kojo Nimo brought charges in the Asantehene's B-grade criminal court against Yaw Amoah for having had a sexual connection with his wife, "contrary to sec. 7 of the Offences under Native Law and Custom, under No. 7 of 1935."

The accused was found guilty and sentenced to a fine of £5 or one month of imprisonment with hard labor. He was also ordered to pay Kojo Nimo's adultery and customary fees.[3]

Obviously, the five adultery cases summarized here, spanning some seventy years of Asante history, have very little in common. The cases differ in the rank, status, and gender of plaintiffs and defendants, in the question of compensation and damages (including who is responsible for paying compensation and who is able to collect), and in the very nature, structure, and proceedings of the courts (the first and second presided over by the king of an independent Asante, the third by a British chief magistrate, and the fourth and fifth by the Kumasihene, later recognized as the Asantehene, whose jurisdiction was defined and circumscribed by British colonial ordinance).

Yet it is precisely these differences that render adultery a remarkable prism through which to explore social change and continuity in Asante. The answers to questions such as who can raise an adultery charge and where, who can collect compensation and to what degree, or what stands as conclusive evidence of or justifiable defense against the charge have not been historically constant in Asante. They have been contested in the ongoing dramas of power and subordination, in relationships between genders and among classes.

Fortunately, the sources for a historical examination of adultery are not limited to the five cases above. While they are certainly not so rich for the precolonial period as for the period after 1896, the early sources provide the social historian with far more than the odd sentence in a fleeting traveler's account and often include information on charges, rank of plaintiff and defendant, and sentences imposed.[4] For the colonial period, the written sources are virtually limitless. Not only are there the detailed discussions of adultery provided by Rattray from the 1920s, with comparative material available in the works of Danquah, Sarbah, and others, but there are volumes upon volumes of recorded case proceedings from chief commissioners, from various district commissioners [DCs], from magistrates, native tribunals, and native courts.[5] Admittedly, each of these sources presents the historian with a particular set of problems. For example, when utilizing sources in legal anthropology from the interwar years, one must always keep in mind, as Chanock reminds us, that its underlying agenda was the adaptation of what was viewed as "primitive law" to the requirements of indirect rule.[6] Moreover, when examining the records of court cases, social historians are confronted with a written record that presents only one limited perspective on what transpired in that case: the perspective of the court recorder, who was often translating proceedings as he wrote or, in the case of British officials, transcribing the testimony as relayed by an interpreter. Nonetheless, if one is able to place a case and a set of actors into a specific historical context and is conscious of the omissions and the silences (both intended and unintended) in the transcriptions of that case, court records can "yield abundant exciting new data about African history," as Kristin Mann and Richard Roberts have recently written.[7] Indeed, they are among the few sources for the early colonial period that allow us to hear subaltern voices—particularly those of women and of commoners—and to chart attempts by those groups to exploit fissures in the structures of power.

Finally, the chronological breadth, the wealth, and availability of sources on adultery in Asante make it possible to bring Asante social history to bear on broader discussions of the nature of so-called customary law in the colonial period. Recent work, particularly Chanock's *Law, Custom and Social Order* and the essays collected in Mann and Roberts, *Law in Colonial Africa*, emphasizes the construction or the "making" of customary law in the colonial period, in contrast to earlier works of legal anthropologists and legal historians that viewed customary law as the twentieth-century survival of "a really African, local law."[8] For example, in examining adultery, Chanock writes that "the claims were fed into the court system, where they were given in evidence and 'proved' and from whence they emerged as customary law."[9] Yet in the case of Asante one is struck as much by the continuities in the jural proceedings between the precolonial and colonial periods, as by the disjunctures and anomalies. Indeed, at least in the case of adultery in Asante, it may be more appropriate to speak not of the "making" of customary law under British colonialism, but of its reformulation or refabrication.

What follows is not a comprehensive overview of adultery and the state in Asante, nor is it a juridical investigation into the nature or evolution of customary law in Asante. Rather, this paper makes a preliminary excursion into Asante social history by examining the "stuff" of which adultery cases were made and situating those cases in broader economic, political, and social contexts. It aims to explore both what adultery can tell us about Asante's past and what Asante's past can tell us about the changes, continuities, and contests evident in adultery proceedings. Its agenda, quite simply, is to make sense of the cases summarized above, to understand the when, how, and why of a private indiscretion in one context standing as a capital offense against the Asante state in another.

Toward a Working Definition of Ayerefa

There is little variation in the definitions of adultery offered in most sources—precolonial and colonial—including in the judgments of colonial courts and tribunals. Although there is much disagreement over what constitutes a fully recognized marriage between a man and a woman, there is general concurrence that the husband's chief prerogative, once such a union is consummated, is the exclusive right to sexual relations with his wife.[10] Adultery, therefore, is *ayerefa* (the taking of someone's wife). It constitutes the theft, "the taking away," of a husband's sexual rights in his wife. That theft usually occurs as a result of a sexual connection and, in such cases, is specifically called *di obi yere* (to make use of someone's wife). However, both Rattray and Danquah list a number of other actions that have been considered tantamount to *di obi yere.* These include sleeping on the same mat, handling a woman's waistbeads, attempting to seduce a woman verbally (*asombo* or *asommo,* literally, to burn a hole in her ear), or "to pull, or play with, a woman's nose, ears, breasts or any part of her body."[11]

As with the definition of adultery, there is much concurrence in the sources on the general procedures for initiating a case. In addition to eyewitness discovery by the husband or a third party, the most common means by which adultery was revealed was by a wife's confession or *wiakyere* (to reveal the theft). Such a confession generally came as a result of the husband asking that the wife "take fetish" before her relatives as to her fidelity and past conduct. As Danquah wrote in the 1920s,

> The best opportunity for knowing the truth from one's wife is considered to be the time of illness or of confinement. The doctor or fetish man is most likely to ascribe her illness or indisposition to some sin she had committed, and she must now confess and get cured, or Death, once so near, will not leave empty-handed.[12]

In many of the colonial-era adultery cases, a husband learned of adultery as a result of his wife's confession. Appearing before the Kumasihene's native tribunal in 1931, Ambah Serwah testified, "By and by my child fell sick and upon consulting an 'oracle' it was revealed that the child's sickness was due to some wrong I had done. I was obliged to confess an adultery."[13] After a wife had confessed, the husband was required to inform his family head or his father who, in turn, would report the matter to the father of the adulterer (*ayerefafo*) and ask for the appropriate compensation.

Compensation was termed *ayefare,* derived from *oyere fa dee* (the thing given for taking someone's wife).[14] For *ayefare* to be collected, it was essential that charges of adultery be submitted through proper channels. In 1946, for example, Kyeame Yaw Pong attempted to collect *ayefare* from Opoku in the Asantehene's D-grade court. Opoku pled not liable on the grounds that he had not been informed by the head of his family as required by "native custom." The court ordered the plaintiff nonsuited and awarded Opoku the assessed costs of 4 shillings.[15]

Although it was the wife, by her confession, who often set an adultery case into motion, she was never a central figure in the proceedings.

Adultery remained, from the precolonial period onward, a suit, a transaction between men. Indeed, in its gender specificity, the Akan term for adulterer (*ayerefafo,* one who takes another's wife) precludes women assuming a central role in a case unless it is through a claim of subrogation, as Ama Kyirewo attempted in 1927. What Danquah wrote of Akyem Abuakwa is pertinent to Asante, as well:

> It would have been thought that rather than allow her to give evidence as a witness on behalf of her husband the wife who accuses a person with an offence should be made a principal party in an action for or in a defence against a charge of adultery. The custom, however, is plain on the point and the husband being the real person wronged—for, in fact, the fidelity of his wife is exclusively his own concern—it stands to reason that he and not the woman must seek redress at law.[16]

Indeed, it was immaterial, as far as the wife's role in an adultery case, whether she consented to a sexual connection or was forced. Consent did not mitigate the basic charge of adultery, even when, as Rattray writes, "the woman had pretended that she was unmarried."[17] The use of force could compound the penalties faced by the nineteenth-century offender, resulting in execution should it involve *ahahantwe* (sex in the "bush"), but it did not transform the wife's position in the case. Her husband, not she, was considered the person wronged.[18]

Both historically and across social class in a given epoch, a number of features—adultery's basic definition, the means by which adultery was revealed, the initial procedures for collecting compensation, and the marginality of wives to the case—have been relatively constant. Where adultery's manifest complexity begins to unfold is in considering the social and historical factors that have determined both compensation (*ayefare*) and the public and/or private sphere(s) in which a case is to be played out. For example, *ayefare* has always been determined by, among other things, the rank and status of the husband and of the offender.[19]

In the nineteenth century, a commoner found guilty of committing adultery with the wife of an *omanhene* (chief of territorial division) was generally executed. Had he committed adultery with the wife of someone of his own rank, he would only have been liable for paying a small fine.[20] What distinguishes these two offenses, and thus accounts in large degree for the disparity in damages, is the sphere in which each was legally positioned. The first case was viewed as *oman akyiwadee*—a crime or taboo against the state which had to be addressed in the public realm. The second case was seen as *efiesem*—a household or domestic matter to be settled by the parties concerned, in consultation with their elders.[21]

It was always possible, however, for a domestic matter to be transformed into *oman akyiwadee* by the swearing of an oath (*ntam*).[22] In this way, as K. A. Busia wrote, "It was possible . . . to get the chief and elders to inquire into a private cause."[23] Indeed, many of the adultery cases heard before native tribunals in the early colonial period were oath cases. A 1916 case before the native tribunal of the Bompatahene was not atypical.

Kofie Fofie swore an oath that he had paid the head-rum on his wife and thus was entitled to the adultery fee paid to him by Cubina Anim. Anim, who claimed Fofie was not entitled to the *ayefare* because his wife was a "mere concubine," replied to the oath.[24] The case thus came before the Bompatahene. Had the oath not been sworn, the case would have been treated as *efiesem* and the status of the marriage privately investigated by the families concerned. As this essay now turns to a historical discussion of adultery in Asante, how *efiesem* and *oman akyiwadee* were distinguished will be of central importance: the line separating the public and the private in Asante was, at once, reflected in and a product of the social construction of adultery at a given historical moment. It was a line that never held firm. It was drawn and redrawn in the shifting sands of power and subordination.

A Tentative Sketch of Ayerefa *Before the British*

Not surprisingly, we know far more about adultery cases played out in the public sphere as *oman akyiwadee* in the nineteenth centuries than we do of domestic cases. The most striking feature of these cases, as T. C. McCaskie has written, is the "evident distinction of power and status between those men who paid physical compensation for adultery, and those who paid for their transgressions with money."[25] Equally striking, one might add, were the vast differences in the amount of money offenders were obliged to pay, were they not among those who paid compensation with their lives. For example, T. E. Bowdich, writing in the early nineteenth century, observed that "a captain generally gives a periguin to the family on taking a wife, a poor man two ackies: the damages for intrigue in the former case are ten periguins; in the latter, one ackie and a half and a pot of palm wine. . . . Intrigue with the wife of a King's is death."[26] Brodie Cruickshank, in the mid-nineteenth century, noted similar variations of between £1 and £10 based on rank, while the cases recorded by P. de Heer at the court of the Asantehene in the 1860s included not only death sentences for adultery with a chief's wife, but monetary damages as high as 25 ounces of gold (over £85).

R. S. Rattray, working in the 1920s, interviewed a number of individuals concerning compensation for adultery in the precolonial period, including one of the Asantehene's former executioners.[27] Aware that his informants may have been "inspired by political . . . motives" because who was entitled to collect what compensation was hotly debated during much of the colonial period, Rattray nonetheless produced a precolonial "table of damages" for officeholders in Kumasi that corresponds closely with nineteenth-century sources. For example, he wrote that the death penalty was automatically inflicted on anyone who "intrigued" with a wife of the Asantehene. The wife herself was also executed, as were "the mother, father and maternal uncle of both parties." Similar sentences were imposed by Asante's *amanhene* (territorial chiefs), although a "Head-Chief . . . who did not wish to decapitate the adulterer . . . would allow the accused to swear an 'oath' that the accusation against him was entirely false." He would then be acquitted, but called upon to pay heavy *Aseda* (thank-offering). Adultery with a wife of one of Kumasi's major officeholders was also punishable by execution, but the officeholder himself could not inflict the penalty. "The culprit had . . . to be tried before the king," Rattray wrote, "and if found guilty handed over to the king's executioner to be executed." The cases recorded by de Heer suggest that the Asantehene could award monetary damages in certain of these instances, particularly if the offender was also an officeholder.[28] For the holders of minor hereditary offices, Rattray maintained that compensation was limited in Kumasi to £24 (one *ntansa* of gold dust), a figure identical to the one recorded by de Heer in 1866. Finally, for "ordinary cases," he wrote, the "damages amounted to about the value of 6s. in gold-dust."[29]

One cannot but be struck by the differences in damages, compensation, and punishment between the nineteenth-century cases falling into the category of *oman akyiwadee* and the case of Bowdich's "poor man" who claimed his one and a half *ackies* and some palm wine in a private, domestic matter. Not only is there no question of "physical compensation" to be paid by the male offender in the latter case, but the *ayefare* is actually less than the marriage fees paid by the husband. In the *oman akyiwadee* cases, husbands appear to have collected sums ten to eleven times their initial investment at marriage.[30] There was also great disparity in the treatment of the offending wife depending on the status of her husband: penalties ranging from death to a token pacification.[31] Bowdich and A. B. Ellis both maintained that a chief had the right to put his wife to death, though he was "expected to accept a liberal offer of gold from the family, for her redemption." Rattray's accounts echo these remarks.[32] In adultery cases treated as *efiesem,* however, the husband's right to punish his wife was strictly limited. Though Ellis offhandedly remarks that the "wife is usually beaten," it appears that in most cases the husband's only recourse was to divorce his wife or to accept a small pacification and remain married. If the wife and the offender "prefer to live together," wrote Cruickshank, "the latter may obtain her as his wife, by the payment of the husband's expenses on her account, without any additional compensation for the injury." As Rattray concluded, "Very often . . . the offence will be condoned and the couple will continue to live together."[33]

The picture that emerges from these precolonial sources is a complex one indeed, one in which class and gender constructions are impossible to disentangle. For those who controlled the Asante state, adultery obviously served to reinforce and reproduce relationships of power and subordination.

This is nowhere more apparent than in the range of compensation available to men based upon their rank. At the same time, the class dynamics of adultery produced and differentiated gender relationships in very specific ways. For example, adultery constituted one of the primary mechanisms by which chiefs controlled and exploited the sexuality of their wives. Wives of chiefs could be killed for having sexual connections with other men. At the same time, some chiefs encouraged their wives, so the sources contend, to "intrigue" with other men in order that they might collect compensation. Dupuis wrote in the early nineteenth century that

> many of the wives and daughters of men in power, were employed in the way of traffic, to practise the seductive charms of beauty, to inveigle the impassioned and unwary of the other sex, in order to create a palaver, which commonly termined in fines or slavery. When the slave trade was legalized on the coast, it was a usual mode of entrapping youth, and those who were incapable of redeeming their persons from bondage, suffered the severity of this pernicious law, and were in most cases sold in the public markets for exportation to the West Indies.[34]

In contrast to Asante's chiefs, men among the commoner ranks could not inflict serious penalities upon their offending wives nor could they collect substantial compensation from their wives' lovers.

Adultery, therefore, was not, nor could it be, a means by which common men (*mmerante* or *nkwankwaa*) exploited their wives' sexuality. It was simply a domestic matter—*efiesem*—involving two men.

Rattray recorded two Asante maxims concerning *ayefare* that shed some light on the gendered class dimensions of adultery in precolonial Asante: "Ayefere sika ntua poka ka" (Adultery gold dust does not pay . . . [a penny] of debt) and "Ayefere sika yenfa nko aban mu" (We don't go to the forts [to trade] with gold dust from adultery compensation). At first glance, these maxims appear to undercut Dupuis' report of chiefs exploiting, for profit, their wives' sexuality. Rattray sought to explain the contradiction between the maxims and the actions of chiefs by arguing that the latter was a result of morality breaking down in the face of "European civilization."[35] Undoubtedly, Asante notions of morality were undergoing change in the nineteenth century, but it is also quite possible that the discrepancy between Dupuis' report and the *ayefare* maxims is simply a (gendered) reflection of the class-specific constructions of adultery in precolonial Asante. In other words, as a domestic matter settled between common men, adultery was not a means to make money. As *oman akyiwadee,* as a crime against the state, it was severely punishable and, for some, potentially quite profitable.

Continuities and (Mis)Understandings in the First Years of Colonial Rule, 1896–1924

In January 1896, the British government arrested the Asantehene and placed Asante under protectorate status. In 1901, following the Yaa Asantewa Rising, Asante was annexed directly to the Crown and subsequently administered as a conquered territory. Thus began more than a half-century of British colonial rule over the former Asante kingdom.[36] How that political rule, and the dramatic economic and social changes accompanying it, challenged and/or reinforced precolonial constructions of adultery in Asante is the focus of the section that follows.

When Chanock examined adultery in colonial Zambia, he was struck by the range of testimony concerning punishment and compensation and by the uncertainty over "how far it was in the 'public' and how far in the 'private' realm." He concluded that while some of the variations in the testimony of elders and chiefs can be explained by "pre-colonial political structure," they are better understood in light of quite contemporary factors, among them, the exigencies of migrant labor, the self-interests of chiefs and elders, and general male concern over "indisciplined women." In short, the wide range of testimony in Zambia, Chanock maintained, had very little to do with what some have termed "precontact native law" and everything to do with the contested colonial moment.[37]

Perhaps because our nineteenth-century sources on Asante speak louder than those for Zambia, giving us a clearer idea of the complexity of, or variations in, *ayerefa* in the precolonial period, it is difficult to sideline Asante's precolonial past in analyses of the early colonial period. While there were certainly debates over and ambiguity surrounding *ayerefa* in the early colonial period, those debates and that ambiguity were of a much different sort than Chanock observed in Zambia. For example, no one contested the rank differentiation in compensation, the fact that a head chief was entitled to a fixed *ayefare* and a lesser chief to a lesser *ayefare.* (Indeed, even the ranked fees in the early colonial period were comparable to those for the mid-nineteenth century.) The question, the contest, played out before the first British administrators centered on who was historically recognized as a head chief and who was not.[38] For colonial Asante, in other words, we must be careful not to assume that all of the variation in and complexity surrounding adultery was the product of an enigmatic, but superordinate colonial presence. What would become Asante customary law was the product not just of a contested colonial present but of a contested precolonial past.

With the exception of Kumasi, the first years of British occupation in Asante (1896–1901) had little impact on the internal government of the outlying divisions. The British Resident was not to interfere in the daily administration of a division and the courts of the *amanhene* were to proceed as usual, "except that in the cases of murder the chiefs were to sit with the Resident and another officer."[39] Because of the basic "hands-off" policy of the British government toward the outlying divisions of Asante during these first years, the proceedings of the *amanhene*'s courts were not recorded. There is no evidence to suggest, however, that domestic cases of *ayerefa* were handled any differently than they had been before the British occupation or that public cases, *oman akyiwadee,* changed dramatically, with the exception, of course, that the execution of adulterers was not permitted.

By contrast, confusion reigned in Kumasi. As Rattray wrote, "it lost not only a King but was deprived of its *Omanhene.*"[40] There may have been continuity in the way in which domestic cases of adultery were handled in Kumasi, but the absence of the Asantehene's court and the presence of a British Resident, Captain Donald Stewart, and of a chief magistrate, meant that there were now alternative venues for the hearing of adultery cases that would have been handled as *oman akyiwadee* in the years before 1896. And these alternative (and often uncomprehending) courts could become sites for staking new sorts of claims and for contesting (sometimes successfully and sometimes not) precolonial constructions of adultery.

Both the British Resident in Kumasi and the chief magistrate heard cases of adultery as civil (not criminal) suits, but adultery cases did not dominate the dockets of their courts. Many such cases were referred to the Native Committee of Administration in Kumasi, set up by Governor W. E. Maxwell to oversee the reconstruction of Kumasi and to try petty cases.[41] Unfortunately, no record of the committee's cases has survived and the record books of the Resident and the magistrate are rather sketchy, often omitting testimony altogether. Yet it is still possible to get some sense of both early British (mis)understanding of *ayerefa* in Asante and of some Asantes' attempts to exploit those misconceptions in the first years of British occupation. For example, in June 1897, Chief Opoku Mensa, a member of the Native Committee, appeared before the chief magistrate in a civil suit in which he charged Yaw Kwaku with entering his wife's room and having a sexual connection with her against her will. In his defense, Kwaku said he knew nothing. Although there were no witnesses, the chief magistrate found Kwaku guilty, but fined him only £5, a penalty far below what would have been imposed two years before in an Asante court. Moreover, the magistrate awarded no *ayefare* to Opoku Mensa, an outcome the subchief had obviously not expected. And chiefs were not alone in seeking judicial remedies in Asante's first British courts. In another magistrate's case that same month, a woman, Akosuah Takyiwa, sought £4 damages from Charles E. Meyer for having "committed her about seven months ago." The magistrate dismissed the case on the grounds that "no action can lie on a case like this, the Plaintiff being the party who alleges adultery with herself." This case is one of the first on record in Asante in which a woman contested the gender-specificity of *ayefare*—an action taken perhaps because the defendant was not Asante (and was presumably British). Despite these new circumstances, the magistrate had no difficulty invoking what was essentially the (precolonial) gender-specificity of *ayefare* in denying Takyiwa's claim.[42]

After the Yaa Asantewa uprising and the implementation of the Ashanti Administration Ordinance in 1902, a structure for British rule in Asante was put in place and the dense ambiguity of 1896–1901 gave way to a more defined, though still no more consistent, court system. The ordinance recognized a chief commissioner's court (replacing the Resident's court) and DC's courts, all of which had civil and criminal jurisdiction. In addition, native tribunals were now recognized by ordinance to hear a variety of land and civil cases up to £100 and could enforce their own judgments as long as those judgments were not "in any way repugnant to natural justice or to the principles of the law of England." Any decision by a native tribunal could be appealed to the chief commissioner or DC's court.[43] Despite these early and rather elaborate attempts to systematize the customary judicial apparatus, the scheme looked better on paper than it worked in practice. As one colonial report lamented years later, the tribunals basically were left to function as they had done before the ordinance and were certainly not confined, as the ordinance required, to head chiefs.[44] Yet it is in the hundreds of record books produced by these courts and tribunals after 1901 that we get a more detailed picture of early British attempts to "administer" law in adultery cases and of Asante attempts to negotiate the terrain of colonial jurisprudence. It is a picture of both continuity and of disjuncture.

While one would expect a great deal of constancy between nineteenth- and early twentieth-century *ayefare* cases handled either domestically or in Asante's "unrecognized" native tribunals, one would also expect to see the most substantial evidence of change—in charges, testimony, and judgements—in the cases heard before the first colonial officials in Asante. This was not always the case. At times, the proceedings and judgments were quite consistent with precolonial cases, with the exception that no physical penalty was exacted. For example; the Edwesohene, Yaw Awuah, appeared before the magistrate several times in 1911 in order to collect compensation from various men whom he alleged had had sexual connections with his wives. Except for the first case in which it was ruled that the woman was a pawn and not a wife, he was awarded his compensation of £100 in each instance.

The *Civil Record Books* for the Kumasi DC and the chief magistrate are also filled with domestic cases of *ayefare,* in which a plaintiff, aware that her or his complaint runs counter to "customary law" is obviously trying to get a sympathetic hearing before a British official. More often than not, however, judgment differs little from what would have been rendered in a nineteenth-century court.[45] For example, in the same court in which the Edwesohene had appeared three months earlier, Yaah Tima sought to collect £5.10.6 from Cobina Buo for "having had connection" with her. She claimed that when she reported the connection to her husband he made her pay £5.10.6 as satisfaction. The magistrate, who well understood the gender specificity of *ayefare,* ruled for the defendant.[46]

At times, however, the magistrate or commissioner ran head-on into a domestic case reflecting practices that "failed the repugnancy test," as Mann and Roberts have called it.[47] In these cases, British officials in Asante were far more likely to revise than to undermine the fundamental premises upon which a particular custom rested. This was particularly true with *ayefare.* For example, in terms of justice and morality, British officials had a difficult time with multiple episodes of adultery involving one woman. Chanock argues for Zambia that there was a general concern among officials about the "morality of compensation" in adultery cases. But in Asante, there is little evidence that officials ever questioned the "morality of compensation" as long as it involved a single "indiscretion" on the part of one wife.

Multiple connections, or *ayefare* for profit, were another matter. For example, Bompatahene Kojo Dakwa, who had been recognized as a paramount chief (*omanhene*) by the British in 1896 and had been placed over Agogo as a reward for his loyalty, married a young Agogo woman. According to his letter to the chief commissioner of Asante [CCA], ten men of Agogo had "misconducted themselves with her." Three of these men had paid *ayefare,* but the others refused on the grounds that the DC in Juaso told them they did not have to pay. The Bompatahene asked for the CCA to intervene, adding that he was "severely struck by this information as all these adultery fees were arranged by Your Honour and I was also appointed by Your Honour. . . . It is rather disgraceful to me if Your Honour give up the matter, as I cannot advise my wives to go round and make money for me."[48] A letter to the DC from another of the Bompatahene's wives, Abena Febi, suggests that the woman from Agogo was not the only one "put to work" by her husband. Febi maintained that she wanted to divorce the Bompatahene but she could not come up with the £20 head money. The Bompatahene, she reported,

> told me to go to Agogo and coax young men so that they will use me. Then he will get plenty money and he will dash me my head money. I agreed and went to Agogo. Soon as I reach[ed] there plenty men used me. One of them is a stranger so he went away. So Omanhin charged me £32.15 adultery fee as the stranger is not there [to pay the compensation]. Now he has sent for me to come "to Bompata so that he will dismiss me." Again he told me that in my coming I ought to bring the £20 with me . . .

> . . . But, your worship, I did not understand him because he told me to go and work for him and he will dash me my head money. . . . He has charged me £32.15, but now he wants to charge me £20 again.[49]

Obviously this case has many nineteenth-century antecedents, particularly in terms of chiefs exploiting their wives' sexuality, and establishing and reinforcing hegemony over a subordinate town via marriage and *ayefare* claims. Despite continuity in "custom," the DC found the Bompatahene's actions repugnant, and he and the CCA refused to accede to the Bompatahene's request. They did not, however, undercut custom altogether. The Bompatahene was warned that he could not "keep women purely for the sake of getting money from them when they were used by other men," but he was not told that compensation must be limited to one claim per wife. Rather, the DC reminded him that the CCA said "he could only claim adultery fees from three men." Such was the British challenge to the "repugnancy" of adultery compensation in Asante—a challenge echoed in many cases in which an official named an arbitrary figure to differentiate acceptable adultery compensation from morally repugnant exploitation. In this case, the number was three. In an earlier Juaso case, it was two.[50] In a Kumasi DC's case in 1907, the number was set at five, with concern being expressed not for the exploited wife, but for her hapless "victims." Captain Korbright ordered that "no claim in respect to the woman will ever be allowed. The young men of this country must be protected from . . . such a woman."[51] As for Abena Febi's complaint concerning her husband, the DC decided to inform the Bompatahene that he must divorce Abena Febi without her having to pay any additional fees. He did not, however, instruct the *omanhene* to return the £32.15 he had already collected from Abena Febi—an amount far exceeding his initial investment at marriage.[52]

Despite the fact that British colonial courts were more likely to reformulate nineteenth-century Asante law than to undermine it, many Asantes increasingly turned to magistrate and commissioners' courts as alternative channels through which to redress various grievances. In fact, according to Chief Commissioner Harper, the Kumasi chiefs complained in 1906 that "their women folk and servants are 'too fond' of taking their cases to the Cantonment Magistrate instead of to the chief."[53] Thus, in the record books of these early government courts we often hear for the first time the voices of Asantes rendered silent in nineteenth-century sources. Women, like Abena Febi, seem particularly inclined to contest the legitimacy of their exploitation through the British courts even though judgment, more often than not, only recast and then reinforced that legitimacy. For example, in Berekum in 1913, a slave wife to the chief of Senase ran away from her master and went to live with a clerk in Sunyani with whom she subsequently had a child. She refused to return to her master/husband. The commissioner of Asante's Western Province was unsure what to do, as "in all cases I have refused ever to put pressure on to a run away slave to return to her master." Yet, he pondered, "not now to allow damages for adultery on account of a slave woman would be to give slave women generally a free license to commit adultery." The commissioner finally decided to allow the claim of *ayefare,* heeding the CCA's advice to "treat slave wives as legitimate wives for once you have done away with 'slavery' the status of wifehood must be one and the same. I make them or their paramount pay satisfaction on the same scale as regular wives."[54] Undoubtedly, the former slave and the Sunyani clerk hoped that, the status of slave no longer being recognized, the woman's right to leave her master would be upheld. But the commissioner could not allow such a transformation in the woman's social status without undermining one of the primary mechanisms by which Asante chiefs exploited their wives' sexuality or without upsetting his own Victorian sense of morality.

If Asante's first British officials were interpreting and applying *ayefare* law in ways nearly indistinguishable from coexisting native tribunals or even precolonial courts,[55] they did not always handle the testimony of litigants in the same way, particularly that of women. Indeed, one of the most notable aspects of sexual contact cases in early native courts was that a woman's testimony was virtually never questioned. That a woman speaks the truth (*Oba na oka nokware*) was a basic assumption in *ayefare* cases; the accused was considered guilty unless he could disprove the woman's allegations with conclusive evidence.[56] In the British government courts, however, even though women thought they had a better chance of challenging custom there than in the native courts, their testimony never carried the same weight. For example, in 1908, Adontenhene J. K. Frimpon took his wife, Adjua Mansa, to the CCA's court claiming £100 damages for infidelity. She denied the charge and maintained that he was responsible for her pregnancy and that she had offered to drink fetish to support her claim. Mansa's mother further argued that "Frimpon is only doing this to make money. He would not allow the fetish to be drunk by the girl." Although Frimpon had no witnesses, the CCA refused to believe Adjoa Mansa or to have her drink fetish in support of her claim. He ruled against Adjoa Mansa for £60. Two months later, Frimpon brought a Mr. John Brew to court and won an additional £50 in *ayefare* compensation.[57]

Crisis, Contests, and Power Consolidated, 1924–1935

If the customs surrounding *ayerefa* survived, remarkably intact, the first two fumbling decades of British administration in Asante, they were to be tried and tested, challenged and reformulated in the decade following the Native Jurisdiction Ordinance of 1924. The ordinance regulated the jurisdiction of Asante's native tribunals and empowered them to hear both civil and criminal cases.[58] Coming under civil jurisdiction were cases involving marriage, divorce, paternity, and child custody. Thus, with the exception of appeals, which went from head chiefs to the DC's court, all *ayefare* cases—whether *efiesem* or *oman akyiwadee*—were heard as civil suits in the native tribunals. These courts, therefore, became one of the arenas in which social contests of power were waged in the context of rapid and often dislocating economic change. Included among them, from 1926 on, was the tribunal of the repatriated Asantehene, recognized only as Kumasihene by the British colonial government.

The rapid spread of cocoa cultivation (particularly after 1920), the expansion of the trade in foodstuffs (a trade women tended to control), and the growth of the mining industry all had profound repercussions on relationships between men and women in this critical decade. Although a full discussion of the impact of economic changes on marriage, divorce, and maternal/paternal responsibilities is not possible in the limited space here, it is important to note that at least for a portion of the colonial period (roughly 1925–35), there is ample evidence to suggest that Asante women had a greater "potential independence from marriage," as Roberts has called it, because of the growing trade in foodstuffs and the possibility of establishing cocoa farms.[59] The initial introduction of cocoa to Asante dramatically increased husbands' demands on a wife's labor—labor that was not compensated by subsistence foodstuffs as it had been in the pre-cocoa economy, but by a rather ill-defined obligation of the husband "to provide part of her subsistence from his own earnings." The conflicts in marriage resulting from this transformation in conjugal obligations saw women searching for more promising options for economic security than that provided by laboring on a husband's cocoa farm and not sharing in the proceeds of that farm or inheriting it if the husband died. Many sought security in the growing markets, some in establishing their own cocoa farms. The assertion of women's autonomy thus forms a backdrop for understanding many of the *ayefare* cases brought before the Kumasi native tribunals of the period—cases in which women not only struggled for a more central position, but contested *ayefare*'s very gender-specificity.[60]

Because the 1924 ordinance placed *all* adultery cases within the jurisdiction of the native tribunals—whether they involved commoners or chiefs, whether an oath was sworn or not—the line dividing the private realm from the public in Asante was dramatically redrawn. Thus, the contests women undertook in the late 1920s were very much public contests waged on a playing field (one might add, a field that was not always very even). What most of these contests had in common was a female plaintiff whose suit was based on some reformulation of *ayefare*. For example, Ama Kyirewo's 1927 claim based on subrogation was essentially aimed at collecting adultery compensation from the defendant because, as she argued, "my daughter's concubine was owing me and as Defendant took her unto himself, I wanted it from Defendant."[61] Kyirewo's case, though rather unique in its use of subrogation, was not an isolated instance of a woman contesting precolonial and early colonial constructions of *ayerefa*. In 1928, Clara Pomah, a sanitary inspectress, appeared before the Kumasihene's tribunal having accused the defendant, Abenah Adutwimah, of having been her husband's lover. She swore the Great Oath in support of her accusation. The defendant denied the allegation and responded by swearing the Great Oath. Pomah's husband testified on behalf of his wife. The court gave judgment for the plaintiff, with costs but no damages, and then reminded the defendant's husband that he could "deal with the witness" if he so chooses.[62] Pomah's accusation of adultery against a woman was thus quickly reformulated as a typical *ayefare* case between the two women's husbands.

Although Pomah's case ended up in court because it was an oath case, not because it involved adultery, some women came to the tribunals prepared to turn the whole notion of *ayerefa* on its head, with or without an oath having been sworn. Amina Badenda appeared before the Kumasihene in 1934 in an attempt to claim a £5 adultery fee from Bekoka Hausa whom she claimed had a sexual connection with her husband. Badenda told the court that her claim was in "accordance with Mohammadan customary law of marriage." After calling in Malam Mahama as an expert witness, the court ruled against Badenda, concluding that "the fact that the Plaintiff's husband has known carnally the Defendant cannot be questioned, but this does not, however, entitle the Plaintiff to sue for an adultery fee which is quite repugnant to both the Mohammadan and the Asante custom, as well as to the English custom."[63]

Some women had better luck convincing the courts of the merit in their rather unorthodox claims. In 1931, Yaa Kwaryie sued her husband, Kwaku Mensah, before the civil court of the Kyidomhene, claiming that Mensah refused to pay her a pacification fee after having a sexual connection "with a certain woman." In what would have been treated as a private marriage dispute in previous years, Kwaryie maintained in the civil tribunal that her husband had claimed £4 pacification from her when she committed adultery and now it was her turn to be pacified. That Mensah did not appear in court that day may go some way toward explaining the court's decision. Kwaryie won her suit, the court ordering Mensah to pay her £2.7—the standard commoner adultery fee, as well as the standard pacification fee for spouses.[64]

In another rather unorthodox case, Ama Jan-Yiadu sued a Mr. Jonsan for £50 damages for having a sexual connection with her daughter. Previously, Mr. Jonsan had been married to the daughter, but had since divorced her and received all of the marriage expenses from Jan-Yiadu. The daughter was about to marry another man, but at the time of the incident was single. Jan-Yiadu's claim challenged the gender specificity of *ayefare* in very fundamental ways in its contention that adultery fees should be collectible on an unmarried woman by the person (temporarily) "owning" or controlling sexual access to that unmarried woman, in this case, her mother. The defendant, Mr. Jonsan did not appear in court and the tribunal, in an unparalleled judgment, ruled in favor of Jan-Yiadu, awarding her an adultery fee of £7.4, damages of £5, plus costs of £3.12.

If some women were challenging constructions of adultery in this chaotic decade by reformulating *ayefare* in customary suits, others simply refused to play their assigned role in the proceedings: that of the third-party confessor. In precolonial and early colonial cases, a woman could refuse to confess the name of the adulterer if she were willing to assume responsibility for paying her husband's *ayefare.* Case after case appears in the civil record books of this period in which women refuse both to name the adulterer and to pay the *ayefare*—a refusal not looked upon sympathetically by the tribunals. In Kofi Boaten v. Yaa Korankyewa, the defendant refused to name the two men, to pay the *ayefare*, or to attend the court session to which she had been summoned.[65] In Yaw Fohuo v. Atta Ya, the defendant would not name the man with whom she had a child, refused to pay the fee, and then defended her actions by arguing that her husband had not provided for her subsistence and therefore was not entitled to *ayefare*. Atta Ya told the court she would not name the adulterer until her husband paid her eight years' worth of subsistence. The court ruled against Atta Ya, ordering her to pay her husband's adultery fee of £9.6.0. According to the court, Atta Ya should have approached her husband for dissolution of the marriage if she were not being maintained.[66] But failure to subsist could in no way mitigate the collection of *ayefare*.

Clearly, the decade following the Native Jurisdiction Ordinance of 1924 was one of intense change in Asante, change highlighted by the prism of *ayefare* cases. Colonial officials had virtually erased the boundary between *efiesem* and *oman akyiwadee* in adultery cases so that all could now be brought to the public realm as civil suits in native tribunals, with or without an oath being sworn. Thus, adultery, regardless of class or rank, was now a public concern. In the confusion that followed, women and men appeared before tribunals and contested, sometimes successfully and sometimes not, the social construction of *ayerefa*. Women were particularly active in this decade, asserting, perhaps, an independence born of sweeping economic changes in the marketing of foodstuffs and the cultivation of cocoa. Sometimes, they were quite successful in their efforts to recast *ayefare* compensation, though this was more likely to be the outcome if their suit was against another woman or if a male defendant failed to appear, than if the case involved a chief or disputed the definition of marriage. Nonetheless, 1924–34 was undoubtedly a period in which the meaning of *ayefare* was widely contested in the public realm and class and gender subordination challenged. In the decade that followed, the long-range victors of those struggles would finally be determined.

Consolidating Moral Order in Colonial Asante: The State, Uncontrolled Women, and the Criminalization of Adultery

For the chiefs who sat upon Asante's colonial tribunals, much of the gender chaos of the late 1920s—from contested definitions of marriage and adultery to a perceived increase in prostitution and venereal disease—was the direct result of uncontrolled women.[67] By the early 1930s, a "moral crisis" had erupted, as Roberts has called it, in which women's "material alternatives" to marriage were often blamed for removing "constraints upon their sexuality." One of the many ways that chiefs and elders responded to this crisis and attempted to reassert control over women's sexuality was through systematic reformulations of *ayefare*.[68] In the nineteenth century and, indeed, well into the colonial period, *ayefare* had provided a mechanism by which Asante's chiefs could both control and exploit their wives' sexuality. *Ayefare,* now fully within the public realm, was easily adapted to the requirements of the 1930s; that is, to the need to (re)establish control over *all* women's sexuality, not just that of chiefs' wives. Informally and often subtly, the imposition of constraints is evident in the circumstances surrounding post-1935 *ayefare* cases, in the testimony of women, and in the judgments of the courts. Formally, it is apparent in the series of official rules and orders under which the native courts operated: orders that criminalized adultery, strictly regulated wives' fidelity and adultery fees, and extended special *ayefare* compensation to Asante soldiers.

The colonial government's restoration of the Asante Confederacy Council in 1935 and its recognition of the Asantehene as the head of Asante created the context in which *ayefare* could be systematically reformulated and then implemented as a mechanism of social/sexual control. It could also be wielded as an instrument for reasserting Asante's hegemony in the region. Indeed, the intimate connections among state power, hegemony, and *ayefare* are dramatically illustrated by the fact that one of the first acts of the newly restored Asantehene was to dispatch messengers throughout the Gold Coast—from Sefwi Wiawso, to Saltpond, Winneba, Oda, and Kwahu—to collect satisfaction fees on behalf of his *nhenkwaa* (servants). In each case, the messenger collected £16, two sheep, and two bottles of gin. One of the Asantehene's messengers reported to the Sefwi Wiawso DC that in every town he delivered a letter to the local *omanhene* that was passed through the local DC. The money collected, he further reported, went to the Asantehene, although if the Asantehene "liked to give some of it to the husband he could do so." A representative letter from July 1935, addressed to the *omanhene* of Sefwi Wiawso, announced:

> It has been reported to me that one of your subjects by name Attah Affukah residing at Essakrome in the Wioso District, has had sexual intercourse with the wife of one of my Nhinkwas by name Kofi Nkuan (my soul washer). The wife's name is called Abina Aduah now residing at Essakrome.
>
> Under the circumstances, I will be very grateful if you will kindly assist my bearer, Kwabena Gyanfi to collect £16.0.0, two sheep and two bottles gin from the adulterer. My bearer will give you two bottles of gin according to native custom.
>
> Many thanks for your assistance please . . .

The DC for Sefwi Wiawso concluded that the "wives of the Asantehene's nhinkwas are distributed round the country and . . . whenever one of them is 'seduced,' £16 is claimed and goes to form part of the Asantehene's revenue."

In one case at Bibiani, the accused adulterer had already paid the local satisfaction fee of £4.13.0, but the Asantehene sent messengers anyway, requesting the amount of £16, as well as a sheep and four bottles of gin, on the grounds that the husband was his *ahenkwaa*. The accused refused to pay more than the local fee. The Asantehene's rather conciliatory reply was most telling: at least £2 for a sheep should be added to the local fee but "in future cases where the aggrieved husband was an Ashanti, the claim for satisfaction was to be referred to him for settlement."[69] Indeed, what the DC failed to appreciate was that the Asantehene was not simply adding to his revenue by collecting adultery compensation throughout the Gold Coast. He was, through the mechanism of *ayefare,* reclaiming (and even extending) Asante's precolonial borders. He was reasserting Kumasi's hegemony over the outlying divisions, as well as Asante hegemony over portions of the colony.[70]

Within the borders of Asante after 1935, *ayefare* was no less important as a mechanism for *restoring* social control. Under the Native Courts (Ashanti) Ordinance of 1935, courts were established for Asante in four grades—A, B, C, D—with civil and criminal jurisidiction.[71] The Asante Confederacy Council, itself, served as a criminal court for hearing major constitutional cases and, after 1936, was empowered to make orders and rules on a number of topics, including so-called native custom.[72] But even before the council was so empowered, a governor's order of 1935, the Native Courts (Offences Under Native Law and Custom) Order, rendered adultery a criminal offense triable in Asante's B- and C-grade criminal courts, with criminal action not prejudicing civil action to collect *ayefare.*[73]

While adultery thus remained an economic transaction between two men, the order added a new dimension of social control by permitting the criminal prosecution of a male adulterer, with the native court able to impose fines and exact penalties including imprisonment with hard labor. Criminal prosecution could thus serve to control the sexuality and, thereby, the options (economic and otherwise) of wives, by deterring men from having sexual connections with the wives of other men. In theory, at least, a woman like Atta Ya would have a far more difficult time finding someone to "subsist her" were that someone faced not simply with a £2.7.0 *ayefare,* but with fines and/or imprisonment.[74] Adultery, whether *efiesem* or *oman akyiwadee,* whether civil or criminal, was now fully in the public realm and available as an instrument of social control.[75]

Other orders aimed at the specific control of sexuality were passed by the Confederacy Council in the decade and a half after restoration. Of direct relevance to this discussion were the council's 1942 resolution (followed by a 1946 order) allowing Asante soldiers who fought in World War II to collect an adultery fee of

£9.6.0, not only for the duration of the war, but for their entire lives. The measure was aimed at encouraging "Ashanti youths to enlist . . . and to discourage any further desertions," but it was also aimed very directly at controlling soldiers' wives. Section 2 of the order required a soldier's wife to pay a pacification fee of £4.13.0 to her husband for "every case of adultery proven against her." If the woman did not pay the fee after civil summons, she was to be imprisoned "for the appropriate number of days."[76]

In 1944, the council standardized a schedule of adultery fees that was subsequently embodied in the Ashanti (Declaration of Native Customary Law) Order of 1946. The lengthy schedule listed adultery fees according to rank for everyone from a "Grade I" *amanhene,* who could collect £111.12. to Kumasi's "Grade III" Gyasehene (£74.8), to the Asantehene's *nhenkwaa* (£7.0), to commoners (£2.7). In ranking, it differed little from what we know of precolonial *ayefare* or from the 1911 CCA's scale. Certainly, the purpose was the same: to reinforce social status differentiation and broaden social control through adultery compensation.[77] The same committee of the council that standardized adultery fees also considered and ultimately recommended that "it should be made an offense, by Ordinance, for women to commit adultery." The Asante Confederacy Council agreed to the recommendation, but no subsequent action was taken. Nonetheless, that the option of criminalizing adultery for women was seriously contemplated in 1944 only shows the length to which the council was prepared to go in order to deter what it perceived as women's uncontrollability.[78] Though adultery was never criminalized for Asante women—an action that would have necessitated the complete regendering and reinvention of *ayerefa*—the council did take a very direct shot at that "uncontrollability" with its 1949 Wives Fidelity Declaration Order. The order made it the duty of every woman married under customary law, "when so required by her husband . . . to make a declaration upon oath of her fidelity." Any woman who failed to carry out her duty was "liable to a fine of twenty-five pounds or to imprisonment for two months or to both such fine and imprisonment."[79] That such an order was considered necessary in 1949 at least suggests that some women were refusing to swear such an oath. By not revealing the theft (*wiakyere*) or not providing the confession upon which all *ayefare* cases were based, wives could undermine the very process of *ayefare* collection. The Wives' Fidelity Declaration Order, with both civil and criminal repercussions, was aimed at reinforcing the essential step between a wife's uncontrolled, extramarital activities and her husband's compensation—the confession.

If the orders passed by the Asante Confederacy Council go a long way toward illustrating the formal actions taken by Asante's chiefs in order to use *ayefare* as an instrument of social control, the treatment of testimony and the judgments of courts during the period provide glimpses of informal, subtle efforts to limit women's options for autonomy by reinforcing relationships of power and subordination. Unfortunately, we do not have material from the nineteenth century with which to compare these domestic cases, but certainly when compared to early colonial cases they show a marked tendency for the courts to undervalue women's testimony and to deflate the responsibilities of men in marriage relationships. For example, Kwaku Boakyi brought his wife before the Asantehene's D-grade court in 1935 charging that she refused both to swear an oath of fidelity and to announce the name of the adulterer. Yaa Mansah responded to her husband, "Do you not remember that you have failed to maintain me for the past six years and hence I offered myself to another man to deal with me and hence I object to point out the particular man . . . to you?" When the court asked Yaa Mansah if her marriage had been dissolved, she said that it had been, in the presence of Chief Kwasi Boakyi. The chief later testified in court that the marriage had not been dissolved before him. The court finally ruled against Yaa Mansah, reasoning that her "contention is rather immaterial to justify her case." She was ordered to swear an oath of fidelity and either reveal the adulterer to her husband or pay the *ayefare* herself.[80]

In a very different sort of case, a similar judgment on men's obligations to subsist wives was made. In the Asantehene's B-grade court, Ama Manu sued her brother-in-law for £8.5.0 being subsistence for herself and her two children for a period of eleven months. Ama Manu's husband had fallen sick for some time and was not contributing to her subsistence or that of their children. The defendant, her husband's brother, did not assist either. Eventually the husband died and Ama Manu technically became the defendant's wife. She was forced to confess the names of the men with whom she had sexual connections during the previous months. This she did and then pacified the defendant with £8. Subsequently, the defendant refused to continue the marriage with Ama Manu and so Manu demanded to be reimbursed for the eleven months of subsistence owed to her by the defendant as her husband. The court ruled against Ama Manu on the grounds that by "her behaviour towards her sick husband and her conduct after the death of her husband, she is customarily not entitled to any subsistence by the Defendant."[81]

The rulings in these two cases give a good sense of the predicament in which some Asante women found themselves when post-restoration native courts ruled on spousal obligations with regard to subsistence and adultery. A man's refusal to subsist his wife—even for as long as six years—did not affect his right to collect *ayefare.* However, even if that wife were willing to cooperate in the collection of *ayefare* (that is, "reveal the theft" and pay pacification) she was still not entitled to demand what was once a husband's primary obligation to his wife: to provide for her subsistence. In other words, for a husband, a wife's extramarital affair was an excuse *not* to fufill subsistence obligations in marriage, but a husband's failure to subsist his wife gave her *no* excuse for refusing to cooperate in her husband's collection of *ayefare.*

Subtle shifts in judgements in *ayefare* cases after 1935 at least partly reflected the courts' changing attitudes toward women's testimony. The days in which a women's testimony concerning sexual encounters was considered uncontestable—*oba na oka nokware* (a woman speaks the truth)—were long gone.[82] For example, in the oath case Yaw Brenyah v. Effuah Frimpoma, Brenyah swore the Great Oath to deny Frimpoma's charge that he had a sexual connection with her. Frimpoma swore the Great Oath in response. The court ruled that "wherein the Defendant prefers a serious charge of adultery . . . the court is not satisfied with the unsupported statement of the Defendant and therefore enters judgement against the Defendant."[83] In a similar oath case, Akua Aframkuma, a boiled-corn seller, had accused Henry Kusi, a cocoa-weighing clerk, of having a sexual connection with her in a cocoa shed. Kusi swore the Great Oath to deny the accusation and Aframkuma swore an oath to support it. Aframkuma first confessed the incident to her husband when she was in labor and both the plaintiff (Kusi) and the defendant (Aframkuma) had witnesses testify on their behalf, though neither witness actually saw what occurred in the cocoa shed. In the end, the court ruled against Akua Aframkuma on the grounds that it was "not possible for any sane man to have a sexual connection with a woman in a cocoa shed in a cocoa season and in the broad day light, at 1 o'clock as alleged by the Defendant."[84] Case closed.

Final Thoughts

Ayerefa in Asante was always about power and subordination: chiefs over commoners, Kumasi over Asante's periphery, and husbands over wives. It was remarkably consistent in the ways it differentiated status and class and marginalized women.

That adultery compensation survived not only Asante's final tumultuous century as an independent power, but over a half-century of British colonial rule certainly testifies to its resilience as an instrument of social control. This is not to argue that *ayerefa* was an immutable social construct, a stable constant in Asante's social past. Rather it is to underscore that its consistence rested largely on its adaptability to economic, political, and social change.

In 1850 *ayerefa* was either a private, domestic matter handled by two men and their respective families or it was a crime against the state (*oman akyiwadee*), punishable by heavy fines or death. In the first case, women's sexuality was certainly regulated, though not controlled. In the second it was regulated, controlled, and exploited. By 1935, *ayerefa* was fully within the public realm and punishable in all cases as a crime against the colonial state, though penalties were far less severe than in the nineteenth century. It was constructed, moreover, to control *all* women's sexuality, not just that of chiefs' wives. In other words, *ayefare* compensation continued to reinforce the class and rank of Asante men, but it no longer differentiated among *wives. All* women's sexuality could now be subject to state control.

Indeed, the 1935 restoration of the Asante Confederacy Council can be understood, in part, as an attempt by the British colonial government to bring order to the chaos in gender relations that erupted during the late 1920s and early 1930s. The Asantehene and his restored council were empowered to stabilize social relations in colonial Asante and one of their many authorized weapons in that struggle was a reinforced and reformulated *ayefare.* This is not to say that *ayerefa*'s meaning was uncontested after 1935, that Asante's chiefs managed, with a few blows, to solve the problem of "uncontrollable" women. Certainly, in much of the testimony cited herein, the meaning not only of *ayefare* but of marriage and divorce were contested at every turn. Indeed, that *ayefare* today, even in the villages, is something about which you consult the historical memories of the oldest inhabitants, is some indication that the contest over meaning was not won by Asante's ruling chiefs and that as an instrument of status differentiation or of social/sexual control, *ayefare* lost its effectiveness. Why that has been the case is outside the scope of this essay, though one would obviously have to consider such wide-ranging factors as changes in the role of chiefs after independence, the impact of education and Christianity, the role of the postcolonial state in mediating gender, economic decline, and its repercussions on conjugal obligations and the broader impact of popular culture. For now, however, perhaps it is best to conclude with the reasonings of an eighty-two-year-old Effiduasi woman. When I recently asked her why *ayefare* was no longer common today, she simply answered, "The men don't take care of the women and the women don't even allow their husbands to come and do the marriage rites! So, who will pay it?"[85]

Notes

As part of a broader study of gender and social change in Asante, research for this paper was supported by the National Endowment for the Humanities, the Fulbright-Hays Faculty Research Program, the Social Science Research Council, the University of Missouri Research Council, and the Institute of African Studies, University of Ghana. I gratefully acknowledge this support.

1. I rely here on T. C. McCaskie's summary of the cases as they appeared in "State and Society, Marriage and Adultery: Some Considerations Towards a Social History of Pre-Colonial Asante," *Journal of African History* 22 (1981): 490–91. For original text, see Instituut voor Taal-, Land-, en Volkenkunde, Leiden, MS H-509, P. de Heer, *Aanhangsel: Journale gehouden to Comassee door eenen tapoeier* (1866–67).

2. Manhyia Record Office, Kumasi [MRO], Kumasihene's Native Tribunal, *Civil Record Book 1,* Ama Kyirewo *v.* Akwasi Poku, 17 Jan. 1927, 134.

3. MRO, Asantehene's Native Court B, *Criminal Record Book 1,* Native Authority Police per Kojo Nimo *v.* Yaw Amoah, 14 Feb. 1936, 210.

4. In addition to P. de Heer's journal cited above, see W. Bosman, *A New and Accurate Description of the Coast of Guinea* (London, 1705), esp. 196–217; T. E. Bowdich, *Mission from Cape Coast Castle to Ashantee* (London, 1819), esp. 252–60; J. Dupuis, *Journal of Residence in Ashantee* (London, 1824), 36–37; B. Cruickshank, *Eighteen Years on the Gold Coast of Africa* (London, 1853), 191–225; A. B. Ellis, *The Tshi-Speaking Peoples of the Gold Coast of West Africa* (London, 1887), 281–89.

5. See R. S. Rattray, *Religion and Art in Ashanti* (Oxford, 1927), 86–93, and *Ashanti Law and Constitution* (Oxford, 1929) 304–23; J. M. Sarbah, *Fanti Customary Laws* (London, 1897), 41–54; J. B. Danquah, *Gold Coast: Akan Laws and Customs* (London, 1922), 145–80. Record books used in this paper are housed either at Manhyia Record Office, Kumasi or at the National Archives of Ghana (Accra and Kumasi).

6. M. Chanock, *Law, Custom and Social Order: The Colonial Experience in Malawi and Zambia* (Cambridge, 1985), 25–47 and passim. See also his "Making Customary Law: Men, Women, and Courts in Colonial Northern Rhodesia," in *African Women and the Law: Historical Perspectives,* ed. M. J. Hay and M. Wright (Boston, 1982), 53–67.

7. K. Mann and R. Roberts, "Law in Colonial Africa," in *Law in Colonial Africa,* ed. Mann and Roberts (Portsmouth, 1991), 47.

8. Chanock, "Making Customary Law," 54.

9. Ibid., 60. Here Chanock emphasizes, perhaps too much, the colonial present in the making of customary law and thereby undervalues the weight of a society's precolonial past in the very contests of the colonial present. In another passage (56), however, he recasts his approach as an effort to understand "the

specific circumstances of the assertion of those forms of male power embodied in systems of customary law." By historicizing male power, therefore, he adds a historical dimension to his framework.

10. See, for example, Rattray, *Ashanti Law*, 317, and *Religion and Art*, 76–77; T. E. Kyei, *Marriage and Divorce Among the Asante* (Cambridge University, Centre of African Studies, 1995), 15–18, 30; Ellis, *The Tshi-Speaking Peoples*, 281–89; and Sarbah, *Fanti Customary Laws*, 41–56. For a discussion of what constitutes a marriage in the postcolonial period, see D. D. Velenga, "Who is a Wife? Legal Expressions of Heterosexual Conflicts in Ghana," in *Female and Male in West Africa*, ed. C. Oppong (London, 1983), 144–55.

11. Rattray, *Ashanti Law*, 317–18; Danquah, *Akan Laws*, 166.

12. Danquah, *Akan Laws*, 155 and 166.

13. MRO, Kumasihene's Native Tribunal, *Civil Record Book 12*, Ambah Serwah *v.* Kojo Piprah, 28 July 1931, 241.

14. Rattray, *Ashanti Law*, 322; J. G. Christaller, *Dictionary of the Asante and Fante Language Called Tshi (Twi)* (Basel, 1933), 587; Danquah, *Akan Laws*, 177.

15. MRO, Asantehene's Appam Court D, *Civil Record Book 33*, Kyeame Yaw Pong *v.* Opoku, 23 Nov. 1946, 42.

16. Danquah, *Akan Laws*, 167–68.

17. Rattray, *Ashanti Law*, 318.

18. The punishments for sexual assault are far more difficult to trace historically than those for adultery. It is virtually impossible for the precolonial period, although the heavy penalties for having a sexual connection "in the bush" suggests that *ahahantwe* virtually implied force because no one would voluntarily commit such an offense. For the colonial period, the picture is quite complex. Certainly, many of the obvious sexual assault cases in the colonial record books are tried in native courts as cases of sexual connection "in the bush," with the male offender receiving a stiff fine or imprisonment. The husband of the woman concerned could also collect *ayefare* compensation from the offender. In the British colonial courts, rapes were treated as sexual assaults under criminal law. See Rattray, *Ashanti Law*, 308.

19. Ibid., 304–8 and 317–23.

20. Rattray, *Religion and Art*, 87–93; Bowdich, *Mission to Ashanti*, 259–60; Ellis, *The Tshi-Speaking Peoples*, 282–83. For a detailed discussion of the many factors that differentiated *ayefare* among commoner classes, see Rattray, *Ashanti Law*, 317–23.

21. Rattray viewed *efiesem* and *oman akyiwadee* as nearly replicating the British legal distinction between "civil" and "criminal." There were, however, several important differences, some of which are discussed in *Ashanti Law*, 286–88. For the purposes of historical reconstruction, it is important to keep the categories distinct in order to understand what happens when Asante notions of *efiesem/oman akyiwadee* collide with British notions of civil and criminal.

22. For full discussions of oath-swearing, see Rattray, *Religion and Art*, chap. 22, and *Ashanti Law*, 379–80; K. A. Busia, *The Position of the Chief in the Modern Political System of Ashanti* (London, 1968; first published, London, 1951), 75–77.

23. Busia, *Position of the Chief,* 75.

24. MRO, Native Tribunal of Omanhin of Bompata, *Record Book,* Kofie Fofie *v.* Cubina Nim, 17 Nov. 1916, 12.

25. McCaskie, "State and Society," 491.

26. Bowdich, *Mission to Ashantee,* 259. A *periguin* or, more commonly, *peredwan* was equivalent to 16 *ackies* or £8.2.0.

27. Rattray, *Religion and Art,* 86–93 and *Ashanti Law,* 307–8.

28. In Asoamfohene Owusu Kwabena *v.* Osei Hyeaman (13 Feb. 1867), the defendant, an officeholder, was ordered by the Asantehene to pay "more than 25 ounces of gold" to Owusu Kwabena. See McCaskie, "State and Society," 491. For the rather famous case of Kwasi Kankam (linguist to the Asantehene) and his "intrigues" with married women, see ibid., 491 and Bowdich, *Mission to Ashantee,* 96–97.

29. Rattray, *Ashanti Law,* 323. Six shillings is roughly equivalent to one and a half ackies—Bowdich's figure for a common man's compensation in the early nineteenth century. Bowdich, *Mission to Ashantee,* 259.

30. McCaskie, "State and Society," 490.

31. On the different penalties faced by men and women, McCaskie explains: "the woman was killed as *punishment* for participation while the man surrendered his life in *compensation* to the offended husband." See "State and Society," 489.

32. Bowdich, *Mission to Ashantee,* 260; Ellis, *The Tshi-Speaking Peoples,* 283. Ellis wrote that if a wife of a chief was from a family "too powerful to admit of the husband putting her to death, he usually cuts off her nose as punishment." See Rattray, *Religion and Art,* 87–91.

33. Ellis, *The Tshi-Speaking Peoples,* 282; Cruickshank, *Eighteen Years,* 199; Rattray, *Religion and Art,* 98.

34. J. Dupuis, *Journal of Residence,* 37. Also see Cruickshank, *Eighteen Years,* 199.

35. Rattray, *Ashanti Law,* 322–23 and *Religion and Art,* 96; Bosman provides a late-seventeenth-century account of this practice in *Description of the Coast of Guinea,* 170–71.

36. See W. Tordoff, *Ashanti Under the Prempehs, 1888–1935* (London, 1965), 67–109. Tordoff's account remains one of the most thorough treatments of the imposition of colonial rule in Asante.

37. Mann and Roberts, "Law in Colonial Africa," 21, borrow the term from J. Starr and J. F. Collier, "Introduction: Dialogues in Legal Anthropology," in *History and Power in the Study of Law,* ed. J. Starr and J. F. Collier (Ithaca, N.Y., 1989), 8–9.

38. For correspondence involving various chiefs and their protests against the scale of adultery fees, see National Archives of Ghana, Kumasi [NAGK], Asante Regional Administration Files [ARA]/848: Principal Chiefs J. K. Frimpon and Six Others to Chief Commissioner, Ashanti dd. 1 Aug. 1917 and Chief Commissioner, Ashanti to Chief Kwesi Nuam and Eleven Others, dd. Kumasi, 13 Sept. 1913. Also see NAGK, SCT/204: Magistrate's Court, *Civil Record Book 7,* Kweku Adeyah *v.* Kojo Fojo, 1 Sept. 1910, 52.

39. Tordoff, *Ashanti*, 79–80, 82–83.

40. Rattray, *Ashanti Law*, 105–6.

41. See Tordoff, *Ashanti*, 83. For examples of cases referred to the Native Committee, see NAGK, SCT/204: Magistrates Court, *Civil Record Book 1*, 1897–98.

42. NAGK, SCT/204: Magistrate's Court, *Civil Record Book 1*, Akosuah Takyiwa *v.* Charles E. Meyer, dd. 25 June 1897.

43. Gold Coast, Ashanti Administration Ordinance, No. 1 of 1902.

44. Gold Coast, *Report of Commission on Native Courts* (Accra, 1951), 31.

45. See, especially, NAGK, ADM/175: Kumasi District Commissioner's Court, *Record Books 1–13*, 1907–14 and NAGK, SCT/204: Magistrate's Court, *Civil Record Books 1–17*, 1897–1917.

46. NAGK, SCT/204: Magistrate's Court, *Civil Record Book 7*, Yaa Tima *v.* Cobina Buo, 7 Mar. 1911.

47. Mann and Roberts, "Law in Colonial Africa," 13.

48. NAGK, ARA/1854: "Claim of adultery fees" by Omanhin of Bompata, Cudjo Dakwa, Bompatahene to Chief Commissioner, dd. Bompata, 18 Sept. 1915.

49. NAGK, ARA/185: Abena Febi to District Commissioner, Juaso, dd. Juaso, 4 Oct. 1915.

50. In the Native Tribunal of the Bompatahene, Kwame Nimakoh sued Cobina Aming for adultery compensation. Nimakoh had already collected compensation from two men, but Aming, the third, refused on the grounds that the DC said that he did not have to pay. Aming dashed Nimakoh 7s. and Nimakoh, claiming he was insulted, took the case before the court. See MRO, Bompatahene's Court, *Record Book*, Kwame Nimakoh *v.* Cobina Aming, 2 Dec. 1916, 14.

51. MRO, District Commissioner's Court, *Palaver Book*, Kobina N'Kansa *v.* Yaw Ewuah, King of Ejisu, 8 Aug. 1907, 34.

52. NAGK, ARA/1854: District Commissioner, Juaso to Chief Commissioner, Ashanti, dd. Juaso, 5 Oct. 1915.

53. C. H. Harper Papers (Rhodes House, Oxford), C. H. Harper, Chief Commissioner, Ashanti, "Native Jurisdiction in Ashanti" (n.d., but probably 1920–21), 21. According to Harper, by 1909, the chiefs asked that all marriage palavers be heard by them. The chief commissioner agreed, ordering that all such cases should be brought to government courts only on appeal. For an important discussion of the ways women used the British justice system in the Gold Coast Colony during this period, see R. Gocking, "British Justice and the Native Tribunals of the Southern Gold Coast Colony," *Journal of African History* 34 (1993): 93–113, but esp. 108–10.

54. NAGK, ARA/238: Commissioner, Western Province Ashanti to Chief Commissioner, Coomassie, dd. Sunyani 5 Sept. 1913; Chief Commissioner Coomassie to Commissioner, Western Province Ashanti, dd. Coomassie, 10 Nov. 1913.

55. The Chief Commissioner's Court, the Magistrate's Court, and the various Native Tribunals in Kumasi all utilized a common scale for adultery fees from

1905 onward—a scale not radically different from precolonial ranked compensation. Although I have not been able to locate a copy of the 1905 scale, several references are made to the "1905 Chief Commissioner's Scale of Adultery Fees" in the early record books. A copy of the 1911 scale can be found in NAGK, ARA/848. The scale closely approximates what we know of precolonial fees, with one important exception. Kumasi's "clan heads," as the British termed them (Kronti, Adonten, Akwamu, Oyoko, Kyidom, Gyase, and Ankobea) were entitled to compensation equal to that of *amanhene*—£50 and one sheep—a reward, no doubt, for their collaboration with British colonial rule. For others, compensation involved one sheep, plus one of the following ranked fees: other Kumasi councillors, £30; heir to *omanhene's* stool, £25; "head linguist, head treasurer, war captain, head sword bearer, head stool carrier, head of cemetery, head court carrier," £20; "minor captains, linguists and elders who are on the council of the omanhene," £9.6; "blood relations of omanhene," £7; "personal servants of omanhene," £4.13; all others, £2.7.

56. Danquah, *Akan Laws,* 167.

57. NAGK, SCT/24: Chief Commissioner's Court, Ashanti, *Record Book 2,* Frimpon *v.* Adjuah Mansah, 26 Aug. 1908 and Frimpon *v.* John Brew, 16 Oct. 1908.

58. Gold Coast, Native Jurisdiction Ordinance, No. 4 of 1924. See part VI, sec. 29–52 for civil and criminal jurisdiction courts.

59. P. Roberts, "The State and the Regulation of Marriage: Sefwi Wiawso (Ghana), 1900–1940," in *Women, State, and Ideology: Studies from Africa and Asia,* ed. H. Afshar (Albany, 1987), 48–49.

60. Many scholars have explored this momentary opening up of options or "avenues of escape," as Chanock calls them, in the first decades of colonial rule. Chanock, "Making Customary Law," 56–57. For the purposes of this discussion, Roberts provides a convincing overview of the impact of economic changes on conjugal obligations in "The State and Marriage," 48–69. See also, D. D. Vellenga, "Matriliny, Patriliny, and Class Formation among Women Cocoa Farmers in Two Rural Areas of Ghana," in *Women and Class in Africa,* ed. C. Robertson and I. Berger (New York, 1986), 62–77; and C. Okali, "Kinship and Cocoa-Farming in Ghana," in *Female and Male,* ed. Oppong, 169–78. For discussions of the broader impact of cocoa, see G. Austin, "The Emergence of Capitalist Relations in South Asenie Cocoa-Farming, c. 1916–1933," *Journal of African History* 32 (1987): 259–79; J. Dunn and A. F. Robertson, *Dependence and Opportunity: Political Change in Ahafo* (Cambridge, 1973); B. Grier, "Pawns, Porters and Petty Traders: Women in the Transition to Cash Crop Agriculture in Colonial Ghana," *Signs* 17, no. 2 (1992): 304–28; P. Hill, *Migrant Cocoa-Farmers of Southern Ghana* (Cambridge, 1963); G Mikell, *Cocoa and Chaos in Ghana* (New York, 1989).

61. MRO, Kumasihene's Native Tribunal, *Civil Record Book 1,* Ama Kyirewo *v.* Akwasi Poku, 17 Jan. 1927, 134.

62. MRO, Kumasihene's Native Tribunal, *Civil Record Book 4,* Clara Poma *v.* Abena Adutwimah, 5 Sept. 1928, 426.

63. MRO, Kumasihene's Native Tribunal, *Civil Record Book 24,* Amina Badenda *v.* Bedoka Hausa, 21 Dec. 1934, 410.

64. MRO, Kyidomhene's Native Tribunal, *Civil Record Book 3,* Yaa Kwaryie *v.* Kwaku Mensah, 8 Dec. 1931, 327. It was common practice for spouses to pacify each other in cases of adultery. The fee for commoners was generally £2.7. See, for example, Gyasehene's Native Tribunal, *Civil Record Book 1,* Yaw Fohuo *v.* Atta Ya, 23 Mar. 1928, 124.

65. MRO, Kumasihene's Native Tribunal, *Civil Record Book 20,* Kofi Boaten *v.* Yaa Korankyewa, 6 Sept. 1933, 45.

66. For a listing of grounds for divorce, see Rattray, *Religion and Art,* 97–98. "Refusal to house, clothe, or feed her properly" is listed as grounds for a woman to divorce her husband.

67. The problem of "uncontrollable" women is a common theme in the broader literature on gender and colonialism. See, for example, M. Lovett, "Gender Relations, Class Formation, and the Colonial State in Africa," in *Women and the State in Africa,* ed. J. Parpart and K. Staudt (Boulder, Colo., 1989), 28 and Roberts, "The State and Marriage in Ghana," 61.

68. For an overview of this crisis and of chiefs' attempts to control women's sexuality, see J. Allman, "Of 'Spinsters,' 'Concubines' and 'Wicked Women': Reflections on Gender and Social Change in Colonial Asante," *Gender and History* 3, no. 2 (1991): 176–89. See esp. 182–83 for a discussion of Asokore's 1929 roundup of all unmarried women. A similar roundup occurred in Sefwi Wiawso in 1929. See Roberts, "The State and Marriage," 61.

69. A. F. L. Wilkinson Papers (Rhodes House, Oxford), Asantehene Osei A. Prempeh II, Asantehene to Omanhene of Sefwi Wioso, dd. Kumasi, 19 July 1935; Memo, District Commissioner's Clerk to District Commissioner, Wiawso, dd. 30 July 1935; DC, Wiawso to Commissioner of Western Province, Sekondi, dd. Wiawso, 30 July 1935.

70. For a prerestoration case in which a man is accused of using the Kumasihene's name in order to demand adultery fees, see MRO, Kumasihene's Native Tribunal, *Criminal Record Book 6,* Native Tribunal *v.* Attah Kwabinah, Kwabena Jaimfie and Akwasi Chaye, 12 May 1923, 203.

71. Gold Coast, Native Courts (Ashanti) Ordinance, No. 2 of 1935. For a summary of the structure of Asante's postrestoration native court system, see W. M. Hailey, *Native Administration in the British African Territories, Part III* (London, 1951), 244–45.

72. See J. N. Matson, *A Digest of the Minutes of the Ashanti Confederacy Council from 1935–1949 Inclusive and a Revised Edition of Warrington's Notes on Ashanti Custom* (Cape Coast, n.d., but c. 1951), 32.

73. Gold Coast, Native Courts (Offences under Native Law and Custom) Order, No. 7 of 1935. Amended by Order 24 of 1943. See also Matson, *Ashanti Confederacy Council,* 42–45.

74. Kojo Nimo's case, cited in the introduction, was one of many cases in which a man was brought to criminal court by the Native Authority Police, acting on behalf of a husband, fined for committing adultery and then ordered to pay *ayefare* in addition to the fine. See MRO, Asantehene's Native Court B, *Criminal Record Book 1,* Native Authority Police per Kojo Nimo *v.* Yaw Amoah, 14 Feb. 1936, 210.

75. In 1943, the council amended its original order on the criminalization of adultery so that prosecutions were limited to those marriages which had been registered. The civil remedy for adultery compensation was not affected. Thus, in civil adultery suits well into the 1940s, a main source of contention continued to be whether or not the husband and wife were *really* married. Increasingly, the only criteria used by the courts was the payment, or not, of *tiri nsa*. For sources discussing the wide variety of recognized marriages and marriage formalities in the precolonial and early colonial periods, see note 11. See also V. Tashjian's article in this volume.

76. The order is discussed and reproduced in full in Matson, *Ashanti Confederacy Council*, 25 and 40–41. Suits filed under this order can be found in MRO, Asantehene's Appam Court D, *Civil Record Books 27–31*, 1943–46. In Ex-GC 54341 John Mensah *v.* Gariba Hausa, *Civil Record Book 31*, 17 May 1946, 552, the court ruled against the plaintiff because it suspected that he "and his wife entered into a mutual arrangement between themselves to put the Defendant in trouble."

77. The order is reproduced in full in Matson, *Ashanti Confederacy Council*, 45–48. While one cannot but be struck by the continuities in *ayefare* over so many decades, the order did differ from the 1911 scale in two important ways. First, the 1946 order held that no husband could claim adultery compensation more than twice "in respect of any one wife." This is, perhaps, the only evidence of a significant British impact on the reformulation of *ayefare*. Second, the 1946 scale returned Kumasi's "clan chiefs" to their precolonial rankings. They were no longer entitled to the same compensation as *amanhene*—a reflection, no doubt, of changed power relations after the restoration of the council and the stabilization of indirect rule. Certainly, the order was a response to the seemingly endless number of cases in which men claimed higher fees than the adulterers believed they were entitled to. For example in Akua Brago *v.* Kwaku Appaw, MRO, Asantehene Appam Court D, *Civil Record Book 10*, 23 Aug. 1937, 353, Akua Brago confessed to two counts of adultery to her husband. One of the adulterers could not be located so Brago was liable for the *ayefare*. Her husband told her that in his status as an ex-*odikro* (village chief) and a "royalist to the linguist Nantwi of Bantama," he was entitled to £11.6. Brago paid this and then became convinced her husband was only due £2.7. The court ruled in Brago's favor and her husband had to refund the difference.

78. This concern was evident in the council's 1938 discussion about changing the laws of inheritance to allow wives to inherit from their deceased husbands—an issue made all the more pressing by the cocoa economy's transformation of conjugal obligations. The Drobohene was able to convince the council to table the discussion, largely by encouraging members' fears of uncontrollable women. "I think you will all agree with me," he argued,

> that the women of these days have no character. Some keep concubines apart from the husbands and some also are wicked; they even go so far as to take the lives of their husbands by means of noxious juju; this is very common in Ashanti and I tell you that a wife can easily poison her husband since she is responsible for his "chop."

Not until 1948, did the council finally rule on the issue of wives inheriting from their husbands, but it was a ruling with no legislative effect. See Asante Confederacy Council, *Minutes of the Third Session,* 7–23 Mar. 1938; Matson, *Ashanti Confederacy Council,* 26–27; Allman, "Spinsters," 184–85.

79. The order is reproduced in full in Matson, *Ashanti Confederacy Council,* 44. Women who were royals of one of the stools scheduled in the order were excluded from the requirement, as were women for whom swearing an oath was "repugnant" to their "religious beliefs."

80. MRO, Asantehene's Appam Court D, *Civil Record Book 3,* Kwaku Boakyi *v.* Yaa Mansah, 23 Dec. 1935, 370 and Gyasehene's Native Tribunal, *Civil Record Book 1,* Yaw Fohuo *v.* Atta Ya, 12 Mar. 1928, 124.

81. MRO, Asantehene's Native Court B, *Civil Record Book 20,* Ama Manu *v.* Kwasi Buo, 25 Sept. 1940, 180.

82. An interesting exception is Yaw Amoah's statement in MRO, Asantehene's Native Court B, *Criminal Record Book 1,* Native Authority Police per Kojo Nimo *v.* Yaw Amoah, 14 Feb. 1936, 210. After several witnesses testified against him, Amoah switched his plea to guilty, saying, "What a woman has said in connection with adultery or sexual connection is always correct and I do not wish to prolong this matter."

83. MRO, Asantehene's Native Court B, *Civil Record Book 4,* Yaw Brenyah *v.* Effua Frimpoma, 13 Feb. 1936, 38.

84. MRO, Asantehene's Native Court B, *Civil Record Book 20,* Henry Kusi *v.* Akua Aframkuma, 19 Oct. 1940, 278.

85. J. Allman, interview with Adwoa Addae, Effiduasi, Ashanti Region, 28 Aug. 1992.

The Naked and the Clothed ESTHER GOODY AND JACK GOODY

At the end of the nave of the great Basilica of Saint Cecilia in Albi, constructed by the Dominicans between the thirteenth and fifteenth centuries as a fortress against the popular movement of the Cathars (miscalled the Albigensians), there is a magnificent fresco of the Last Judgment. The scene is divided horizontally into three layers with Heaven on high, and Hell below. In the middle lies Purgatory, the inhabitants of which are nude, except for the Book of Life hung around their necks. If they are condemned, they are encompassed by the waters and the flames of Hell, but without their books. Those who have reached Heaven are heavily clothed, either as royalty, as priests, or as good bourgeois. So too the saints and the angels. Even Christ and God the Father carry a light cloth to cover their modesty, although their bodies are otherwise largely exposed. The contrast is dramatic between the saved, who are well clothed, and the damned, who are nude.

That contrast had a long history in the Near East. When Adam had eaten the forbidden fruit he then became ashamed of his nakedness. While nudity was man's original state, as a sinner he felt he needed to clothe himself and cover up his genitalia. The relationship among nakedness, sex, and sin was established right at the beginning of the Jewish Bible.

Islam is no less severe upon nudity, even partial nudity, than Christianity. When Ibn Battutah visited the Maldive Islands in the fourteenth century he was disturbed by the girls dressed in sarongs and refused to act as *qāḍī* in judicial disputes, unless the women before him had their bodies covered.[1] While tropical India and Southeast Asia were distinguished by the wearing of a small amount of cloth, northern India followed Islamic patterns in insisting that the whole body should be covered. In the extreme form in West Asia that meant covering the head, especially the hair, and the face of women too by means of a veil, except in the privacy of the house or tent. Once again this practice had its counterparts not only earlier in Judaism and westward in the East Mediterranean but also in northern India. The total covering of women in this fashion went along with their seclusion from men outside the family. While such complete covering was rare in Europe, the veil was in use until recently among some women of the bourgeoisie and head covering was always worn by women (in contrast to laymen) in Catholic churches. Most advanced civilizations regulate dress in this way as part of the process of making the inhabitants "civilized." During the extensions of the Han government to northern Vietnam, local people were instructed in "justice and ritual," being required to accept Chinese marriage rites and to wear hats and sandals.[2]

Peoples With Cloth, Peoples Without

To be clothed is not, of course, always the same thing as to wear cloth, even though the distinction is difficult to make in English.[3] In all human societies, men and women past the age of childhood wear something: beads, bark-cloth, skins. Such was the case in northern Ghana where Fortes has drawn attention to the importance of apparently small items of dress, including leaves, not only in covering one's nudity, usually the sexual organs, but also in distinguishing people's status, especially that of women as unmarried, married, widowed. While some cloth was also being worn by the Tallensi when he worked there in 1935, the people did not themselves weave cloth, and they purchased what they then used, either the European variety mainly from stores, or the local (Mossi) cloth from market traders. Traditionally, like the LoDagaa farther west, they wore no cloth but used the skins of animals in various forms; in the case of women it was waistbands of grass for unmarried girls and of leather for married women, usually supplemented by leaves.

In clear contrast to these clothless and relatively unclothed peoples were the inhabitants of the kingdoms of the area, the Mossi, the Mamprusi, the Dagomba and Gonja of the savannahs, and the Asante and other Kwa speakers in the forest. Here we find producers of narrow strips of cloth, which were sewn into clothes for both men and women. In the forest region bark-cloth was widely used before the advent of cotton goods, whereas in the savannah it was animal hair. Royalty naturally wore more than others, but Muslims in particular were marked by their use of cloth on all occasions, even on the farm. In fact in these kingdoms, not to wear cloth was a sign at once of the pagan ("those who do not pray to God"), and of the savage (the wild, the "men of the bush"), of those who live without the law of God or of man, at least the law of citizens. On the other hand, for the "tribal" societies cloth was at times the sign of the domination of the centralized power of states, which was opposed to the earth in its spiritual aspects. In the rest of this essay, we pursue this contrast that is important not only in an ethnographic context, practically, morally and symbolically, but also for the history of mankind.

While we do not develop the theme in this essay, cloth and clothing were the subject of much early exchange and manufacture. Early records of Mesopotamia provide evidence of its importance in the external trade for metals,[4] and in the development of forms of workshop production. In India in precolonial times cotton played a central role in internal consumption and in external trade throughout Asia as well as to Africa and even Europe. In China the weaving of silk was an early achievement of its technology, and the product was subsequently gathered by the state in the form of taxes to be used for internal consumption as well as to supply the overseas markets. Much later, from the thirteenth century, cotton entered this system of taxation. In the development of first mercantile, then industrial capitalism in Western Europe, cotton played a critical part.[5] In West Africa too it was a major feature of exchange within and between communities. This fundamental role of cloth in the development of human society was partly related to the control of body temperatures but more to its moral and status implications, for reasons to do both with sexuality and with the maintenance and assertion of identity, including the temporary boost to self-esteem that adherence to "fashion" provides.[6]

Clothing but Not Cloth among the LoDagaa

However, there are obviously many forms of bodily covering other than cloth. Among the "tribal," acephalous peoples of northern Ghana, an adult man was uncovered if he did not wear a penis-sheath (a covering of skin), and sometimes a short apron of hide.[7] Even recently a LoDagaa youth who had not reached puberty would sometimes go nude, although he might hitch his penis under a waistband made from a single stalk of grass; after puberty only a madman would go around like that. An old man may wear a conical straw hat with bound leather edges and very occasionally a cowskin as a cloak, especially at ritual gatherings. Indeed one of the benefits provided by the Bagre association was just such a covering for those old members who could not afford one.

Women have more distinctive items of wear, which are closely linked to their sexual status. A young girl would run about without clothing. When she approaches puberty, she will wear fiber waistbands, the ends of which hang down to her knees in front of her (*ganzuole*). Once she is married she changes to a much thicker set of bands made of fiber or of goatskin (*gamie*). These no longer hang down in front but are decorated with leaves, mainly at the back, which is said to be the favored sexual approach.

The absence of cloth in no way inhibits the presence of moral attitudes toward covering the body. Nobody would wear the covering that was inappropriate to their social position, for they would be subject to the strongest pressures of ridicule. But such practices were also strongly internalized as they were closely linked to sexuality as well as to self-esteem. For a young girl to let her vagina be seen after puberty was highly immodest. Nor would any adult woman be seen without her leaves, newly plucked, for similar reasons. Only the very old would be past feelings of modesty or the desire to look attractive, but even they would always put on their waistbands. In the past an adult man would wear his penis sheath and nowadays his shorts. Although these people were sometimes referred to, not only by Europeans, as "the naked Lobi," nudity was for children, not for adults. Certainly one did not go unclothed in front of members of the opposite sex, especially those with whom one might have sexual relations. But such reluctance extends more widely. Even though among the Nuer of the southern Sudan, men normally have no covering, a man would not appear naked before a kinswoman of his wife.[8] One is reminded of biblical taboos on going naked before kin.

The link of morality to the wearing of correct coverings is doubly entailed. First, as the link to sexuality, "uncovered sexuality" (however defined) is equivalent to potentially uncontrolled and hence dangerous sexuality. Second, the rejection of the correct wear for one's position implies the rejection of the system of statuses by which people relate to one another. Children wear nothing as they are not considered sexually active, nor do they yet hold significant social roles. Normally the achievement of sexual and social adulthood is reached by the assumption of clothing that is "correct" for the sex and for the marital status. Correct for oneself too, since this is a matter of identity as well as of status, internal as well as external. Indeed the English word "habit" stands both for external appearance and internal disposition in much the same way as "custom" and "costume."

Ethnographically that was the situation in northern Ghana at the beginning of this century and one that continued in some pockets until recently. At the time of our fieldwork among the LoDagaa in the early 1950s, cloth was increasingly used by men for shorts as well as for smocks, the latter always made of "Mossi" cloth purchased in the local market. For the neighboring Tallensi, Fortes has emphasized how closely cloth was associated with foreigners: Mossi cloth with the savannah states who produced it, as was the Manchester or Yoruba cloth worn by women, the first imported from Europe, the latter from Nigeria. As foreign items, these were prohibited at certain major festivals; indeed the Earth priests of the Talis wore only a cow's hide at all times.

The situation was much the same among the LoDagaa. However, there was one occasion when cloth did come into its own and that was at funerals. In the 1950s the corpse of an adult who had a "good" death was always "dressed up" in the finest available costume of the kind that chiefs and elders would wear in the states, including a fez, while the funeral stand was draped in lengths of cloth. These were all provided for the occasion; the corpse was buried nude in a mat, accompanied only by a short strip of white cloth as a token. The fez and the lengths of cloth of local weave associated the dead with the richer and status-conscious states of the savannah region, where Muslim influence was strong. In no other context would the fez be worn, although the heavy smocks and trousers are nowadays part of the apparel of the local "chiefs" whose positions were virtually created with the establishment of colonial rule at the beginning of the century.

Some cloth was undoubtedly worn by richer members of LoDagaa communities in earlier times. Along the main trade routes groups of Muslim traders included weavers of cloth as well as importers. But it was not widespread, except for the small piece of cloth buried with the corpse as an indication of his or her position in the society as well as of the position it was hoped he would hold after death. In some adjacent areas pagan tribal peoples used complete shrouds for burial, in the manner of Muslims, the cloth being purchased from trading centers.[9]

In other ritual situations cloth carried a negative value. Some taboos of the patrilineal clans forbid its handling in certain ways, for example, throwing it from one person to another.[10] Some situations prohibited any covering at all. In the course of initiation into the Bagre society of the LaDagaa, as with other rites of entry, the neophytes have to strip, in order to put themselves in the status of "unclothed" infants, ready to receive instruction. But most important of all were the frequent taboos on clothing in conjunction with rituals at the Earth Shrine. Visitors to the Tongo shrine of the Tallensi had to unclothe themselves, while the custodian of the Earth Shrine himself would wear only a skin, at least when approaching the altar of the deity.[11] Here the religious and the political combine; part of the rejection of cloth was an opposition to those states with whom it was associated as well as to their traders, who were seen as legitimate prey by the acephalous peoples.[12] The wearing of cloth was thus doubly valued: it was a sign of wealth and status, especially in recent times, but for the tribal peoples it could also carry the implications of "foreign luxury," of a betrayal of local roots.

Cloth as Clothing among the Gonja

Among the states of the region, cloth had none of this ambivalence. It is used unequivocally as a marker of status and as a protector of modesty; it plays much the same role as covering does among the tribal peoples but in a more complex way.

There is no doubt that cloth was highly valued both religiously and politically in the kingdom of Gonja. The white dress of the Muslims was highly distinctive and the style of clothing, if not cloth itself, was strongly connected with that religion. Muslims were never naked, in public, and their women always covered their breasts. The special headdress worn by the paramount chief, the YagbumWura, to cover his face when he appeared on state occasions was in the style of the burnous of the Saharan peoples. Chiefs' smocks are sewn of narrow strips patterned in deep blue and light blue (from indigo) and white. It is these above all that represent the wealth and power of office. However these vivid and subtle patterns are laid aside at times of ritual significance, such as rites of passage. A corpse is shrouded in plain white cloth (*wadza fuful*), and when a senior man or woman dies, the eldest son and daughter (*wurikung* and *wurikunchte*) are secluded for seven days during which time they wear only white cloth. In her much longer period of seclusion a widow also wears white. Unlike the LoDagaa, feet were traditionally shod with sandals and those of the chiefs were of a special elegance, as were his robes generally.[13]

The association of the state with cloth meant that the inhabitants looked down on those who had none, considering them naked and "unclothed" in the literal sense. Those were the tribal peoples who in the past had been raided for slaves or incorporated into their states, handing down to them some of their own "civilized" ways. The Gonja take a rather similar attitude to the Asante, who had beaten them in battle several times with the aid of guns obtained from European traders in exchange for gold and slaves. Of these, their southern neighbors, one sometimes hears the comment, "they wore bark-cloth until we showed them how to weave."

The political role of cloth emerges most clearly in the process of installing a chief among the Gonja. That is accomplished by placing a gown over the man's head before an assembly of chiefs, courtiers, Muslims, and commoners (including the people of the land). Significantly it is the representatives of the latter two groups who actually perform the critical act of installation by placing a plain white gown over his head. To install a chief is to "enrobe" him (*bu kawura*), but this involves placing over his head the white robe of mourning and of Islam before he is secluded in a room for seven days with the spirits of former chiefs. At the end of this time he emerges in the full glory of the indigo-patterned gown of chiefship.[14] These chiefly gowns often contain many yards of cloth, which are swirled about in dramatic movements, often as if the wearers were riding on the horses that were formerly their prize possessions, as they dance before their seniors at court. Even the paramount himself makes mincing steps as he appears in public surrounded by courtiers who move around him in rhythmical progression. But senior chiefs are more danced at than dancers.

The use of cloth was not confined to chiefs and Muslims; men of all three estates wore brown-dyed smocks for hunting and war, and simple shorts and sometimes short smocks for farming, with longer, fuller ones for important occasions. While some sorts of cloth were always imported—in precolonial times across the Sahara and as trade goods on the coast, as well as from the Sudan and Nigeria—cloth itself was not considered a foreign product. On the contrary, Gonja say that men have always woven on the narrow looms characteristic of the West African savannah.[15] The diffusion of these skills throughout Gonja, even in villages that are today very remote, supports this belief that they have long made cloth. Virtually every old woman of the Muslim and ruling estates can spin, and many make particularly fine and even thread. Spinning is especially "the work of old women." It was still common in the mid-1950s to find one or two weavers in a village of any size; even today this is not unusual, although most are now concentrated at Daboya, the old center of indigo dyeing.[16] Cloth woven locally on narrow looms is called *gbanya wadze,* Gonja cloth. For hunting, white smocks were dyed brown as a kind of camouflage. In warfare, they were covered with Muslim *safi,* verses from the Quran sewn into leather patches that were thought to prevent the arrows and even bullets of the enemy from harming the wearer.[17] In the early 1970s such smocks might cost as much as one hundred pounds, and even more might be paid for the light cotton smocks on which such verses had been directly written. The patterned cloth worn by men at the annual political rituals, especially for the festival of Damba that celebrated the birthday of the Prophet, were woven in a limited number of designs that left a slight opening for a new creation but whose political role leaned heavily on the side of tradition. They were often presented to a man by his sisters and his wives who took great pride in seeing him perform, at times crowding around him when he danced on his own and praising him with their own rhythmic movements.

Because women of the ruling and Muslim estates have important roles in the complex political-economic-religious structure of the Gonja state, cloth for them has many kinds of meaning. A girl expected to receive a matched pair of *gbanya wadza* on her marriage, and a husband was supposed to provide his wife with a new cloth for Damba each year. For Gonja women, commoner, Muslim, and ruling estate alike, cloth of some kind was a necessity for decency's sake. All respectable women wore at least a cloth wrapped around the waist while working, or under the arms for greater formality. A single cloth usually sufficed for ordinary wear, and a woman had several ranging from the newest

Damba cloth to old and well-worn cloths of her mother's. Some of these would be *gbanya wadza* and the others of cotton cloth manufactured and brightly dyed in Holland or England and recently in Ghana or Nigeria. *Gbanya wadza* were, and are, preferred for tying a baby at the back as they are stronger than manufactured cloth.

To have new cloths is important to women for complex reasons. Traditionally a woman should receive a new cloth (or the money to buy it) from her husband at Damba.[18] Because it is a time when minor chiefs publicly pay homage to the divisional chief (and when men without office scheme to have it), at Damba people converge on the divisional capitals from the villages. Everyone dresses in their finest attire, especially for the all-night dance that marks the close of the festivities. It is a time to see and be seen. So a woman wants to have a new cloth to show off at Damba. Sometimes a group of women—perhaps those from a certain neighborhood, those trading in the same commodity, or women who are just friends—will arrange to buy cloth of the same pattern so that when they dance together they make a striking and easily recognizable sight. Here the element of display, both for each individual and as a member of a group, is important. If her husband does not provide a cloth for Damba a woman will try to get one herself. This is both because she wants to be proud of her appearance, and so that people do not wonder whether her husband has become too poor to buy a cloth—or perhaps lost interest in her and is buying cloth for another woman.

Although manufactured cloth is widely available today in many styles and colors, new and old, the relative price has probably not changed very much. It is still extremely expensive for the ordinary man or woman to buy (C17,000–C34,000 = £25–£50 in 1992).[19] Indeed it was probably easier in the past for a woman to spin the thread for *gbanya wadza* than it is today to earn the money to buy cloth.

As their cloths wear out women become obsessed with the problem of where and how to get a new one. Old women make pointed hints to sons and daughters, or undertake the heavy work of collecting firewood and bringing it to the town to sell. Petty trading is preferred both to making shea butter and to collecting firewood, but this requires capital, and nowadays the profits are extremely low and uncertain.[20] Girls and young women are particularly keen to find money for new cloth, and to pay a seamstress to make it up into the latest style of *kubba* (blouse). All agree that it is the pursuit of money for nice cloths that lures them to Abidjan and Lome to seek "work" and money for finery. Indeed, the number, style, and newness of clothes was considered to be the best index of a woman's social position (not simply of her wealth) in a recent survey in Bole (western Gonja).

This concern with fashion and appearance is unlikely to be a modern phenomenon. Cloth was used very early in the trade between Europe and West Africa. In fact special orders were being placed with English factors in India for cloth suitable for the West African trade in the seventeenth century. As this suggests, cloth has long been desired by West African traders, who in turn were responding to local demand. Indian and Indonesian designs were very popular, and during the nineteenth century were incorporated into cloth manufactured for West Africa. As these became more widely available inland during the middle part of the twentieth century, women came to treasure and to covet this figured and brightly dyed material. In Gonja in midcentury it was, however, too expensive for most people, and women continued to wear *gbanya wadza.* One alternative, which was extensively used, was imported unbleached cotton that was locally tie-dyed with indigo. Even these simple resources were subject to the influence of fashion. In the mid-1970s people remembered that the name of one design from the 1930s was "all Daboya," so-called because all over Daboya women were wearing it.

Cloth and the Local Market

Traditionally, body covering was firmly linked to morality, especially that associated with sex and gender, with identity and status. That was true both in the kingdom of Gonja and among the tribal LoDagaa. But in the relations between these neighboring peoples, it was cloth itself that became a central point of reference for moral judgments in these two spheres. Those without cloth were not only seen as politically inferior, lacking the attributes of the civilized, and lacking status, but as lacking sexual control. In earlier days to capture them as booty was part of the way of life; as slaves, they were objects of exchange, of labor, and of sexual access. In other words, while internally the morality of covering held sway in both groups, externally the clothing became invisible to the Gonja if it was not cloth. The "Lobi" were naked,[21] morally condemned, while, much more ambivalently, the tribal peoples identified cloth with tyranny and exploitation.

The presence or absence of cloth in the past depended mainly on the ability to produce and purchase it. Production depended upon the purchase or planting of cotton, which tribal peoples did not undertake, and the presence of the narrow loom, together with techniques of spinning, dyeing, weaving, and tailoring. Since the production of cloth was specialized, it also depended upon an active market, internally and externally.

The local cotton was planted in between food crops. It was women who spun both homegrown and purchased varieties into thread. The older ones, whose children had grown up and now fed and cared for their mothers, had time to spin as they sat in the shade in front of their rooms. This thread they sold in the local markets or gave it directly to the specialist weavers to be made into cloth.

The narrow strips in which cloth comes off the West African looms were used as a kind of currency throughout the Sudan, though it was never entirely drawn from the domain of consumption. They might be sold in the form of a large disc (Ngbanyito, *k'baw*) in which the cloth from an entire warp was stored and carried to market. Alternatively the strips could be cut into lengths of a hand-span, or of the width of a man's or a woman's cloth. It seems unlikely that cloth currency was anywhere standardized in width, for such strips varied considerably, from as narrow as two inches to ten or twelve, although in northern Ghana most strips are from three and a half to five inches. These strips were used to purchase other commodities such as pottery, metal bangles, and hoes. But they could also be made up into cloth for wearing, or for shrouds (always in demand, since they are necessary gifts from kin at a funeral). And conversely, made-up cloths could be unpicked and converted into currency as the need arose. These rolls of cloth were carried over long distances by traders from various groups; in northern Ghana they were often Yarse traders from Mossi of "Mande" origin. Binger's careful observations from the 1890s, before the advent of colonial powers, gives details of the different prices obtained in different localities. These were affected by local market conditions at any one time, including the state of the roads and preferences for one type of cloth or another. As the colonial authority in the savannah area, the French regarded it as the major currency (apart from cowries) and were forced to accept it as the medium in which taxes were paid. Since they had no use for these narrow bands of fabric, they accumulated in warehouses and much rotted there.[22]

While it was the product of a laborious technical process and its supply was limited, production was not controlled. Any farmer could grow cotton, and the nature of the administration of kingdoms was not such that this produce could readily be taxed except perhaps around a few capitals. Any woman could learn to spin. Today some women of the groups that did not formerly weave or wear cloth, spin cotton for petty cash, although they do not wear the handwoven cloth for which it is used. Dyeing was a specialist operation in the hands of particular groups of weavers who produced much colored cloth. But the plain white strips were more straightforward and within states and in trader communities individuals could learn to make them by working for a short time with a weaver. A survey of Zabzugu in the state of Dagomba in 1958 showed 298 looms among 167 households, mostly used part-time by farmers. Weaving meant training as well as looms; the LoDagaa had neither. Like the growing and spinning of cotton, the preparation of dyes and the complex marketing arrangements, this was part of a whole social organization of production that could not be transferred in a day and of which the LoDagaa were ignorant.

Changing Patterns of Use and Consumption

The movement of cloth between different areas of West Africa has been part of a long-standing trade of a local and regional character. But cloth has also long been imported from outside the continent. Just as they broke down and reshaped Venetian beads, so too the Asante unraveled colored cloth imported across the Sahara and rewove the threads into the famous kente cloths. In East Africa Indian cottons had been imported for many centuries and before they rounded the Cape, these *pintadoes* were purchased by the Portuguese by way of the Near East in order to sell to the peoples on the Guinea Coast in exchange for gold. European traders continued to import cloth for the Guinea trade until their own manufactured materials began to be produced by cotton mills in the eighteenth century. The resulting Manchester cloth and Dutch wax prints retained many of the basically Indian (or Indo-Javanese) designs that had attracted earlier customers, and that often holds true today.[23]

At first these were luxury goods, destined for the wives of traders and chiefs in the south. Gradually with the wealth from cash crops, and specifically from cocoa in Ghana, imports expanded. The export of cloth from Europe was a mainstay of the trade with Africa for much longer than India, which itself became a net exporter during the latter half of the nineteenth century. Factory cloth is now made in Ghana, but it is also imported from abroad. The bulk of the clothing expansion has taken the form of manufactured cloth but, while the production of the handwoven varieties has declined, it has by no means been extinguished, thanks to long-established preferences and ceremonial usages.

In the contemporary world, many "tribal" men wear clothing of a European type, in particular shorts and a shirt, except at festivals. That is the dress of most schools and most offices, extinguishing earlier status markers. During the early 1940s there was a strike at the newly created Teachers Training College in Tamale, capital of what was then the Northern Territories, against the regulation that pupil-teachers must wear the traditional northern smock. Many of the pupils came from "tribal" groups that did not earlier wear such smocks, since members of these groups often found school education easier to accept in the initial phases.[24] However, it quickly became the correct dress for northern men, while women generally adopted a type of southern dress of colorful Manchester cloth. Today, with "the coming of politics," even southern politicians, when campaigning in the north, often wear a light smock to indicate where their loyalties lie. The same smock has been adopted by many expatriate teachers and voluntary workers.

That usage indicated a general change among the tribal population. Missionaries often put pressure on their converts to wear some covering, not necessarily European. Indeed the major missionary group, the White Fathers, wore an adapted Muslim dress, including a fez and rosary on special occasions, which they had adopted in North Africa as a means of identifying with the local Islamic population. But more important influences were (1) the new government schools that were springing up; and (2) the consciousness, arising from the earlier ambivalence, that the rest of the world was different and looked upon them as "primitive." Those notions came to the fore when international attention was directed to Africa at the time of independence, that is, in 1957 for Ghana. Many diplomatic visitors from abroad were not used to seeing "naked" women on the paths; even sympathetic black Americans were somewhat taken aback by this practice that was at once "natural" and "primitive." Meanwhile many southern politicians now traveled extensively in other areas for the first time and were apprehensive about the image of backwardness that such frankness might encourage. It was a moment in history when it was felt that "backwardness" could and must be banished in a matter of years.

But it was the newly elected members of Parliament from the north who exercised the greatest pressure, although it was not confined to them. In the words of the subsequent report on the subject entitled "Nudity as a Social Problem in Ghana,"

> Patriotic people from all sections of the country who feel that the presence of unclothed people elicits ridicule and scorn from foreigners; Northern Members of Parliament who feel that "nudity" stigmatises their area as backward; members of the Northern Regional Assembly's women's leaders who feel that it is a symbol of the subordination of women; and some Christians and Muslims who consider lack of clothing a sign of paganism and immorality—all have, in recent months, begun to organise public support for a campaign to eradicate nudity from Northern Ghana.

The problem fell within the purview of the Department of Social Welfare and Community Development, who in turn asked the Department of Sociology at the University College of Ghana to assist in gathering information that might provide a basis for understanding the reason why some people in the north did not wear clothing. For this purpose twelve second-year students were asked to carry out surveys during the Christmas vacation of 1957–58, under the practical supervision of Dr. P. T. W. Baxter, though the report was written by the head of the department, the well-known Afro-American anthropologist, Prof. St. Clair Drake. The individual reports are often very detailed and contain a mass of information on the various areas studied, apart from that on clothing or its absence.[25] One particular factor stood out. While men in "tribal" areas had often adapted to modern practice, women in some parts, especially the "Lobi," still went about clad only in perennial bands and leaves. And their "nakedness" was associated in turn with the use of bodily marks as well as lip-plugs and female excision. The practice of body marks is not confined to the "nude," though it is disapproved of by the Akan to the south and by the Muslims to the north, and partly concealed by clothing. Each of these practices is in turn linked to "male attitudes of superiority and dominance." The women themselves were described as being an "eyesore," as "backward," "disgusting," and "undesirable." At a time when the tourist industry was being encouraged it was felt that visitors should not be given the opportunity to take photographs that would reflect adversely on the country. As a result of these considerations a campaign developed to provide free clothing for the inhabitants to wear in public places (private conduct was not at issue).

In recent decades most men of the unclothed peoples have taken to wearing some cloth, and women, even the older ones, wear cloth over their traditional dress when they go to the market. That has long been the case not only because of the scorn of other peoples in a public place but also because "dressing up" and using cloth was what one did on special occasions—for the dead at funerals or for the initiates emerging from the Bagre ceremonies. Fortes reports this trend toward wearing cloth on public occasions such as markets among the Tallensi in the mid-1930s, even though cloth had specifically to be rejected by males during the Great Festivals, part of the long-standing opposition of "states" and "tribes." According to the survey, such an opposition was still to be found among the "Lobi" (LoBirifor) who had migrated into western Gonja; the more they were "despised" by others, the more they stuck to their own ways. As with lip-plugs (which it has been suggested were originally adopted as a means of discouraging slave raiders) the traditional apparel is positively valued by many. "This is custom. We must obey it," remarked one, while another claimed, "The custom of not wearing clothes was given to us by God."

But as we have seen, changes have long been taking place, especially among the wives of those groups who have been heavily involved (more than the members of states) in wage labor outside their communities. The women were more "conservative" partly because they did not then engage in wage labor to any extent and were largely dependent upon cash from males to purchase cloth. There is little or no indigenous production of cloth in the tribes; all has to be imported and paid for. And it is males rather than females who have had the opportunities for wage employment, although young women increasingly leave for prostitution, which involves both having clothing and being willing to remove it. Women's lack of access to ways of earning money has brought real problems at the level of the domestic economy. In Birifor today husbands accuse their wives of selling grain meant for food in order to get money for clothing. (Wives accuse their husbands of not giving them anything with which to buy clothing, and of spending their cash on drinking.) In the states, husbands have a traditional obligation to give clothes to their wives on annual occasions such as Damba, the birthday of the Prophet. While two cloths were given to the bride herself, the groom's family does not provide bridewealth at marriage. Among the tribes, bridewealth payments are very high and men explicitly adduce this expenditure as a reason for not providing their wives with cloth.

In any case, tribal peoples were generally less well off than the average citizens of states, who were more concerned with trade and with appropriations of various kinds. While economic considerations were not decisive, they are certainly relevant. Women did not think it worthwhile to wear cloths for dirty work, especially as soap costs money and water was often scarce or available only at a distance. Indeed the absence of cloth was sometimes attributed to their "hard work," which was contrasted with the laziness of the women in the states, who were unused to heavy work. For tribal women to wear much cloth might even attract the envy of others, and hence an attack of witchcraft. The whole notion of fashion in clothes was foreign to the "Lobi" of whom it was said that they "do not believe in displaying wealth through dressing and in impressing anyone."[26] It is true that some use was made of ornaments including facial marks to attract men. But any display deemed excessive would bring about retribution.

While change was clearly taking place over the long term, especially when people went to the markets or to the main towns, women in some tribal areas clung to earlier customs, partly because of economic reasons (they received no gifts and gained no cash), partly because they were engaged in agricultural work that inevitably promotes different standards of clothing and cleanliness from the towns, partly because there seemed little need for further (imported) covering that might lay them and the community open to mystical dangers. But the Nudity Survey was part of a wider campaign that did not stop with the writing of reports. In the long run, it was believed that economic change and the presence of schools (where cloth was de rigeur) would bring "civilized" behavior to these groups. In the short term other measures had to be taken.

Mass Educations Officers, one of the designated instruments of social change ("education") at the local level, were asked to attend markets to see that women (men had long since changed) wore appropriate clothing. If not, they were to be fined. The ruling Convention People's Party mobilized its members to the same end. One day in 1964 we made a roadside stop at a LoBirifor village south of Wa, where we were not known; it was market day and we had the camera ready to take some photographs. A schoolboy, obviously a Young Pioneer, a member of the Party's junior branch, came up and told us we were not allowed to take photographs of these people as they were "primitive." He was from the same group, but wore the civilized clothes of the school, whose pupils have to provide themselves with shorts and shirt, or blouse and skirt, often at considerable expense for the parents. All this was not accomplished without some violence. It is reported that in Bole market lip-plugs were forcibly knocked out and that roughness occurred at other markets. At similar campaigns in the neighboring Ivory Coast, police were said to have removed women's leaves, leaving them "naked," so creating further resentment against the authorities and their clothing.

The result of all this pressure was a change in the clothing worn. Increasing prosperity has meant more money to buy commercial goods. Even in the first stores in the area bales of cloth were one of the most important items. Gradually the tribal people have clothed themselves, although women worry less about what they wear above the waist. They have been literally shamed into conformity and given new ideas of modesty, as well as new ideas on the consumption of commodities.

Conclusion

Important differences exist to this day in the uses of cloth in northern Ghana. Although the LoDagaa make much use of cloth, women, especially old women, still sometimes appear in their traditional garb, especially among those people descended from immigrants from Burkina Faso, mainly LoBirifor, who are often thought of as foreigners, as "leaf people." They do not have the same respect for cloth, except among those who have been to school. The Gonja continue to look down upon them, partly as pagans, for Muslims are as keen on cloth as Christians, partly as uncivilized, for they come from beyond their dominion. In this the chiefs and the government are of one mind. For the Gonja the LoDagaa are uncivilized partly because the absence of cloth is seen as involving an absence of rank and order (in the Shakespearean sense) as well as a lack of modesty. But the LoDagaa, while formerly "unclothed," were never naked, though this is how their chiefly neighbors saw them. They too used coverings both for modesty, for self-esteem and to differentiate positions and even individual identities. Their general thinking about covering the body was similar to that of their neighbors. But with the advent of woven cloth to the north, closely associated with states and with Islam, the results were very different, leading to a moral depreciation of one group by the other that was in part reciprocated. As a consequence, external pressures and internal ambivalences have led even the acephalous peoples of West Africa to become part of the extensive market in cloth. That is the case not only for the local and regional market, which was of such longstanding importance to the states of the area; but more recently for the international market, which was a central pillar in the development, first of industrial capitalism in Western Europe and then of its extension to South and East Asia. There are even pressures to reshape the past to fit the standards of the present. On a visit to the chief of Tongo in January 1993, Dr. Spens inquired about the photographs taken by Fortes (in the 1930s), which used to be prominently displayed in his hall. They have now been thrown away, she was told, because "our fathers were not wearing clothes."[27] When the opposition between "states" and "tribes" began to be modified under the impact of international trade, the colonial presence, and new notions of acceptable behavior, all tended to become subject to the same definition of the naked and the clothed.

Notes

1. K. N. Chaudhuri, *Asia before Europe* (Cambridge, 1990), 185.

2. K. W. Taylor, *The Birth of Viet Nam* (Berkeley and Los Angeles, 1990) quoted by C. F. W. Higham, *The Archaeology of Mainland Southeast Asia* (Cambridge, 1989).

3. We make an analytic distinction, based upon European usage, between being clothed, that is, *habillé*, "covered" in material (clothes, costume) of any sort cognate with "habit," dress, "habitude," habit, and "habitat," living conditions (not habitat), and on the other hand wearing cloth, which is woven (*tissu, tisser, tisserand*) rather than beaten (bark-cloth) or stretched (hides). Clearly the two are often conflated in cultures with cloth; that is so among the Gonja who equate nudity with the absence of cloth.

4. M. T. Larsen, *The Old Assyrian City States and its Colonies*, (Copenhagen, 1976); A. L. Oppenheim, *Ancient Mesopotamia: Portrait of a Dead Civilization* (Chicago, 1964).

5. E. Goody, introduction to *From Craft to Industry: The Ethnography of Proto-industrial Cloth Production*, ed. E. Goody (Cambridge, 1982).

6. For references on the manufacture and use, symbolic and otherwise, of cloth, see E. Goody, *From Craft to Industry* (Cambridge, 1982), and A. B. Weiner and J. Schneider, eds., *Cloth and Human Experience* (Washington, D.C., 1989). Both these works discuss cloth and clothing (covering) in human societies, whereas we are here concerned with the contrasts made by the actors between the clothed and the "nude" as they are differently perceived in adjacent societies. The essay does not employ regional comparison in the usual sense of the word (that is, made from the observer's standpoint). Nor does it attempt to look at the ways different groups, usually "tribes" and "states," interact, as we have earlier tried to do for politics, warfare, and population; see J. Goody, *Technology, Tradition and the State in Africa* (London, 1971), and "Population and Polity in the Voltaic Region," in *The Evolution of Social Systems*, ed. J. Friedman and M. J. Rowlands (London, 1977). We are attempting to analyze "the articulation of modes of thought" in an effort to widen the restricted framework of much cultural, symbolic, and cognitive inquiry.

7. See the photographs in H. Labouret, *Tribus du rameau Lobi* (Paris, 1932), and R. S. Rattray, *Tribes of the Ashanti Hinterland* (London, 1932), and earlier in von François, "Aus dem Schutzegebiet Togo," *Mitt. Von Forschungreisenden und Gelehaten aus den Deutschen Schutzegebieten*, 1888, 143–71.

8. E. E. Evans-Pritchard, *Nuer Religion* (Oxford, 1956), 20.

9. R. Launay, *Traders without Trade: Responses to Change in two Dyula Communities*, (Cambridge, 1982). That is also said to be the case among the LoBirifor inhabitants of Vieri, west of Wa. See S. Drake, P. Baxter, et al. "Reports on the Problem of Nudity in Northern Ghana," (African Studies Centre, Cambridge, 1958).

10. See the list of patrician prohibitions in Rattray, *Tribes.*

11. M. Fortes, *The Web of Kinship among the Tallensi* (London, 1949). From one point of view the act of wearing skins rather than cloth resembles the use of bark-cloth rather than woven cloth by the ruler of Asante in the rites of investiture. Such an act may reflect the "conservative" nature of much ritual activities (for example, in the case of rice in the Gonja Damba ceremonies, see J. and E. Goody, "Making Way for Cabbages," in *Cavoli e Mereda* (forthcoming). But with clothing there is also the aspect of "denuding" oneself in the course of ceremonies that involve the notion of rebirth into a different status. That is certainly the case with the initiates into the LoDagaa Bagre and the Tongo shrine of the Tallensi.

12. L. Binger, *Du Niger au Golfe de Guinée* (Paris, 1892); J. Goody, *Technology.*

13. This contrast between the clothing in states and "tribes" is vividly brought out in the photographs in von François, "Aus dem Schutzegebiet."

14. E. Goody, *Contexts of Kinship: An Essay on the Family Sociology of the Gonja of Northern Ghana* (Cambridge, 1978).

15. There is some evidence that most weaving used to be done by slaves. In Daboya, for instance, men of the Muslim Sakpare group never weave because they say this was the work of slaves. However, today few people are aware of this past association of weaving and slavery.

16. See E. Goody, ed., *From Craft to Industry,* for an account of the history and organisation of Daboya textile manufacture.

17. Such smocks were especially associated with the Mbongwura and his followers, who were the gunmen; they were also the proud possessions of those men of other estates who were leaders in warfare. At the Jentigi festival in 1992, the Bole Gonja feared attack by the Konkomba (recently immigrant farmers in Eastern Gonja). The BoleWura offered to provide smocks of this kind to any member of the ruling estate who would bear arms.

18. The last few years have seen intensified interest in, and proselytizing for Islam in northern Ghana, as elsewhere in West Africa. A few women of the ruling estate have now been to Mecca, and they usually wear full-length smocks of manufactured cloth, which they consider more modest than traditional styles. The senior Bole Ewuritche has recently been putting pressure on the other women chiefs to wear smocks and veils at Damba instead of the *gbanya wadza* traditionally associated with their office.

19. The most frequent way for a women to earn money, by processing shea nuts into shea butter for sale, yielded in 1992 a profit ranging from C100 to C500 for three days' hard work. And often this money is needed for daily foodstuffs like maize, cassava, tomatoes, or dried fish.

20. One elderly woman with a reputation as a wealthy and successful trader told me that she no longer trades at all because the profit margins are so small. She used to specialize in providing commodities to retailers but now they only take them on credit, and then claim they cannot pay her.

21. The Gonja do not have any way of describing "naked Lobi" except by saying "they don't put on cloth."

22. M. Johnson, "Cloth as Money: The Cloth Strip Currencies of West Af-

rica," in *Textiles of Africa,* ed. D. Idians and K. G. Ponting (Bath, 1980). She discusses distribution of cloth currencies in West Africa and factors related to different standards of width and length, as well as fluctuations in equivalence between cloth strips and various other currencies.

23. See for instance B. W. Hodder, "Indigenous Cloth Trade and Marketing in Africa" in *Textiles of Africa,* ed. Idians and Ponting.

24. See S. W. D. K. Gandah, *Silent Rebel,* MS.

25. These reports were kindly made available by St. Clair Drake and Paul Baxter. They are deposited in the African Studies Centre, Cambridge University.

26. This was part of their general egalitarianism reinforced by fears of arousing jealousy by "standing out."

27. Personal communication.

The Individual as Stranger in Nineteenth-Century Anlo: The Politics of Identity in Precolonial West Africa

SANDRA E. GREENE

Studies on the social composition of precolonial African societies have identified numerous ways in which Africans within the same political community differentiated themselves from one another. Language, gender, age, religious affiliation, social status, economic and/or productive roles, political and military position, time of settlement, the nature of one's affinal and natal ties—all served as important markers of social identity within these early communities. Many of the studies that have examined this phenomenon have also explored the permeability of the boundaries that separated one group from another. We know, for example, that in a number of societies, women could assume the traditionally male role of husband. Young men, slaves, and strangers could transcend their socially defined position within the societies in which they lived and acquire prominent political and religious positions if their talents, skills, and knowledge so warranted the same. Outsiders, whether slave or stranger, could become integrated socially into a kin group in their host communities through the institutional practice of fictive kinship, and even become heads of their adopted families if circumstances permitted.[1]

These studies also indicate that similar conditions influenced the status of individual slaves and strangers in precolonial African societies, but important differences between these two groups existed as well. Slaves, particularly first-generation slaves, lacked a social identity outside that which they were given upon entrance into the households of their masters. Bereft of the web of kinship ties that would have allowed them as free individuals to move between and manipulate, for their own benefit, at least their maternal and paternal relations, they suffered initially from a lack of social networks. Strangers, on the other hand, existed socially as members of their host communities, while also retaining an association with their communities of origin. This position permitted strangers a number of choices unavailable to slaves and other individuals such as refugees, who, because of the way in which they entered their new locations, were deprived of their previous social identities and/or networks. Strangers, theoretically, could opt to remain in their host communities or return to their homes of origin. They could choose to establish closer or more limited relations with the people and political leaders of the societies in which they lived. This fact has received little attention in the literature, however. One of the consequences of this neglect is that the complexity of the stranger/host relationship is reduced to a recounting of how individual strangers and those within their host communities benefited from the manipulation of certain historical conditions, societal institutions, and the skills of strangers. That these types of outsiders could also, in certain circumstances, define their own identities and influence the nature of their relations with their host communities has been ignored.

This essay will explore the importance of choice, and the power that this choice gave to strangers when combined with particular kinship ties, residential affiliation, the skills of the individual stranger, and specific historical conditions. I shall examine these issues by comparing the histories of two different strangers who were resident among the Anlo-Ewe during the nineteenth century. Both individuals are remembered officially or unofficially as strangers who gained particularly influential positions within the political hierarchy of Anlo society. Both made use of the various social and economic networks at their disposal to achieve their positions. Each, however, made quite different choices in terms of how they would interact with Anlo society, a choice that, I argue here, made a major difference in the way in which they were socially defined and interacted with members of the Anlo political elite. I begin this essay with a discussion of the impact of the European effort to abolish the slave trade in West Africa, for it was this event that provided the two individuals discussed here and their families with the opportunity to gain economic clout within Anlo society, and then to translate that financial status into political influence. This section is then followed by a detailed history of the two strangers who are the subject of this study. The first, Togbui Gbodzo of Woe, rose from the socially marginal position of being a patrilineal descendant of a stranger to become the right-wing commander of the Anlo army. The second individual, Geraldo de Lima, used his success in business to transform his official identity from that of stranger, originally from the Slave Coast town of Agoue and affiliated with Portuguese slave traders, to that of being a member of the Anlo clan (*hlo*) that provided on an alternate basis with another clan, the highest political and religious leader in the Anlo polity. A comparative analysis of their respective relationships with the Anlo polity follows, in which I argue that the differences that emerged in the way in which each of these individuals interacted with and were defined by the Anlo political hierarchy had to do, in part, with their respective decisions as to how they wished to manage their relations with Anlo society.

Anlo and the Export Trade in Slaves during the Nineteenth Century

One of the most influential events affecting the social composition of Anlo society in the nineteenth century was the European effort to abolish the Atlantic Slave Trade. For although the volume of slaves passing through this polity during much of the eighteenth century had never been so great as that which was occurring in other coastal areas to the east and west of Anlo,[2] this situation changed dramatically after the various European powers on the lower Gold Coast and upper Slave Coast began to interdict the trade from Africa. To understand why this was the case, and how it affected Anlo society, I shall begin in this section with a brief review of the European efforts to abolish the slave trade in the mentioned region.

In 1792 and 1807, two of the major powers operating on the lower Gold Coast and upper Slave Coast, Denmark and Britain, officially abolished the slave trade, and enacted laws forbidding their nationals to engage in the same after 1803 and 1807, respectively. The Netherlands followed suit in 1814.[3] Thus, by 1815 when the Napoleonic Wars, which had dominated the European political scene since 1795, came to an end and shipping to the West African coast resumed, significant legislative strides had been made to limit the traffic in humans. None of these powers, however, was able to influence significantly the trade in slaves from the lower Gold Coast and upper Slave Coast until the 1840s when more aggressive measures were enacted.[4] In the intervening years (between 1803, when Denmark outlawed its citizens' participation in the trade, and 1841–42, the time by which Britain had added more ships to the antislave squadron and all the major European powers had signed treaties allowing the squadron to seize any vessel fitted with equipment to carry slaves) the buying and selling of human beings continued as independent local merchants—European, African, and Afro-European—filled the vacuum created by the departure of the European governments and trade companies. C. Reindorf describes one such independently operated business in Accra and its confrontations with the English who were attempting to suppress the trade.

> After [1815/16] . . . the country enjoyed peace, but then the slave-trade with the Portuguese became brisk. Chief Ankra was the general broker for the slave dealers. . . . As there was no commandant in the Dutch Fort at that time, Dutch Town was made the depot. Slaves were sold during night, and Ankra had the charge to keep them till a slaver arrived, and the poor people were shipped in the night, all to avoid detection by the English and Danish governments.[5]

As English opposition to the trade intensified in the Accra area, many traders shifted their business to the east, particularly to communities on the upper Slave Coast, to which they brought their slaves for sale. The attractiveness of this area was due, in part, to the existence of long-standing trade ties between this region and the Accra area. Since the late seventeenth century, a thriving trade in livestock had existed between Anlo and the lower Gold Coast; and those who traveled along the coast throughout this same period to Anexo and Whydah to purchase the much-valued aggrey beads necessarily passed through the Anlo area and were therefore quite familiar with the same.[6] A second factor contributing to the increased movement of strangers into the Anlo area during the early nineteenth century had to do with the fact that enforcement of the antislave trade laws by the European powers operating in the areas east of the Volta was poor. For example, in the Anlo area where the Danes claimed exclusive trading rights, this country virtually abandoned any active involvement after 1807.[7] To the east where the French and Portuguese frequently traded, these two refused to refrain from the trade in humans at Whydah because this port had proven to be such a lucrative source of enslaved Africans. Accordingly, when Portugal agreed in its treaty of 1810 with England to abandon trade in areas outside its claimed dominions on the African coast, Whydah was specifically reserved as a port at which it could continue to buy slaves. This "special reservation" ended in 1815, but independent Portuguese and Brazilian merchants continued to operate at the port through the 1860s. Similarly, France stipulated in its 1833 treaty with England (which permitted the search and seizure of each other's ships suspected of carrying slaves) that any French ship docked at Whydah would be immune from the provisions of this treaty.[8] Thus, slave ships continued to dock at the ports on the lower Slave Coast after such contacts to the east became more problematic. This movement of slaves from towns to the west of the Volta to the upper Slave Coast was still the case in 1845 when Governor Carstensen noted that

> what supposedly has been happening all the time is now clear: negroes are carried from [Accra] here and from all the towns [on the littoral as far west as] Cape Coast to the market in Vay [Woe in Anlo]. [For example, in] Dutch Accra . . . [are resident] several slave trade agents, especially immigrated Brasilian negroes who have correspon-

> dents in Vay and Popo [Anexo]. Three months ago two negroes were thus caught in Ningo (Fredensborg). They were to have been brought to the lower coast escorted by a Brasilian negro. But if one is caught and liberated, hundreds get through without interference.[9]

This development contributed to a number of changes in the Anlo area. Included among these was a large-scale immigration of traders, African, Afro-European, and European, into the Anlo area, who then established close relations with local political, religious, and economic leaders as a means of protecting their newly established businesses. Among these strangers was one Tettega, an Adangbe trader who married during the late 1700s or early 1800s into a wealthy family based in Woe. As a result of this marriage, a son, later known as Togbui Gbodzo of Woe, was born c. 1800, who because of his father's non-Anlo origins was technically a stranger (*blu*) and a member of the Blu clan. Despite this status, he rose to become the right-wing commander of the Anlo army.[10] By examining the history of Gbodzo and his family, I hope to define which circumstances and actions taken by them were critical in propelling this individual into such a prominent position within the Anlo political and military hierarchy, and how these variables also impacted upon the identity of Gbodzo as the descendant of a stranger.

Gbodzo and Family, and the Economy of the Upper Slave Coast

The history of the Gbodzo family is one of wealth generating additional wealth, as members of the family successfully established ties to some of the most prestigious groups in Anlo society. We begin with Gbodzo's father, Tettega, who is said to have first entered Anlo as a trader from Ada, specializing in the buying and selling of beads. Involvement in this particular enterprise suggests that Tettega was fairly wealthy on his arrival: beads were a commodity that was highly valued and for which the purchase and resale involved great expenditure and great profits. The most valued form of this jewelry was the aggrey bead, purchased from the upper Slave Coast towns of Anexo and

Whydah, and marketed along the littoral to the west as well as in the interior. Extensive sales of these beads were noted by the Danes in 1810, the period when Tettega is also said to have participated in this trade.[11] Their great value was also noted by the German missionary, J. Bernhard Schlegel in 1853, and in a English report written in 1883:

> What are known as Aggri beads usually met with among the tribes on the Gold Coast, are highly valued by them, and form part of the royal jewels of the Kings of Ashantee . . . they have probably been given in barter for slaves, gold dust and nuggets; they fetch at the present day an equal weight in gold and the rarer sorts one-and-a-half to twice their weight in gold dust.[12]

> [They] are the most precious ones that the Negro knows; females, especially virgins generally hang or often load themselves with . . . the so-called "beads." The more one is able to do this, the more certain and firm she fastens the eyes of the males on herself. The complete clothing of a real Ewe-virgin consists of a rich pearl decoration around her loins; the more she can get, the more she puts on.[13]

Given the period in which Tettega operated along the upper Slave Coast and lower Gold Coast, between the late 1700s and early 1800s, and the fact that his involvement in the trade in beads took him from the Ga-Adangbe area to Anexo and Whydah, one may assume that he was also deeply involved in the movement of slaves within this same region. As noted above, beads were often exchanged for slaves, and after the British abolished the slave trade and began to interdict the same in the Accra area, many traders based in the Accra and Ada area simply transported their slaves across the Volta and sold them at ports on the Anlo coast or farther east. It was also at this same time that gold, used by the Asantes to purchase the much-demanded aggrey beads, began to appear in the towns on the upper Slave Coast.

According to oral accounts, Tettega's principal base of operations in Anlo was the town of Woe.[14] His ability to establish himself in this community can be attributed to his affiliation with Amegashi Akofi of Woe, the son of an Alakple fisherman and member of the Ame clan who immigrated to Woe in the mid-1700s. Akofi, who is also said to have been "a rich man indeed," gained his wealth by supplying slaves to the Europeans operating on the Anlo coast. In such a position, he was able to attract wealthy traders like Tettega, whose involvement in the slave trade complemented his own, and whose presence in the community under his auspices served to strengthen his own prestige. That a close association between Tettega and Amegashi Akofi did exist is indicated by the fact that Tettega was married to Amegashi Akofi's daughter, Kpetsimine. This union, which ultimately led to the birth of Gbodzo, appears to have served quite well the interests of both Tettega and Amegashi Akofi. It strengthened the former's association with the community of Woe, and with one of its more influential citizens. It secured for Amegashi Akofi an additional buyer for his slaves; and it is likely that through his wife Kpetsimine, a member of the Nyigbla religious order that served as the war god of the entire Anlo polity, Tettega obtained access to the young women whom this order had begun to sell to the slave buyers exporting human beings from the coast.[15]

Tettega and Amegashi Akofi, father and maternal grandfather of Gbodzo, were not the only members of Gbodzo's family who were known for their wealth. Gbodzo's mother, Kpetsimina, and his mother's brother, Kuwo Nunya, both had similar reputations in their own right. Nunya acquired enough slaves to create for himself a *hozikpui* or wealth stool.[16] Kpetsimina was also financially well endowed. Her wealth, according to some oral narratives, came from marketing in the Anlo area to the east the beads that her husband purchased, as well as from the wholesale buying of foodstuffs from communities on the northern side of the lagoon, which she then marketed in the Anlo towns on the coast. It is likely, however, that she too was deeply involved in the Atlantic Slave Trade. She is known to have owned her own boats, vessels with which she would have been capable of transporting between the shore and the awaiting European vessels off the coast of Woe, her slaves and the goods purchased from the European merchants. And it is these boats and the implied riches they conveyed, that are mentioned in the following praise poem about her, where she is referred to as Gbodzo's mother.

Gbodzono fe de, menye nuka da ge woala o.
Wutregodidi menye asiku o, Gbodzono fe wu le megbe gbona.

(Gbodzo's mother's oil palm, one does not know what it will cook.
The first boat to arrive is not the right one; Gbodzo's mother's boat is on the way.)[17]

The wealth generated by Gbodzo's paternal and maternal relatives provided Gbodzo with a particularly strong financial base upon which to establish his own business activities. As the son of Tettega, an Adangbe who like the Anlo practiced patrilineal descent, Gbodzo should have inherited much of this initial capital from his father. Tettega, however, did not remain permanently in Woe; as did other traders during this period, he moved continually up and down the coast, staying for only limited periods of time at his various trade stations, while maintaining wives in each location to conduct his business on a more regular basis. Gbodzo, instead, remained in Woe and through residency, affiliated not with his father's relatives but with his mother's. Although there is no record of the family from whom he inherited the bulk of his wealth in order to embark on his own business activities, we can assume that given the absence of any known legacy left in Woe by his father other than his reputation and a single son, Gbodzo probably obtained the majority of his training, the labor force, and the capital to engage in trading from his maternal relatives.[18] Like them, his reputation for great wealth, which he displayed through the creation of his own *hozikpui,* was based on his involvement in the slave trade.[19] It was Gbodzo who erected the holding cells near the Woe beach on the Atlantic Ocean from which the slaves were moved when the European ships anchored off the coast;[20] and it was these slaves who are said to have composed the following song while awaiting their transfer.

Avie mata na Gbodzo yee
Avie mata na Gbodzo yee
Fu nade gbe
Ga nade gbe yee
Nye wukula meva hade o

Avie mata na Gbodzo yee

(I shall rub Gbodzo with tears
I shall rub Gbodzo with tears
The sea may roar
The irons may clank
The rower has not yet arrived

I shall rub Gbodzo with tears)[21]

Gbodzo and the Europeans

Residence with and inheritance from his maternal relations was only one of the many factors that contributed to Gbodzo's success in trade. A second factor involved his and his family's successful cultivation of close ties with the Spanish, Portuguese, and Brazilian traders to whom he and others on the Anlo coast sold their slaves. Evidence of the closeness of these relations is found in the history of the Danish efforts to stop the export trade in slaves in the Anlo area. As noted previously, Denmark prohibited its citizens from buying and selling human beings in 1807, but because of the Napoleonic Wars, the government was unable to maintain communication with its forts and lodges in Africa, and little was done to enforce the legislation locally. After these wars ended in 1815 and communication restored, the Danish government still did little to suppress the export in human beings, and instead focused their attention on cutting the costs associated with the maintenance of their forts and lodges by reducing the already small garrisons posted to their out-forts at Ningo, Ada, and Keta.[22] Only when these soldiers informed officials in Accra that the actions of the slave traders had become particularly blatant, would the Danish governor dispatch local troops to the area to confront and drive out or arrest the offenders. Three such encounters occurred on the lower Volta between 1839 and 1845; all involved the Spaniard, Don Jose Mora.

> In 1839, Governor Hans Angel Giede was informed that one Don Jose Mora, had established a depot at Bato [Bator] on the bank of the Volta. The governor, at the head of about 60 soldiers and some armed men, . . . marched to Bato to apprehend Don Jose Mora. He tried to fire a pistol at the Governor, but failed and was captured with his weapon. His goods and a few slaves he had bought were confiscated. After promising never to carry on slave trade in the jurisdiction of the Danish government, he was set free.
>
> Don Jose Mora shortly after opened the slave trade at Wei [Woe] in Angula [Anlo]. In 1842, the Danish governor Wilkens . . . and 150 soldiers set sail in an American trading vessel to apprehend the malefactor. They landed at night, and marched to attack Don Jose Mora, who managed, however, to jump through a window of his house and escape.
>
> In 1844, Sergeant J. C. Hesse was appointed commandant of Keta to relieve H. Meyer. On Mr. Hesse's arrival he was informed that the old Don Jose Mora and two other slave dealers were still at Wei, carrying on that nefarious traffic. He according to his instructions, prepared to attack them at that place; but they heard of his intentions.[23] [Mora] escaped eastward to Popo or Whydah[24] . . . out of . . . Danish jurisdiction, . . . [leaving] a young Spaniard . . . as a manager.[25]
>
> [Later, in 1845], Mr. Hesse one night saw old Don Jose Mora passing by the fort with a gang of slaves. . . . Joined by Mr. Walter Hansen and some young men from the town, he overtook the gang and ordered them to halt, upon which Don Jose pointed his pistol at Mr. Hesse, and three times attempted to fire, but without effect. He was then caught and the pistol taken from him. The slaves were brought to the fort, but the dealers were suffered to depart.[26]

In the last two incidents described above, Mora was actively assisted by the people of Woe, where he resided. In the 1844 incident, it was "the old men of the town," no doubt the advisers of Gbodzo who by this time was chief of Woe, who urged him to relocate temporarily to towns east of Keta[27] and who later sent a message to the Danes, via an English ship's captain, "that they were going to show the Danish governor that they could use their flint-locks if he should visit them." After Mora was captured and released in 1845, it was also probably Gbodzo who obtained support from the leadership in Anloga to defend the Spaniard's interests, by storming the Keta fort, taking custody of the slaves being held therein, and returning them to their owner.[28] Gbodzo's willingness to engage in such action is indicative of the close economic relationship that had developed between himself and Mora. These economic ties were strengthened by the establishment of social bonds. Gbodzo's maternal cousin, Afedima, according to Anlo oral traditions "was a wealthy woman . . . whom the European merchants used to entrust with money to buy slaves for them; she was [also] the first black woman [in Anlo] to befriend a white," and is remembered as the wife of Don Jose Mora.[29] Gbodzo himself chose to commemorate the close relations he had established with another Iberian or Brazilian trader remembered only as Antonio, by giving one of his sons this name.[30] Establishing such close relations with Mora and other European slave traders operating on the upper Slave Coast allowed Gbodzo and his family to sustain their position within the Anlo polity as one of the wealthiest families in the area.

The Issue of Choice

The opportunity for Gbodzo to obtain a position of power within the Anlo political hierarchy came with the 1831–33 Peki war.[31] This conflict began as a local dispute in the interior, north of the Anlo littoral between Atikpoe and Nyive, the latter of whom hired the polity of Agotime to assist it in the war with their enemy. In the battle that followed, Atikpoe was defeated, but only because Agotime continued to fight after the Nyives fled the field. In compensation for the heavy losses suffered by the Agotime because of their desertion, the Nyive chief gave his daughter in marriage to the brother of the Agotime chief. Several years later when the daughter returned to Nyive with the children conceived from the marriage, and the Nyive chief refused to send her back, Nyive and Agotime went to war. Each sought allies. Nyive obtained the assistance of a number of Krepi towns including Shia, Tove, Agu, and Atigbe; Agotime requested and received assistance from Accra, Akwamu, and the latter's subordinate ally, Peki. In the ensuing battles, Agotime and its allies defeated Nyive, but conflicts among the victors led to another series of disputes, the most serious of which involved Peki and Akwamu. The numerous differences that placed Peki and Akwamu in opposition to one another during this period have been discussed elsewhere.[32] More significant for our understanding of this event is the fact that their unwillingness to resolve these conflicts peacefully brought both to the battlefield in 1833, each again with its own allied forces. Peki gained support from Anum and Boso; Akwamu received troops from Anlo. Among the latter were Togbui Zewu, interim commander of the entire Anlo army, Adedze Gbekle of Woe, leader of the right wing (*dusifiaga*), and Gbodzo, who was serving under the command of Gbekle.[33] Although their first encounters with the enemy were successful, subsequent battles took a heavy toll on Akwamu and its Anlo ally. The latter suffered particularly large casualties.[34] As a consequence of the heavy loss of life and the paltry reward in slaves acquired from the conflict, Adedze Gbekle, leader of the right wing of the army, resigned as *dusifiaga*. Gbodzo assumed the position thereafter.

Gbodzo's elevation to this post raises a number of questions. How, for example, did the Anlo leadership, who confirmed Gbodzo as *dusifiaga,* handle Gbodzo's identity as a stranger? How did Gbodzo himself, manage this affiliation? We know, for example, that those in Anlo society with such an identity were viewed with suspicion, for many felt that association through kinship with another polity or culture compromised one's ability to identify and support wholly the interests of Anlo. Those who held such views would have been able to cite a number of examples to substantiate their opinion. In 1750, for example, when Anlo successfully extricated itself from Anexo control, the then *awoamefia,* Anyage (who had been born and raised in Anexo, his mother's home, and who was also known as Kofi Adzanu and Fiayidziehe), resisted this move, and invited the Anexos and Adas to attack Anlo. He subsequently fled into exile after a failed assassination attempt.[35] German missionaries recorded vivid accounts of this betrayal as late as the end of the nineteenth century. They recorded similar sentiments about foreign *trowo* (gods), as indicated in the following account.

> Apart from Nyigbla . . . [alien *trowo*] were . . . looked upon by their worshippers as foreigners and intruders, who, as they say, "were not one" on the side of the Ewes. In times of war, for instance, they were never on the side of the Ewes, and were, therefore, not taken with them to war. One could not trust them totally. Their nature was bad and they paid in general, no heed to the lives of men.[36]

The Anlo political and military leaders who elevated Gbodzo to *dusifiaga,* could have, of course, set aside these generally held sentiments by emphasizing the fact that (1) Gbodzo was a maternal nephew to Amegashi Akofi, an Ame clan member, and as such was in a recognized position of kinship to an Anlo clan, the same relationship that by this period is said to have obtained between the Bate and Adzovia clans, which provided the *awoamefia* or political and religious leader of the Anlo polity; (2) Gbodzo had lived in Woe his entire life, and therefore was an Anlo, not only by matrilineal descent but also by residence; (3) his military involvement in the Anlo war in Peki demonstrated his willingness to risk his own life and the lives of his slaves for the economic and political interests of Anlo; and (4) Gbodzo's support of the *awoamefia* by supplying the Anlo military with munitions, and his ability to continue to do the same because of his close ties to the various Afro-European and European slave traders on the coast was significant enough to warrant such recognition. That both the Anlo elders and Gbodzo may have used these very arguments to rationalize away Gbodzo's identity as a *blu* is suggested not only by the fact that the antistranger sentiments in existence in nineteenth-century Anlo would have required such action, but is also indicated by the ways in which Gbodzo's connection to the *dusifiaga* position is remembered in the oral traditions of Anlo. When I made inquiries about Gbodzo in 1978 and 1988, it became quite clear that his descendents were still quite sensitive about their stranger origins, and were unprepared to discuss the same with other Anlos who might use this fact against them. In addition, some of the most knowledgeable elders in Anloga, the political and ritual capital of Anlo, were either unaware of or unwilling to discuss Gbodzo's membership in the Blu clan. Instead, that which was most readily recalled about Gbodzo involved everything but his identity as a stranger. Emphasized was his close affiliation with his maternal relatives, his legitimate acquisition of the *dusifiaga* position because his predecessor, Adedzi Gbekle, was unwilling to continue or to have his own family members continue to hold the position, his supposed affinal ties to the Gbekle family, his great wealth, his reputation as a force in Anlo society, and the fact that his mother, Kpetsimina, was a Nyigbla member and therefore closely associated with the political and religious leadership of Anlo. The omission of his clan affiliation during these interviews, though readily detailed on further inquiry, suggests that when the elders of Anlo chose to elevate Gbodzo to the position of *dusifiaga,* this was done in recognition of the fact that his stranger origins were a potential liability and that his identity as a *blu* was to be ignored. Emphasized instead were those other qualities so valued by the Anlo. Accordingly, the most common reason given currently for Gbodzo's position within the Anlo political and military hierarchy is the fact that "there was nothing they [the *awoamefia* and his advisers] could ask that he would not give."[37] This statement is then often concluded with the following praise poem about his great political influence and military prowess:

Ablodoa bla
Dzogbede xewo dui gli
Tomeseklonui be yenyro wu amega kple atowo
Ablodoa bla

(The savannah palm which birds eat and lose their self-control
The river that is knee-deep, yet capable of sinking both captain and crew)[38]

In accepting the position of *dusifiaga,* Gbodzo not only agreed to help finance Anlo's wars and to accept the political and economic benefits associated with such a position;[39] he also assumed the risks that accompanied positions of military leadership among the Anlo. As Anlo elders noted: "[In the past (that is, during the nineteenth century)], we [were] fond of war; kill some and catch some and chop and marry their women"; yet, it was difficult to get anyone to agree to lead the army to war: "people used to run away [from the positions] because of the wars and the problems associated with them."[40] The accuracy of this latter observation is apparent from the history of those who assumed such posts. After suffering heavy casualties in the 1784 Sagbadre war against the Danes, the Adas and their allies, Adagla, a member of the Tsiame clan and the then *awadada* (military commander of the Anlo military) preferred to delegate his office to another and then drown himself in a river rather than return home after such a terrible defeat. In 1792, when Awadada Kwawuga found himself completely surrounded by his Keta enemies and then saw his forces fleeing the field in disorder, he also chose to commit suicide. In 1833, Adedzi Gbekle gave up the position of *dusifiaga* after the disastrous Peki campaign. In 1860 and in 1866, when the Anlo participated in a war in Anexo after being invited to do so by one of the political factions therein, their defeat in both years led the then Awadada Axolu to remain in self-imposed exile for approximately ten years, and when he did return after the 1869 Agotime war, he refused to continue in the position as the Anlo military commander.[41]

Why then would Gbodzo accept the office of *dusifiaga?* In the absence of Gbodzo's own testimony on this question, it is obviously difficult to determine the answer in full. Any number of factors may have been in play: a sense of loyalty and/or obligation to the *awoamefia* and the polity of Anlo, confidence in his own abilities to avoid the difficulties that had plagued others, a personal inclination for risk-taking, a willingness to respond to the accolades that would have accompanied his acceptance of the position, the political and material rewards associated with the *dusifiaga* position. All of these factors may have contributed in some way to his acceptance of the position, but perhaps more revealing is the fact that his decision to assume this office was consistent with his previous efforts not only to interact with the Anlo for economically utilitarian purposes (as was typical of his father and other strangers trading in the area), but to identify actively with his maternal home. He chose to affiliate with his maternal relations rather than seek out and associate with his paternal relatives. He decided to become involved physically in the wars in which the Anlo were engaged even though there was no obligation for strangers to do the same. He opted to maintain his base in Woe rather than relocate to one of the towns east of Anlo, as did other residential strangers involved in the slave trade when the actions of the Danes and later the British made it increasingly difficult to conduct this business in Anlo. And I would argue he chose to accept the *dusifiaga* position, specifically, because of his decision to participate as fully as possible in this particular society, and because military leadership constituted one of the very few ways in which strangers could gain access to positions within the political hierarchy of Anlo society.[42] I would also argue that it was this demonstrated commitment that encouraged the Anlo political elite to ignore his social status as a stranger and to emphasize instead all other attributes that could be used to justify their decision.

The plausibility of this analysis is strengthened if one compares Gbodzo's choices, and those of the Anlo political elite, with those associated with another trader of foreign origin, who was equally wealthy and also quite influential in Anlo affairs, but whose relationship with Anlo was quite different from that of Gbodzo. This individual, Atitsogbi, more commonly known by his assumed Portuguese name, Geraldo de Lima, achieved prominence in Anlo between the 1860s and 1880s. Much has been written about Atitsogbi and the Brazilian with whom he worked, Cesar Cerquira de Lima,[43] but in this discussion, I shall focus only on the early years of Atitsogbi's life and how he chose to establish and strengthen the bonds between himself and this polity; it was these actions that bear comparison with those of Gbodzo.

Atitsogbi (alias Geraldo de Lima) as "Brother" and Entrepreneur

Born during the late 1830s or early 1840s in Agoue,[44] Atitsogbi, like Gbodzo, lived in Anlo for a considerable part of his lifetime, and he, too, was considered to be a stranger.[45] His residence in the area stemmed from his position as a domestic slave of the Portuguese trader, Cesar Cerquira, the latter of whom had taken advantage of the more open conditions for the export of slaves on the upper Slave Coast in the first half of the nineteenth century to establish a trade station in the Anlo town of Vodza, three miles east of Keta on the Atlantic coast. It was from this town that Atitsogbi operated as an agent for Cerquira, buying from the local community the salt produced there in large quantities. He combined this with European manufactures, all of which he then conveyed to all the towns along the Volta River, where they were exchanged for slaves. The latter were then marched to Vodza or to the other less well patrolled ports to the east where they were sold to passing slave ships. By 1862, Atitsogbi's relationship with Cerquira appears to have evolved into one in which he was regarded as a trusted business partner and family member: on Cerquira's death in that year, Atitsogbi inherited both the business and Cerquira's wives as was the custom in nineteenth-century Agoue when a "brother" died.[46] By assuming his "brother's" place, Atitsogbi not only inherited the latter's property; he also adopted his former master's surname, and became known as Geraldo De Lima. In this way he was able to establish in more obvious form his relationship to Cerquira and to continue to conduct business with the latter's Brazilian contacts.

Geraldo did more, however, than simply continue the business as it had previously operated. He modified its operations in response to the fact that economic conditions on the lower Gold Coast and upper Slave Coast were becoming increasingly difficult for those involved in the export trade in slaves. As noted previously, the British, the Danes, and the French had begun to expand their efforts to extinguish the export trade in slaves from the upper Slave Coast during the 1830s and 1840s. In the Anlo area this took the form of land-based military expeditions launched by the Danes in 1839, 1842, and 1844 to drive out of the region the Spanish and Brazilian merchants operating in various towns on the Anlo littoral.[47] After their efforts largely failed, the Danes sold their claimed possessions on the Guinea Coast, including the Anlo area, to the British in 1850, and the latter country continued and expanded the antislave trade export campaign. A larger contingent of soldiers was assigned to the Keta fort, which then forced many of the local traders as well as the Brazilian and Spanish merchants still involved in the export of slaves to relocate their businesses. Most moved to the littoral villages of the Vodza and Kedzi on the eastern edge of Anlo territory and to the Agbosome coastal towns of Blekusu and Adina, all of which were outside the reach of the British soldiers stationed at Keta.[48] By the mid-1860s, the trade had come to an end. The few remaining Brazilian and Spanish traders had died or left the area completely. A number of local traders shifted their emphasis to the production and trade of local agricultural products using slave labor. Others began to sell slaves on the domestic market where there was growing demand for labor to be used in trade as carriers, and in the cultivation and processing of agricultural products in demand both in Europe and in the local economy.[49] Gbodzo of Woe, for example, abandoned the export trade in slaves and emphasized instead their use in the production and sale of animal and fish products.[50] Geraldo shifted to the export of rubber, cotton, and vegetable oils, from which he made tremendous financial gains.[51]

Geraldo's success can be explained in the following way. Between 1861 and 1866, profits from the export of palm oil were particularly high in the Anlo area, because the Krobo (who were the principal producers) were boycotting at that time a number of agents contracted by the English government to collect a fine imposed on them. In an effort to market their oil through other agents, the Krobo began to sell the same to traders operating in the coastal towns east of the Volta River.[52] Geraldo was able to capture a significant amount of this trade. His achievement in this latter venture was due, in part, to the fact that in 1855, Britain raised the ad valorem duties on exports from Britain to the Gold Coast from ½ percent to 2 percent. This policy forced the merchants operating on the British-controlled Gold Coast to increase the amount of money they demanded from customers for these goods in order to offset the higher duties.[53] Those like Geraldo, who obtained their European goods from non-British ports, were clearly placed in an advantageous position to offer lower prices for these same commodities to their customers, and thereby increase their own profits by attracting more customers, including those with palm oil to sell. Another factor contributing to Geraldo's economic success had to do with a second set of policies implemented on the Gold Coast by Britain. In 1862, this country imposed a ban on the importation of firearms and ammunition. The events that prompted this action involved the deterioration in relations between Asante and the English, the latter of whom had increasingly come into conflict with Asante over the question of which power had ultimate jurisdiction over the provinces to the south of this inland state. In that year, the English refused to extradite from the coast to his home country Kwasi Gyani, an Asante citizen who had been accused of hoarding gold nuggets in violation of local law. Anticipating that his actions would precipitate war, the governor of Cape Coast Castle, Richard Pine, ordered the immediate cessation of firearms and ammunition sales to Asante from British sources.[54] In 1863, Asante invaded a number of the southern provinces, thereby demonstrating their ability to overwhelm militarily British defenses on the coast, but the British refused to relinquish Gyani and other refugees to Asante authority. Tensions continued between the two powers through 1866, when British officer Conran noted the economic consequences of the conflict.

> There can be no doubt as to the great sufferings the Ashantees have undergone during the last 2½ years consequent on their being blockaded within their own territory, all communication without long line or sea coast have been shut out from them, depriving them therefore

> of the means of obtaining supplies such as arms, ammunition, cotton goods and salt being articles of trade, to them indispensable.[55]

> There are but two modes through which the Ashantees . . . can receive supplies from the coast . . . the Assinee and Volta.[56]

References to a traffic in arms on the Volta could have only meant sales made to Asante by the Anlos. The latter had traditionally provided such materials to Asante under similar circumstances throughout the second half of the eighteenth century, and this relationship was strengthened during the first two decades of the nineteenth century. For example, when Britain refused to buy Asante's human exports and then between 1807 and 1817 imposed restrictions on the sale of firearms to cut the flow of slaves to the coast, Asante traders resorted to Atoko and other towns on the Anlo littoral.[57] Thus, when Britain again restricted the flow of munitions to Asante in 1862, the latter resorted once more to the Anlo area. Geraldo, who had his base of operations in this district was in a particularly good position to meet the Asante demand because of his extensive contacts in Keta, Anexo, Agoue, and Grand Popo where he was able to obtain from independent traders, the European war supplies in demand in Asante.[58] His residency in Vodza, a salt-producing town on the Anlo littoral, also gave him ready access to this commodity, a stockpile of which the Asante deemed necessary to have in the event of war.

By taking advantage of the opportunities that emerged in Anlo because of the Krobo oil boycott and British trade policies, Geraldo was able to shift his emphasis from the export of slaves to the export of palm oil. In so doing, he sustained the economic legacy left him by his former master and "brother" Cerquira, and became in his own right, one of the most important traders in the area.

Geraldo and the Anlo Political Hierarchy

During the same period in which Geraldo was establishing his dominance in the palm oil trade east of the Volta, he also began to develop close ties to the political and religious elite of Anlo.

One of the ways he did this was to do more than was necessary in the customary relations that obtained between himself as a stranger and the Anlo leadership. For example, during the eighteenth and nineteenth century, all foreign traders who operated in the Anlo area were expected to send to the *awoamefia,* certain gifts in acknowledgment of the latter's authority. Geraldo exceeded these expectations by not only providing such gifts, but also selling munitions to the Anlo army at particularly advantageous terms of trade.[59] He then used this relationship to recast his position as stranger into one which he would be accepted as an Anlo citizen. He did so sometime between 1862 and 1865, by participating in an induction ritual that made him a member of the Adzovia clan (which supplied the Anlo *awoamefia*), and by becoming a major patron of one of the most prestigious gods in Anlo, the Adzovia deity, Tomi.[60] Thereafter, he added to his name the appellation Adzoviahlo, or Adzovia clan, to make explicit his affiliation with this politically and religiously influential social group.

Geraldo's motivation for taking such a course appears to have involved his desire to protect his business interests. As noted above, Geraldo benefited tremendously from the Krobo oil boycott, but he did so at the expense of the firms and individuals who had been contracted by the British government to collect the fine imposed on the Krobo. The latter group, which included the firms of F. and A. Swanzy, and Forster and Smith, and the independent merchant William Addo, responded to their inability to purchase oil at monopoly rates from the Krobo by pressuring the British government to intervene. Britain responded to this pressure in 1863 by posting government troops to interdict all trade with the Krobo area. These forces were withdrawn shortly thereafter, however, and the oil was again diverted to Geraldo and others operating in the Anlo littoral towns and at Kpong and Ada on the lower Volta River. F. and A. Swanzy and Forster and Smith then resorted to their own forces, which began to blockade the Krobo area in an effort to force the Krobo to bring the oil only to them. The use of such troops by both the government and the firms contracted to collect the Krobo oil must have impressed Geraldo with the need to have at his disposal similar military forces to defend his interests. It was this, I would suggest, that prompted Geraldo to renegotiate his status as a stranger in Anlo by becoming a member of the Adzovia clan. Affiliation with this clan brought him not only the benefits that would have accrued to any member of such a social unit in Anlo (the ability to obtain support, both military and political, from fellow members), it also placed Geraldo in a position to gain such support from the clan that provided, in alternation with the Bate clan, the *awoamefia* of Anlo (which had custody of the god Tomi, one of the most respected and feared in Anlo).

The year 1865 brought the first occasion on which Geraldo probably sought support from the Anlo. In March of that year, a dispute erupted between Geraldo and a trader from Ada, whom Geraldo claimed had refused to settle a debt. After failing to get satisfaction, Geraldo panyarred eight canoes belonging to a second Ada trader. When the Ada leaders ordered Geraldo to return the canoes and their contents, Geraldo refused and the dispute escalated into a much wider conflict that saw Geraldo and his Ada adversaries seizing each other's people, and killing and wounding a number of others. It was at this point that Geraldo requested protection from the Anlo, perhaps reminding them of his status as an Adzovia and his close relations to many of the political and religious leaders. The Adas, along with the Gold Coast traders who operated in the area, requested the assistance of the British, citing their business rival, Geraldo, and the Anlo as threats to their own security and that of the Gold Coast. Both the British and the Anlo responded to the call to arms. In May 1865, the British sent first the H.M.S. *Lee* and then later, the H.M.S. *Dart,* commanded by Captain Richards, to negotiate the retrieval of Geraldo from the Anlo. The latter refused to comply; this was then followed by a series of battles known as the 1865 Funu or Atitetti war, and the 1866 Adidome and Datsutagba wars.[61]

Of particular interest for our understanding of the relationship between Geraldo and the Anlos is the fact that, despite their involvement in these battles, several firsthand accounts, both oral and written, indicate that the Anlo's support of Geraldo was lukewarm and that the reason they became involved in these conflicts had little to do with a felt desire or obligation to defend Geraldo's interests because of his status as an Adzovia clan member or because of his business associations with the military, political, and religious leaders of Anlo. In an account published in the Norddeustsche Missionsgesellschaft's monthly publication, the German missionary Brutschin indicated that when the British arrived at the mouth of the Volta on 17 May 1865, following the appeals of the Adas and merchants operating in the area, they demanded that the Anlo hand Geraldo to them in three days. The Anlo promised to do so and then informed Geraldo of the British request, but they made no effort to apprehend him. They then contacted Asante and Akwamu, and requested their assistance in the event of war with the Accras and Adas. The Anlo sent only ten sheep, however, an offering Brutschin stated was considered quite paltry.[62] It is possible that the Anlo were simply stalling for time when they agreed to honor the British request to release Geraldo; and it is also possible that the rather small offering to the Asante and Akwamu was indicative of the fact that they did not take the threat of war and the need for allied assistance seriously. A different explanation, however, is offered in oral accounts delivered to a 1912 commission of inquiry by a number of Anlo military leaders and participants in the 1865 Funu war. These leaders indicate that it was, rather, indecision that prompted the Anlo's response to the British and the rather curious request sent to the Asante and Akwamu. In previous years, the Anlo had had some rather nasty encounters with the various European powers on the coast. Keta was bombarded and completely destroyed by the Danes in 1847, after a dispute erupted between the Danish garrison in the Keta fort and the military leader, Dzokoto of Anyako. In 1850, when the British assumed control of the Keta fort, they posted a larger contingent of soldiers in the town than had been assigned to this place by the Danes, and these soldiers immediately began to take a more active role against the slave trade by confiscating slaves destined for export. They also gave asylum to domestic slaves who fled to the fort for protection. In 1853, when the Anlo refused to pay the recently imposed British poll tax, they were eventually persuaded to do so by the British commandant in Accra, presumably, under the threat of force. In 1855, German missionaries Brutschin and Plessing experienced just how much the Anlo had come to fear and dislike the British when they attempted to obtain from the Anlo leaders permission to build a station in Keta. In their negotiations, they had to distinguish themselves clearly from the British in order even to enter into a dialogue with the Anlo leadership; only after they had declared their nonwarlike intentions was a ban that forbade any citizen to sell to them foodstuffs or durable goods lifted and permission granted for them to establish a station in the town of Anyako.[63] Thus, when the British in March 1865 demanded that Anlo hand over Geraldo to them, Togbui Acolatse, a military leader from the Anlo town of Kedzi, noted that of the *asafohenewo* (military leaders) present—a group that included Tamaklo of Wuti, Dzokoto of Anyako, Agbozo of Anyako, and Nyaxo of Keta—half were prepared to do so, presumably to avoid a conflict with the British, with whom they had already had great difficulty. The other half refused to honor the British request, and it was they who prevailed in convincing their more reluctant comrades that they should engage the British, the Adas, and the Accras in battle. According to Acolatse the argument did not revolve around the issue of Geraldo's citizenship as an adopted member of the Adzovia clan; rather, it had to do with their chances of victory. As Acolatse noted, "Awuna [Anlo] had no money then . . . we are fond of war; kill some and catch some and sell and chop and marry their women; there was no work, we had to sell slaves." Accordingly, when the Anlo were defeated, having lost approximately one hundred men and capturing none of the enemy, they refused to continue to support Geraldo.[64] They saw no profit in such a venture, and they had much to lose. Instead, the majority of the Anlo leaders broke off the campaign and shifted their forces to the east where they had agreed to assist one Kuadzo Landzekpo of Agoue, who was engaged in a conflict with a business partner.[65] This conflict, known as the second Agoue war, probably took place between mid to late 1865 and the very first weeks of 1866.

While still in Agoue, the Anlo heard that Geraldo and his Anlo ally, Akroboto of Srogboe, had continued to harass the Adas, by attacking the Volta River towns of Adidome, Amedika, and Kpong. By February 1866, the conflict had escalated to the point where the British were preparing to invade Anlo in order to open the trade routes that had been closed by Geraldo's activities. Again, Anlo's participation in the subsequent conflict, known as the 1866 Datsutagba war, was less a result of their support of Geraldo as an Anlo, and more a response to the urgent need to defend their homes from their enemies. As Anlo military leader Acolatse noted, "we knew that if we stayed at Agoue, the Accras and the Adas would take all our properties." Descriptions of this battle exist elsewhere;[66] of significance here is that both sides claimed victory. Thus, when Anlo negotiated with the British, they were unprepared to do anything that would suggest that they had been defeated or intimidated.[67] They refused the British demand that they pay an indemnity to cover Britain's war expenses. They also refused to comply with the renewed request that they hand over Geraldo. The explanation given by the Anlo for their latter action was that because Geraldo was a stranger, they had no right to capture him and give him to those whom he had wronged. This rationale was based on nineteenth-century Anlo customary law that required a lineage and/or clan to hand over to an offended party that person from among their ranks who had committed an offense.[68] By declaring Geraldo a stranger, the Anlo political and military leaders absolved themselves of the need to comply with the British request according to their own laws. That this declaration of Geraldo's status as a stranger was more than a political ploy on the part of the Anlo is indicated by the fact that while Geraldo continued to reside in Anlo, support for him among the Anlo, particularly from those who were resident on the littoral and who were most vulnerable to British bombardments from the sea, was largely absent in the subsequent encounters that occurred between Geraldo and the British.[69] In addition, while he is remembered among the Anlo as having become a member of the Adzovia clan and to have assumed the name Adzoviahlo as a marker of the same, he was always described in both late nineteenth-century and early twentieth-century accounts, by supporters and adversaries alike, as a stranger who was originally from Agoue.[70] Thus, the Anlo statement to the British in 1866 about Geraldo's status as a stranger indicates that his induction into the Adzovia clan failed to alter the boundaries that defined his position in Anlo as a stranger. I would suggest that this was the case because Geraldo himself had sought not to deemphasize or alter his identity, but rather to supplement it for purely self-serving reasons. Geraldo wanted to maintain his connections with the Afro-European and European trading sector, and he did so symbolically by taking and retaining his Portuguese name. But he also needed the military support that Anlo could provide because the business climate in which he operated required that he be able to defend his interests in this way. The Adzovia clan accommodated him by making him a member because it stood to benefit economically by responding to the interests of reportedly one of the wealthiest individuals in Anlo. But very little, in fact, changed. And Geraldo would not have had it otherwise. By operating within the interstices that separated and connected Anlo society with the Atlantic trading world, Geraldo successfully manipulated both systems for his own interests while actively and intentionally remaining on the margins of both.

Gbodzo and Geraldo Compared

In reviewing the relationships that existed between Anlo society and Gbodzo and Geraldo as these shifted and changed throughout the nineteenth century, it is apparent that a number of similarities and differences existed in the ways in which the Anlo and these two individuals managed their association with one another. With regard to the similarities, both Gbodzo and Geraldo had reputations in Anlo as wealthy traders who obtained their wealth initially by working closely with Spanish and Brazilian traders in exporting slaves to the Americas. Both were considered strangers by the Anlo during their initial years of active association as independent traders. Gbodzo, by the rules of descent among the Anlo-Ewe was considered a *blu* (stranger) from Ada, because those were the origins of his father. Geraldo is remembered as having come from Agoue. Both also had and/or developed ties of kinship that strengthened their association with the political, religious, and military leadership within the Anlo polity. It is likely, for example, that the relationship that existed between Gbodzo's mother, Kpetsimine, and the priest of Nyigbla, the war god of the Anlo polity; her father's position as a priest, who would have also had relationships with other priests in the area, including those in Anloga; and Gbodzo's relations with the European and Afro-European slave traders all contributed to Gbodzo's becoming the *dusifiaga* (right-wing commander of the Anlo army). Geraldo gained admission to the Adzovia clan and became a particularly strong supporter of the Tomi fetish. This, in turn, strengthened his association with the political, military, and religious elite of Anlo.

One of the major differences that distinguished Gbodzo's relationship with Anlo from that of Geraldo's had to do with the way in which each was socially defined, officially and unofficially. I noted above that while the community of Woe still clearly identifies Gbodzo as a *blu,* and Gbodzo's ancestors continue to exhibit a certain amount of hesitancy in discussing in detail their affiliation with the Blu clan, particularly to other Woe residents, they have been fairly successful in muting this association with the stranger's clan outside the town of Woe. In 1912, for example, Anloga elder Davodzi Banini, an individual who was noted for his knowledge of Anlo history and culture, stated erroneously that the son of Gbodzo, Antonio, who had inherited the *dusifiaga* position from his father, was a member of the Lafe clan. This latter *hlo* was at one time noted for its leadership in war, but this was not the clan with which Gbodzo or Antonio were affiliated.[71] Banini's error, I would suggest, was a result of the fact that Gbodzo and his relatives did not publically associate themselves with the Blu clan. This supposition is supported by the fact that in 1978 when I conducted interviews in Anloga with Mr. T. S. A. Togobo, the individual who at that time was identified by the residents of the town as one of the most knowledgeable about Anlo history and culture, he too was unable to answer correctly the question as to which clan Gbodzo and Antonio were affiliated. These examples suggest that Gbodzo and his descendents have been fairly successful in deemphasizing their position as strangers. In contrast, Geraldo's status as a stranger was strongly articulated as such by the Anlo leadership during the late nineteenth century, and this has continued to be the case to date, despite his formal admission into the Adzovia clan.

This difference can be explained, in part, by the distinctions that existed between Gbodzo and Geraldo in terms of their kinship and residency relations. Gbodzo was a direct descendent of an Anlo woman, Kpetsimine, who in turn was a descendent of those who had been captured in war and incorporated into Anlo society between 1730 and 1742, some sixty to seventy years before Gbodzo was born. He lived in his maternal grandfather's household and remained a resident of the Anlo town of Woe his entire life. In contrast, Geraldo was born in Agoue of local parents, entered Anlo only after joining the household of the Brazilian trader, Cesar de Lima, himself a stranger. He began to develop a close association with members of Anlo society only after he inherited the business of his former master and became a wealthy trader in his own right. These differences in kinship and residency, and the fact that Gbodzo was able to limit, outside his home community of Woe, his identification with the Blu clan—while Geraldo was and is still considered to be a stranger, despite his formal incorporation into the Adzovia clan—suggests that the Anlo maintain a mechanism for ordering social relations that distinguishes putative versus real kinship, at least in the short term, and that they also took into consideration residential affiliation when ordering their relations with individual strangers. I would argue that a third and perhaps even more critical factor was the Anlo polity's reading of what level of commitment each individual stranger made to support the interests of the community. As a young man, Gbodzo opted to affiliate with his maternal rather than paternal relations, and he participated both physically and materially in wars sanctioned by the Anlo military, political, and religious elite. Geraldo, on the other hand, participated only in those wars that were of his own creation, provided arms and munitions to the military in ways that were designed principally to further his own business interests, and became a member of one of the most politically and religiously influential clans of Anlo for seemingly self-interested reasons only. By elevating Gbodzo to the position of *dusifiaga* while also deemphasizing his official affiliation with the Blu clan, the political, military, and religious leaders of Anlo chose to recognize Gbodzo's choice to identify completely with the polity and to take advantage of the same. By inducting Geraldo into the Adzovia clan while still continuing to define him unofficially as a stranger, this same Anlo leadership responded to Geraldo's own desire for this type of association.

Conclusion

This comparison of the historical relationship that developed between the polity of Anlo and two of its most prominent strangers in the nineteenth century—Togbui Gbodzo of Woe and Geraldo de Lima of Vodza—illustrates the complex conditions that determined the social identity and status of strangers in precolonial African societies. Kinship ties (whether fictive or real), residency, wealth, unusual skills, or "outside knowledge" all played a role in determining how strangers were viewed by and interacted with their host communities. These same factors influenced the status of slaves and refugees, groups that were also defined as outsiders because of their social origins. But what distinguished strangers from the latter groups was the fact that only strangers had the option under particular circumstances to determine the degree of their own identity and social incorporation. Gbodzo opted to affiliate with his maternal rather than his paternal home. He then used these kinship ties, his residency, and wealth to minimize his identity as a stranger so as to obtain the socially prestigious position of right-wing commander of the Anlo army. Geraldo de Lima opted to maintain his affiliation with the Afro-European and European communities with which he was associated, even as he became a member of one of the most powerful clans in Anlo. These histories indicate the extent to which strangers could, under specific conditions, define their own identities and the degree to which they could control the extent of their incorporation into their host communities.

Notes

1. On the issue of gender transformation, see Denise O'Brien, "Female Husbands in Southern Bantu Societies," in *Sexual Stratification*, ed. Alice Schlegel (New York, 1977), 109–26; Regina Smith Oboler, "Is the Female Husband a Man," *Ethnology* 19 (1980): 69–88; and Ifi Amadiume, *Male Daughters, Female Husbands: Gender and Sex in an African Society* (London, 1987). Studies that examine the social incorporation of slaves include Suzanne Miers and Igor Kopytoff, eds., *Slavery in Africa: Historical and Anthropological Perspectives* (Madison, Wis., 1977), Paul E. Lovejoy, ed., *The Ideology of Slavery in Africa* (Beverly Hills, Calif., 1981); Martin Klein and Paul Lovejoy, "Slavery in West Africa," in *The Uncommon Market*, ed. A. Gemery and Jan S. Hogendorn (New York, 1979); and Claude Meillassoux, *The Anthropology of Slavery* (Chicago, 1991). For a general discussion on strangers in precolonial Africa, see the rather dated but nevertheless useful studies by M. G. Smith, "Pluralism in Precolonial Africa," in *Pluralism in Africa*, ed. Leo Kuper and M. G. Smith (Berkeley and Los Angeles, 1969), 91–151; Ronald Cohen and John Middleton, *From Tribe to Nation in Africa: Studies in the Incorporation Process* (Scranton, Pa., 1970); Meyer Fortes, "Strangers," in *Studies in African Social Anthropology*, ed. Meyer Fortes and Sheila Patterson (London, 1975), 229–53; and Monica Wilson, "Strangers in Africa: Reflections on Nyakyusa, Ngoni and Sotho Evidence," in *Strangers in African Societies*, ed. William A. Shack and Elliot P. Skinner (Berkeley and Los Angeles, 1979), 51–66.

2. See W. E. F. Ward, *The Royal Navy and the Slavers* (New York, 1969), 63; and Edward Reynolds, *Trade and Economic Change on the Gold Coast, 1807–1874* (London, 1974), 40–41.

3. For a discussion of the Dutch role in the Atlantic Slave Trade and its abolition, see Johannes Postmas, *The Dutch in the Atlantic Slave Trade, 1600–1815* (Cambridge, 1990). Danish activities are described in Georg Nørregård, *Danish Settlements in West Africa, 1658–1850* (Boston, 1966); and Edward Carstensen, *Guvenor Edward Carstensen's Indberetninger fra Guinea, 1842–50* (Copenhagen, 1964). See Ward, *The Royal Navy*, for a detailed discussion of British efforts.

4. Ward, *The Royal Navy*, 39, 121, and 162.

5. Carl Reindorf, *History of the Gold Coast and Asante* (Basel, 1895), 152–53; see also Susan B. Kaplow, "The Mudfish and the Crocodile: Underdevelopment

of a West African Bourgeoisie," *Science and Society* 41, no. 3 (1977): 317–33, who discusses the fortunes of a number of Afro-European traders during this period who were supposedly involved solely in "legitimate" trade; Susan B. Kaplow, "Primitive Accumulation and Traditional Social Relations on the Nineteenth-Century Gold Coast," *Canadian Journal of African Studies* 12, no. 1 (1978): 19–36; and Raymond E. Dumett, "African Merchants of the Gold Coast, 1860–1905: Dynamics of Indigenous Entrepreneurship," *Comparative Studies of Society and History* 25, no. 4 (1983): 661–93.

6. J. E. J. M. van Landewijk, "What Was the Original Aggrey Bead?" *Ghana Journal of Sociology* 6, no. 2, and 7, no. 1 (1970–71): 90–91; see R. A. Kea, "Akwamu-Anlo Relations, c. 1750–1813," *Transactions of the Historical Society of Ghana* 10 (1969): 50, who describes an alternate route to the eastern ports that passed north of the Keta Lagoon.

7. The Napoleonic Wars prevented any shipments of trade goods between that year and 1814; thereafter only a small garrison was posted in Keta, and this was further reduced in 1834 to a single soldier; see Nørregård, *Danish Settlements,* 190–205.

8. Ward, *Royal Navy,* 58, 78; see also Lawrence C. Jennings, "French Policy Toward Trading with African and Brazilian Slave Merchants, 1840–1853," *Journal of African History* 17, no. 4 (1976): 515–28, for a discussion of French policies toward the independent slave traders on the coast.

9. Carstensen, *Indberetninger fra Guinea,* 106–7, 141–42. This diversion of the trade in slaves to the upper Slave Coast was also facilitated by the fact that certain goods that were in demand in the interior, the area from which many coastal traders obtained their slaves, were easily available on the Anlo coast. One such commodity was firearms. In 1807, Britain enacted legislation prohibiting the sale of war munitions at their establishments in Africa, including those on the Gold Coast, "because it was thought that [munitions] promoted the export of slaves." One of the consequences of this policy was that Asante traders operating in the southeast began to bypass the Akwamu middlemen who had previously supplied them with firearms and salt from the lower Volta, in order to purchase these same goods directly from Anlo. Thus, in the first decade of the nineteenth century, gold was reported to be available in sizable quantities for the first time in Keta. A second commodity in demand in the interior was tobacco. As T. E. Bowdich noted in the early 1800s: "the Asantees will purchase no tobacco but the Portuguese, and that eagerly even at 2 oz of gold, the roll." Available primarily from the Portuguese and Spanish ships that dominated the illicit trade in slaves after 1810, the British in Accra were prohibited from purchasing this commodity, because the sellers were involved in slave trading, and after 1818, when the Dutch closed all their forts and posts in the Accra area, tobacco was no longer available from these outposts either. Thus the only reliable source of Portuguese tobacco on the lower Gold Coast and upper Slave Coast was along the Anlo littoral and at ports further east. See Carstensen, *Indberetninger fra Guinea,* 106–7, 141–42; Reynolds, *Trade and Economic Change,* 59–60; Kea, "Akwamu-Anlo Relations," 60; and T. E. Bowdich, *Mission from Cape Coast Castle to Ashantee* (London, 1819), 337. Portuguese, specifically Bahian, tobacco was distinct because of its

"harsh" quality and because it was cured with molasses; see Joseph C. Miller, *Way of Death: Merchant Capitalism and the Angolan Slave Trade* (Madison, Wis., 1988), 462; and Reynolds, *Trade and Economic Change,* 38 and 50.

10. Sandra E. Greene, Field note 5: interview with Mr. T. S. A. Togobo, 20 June 1978.

11. For a discussion of the origins and manufacture of aggrey beads, see van Landewijk, "Aggrey Bead," and Kea, "Akwamu-Anlo Relations," 50.

12. Cited in Reynolds, *Trade and Economic Change,* 33.

13. J. Bernhard Schlegel, "Beitrag zur Geschichte, Welt- und Religionsanschauung des Westafrikaners, namentlich des Eweer," *Monatsblatt der Norddeutsche Missionsgesellschaft* 7, no. 94 (1858): 406; see Maxine Kumekpor, "Some Sociological Aspects of Beads with Special Reference to Selected Beads Found in Eweland," *Ghana Journal of Sociology* 6, no. 2, and 7, no. 1 (1970–71), for a more complete description of the uses of beads among the Anglo-Ewe, as well as Greene, Field note 96: interview with Togbui Anthonio Gbodzo II and councilors, 24 Feb. 1988.

14. Greene, Field note 96, ibid.

15. Greene, Field notes 53, 55, and 65: interviews with Togbui Alex Afatso Awadzi, 16 Dec. 1987; Togbui Kosi Axovi, 17 Dec. 1987; and Togbui Dzobi Adzinku, 6 Jan. 1988, respectively. See also J. Spieth, *Die Religion der Eweer in Süd Togo* (Göttingen, 1911), 146; and Carl Spiess, "Ein Erinnerungsblatt an die Tage des Sklavenhandels in West Africa," *Globus* 92 (1907): 207.

16. A *hozikpui* is a wealth stool carved in the shape typical of those made by the Akan, around the base of which cowries are strung in the number of slaves owned by the stool holder. See E. Y. Aduamh, *Ewe Traditions No. 1,* Institute of African Studies, University of Ghana, Legon (1965), 14: Greene, Field notes 34 and 70: interviews with Togbui Alex Afatso Awadzi, 3 Oct. 1978; and Mr. Kwami Kpodo, 12 Jan. 1988.

17. Greene, Field notes 70 and 96: interviews with Mr. Kwami Kpodo, 12 Jan. 1988; and Togbui Anthonio Gbodzo II and councilors, 24 Feb. 1988. Note that this same saying is also used to praise Gbodzo; see Aduamah, *Ewe Traditions,* 13.

18. The practice among the Anlo at that time of nephews working for and inheriting the acquired wealth of the maternal uncle, and the practice of mothers bequeathing their wealth to both sons and daughters, would have been the means by which Gbodzo could claim to be a rightful inheritor of his mother and uncle. See Sandra E. Greene, "Women, Marriage and the Family in Precolonial West Africa: An Essay on Social Relations in Eighteenth- and Nineteenth-Century Anlo (Ghana)," presented at the 1992 African Studies Association Conference in Seattle, Washington.

19. Greene, Field note 76: interview with Togbui Anthonio Gbodzo II and councilors, 24 Feb. 1988.

20. Greene, Field note 76, ibid.; Carstensen, *Indberetninger fra Guinea,* 141.

21. Aduamah, *Ewe Traditions,* 13–14.

22. Nørregård, *Danish Settlements,* 205. The government of Denmark exhibited little interest in continuing to support what had been a losing business venture on the Guinea coast; therefore, it was not prepared to invest or support any

activity that necessitated large expenditures. After its abolition of the slave trade, they concentrated their efforts on supporting the ventures of various Danes to develop plantations in the areas they had claimed as Danish territory; see Nørregård, *Danish Settlements,* chaps. 19–22.

23. Reindorf, *History of the Gold Coast,* 154–55.

24. Nørregård, *Danish Settlements,* 209.

25. Carstensen, *Indberetninger fra Guinea,* 87.

26. Reindorf, *History of the Gold Coast,* 155–56.

27. Carstensen, *Indberetninger fra Guinea,* 87.

28. The details of the retrieval and the involvement of the Anlo *awoamefia* are noted in Carstensen, *Indberetninger fra Guinea,* 149; Reindorf, *History of the Gold Coast,* 156.

29. Greene, Field notes 70, 76, 94, and 96: interviews with Mr. Kwami Kpodo, 12 Jan. 1988; Togbui Anthonio Gbodzo II and councilors, 20 Jan. 1988; Mr. Klevor Abo, 29 Feb. 1988; and Togbui Anthonio Gbodzo II, 24 Feb. 1988.

30. See Greene, Field notes 5 and 70: interviews with Mr. T. S. A. Togobo, 20 June 1978; and Mr. Kwami Kpodo, 12 Jan. 1988. The name Antonio has been retained as part of the stool name for the Gbodzo family.

31. For detailed descriptions of this conflict, see Reindorf, *History of the Gold Coast,* 305–14; C. W. Welman, *The Native States of the Gold Coast, History and Constitution: Pt. 1, Peki* (London, 1965); and Christian Hornberger, "Etwas aus der Geschichte der Anloer," *Quartal-Blatt der Norddeutsch Missionsgesellschaft* 85 (1877): 460–61.

32. See Welman, *Native States;* and Reindorf, *History of the Gold Coast,* chap. 26.

33. L. P. Tosu, *Anlo Traditional Council Document: A Short Account of the Awada-da Stool of Anlo* (n.d.), 5; Greene, Field note 76: interview with Togbui Anthonio Gbodzo II and councilors, 20 Jan. 1988.

34. Reindorf, *History of the Gold Coast,* 313–14.

35. Greene, Field notes 5, 30, and 42: interviews with Mr. T. S. A. Togobo, 20 June 1978 and 3 Aug. 1978; and Boko Seke Axovi, 1 Nov. 1978; Carl Spiess, "Könige der Anloer," in *Weltgeschichte 3: Westasien und Afrika,* ed. H. J. Helmot (Leipzig and Vienna, 1901), 574; R. S. Rattray, "History of the Ewe People," *Etudes Togolais* 11, no. 1 (1967): 93.

36. J. Spieth, *Die Religion der Eweer in Süd Togo* (Göttingen, 1911), 145.

37. Greene, Field note 5: interview with Mr. T. S. A. Togobo, 20 June 1978.

38. Aduamah, "Ewe Traditions," 14.

39. By assuming such a position, not only did Gbodzo enhance his power within the political and military structures of Anlo; he also gained the opportunity to lead a section of the Anlo army into battle when such action supported his own economic interests. When the inland polities retaliated against Anlo for its 1833 support of Akwamu's campaigns in the Krepi district by refusing to allow Anlo traders to operate there, it was probably Gbodzo, with the success of his business dependent on access to these areas, who led (as the commander of the right wing of the Anlo army) a second foray into the interior in 1837. This time the military results were much more favorable to the Anlo, and as Anlo accounts recorded by a German missionary in 1877 indicate, they "returned home with a

rich booty." One of the major beneficiaries of this capture of "old and young and all who couldn't flee" would have been Gbodzo, whose male slaves would have supplemented the efforts of his own family members and followers in capturing people to sell or to absorb into their own ranks and thus increase the number of those over whom he had authority. His assumption of the *dusifiaga* position also enhanced his reputation within the society. No longer just an *hozikpui fia* (a chief whose influence was based on his wealth), Gbodzo was now also an *awafia*, a leader who by virtue of his military performance in war, was to be accorded a voice—and in Gbodzo's case, a leading voice as *dusifiaga*—in the political, military, and economic affairs of the Anlo polity. See Greene, Field note 76: interview with Togbui Anthonio Gbodzo II and councilors, 20 Jan. 1988.

40. ADM 11/1661: Notes of Evidence, Commission of Enquiry, 1912: Awuna, Addah and Akwamu, National Archives of Ghana, 35; Greene, Field note 9: interview with Mr. T. S. A. Togobo, 3 Aug. 1978.

41. Anlo State Council Minute Books, 9 Jan. 1935, Awunaga, Chiefs Kata, Adaku, Avege, and Agblevo per Samuel Nutsuga for themselves and on behalf of the Tsiame tribe of Anloga, Atoko, Atsiaveie, and others *v.* Chiefs Zewu, Agbozo, Anakoo Attipoe and Zioklui, Davodji Banini and others for themselves and on behalf of Agave Tribe of Anloga, Djelukopwe, Anyako, etc., 378–88; Greene, Field note 57: interview with Mr. Robert Kofi Afetogbo, 22 Dec. 1987.

42. Strangers could also gain entrance into the Anlo political hierarchy through their possession of particularly popular gods whose services the Anlo believed could benefit the entire polity. See Sandra E. Greene, "Conflict and Crisis: A Note on the Workings of the Political Economy and Ideology of the Anglo-Ewe in the Precolonial Period," *Rural Africana* 17 (1983): 83–96.

43. See, for example, G. A. Sorkpor, "Geraldo de Lima and the Awunas, 1862–1904," M.A. thesis, Institute of African Studies, University of Ghana, Legon (1966), and "Notes on the Nayo Friko Shrine in Awuna," *Research Review* 2, no. 3 (1996): 87–98; W. Walton Claridge, *History of the Gold Coast and Ashanti* (London, 1915); Charles M. K. Mamattah, *The Ewes of West Africa* (Accra, 1979); D. E. K. Amenumey, "Geraldo de Lima: A Reappraisal," *Transactions of the Historical Society of Ghana* 9 (1968): 65–78; and J. B. Yegbe, "The Anlo and Their Neighbors, 1850–1890," M.A. thesis, University of Ghana, Legon (1966).

44. The estimated date of Atitsogbi's birth is based on an account by the chief of Kedzi, Acolatse I, who stated in 1912 that Geraldo was several years older than himself, he having been born some time around 1850: ADM 11/1661, 34. Acolatse IV claimed that Acolatse I was born in 1840; Greene, Field note 81: interview with Tognui Joachim Acolatse IV, 26 Jan. 1988. See also Sorkpor, "Geraldo de Lima," 4, who obtained similar dates for Atitsogbi's birth from the grandson of Atitsogbi's wife; see Mamattah, *The Ewes*, 368, for a local version of Atitsogbi's genealogy.

45. We have no information on when Atitsogbi joined Cesar Cerquira as a servant in Vodza, but according to the grandson of one of Atitsogbi's wives, he had been with Cerquira long enough to have been introduced into the Christian faith and to have adopted by 1855 the name Geraldo de Vasconcellos. See Sork-

por, "Geraldo de Lima," 4; and Claridge, *History of the Gold Coast and Ashanti,* 1:548. Geraldo remained in the area until his death in 1904.

46. Madeline Manoukian, "The Ewe-speaking People of Togoland and the Gold Coast," in *The Ethnographic Survey of Africa: Western Africa, Part VI,* ed. Daryll Forde (London, 1952), 28.

47. See Carstensen, *Diary,* passim; Reindorf, *History of the Gold Coast,* chap. 11; and Claridge, *History of the Gold Coast and Ashanti,* 457–58.

48. Yegbe, "The Anlo," 19–38.

49. See Sorkpor, "Geraldo de Lima," 2–21; Amenumey, "Geraldo de Lima," 67; David A. Ross, "The Career of Domingo Martinez in the Bight of Benin, 1833–64," *Journal of African History* 6, no. 1 (1965): 88–89.

50. Greene, Field note 76: interview with Togbui Anthonio Gbodzo II and councilors, 20 Jan. 1988.

51. Greene, Field note 97: interview with Mr. J. G. Kodzo-Vordoagu, 24 Feb. 1988.

52. For a discussion of the Krobo oil boycott, see Freda Wolfson, "A Price Agreement on the Gold Coast—The Krobo Oil Boycott, 1858–1866," *Economic History Bulletin* 6, no. 1 (1953).

53. Reynolds, *Trade and Economic Change,* 131–32.

54. Ivor Wilks, *Asante in the Nineteenth Century* (Cambridge, 1975), 220.

55. Cited in Reynolds, *Trade and Economic Change,* 171–72.

56. Cited in Wilks, *Asante,* 224.

57. Reynolds, *Trade and Economic Change,* 59–60.

58. See John Duncan, *Travels in Western Africa in 1845 and 1846* (London, 1847), 137–40, whose descriptions of the traders in Whydah is representative of the individuals with whom Geraldo and others conducted their business. He mentions Spaniards, Portuguese, Sierra Leoneans, English descendents, and French merchants.

59. Greene, Field note 83: interview with Mr. K. A. Mensah, 27 June 1988.

60. See Mamattah, *The Ewes,* 372–73; and Sorkpor, "Geraldo de Lima," 23–24, who collected traditions indicating that he had obtained membership in the Adzovia clan before the Anlos came to his assistance in the Funu war of 1865; these accounts contradict Amenumey, "Geraldo de Lima," 65, who states that Atitsogbi was given the name Adzoviahlo at birth.

61. For descriptions of the battle, see Africanus Horton, *Letters on the Political Condition of the Gold Coast* (London, 1970), 75–89; ADM 11/1/1661, 34–36, 93, 134–39; Yegbe, *The Anlo,* 56–67.

62. B. Brutschin, "Keta and Anyako," *Monatsblatt der Norddeutsche Missionsgesellschaft* 16, no. 184 (1866): 806.

63. Friedrich Plessing, "Briefe aus Keta," *Monatsblatt der Norddeutsche Missionsgesellschaft* 5, no. 57 (1855): 244; and "Station Quitta in West-Afrika," *Monatsblatt der Norddeutsche Missionsgesellschaft* 4, no. 42 (1854): 176–77.

64. The Anlo forces suffered this defeat, despite their superior numbers because the British were able to use their gunboats to keep the Anlo at a distance, while inflicting heavy casualties. Geraldo continued to seek revenge for the Ada's actions, by attacking the Volta River towns of Adidome, Amedika, and Kpong,

and forcing the cessation of all trade from the Krobo and Krepi district that was conducted along the Volta River. Only the Anlo military leader Akroboto of Srogboe was prepared to assist Geraldo. Geraldo supplemented his own forces and those of Akroboto by obtaining the assistance of the Malfis, located on the east bank of the Volta; he also traveled to the town of Adele, in the present Republic of Togo, to consult the priest of the war god, Nayo Friko, so as to gain assistance in battle; for information on this, see Sorkpor, "Notes," 87–89.

65. For a description of this conflict, see Kue Agbota Gaba, "The History of Anecho, Ancient and Modern," Balme Library, University of Ghana, Legon (1942), 127–39. Note that the first Agoue war of 1860 is also described in this account. See also Pierre Bouch, *La Côte des Esclaves* (Paris, 1885), 303; *Anlo State Council Minute Book,* 9 Jan. 1935, Awunaga: Chiefs Kata, Adaku, et al. on behalf of the Tsiame tribe *v.* Chiefs Zewu, Agbozo et al. on behalf of Agave Tribe, 378.

66. The most detailed description of his conflict can be found in Horton, *Letters,* 78–89.

67. According to the British, they were able to persuade the Anlo to agree to another treaty because they had frightened the Anlo by bombarding and destroying Geraldo's house in the coastal town of Vodza. See Claridge, *History of the Gold Coast and Ashanti,* 574–75; ADM 4/1/2: District Office Records, Keta, 250–52; ADM 11/1/1661, 93.

68. See D. Westermann, "Die Glidyi-Ewe in Togo," *Mitteilungen des Seminars für Orientalische Sprachen* 38 (1935): 142–45; Aliwodsi, "Ein Sittenbild," 28–29.

69. Another reason why the Anlo may have shied away from supporting Geraldo had to do with the fact that during the second Agoue war they suffered heavy casualties after Landzekpo's adversary sought the support of the British and the latter bombarded the Anlo from the ocean.

70. ADM 11/1/1107: Awuna Native Affairs (1878–1901). Letter of Evidence, 8/5/89: Chief Tete Mamimey to Tamaklo, 5 July 1888; ADM 11/1/1661, 34–35.

71. ADM 11/1/1661, 3.

The Native Tribunal of Okorase-Akwapim: Selected Land Cases, 1918–1919

POLLY HILL

Introduction

Would that my friend and exact contemporary the late Marion Johnson (1914–88) were available to discuss the subject matter of this fragile article with me; would, indeed, that Eugene Ohene Walker (1895–1975) of Larteh-Akwapim, who introduced me to so many of the Akwapim migrant cocoa farmers and to the bridge at Mmetiamu, might continue to unravel further my misapprehensions.[1] In their absence I seem to make little progress in studying one of the most astounding migrations that ever occurred in the history of sub-Saharan Africa; but at least I can pay tribute to each of them at the end of this article.[2]

One of the unresolved questions at issue is whether it is true, as we all seem to take for granted, that oil palm "plantations," which had been established by the Akwapim farmers, were converted into cocoa "plantations" in the last years of the nineteenth century. Did the Akwapim farmers, in other words, resemble the Krobo, whose *huza*[3] were gradually (though not necessarily entirely) turned over from the oil palm to the cocoa tree?

While Marion Johnson, in her remarkable pair of articles "Migrants Progress,"[4] sought to view the "cocoa migration as part of a larger movement extending back in time and in place far beyond the crossing of the river Densu[5] by cocoa farmers late in the nineteenth century," she yet contended that most of the land acquired before 1890 for "oil palm and commercial food production" was "never used for cocoa at all." She argued that the migrant farmers concerned with cocoa were "understandably averse to cutting down fruitful oil palms" and that it was the "very extent of the pre-cocoa migration which made it necessary for farmers to look so far afield for their cocoa farms." I suggest that, on the contrary, so far as concerns most of the land that lay in the zone east of the river Densu and west of the Akwapim ridge, where many oil palm plantations were established, the agronomic conditions, affecting soil, forest cover, and so forth, had been unfavorable for cocoa cultivation. As for trans-Densu lands, the high cost of transporting palm oil to the coast for export had always been prohibitive.

Marion Johnson relied heavily on the missionary Andreas Riis, who flourished in mid-century; the "plantations" he visited lay mainly to the east of the Akwapim ridge. But in 1839 he went to Akim, "travelling by the usual route, which at this time led through Ahabante and Kukurantumi."[6] Later he reported that "the whole land" of Akim was "densely overgrown with strong and unbelievably tall trees,"[7] and that "the useful palm-tree" was less in evidence there than in Akwapim. The word "plantation" derives from the Twi portmaneau word *akuraa,* which was defined by Christaller as "a hamlet, a village on a plantation inhabited by the family and the labourers of the proprietor."[8] But the definition provided in a dictionary by H. N. Riis, nephew of A. Riis, was longer and read: "the hamlet in a plantation, where its owner keeps his family, his slaves, and the chief part of his property, in contra-distinction to *man* or *krom,* the town which is the common centre of a greater or smaller number of plantations."[9] This is a definition, be it noted, that implies "dual residence"—though not of the type followed by most migrant cocoa farmers who made cottages in the distant forest their usual habitations, while retaining Akwapim, where they built proper residences (many of them grandiose), as their foundation.

Referring to earlier times,[10] Marion Johnson emphasized the existence of a great tract of "empty" country, between Akim on the west, and Akwapim and Akwamu on the east.[11] Only on the Kukurantumi-Ajisu-Opanto-Ahabanti line was there "a nearly continuous string of villages"; this was on the main trade route from Asante to Accra, being situated on Ivor Wilks's Route V.[12]

According to Nana Dabera Appraku II,[13] Mankrado of Larteh-Kubease, Larteh farmers made one of their very earliest purchases of land to the west in the early 1890s at Adweso (shown in the Ghana Survey as Ajiso) a few miles south of Koforidua—lying on a southward continuation of the above-mentioned line running south of Kukurantumi. I cannot now vouch for the accuracy of my notes, which record that the Mankrado said that this land was for oil palm and foodstuffs, that it was several square miles in extent, and was paid for in cowries. But it is certain that somewhat later Paul Yaw Kuma, also of Larteh, who had been a sawyer at Senchi, acquired[14] a large land in the neighborhood of Okorase,[15] much of which he resold to other Larteh farmers. Situated in Akwapim, Okorase became a real home away from home (not a ramshackle habitation in the forest) for many migrant farmers from Larteh and also provided them with a springboard for the westward movement over the river Densu, which formed Okorase's western boundary.

At some early, though unascertained, date (which E. O. Walker believed might have been as early as 1900) the chief of Okorase established his own native tribunal[16] and in 1964, or perhaps somewhat earlier, E. O. Walker led me there to visit the chief who permitted me to take extracts from the volume of the excellently kept records of his court relating to June 1918 to 1920. The tribunal sat very often and as the record of the proceedings was apparently verbatim the 1918–20 volume consisted of seventy large pages in small handwriting.[17] Included in this mass of material were the records of some interesting land cases, throwing light on the early migration of Larteh cocoa farmers. Heavily edited[18] extracts from five of these cases, together with explanatory footnotes, are presented here. These were originally prepared with the help of E. O. Walker, who fortunately remembered most of the personalities involved.

Rereading (which is not easy) these extracts today, I am struck by some of their odder features: by their somewhat dreamlike, or timeless,[19] quality, as though all concerned were sleepwalkers groping in the dark, sometimes over a couple of decades or more; by the unsatisfactoriness, in the expert opinion of E. O. Walker, of some of the judgments and statements; and by the feelings of uncertainty that pervaded the proceedings. As was well known to all concerned, certain land had been salable for some time, but it was as though the implications of such a fundamental change had not yet been properly foreseen or thought through.[20]

I now much regret that I failed to ask E. O. Walker many important questions. When had Paul Yaw Kuma died, when had he bought the land, and who had been the original vendor? There are many other unanswered questions lurking in the text and footnotes. But, at least, there is no evidence, even an unlikelihood, that the land had been an oil palm plantation before it was planted with cocoa.

The Proceedings of the Native Tribunal of Okorase-Akwapim

Case A

7 July 1919. Kwadjo Kuma *v.* Theo Adu

After the death of Akrofi, Benkumhene of Akwapim in 1900, some of his land was resold by his brother, Oheneba Awusi, to meet Akrofi's debts. However, Awusi was permitted to retain a farm, which he had made within the land, for use during his lifetime. When Awusi died, plaintiff who had purchased the land within which the farm lay, was prevailed on to allow defendant, a son of Awusi, to pluck the cocoa on it, retaining half for himself. Defendant failed to pluck, and when plaintiff employed laborers for the work defendant was arrested for trespass. Judgment having been given for plaintiff, it certainly seemed that defendant had been treated with unusual severity, as E. O. Walker commented. (See note 23)

The Plaintiff stated: I am native of Larteh living at Densu-side as farmer. It was in the time of Benkumhene Akrofi [1894–1900] who owned a land at Miawami, Densu-side and he had a [legal] case at Accra, which ran him to a heavy debt. After the death of the late chief his brother Awusi determined to sell the said land in payment. . . . The land was measured and divided into two parts: ten men took one side and seven of us on the other side;[21] meantime late Asamoa[22] stated that so far as late Awusi had already got a farm there before the division, the party in whose share that farm will be included must favor the old man allowing him to enjoy the farm until his death and afterward the farm must be that man's property.[23] The farm indeed came into my possession and . . . I did him [Awusi] the favor of allowing him to enjoy it until his death. I did not share the proceeds with him. He thanked me with one sheep. It is now 15 years since the land came to our possession. It was last year the said old man Awusi died. It was in last passion days [Easter] that I went to defendant to come and talk about the farm, because he had enjoyed the last season after his father's death . . . and now that the said father had died defendant must leave it alone and should not stop on it. Next morning . . . the mother of defendant (being wife of late Awusi) went . . . to beg me to allow her to work the farm as before under her late husband so that she may have something for her living. For it was true the land was not her late husband's property, but it was through my mercy.[24] Next morning again defendant came . . . warmly begging me to give them the farm for working. I agreed that I would do so, but that I should share the proceeds with defendant, he enjoying one-third and two-thirds for me.[25] After many humiliations of entreatment I agreed to share equally with defendant. And as defendant was asking about a certain *ntome* [boundary plant][26] in the land I was vexed and explained that it was a dispute between his late father when the farm was under his engagement . . . and that I fixed in the *ntome* to curtail any further dispute. Defendant was found guilty . . . and 2 bottles rum was charged from by the arbitrators and defendant ordered to pacify me one sheep which he hasn't till now. . . . Now after this defendant left the fully ripened pods unplucked and so I hired laborers to do the work and put the pods aside awaiting his coming before sharing with him and then paying the laborers. Then about a month ago when coming to my village I was arrested by constables directed by defendant's brother Offei that I had trespassed on his late father's property. I was not allowed to make any explanation than to pay £50 and go home for further investigation as it is a land matter. Thereafter I called him here for his explanation.

Defendant stated: I am native of Larteh living at Densu-side as blacksmith. . . . [After the sale and sharing of the land] my father's farm came in plaintiff's possession of the share and it was decided by the elders assembled that whosoever will have such farm must favour my late father for his enjoyment. Plaintiff indeed gave the land to my late father and he charged a sheep and a bottle of rum. . . . My late father asked plaintiff to fix in *ntome*[27] for him. . . . The land was given in presence of myself and my brother Offei and others.

The Witness Kwame Appiah as Sannah[28] *for Benkumhene stated:* About 15 years ago we the Awurade tribe[29] shared a land belonging to late Akrofi at Miawami; there was an old farm on the shared land and we know that it belonged to . . . Awusi. He was asked to take a part in the payment[30] so as to inherit the land but couldn't because of being poor. It was begged of the community in his favour to allow him to enjoy the farm from the one whose allocation the said farm will come to. After the division the said farm came to plaintiff's possession as his share. . . . [Plaintiff said Awusi] must simply enjoy the farm until his death and leave land alone.[31] And he has no right to secure or pledge the farm to himself anywhere; if the said old man did so, then the plaintiff will deprive him of the farm. Plaintiff then went and measured the land which was six ropes[32] and some forest behind an ant hill; plaintiff excluded the forest from the farm . . . and gave the farm to the old man's use. We the assembly consulted the old man that what plaintiff had done was all right for allowing him not for any accounting[33] and must therefore give a sheep as thanks. . . . It was last year when the old man and his son Offei came to me saying that he has been indebted by Offei's seduction matter and was coming for money from me as to pledge the farm to me. I refused because of the formal arrangement I knew of.[34]

Judgment: Judgment against the defendant, on the ground that he in statement clearly stated that the farm was made by his late father before the general division of the land, that the said farm, not all but a part,[35] came to plaintiff's possession in addition to the forest as his share and for that reason the old man approached plaintiff for the enjoyment of the farm so given to him as his share only in lifetime. If the farm was not plaintiff's how can defendant engage the witnesses mentioned for assistance and pleading on his behalf, asking that plaintiff should endeavour to continue the favour he has done to the late father, the same to be done to himself and his mother the widow?

Case B

9 October 1919. Kwame Asiam *v.* Akrong Kofi (Oath Case)

The most fascinating feature of this case was plaintiff's bland assumption that land he had purchased on borrowed money, before traveling to Nigeria some twenty years or more previously, would be "waiting for him" on his return. The defendant had acted as surety for the loan and in plaintiff's absence had himself paid off the £10 debt equal to the purchase money—thus freeing two young men, one of them his son, from service as pawns. But plaintiff had invested a further sum of £6 5s in the land, in the form of sheep and drinks, at the time of purchase; as the court found that this sum had not been repaid by defendant, judgment was given in favor of plaintiff's continued rights in the land.

Plaintiff stated: I am a carpenter living at Larteh. About 26 years ago I sent rum to late [Paul] Yaw Kuma and put before him that I want land and he indeed agreed. He asked me for one sheep and one case of rum as native custom allows. I went to Kwaku Botwe and asked loan from him. I reported to defendant about the loan and [he] secured me for the amount [£10]. . . . I went to Bights.[36] I made up my mind to return home. As I took up train[37] . . . sent men for the information of defendant. The reply he gave to the messenger was that if I meant to come he was coming to my land, as the land is lying for me.[38] My brother sent for me with hammock. . . . From my brother's village I came to my land at Kentenkren[39] being the land in dispute. . . . Some days passed and defendant never called to my place; he once then came and welcomed me simply and left off. Three or four days later he returned to me again. Defendant informed me all news at back during my leaving away. I then asked how my land that I left before going away and defendant said he had paid Kwaku Botwe the amount and so I have no more here. And the owner late Paul Yaw Kuma has sold 2 ropes[40] of the land proposed to be purchased by me and so I can go and enquire of it. I said that 2 ropes piece of land was not paid for by me, for only one rope was what I paid that one is what I am claiming. . . . Defendant gave the reply that I had no money in the land and have not purchased any land at all. Thereby I swore that I had money in the land for he, defendant, was only surety for me on the amount loaned by me from Kwaku Botwe. Then he too swore that my land is with late Paul of Okorase.

Plaintiff questioned:

Q: Before buying this land did you assemble before the family?

A: No, only Yaw Mante, Kwadjo Yirebi.

Q: The money from Kwaku was only a loan or was a man served for it?[41]

A: Mante and Kwadjo Yirebi were served for it—defendant was surety.

Q: If these two men are for £10 and also the land was for £10, how you managed to have a portion?[42]

A: Because I incurred the expenses, sheep and drinks of the land.

Q: How long you purchased the land from late Paul?

A: Twenty-five years.

Q: Did you purchase the whole land?

A: Yes.

Q: Did you cut *guaha?*[43]

A: Yes, and paid £10 on account the balance note.

Q: Did you ask for time on the balance?[44]

A: I did not pay the balance and so that land left was not mine.[45]

Q: Defendant's money was not included in buying the land?

A: No, but he was surety for the loan raised from Kwaku Botwe

Defendant questioned:

Q: You made company and bought land from late Paul?
A: We all agreed from home and plaintiff was the leader.[46]
Q: How much you gave in assistance to plaintiff for the purchasing?
A: Mante and Kwadjo were pledge on the amount. Mante is my own son and his money pledge for is my money.
Q: Men were pledged?
A: Yes, as servant for payment within a year.[47]

Judgment: Judgment against the defendant for the reason that he indeed never denied plaintiff to be the leader when such land was being purchased; for if so, however it is, his small amount will be contained in the sum paid as purchase money Even if he has none, defendant ought to be patient until a close account be entered by both of them. . . . Of course from defendant's statements we know that plaintiff borrowed an amount for which he gave two young men for servitude, for which said amount defendant was surety; defendant tried and paid that sum during plaintiff's absence and redeemed the two young men, who thereby enjoyed the land for themselves. Plaintiff in his statement meant the same, but also speaks of further expenses of a sheep and drinks bought against the purchasing which sum was also borrowed by him. . . . Such extra expenses were not paid and he can therefore also enjoy land for such sum. So far defendant knew this he should allow plaintiff his share.

Case C
Robert Kofi[48] *v.* Kwabena Daniel
12 November 1918.
(Oath against defendant depriving him of the land belonging to plaintiff)

The financial and working relationship between cocoa-farming brothers who cultivated purchased land was often very vague, as this case so clearly illustrates. Thus a resident brother might have been entirely responsible for farming land purchased by his nonresident brother, even though there had been no discussion between them regarding the division, if any, of the future proceeds; such a resident brother would have had full status as a "farm owner" in the eyes of both the local community and (later) the Department of Agriculture. It is interesting that, in this case, the proceeds from the land were sometimes paid to the brothers' mother (they had different fathers), who may have been notionally responsible for the general management of the family finances. Although there are many obscurities surrounding the brothers' financial relationship, it does seem clear that the defendant, Kwabena Daniel, was free to reinvest the proceeds from growing cocoa on land he did not own in the purchase of another land for his own use. As for the judgment, considering that defendant had been busy establishing a cocoa farm at Osabene, for some twenty years and had cut guaha *on the land, so that he would generally have been considered to be the owner, the judgment against him seems rather harsh, especially as plaintiff had been a trader during that time.*

Plaintiff: I am native of Larteh as trader, defendant is my own brother. I have got a piece of land situate at Osabene near Okorase and I gave the land to him to overlook it and render all accounts to me.[49] It is more than sixteen years ago I did so.

Defendant: I am native of Larteh living at Osabene as farmer. . . . I was at Fante as labourer and when coming home met with plaintiff . . . and gave him £6 for safekeeping. . . . I saw a woman whom I wanted to marry, so I told him to give the £6 to me for her marriage. Plaintiff said "no, I was too young" and was going to trade with the £6 at Ayikuma: he did so. Not long he consulted me in assisting to purchase the land in question from late Emmanuel Asiedu;[50] I was the man who cut the *guaha,* myself and Charles Kwaku Poku. Plaintiff said I must work on the land for he was going to trade. A year after my settlement on the land I wanted to marry a woman but he said not, so I went off on an inspection journey; shortly plaintiff wrote that I should come for he has married the said woman for me.[51] I then resumed my farming as before, almost to twenty years. Then plaintiff showed me another land which he had bought and instigated me to persevere to work in this one in question and from the yields of this one he will share all and every land he had already bought with me. When the railway line was made through the land I claimed compensation of £70 and £50 was the net balance[52] . . . and gave to my mother for safe-keeping; he then at my absence went for it. Meantime I had already given £30 as proceeds in this land in question as advance to Odei Gad[53] for purchase of another land. I also gave £30 to Asamoa Yirebi[54] as advance against a new land. I again paid £180 for a land at Mmease[55] from this land in dispute. I have never disputed with and put plaintiff to blame before. . . . The ground of my not quitting is that my money was included in purchasing the land and he has no right to scream for my removal. Plaintiff during my absence took my money of £260 for safe-keeping from my mother. This money is proceeds from this very land.

Defendant questioned by plaintiff:

Q: You joined me in buying the land?
A: Yes, I am included.
Q: How we came to purchase it?
A: Because my money of £6 was entrusted to you for trade and other purposes.
Q: Where we made this agreement?
A: At your house at Akyremade.[56]
Q: In whose presence?
A: Before our mother, only three of us.
Q: When the land was bought was I at Larteh or Ayikuma?
A: Ayikuma.
Q: Was I already a trader or did I become so during that time?
A: The trade was already started.
Q: Do you inherit with me in enjoying property?
A: No, because we are not of one father.[57]

Plaintiff questioned:

Q: How long you purchased the land in dispute?
A: About 20 years as I may say.

Q: How much you bought it for?
A: £25.
Q: From whom you purchased?
A: Late Emmanuel Asiedu.
Q: Not you and defendant joined in buying?
A: Never.
Q: You never asked defendant's assistance of an amount in buying it?
A: No, but rather late Yau Kuma[58] and Awua Sono[59] bought and paid for me.
Q: Was it you who settled defendant thereon?
A: Yes.
Q: How long he settled there?
A: I can't definitely mention.
Q: To stay there for what?
A: To work and render accounts for me.
Q: Did you not tell defendant his share is a rope[60] or that you entirely bought it for him?
A: Never.
Q: Why can you forcibly swear depriving him?
A: Because he has stopped rendering account and is now abusing and insulting me that the land is rather his.
Q: Has defendant never given you £6 before?
A: He really did, but he has long got it from me.

Defendant questioned:

Q: Since those 20 years have you ever asked for your share?
A: No, because he has never sworn on me.
Q: What is your yearly returns to him?
A: I do to my mother and not he.[61]
Q: Have you used some proceeds for another thing before?
A: Yes, in buying another land at Akem.

Judgment: It is clearly evidenced from the statement of defendant and in his cross examination that he cannot definitely prove his reason for claiming the property in question as shareholder with plaintiff. In reality he is a brother to plaintiff, but does not join in inheritance. Besides we see if defendant had given an amount to plaintiff it is not for this purpose, meanwhile that amount has already been spent on his behalf as dowry of a woman defendant married.

Case D
19 November 1918, Ofusu *v.* Ling Kwadjo
(Oath against defendant)

Although significant aspects of this confusing case are unclear, it is included here owing to the importance of E. O. Walker's comments and because there are indications that the tribunal itself failed to understand the inheritance system per stirpes *which was such that the* set *of brothers of each mother should be benefited equally. Plaintiff was a schoolboy at the time of his father's death and it must be said that everyone (actors and observers alike) is apt to be baffled by the problem of "delayed inheritance" due to youthfulness at the time of death.*

Plaintiff stated: I am native of Okorase as sword bearer. About 8 to 9 years ago when I was at Aburi as a school boy . . . I came here and was informed that the land that belonged to our deceased father at Osabene, Okorase, had been divided amongst us. When I asked my elder brother Kwame,[62] who has since died, why the land was shared like that, he said he didn't know, for he being the eldest was given a small portion of which defendant's share was more pleasing than his and that myself and my surety Tawia also got an old farm made by Agya Opuko, two farms cultivated by Atta Kofi and one by another man from Larteh. It was not long before my elder brother [Kwame] died. . . . Defendant then being the next [in age] to the deceased, overlooked [oversaw] all these farms for many years. After the death of my late brother, defendant pledged his portion, so shared and owned by him, to Johanes Awua Sono[63] for £50, because he [Kwame] had been indebted; then I have nothing to enjoy at all. All that was shared and given to myself and others as our portion is in his hands, enjoying same and not caring after the rest of my sisters, Ata and Afua.[64] At yearly festivals and Christmas he takes no care of them, whilst we all take the trouble every year, plucking, carrying, fermenting, drying the said cocoa for him. And as I was displeased with the treatment, I went with Ansah to him this morning asking him why, as the land has been shared amongst us individually, he enjoys mine in addition to his and refused or disliked to care for my brothers and sisters: mine, which he overlooked for more than 8 years, I was today claiming back from him. What was his reply? His reply was that I had no portion at all, for through grace I was mentioned amongst them.[65] This caused me to swear on him for the detention of the loads [of cocoa] so dried. . . . We all have one father, my mother was the one who cultivated the land[66] and now he wanted to deprive me of the property. A piece of the farm also which is under Anang, he must leave that alone for it is mine. . . . Also that piece enjoyed by our mother Aka is mine, but presently . . . she must enjoy it and after her death it is mine.

Plaintiff questioned by defendant:

Q: Can you tell me the mothers of us all?

A: You and late George are of one [mother] and myself, late Kwame and Tawia are of one—women (or daughters) exclusive.

Q: If two sons of one father and different mothers share a thing how do they do it?

A: Division is in different ways: every one enjoys his own.[67]

Defendant: I am linguist for Chief Kumi of Okorase. About 10 years ago my father died: he had done a fine[68] work and the work was handed over to my elder brother Kwame. Myself and Kwame then went to Larteh and informed one Yaw, our elder brother or cousin,[69] that we are sons of the late father by different mothers . . . so that the land must be divided amongst us.[70] And [so we were] . . . with our elder brother Yaw . . . putting the matter in presence of the elders, who charged £3 on each side as divisional fee. One land is at Larteh-Bompong[71] and Yaw, being senior in the place of our father, must inherit that as family land; and this one in dispute should be divided[72] amongst plaintiff's late brother Kwame and the other brothers—these being plaintiff and others on one side (of the same mother)—and myself and my brothers on the other side (of another mother). The cocoa was divided but the forest not.[73] Kwame, being the senior son, was placed towards Johanes Awua Sono, then myself and my brothers were next to that.[74] Myself and my late brother George [who had the same mother] worked and cultivated some additional farms to the old ones.[75] What plaintiff is now claiming to be the farms made by Opoku, Atta Kofi and others are mine; I cultivated them and when my late wife Opokuwa was alive they were under her care, after her death I properly managed and worked them.

After the division my late brother Kwame . . . went to Dodowa and was advanced some cash from S & B[76] for purchasing produce; meantime he got some from Capt. Asare and one Mensah, Mr. Oboo[77] and another man. . . . After the death I was made to understand that as he was indebted to the above named people he secured the portion alloted to him and brothers to S & B for advances and that Obeng Tia was the personal surety. Then after the death [of Kwame] Mr. Kofi Mensah was sent with a writ for the sale of the property there being an amount of £60 due unpaid by plaintiff's brother;[78] I tried and paid what was due to the blacks,[79] leaving that of S & B; and when it was time to be sold I called plaintiff and Amma Apam to Yaw Kumi's house and put the matter before them that I was going to pledge them[80] for a loan in payment of the debt due by their late brother, for if the land he sold them they have finished;[81] plaintiff and other refused to be in servitude. I then put the matter before Mr. Awua Sono and gave him the cocoa farm as pawn and any time that will be convenient I shall claim it back.[82] He gave me £50, the £10 to make £60 [due to S & B] was paid with cocoa by myself. Plaintiff was present, as well as Leader John Anang when raising the loan;[83] and when paying the debt at S & B plaintiff was present too. I did not pledge the whole farm to Mr. Awua Sono, but as assistance to plaintiff left a portion for him in order that he may get that for his living. After the death of my own brother George (whom I am of the same mother), I gave his portion under his care to plaintiff to use until the redemption of their own [farm] from the pledge and then I would reclaim back.[84] . . . It was this morning that he came and swore on me that the cocoa the drying place was his and I must not touch it.

The witness E. J. Kumah, for the defendant, stated: I am pastor in charge of the Wesleyan Mission Station here. Some years ago we went to share the land of both parties' late father amongst themselves. We did not divide the land that is the forest, but only the cocoa farms; then a new farm was lying on the right side of the cocoa farm, but that was not given to anyone but to Ofosu and his young brothers to go and visit them as a joy.[85] The farms were shared into 2 parts; one was for Kwame and the other for defendant.

Witness questioned:

Q: Was it [the new farm] given to them [the boys] as their entire heritage for ever?
A: No, only to play and pluck for pocket money.
Q: How many boys were those the farms were given?
A: George, Ofosu and Tawia[86]

Judgment: Against the plaintiff. Witnesses have proved that the farms were divided into 2 parts . . . and that no special portion was elected for plaintiff.[87] . . . if so he cannot swear that the cocoa collected from that farm was his. If it was because the cocoa in question was from the new farm not so added to any one's portion, but by perseverance defendant had tried and put it up[88] and plaintiff was not pleased, then he must ask for a share in that, but cannot claim it to be his alone.

Case E

4 April 1919. Joseph Siaw *v.* Kofi Nyako

(The plaintiff claimed £25 damages from defendant for trespass for having unlawfully ploughed a portion of land.)[89]

On the death of Akrofi, Benkumhene of Akwapim, in 1900, his creditor, Asamoa Yaw,[90] claimed the repayment of a £70 debt. Akrofi's brother, Oheneba Awusi,[91] decided (though not without prior consultation with the "sons and daughters") to sell land owned by Akrofi in settlement of the debt. A number of people, among them plaintiff and defendant, bought portions of land, the whole being divided between them according to their contributions. Plaintiff lacked money and actually borrowed from the creditor, Asamoa Yaw, to pay for his portion, promising quick repayment from the proceeds of selling planks. The usual existence of friendly and complex relationships between creditor and debtor is indeed well emphasised by this creditor's activities, for he played a prominent part in selling the land, marking the boundaries—even fixing the price of the portion acquired by plaintiff. When land is resold, it is usual for a portion to be retained for the relatives, as happened in this case.

Plaintiff stated: I am native of Larteh living at Densu-side, Miawami, as sawyer. I bought a piece of land from late Oheneba Awusi more than twelve years ago. . . . [The creditor, Asamoa Yaw, had been responsible for fixing the boundaries of this land, on which it was alleged defendant, from his adjoining land, had trespassed.]

Defendant stated: I am native of Larteh as linguist for Benkumhene. About 14 years ago I was informed by my brother-in-law, Johanes Awua Sono,[92] of a land, being land of the late Benkumhene Akrofi, to be divided on payment of certain debts. . . . I replied that I would have it and £10 was paid as advance for it. A general meeting was held at old late Akrofi's house and payments were made and a day was fixed for the division of the land. It was a Monday when we started for the division and a messenger was sent to inform late Asamoa Yaw because he was the leader to show the lying and situation of the said land.[93] Late Asamoa was obliged to show all the sides, but the side touching old Gyebi Kwame,[94] down to the river Dedewa, was missed. And as old Gyebi Kwame was the party who first bought his land and bought this said land in dispute for the Benkumhene late Akrofi,[95] he was sent for to come and show the boundary between them.

The witness, Johanes Awua Sono, for the defendant stated: I am native of Larteh and councillor at Okorase. . . . During the time of late Akrofi a debt was incurred and late Asamoa paid £70 and therefore old Akrong[96] and [my] father Awusi met and late Asamoa was claiming amount after the death of Akrofi;[97] so the whole sons and grandsons were assembled and proposed to share the land in payment of the debt. I paid £55 of the amount all the others paid according to their abilities. . . . [After determining the boundaries] we then measured the whole land and shared it according to the amounts paid. When all those who paid got their shares a part was alloted aside the children of late Akrofi, Amoako and late Awusi . . . I asked to be the last man in sharing.[98] After the division defendant . . . asked me to offer him that portion of mine. I sold to him for £20. . . . Defendant was present when we shared the land and got my portion returned to him. Two pounds was claimed from every man paying £10 before affording certificate.[99]

The witness Wesley Asiedu stated: I am native of Larteh as leader of Methodist Society. . . . Plaintiff . . . told me that he was going to purchase some [land] from late Awusi. As he had no money to pay ready cash, late Asamoa will not agree that the land he sold to plaintiff. So plaintiff took me to late Asamoa to ask his pardon to give him credit for the land and was going to sell some planks in payment for it. Late Asamoa agreed. . . . The land was priced at £21. . . . I was surety for the amount and asked for time to pay; and at once plaintiff at home paid £10 on account to Awusi and delivered to Asomoa; and a time was fixed for the balance; later on the rest was paid. That's all I know.

The witness questioned:

Q: Asamoa and Awusi who was the vendor?

A: Late Awusi.

Q: If so how can Asamoa tell you the price and fix the price?

A: Asamoa did this, as the money was to be paid as a debt due to him.[100]

Q: Were you present when the balance was paid?

A: Yes, to Awusi.

Judgment: The chief with the councillors with 2 parties went to the land in dispute, including witness. [The boundaries were indicated.] . . . Judgment was given for the plaintiff.

Marion Johnson

For a large part of her life Marion Johnson (1914–88) had led a maddeningly peripatetic existence as a wife and mother (three sons who were followed, in 1956, by a daughter). Her itinerary was Achimota (1937–39), Tanganyika (1940–45), Kenya (1945–49), Manchester (1949–55), Sudan (1955–61), and Ghana (probably 1963–67). Originally trained as a geographer at Oxford, at no stage, until she finally arrived at the Centre of West African Studies in Birmingham in 1969, did she have any formal attachment to an academic institution—though, encouraged by Thomas Hodgkin and Ivor Wilks, she knew how to "frequent" the Institute of African Studies at the University of Ghana—and she was consequently always quite immobile. It is ironic that one of her chief claims to fame, at least in my opinion, was her historical work on the mobility of farmers in southeastern Gold Coast, an adventure that had developed in her mind and in her imagination while she was living in East Africa and the Sudan.[101]

I was unable to acknowledge her pioneer spirit in *MCF* because she had published nothing before that book appeared in 1963. I think, though I cannot be sure, that I first met her by chance in the Institute of African Studies in 1963, the year when she somehow managed to travel to interview a very old man at Pampanso Kese, on the "Middle Densu,"[102] whose grandfather had been a canoe-builder who had been named Mankata in 1824 after Sir Charles MacCarthy.[103]

Our first meeting will remain forever in my memory. My ideas on the migration of cocoa farmers had been badly received by large numbers of people at the University of Ghana (at least before my book was published) who insisted, and went on insisting, that land had never been salable[104]—and here at last was someone who not only understood what I was driving at, but who, in the objectivity of her imagination (aided by few maps or libraries), had been able to thrust back the migratory story to the beginning of the nineteenth century.[105] How she did this I will never know for during the two years (1937–39) when her husband, Frank Johnson, had been on the staff of Achimota College, she had been dragged down by domestic responsibilities. Somehow, the existence of the "empty forests" of southeastern Gold Coast, which she had presumably never seen, had then presented her with a problem from which she could not subsequently escape.

As there is a Festschrift commemorating the encyclopedic scope of Marion Johnson's historical work in the last two decades of her life,[106] there is no need for me to emphasize that she became a scholar of international renown, whose African[107] interests knew no internal boundaries—geographical or disciplinary. No subject was too small or too large. "The Ounce in Eighteenth Century West African Trade"[108] heralded her two definitive articles on the West African cowrie currency[109] and the fruitfulness of her collaboration with the economist J. S. Hogendorn on West African slavery is well known. She even had time for a somewhat technical article on Shai pots which, as it happened, had been used to carry palm oil from Krobo and Akwapim country to the coast in the 1850s.[110] The Shai people had been expelled from their hills, or inselbergs, on the Accra plains in 1892 and had never returned there; hence, they were of particular interest to Marion Johnson.

When, in 1987, she received the news that she had inoperable cancer, Marion Johnson repaired to a Birmingham hospice, together with her books, papers, and computer, where business was carried on as usual; many people called and it is almost true to say that she was holding a seminar on her deathbed.[111]

Eugene Ohene Walker

For myself, as a fieldworker, Eugene Ohene Walker (1895–1975) was the ideal guide and friend. I had always found that the aura of formality surrounding dignitaries had impeded the uninhibited flow of conversation—after all, it is one of the main functions of such personages to tell people what it is good for them to know. In my particular case such problems were compounded by the awe (in the dictionary sense of "dread mingled with veneration") in which I held my father.[112]

E. O. Walker was the ideal purveyor of information because he moved in chiefly circles, while not being a chief himself; indeed, he was the *elder* brother of the Benkumhene of Akwapim, Nana Okanta Obrentri, with whom he resided (before the early death of the latter) in a handsome mansion on the edge of the Larteh ridge, with a wonderful view of the Accra plains and of the distant ocean beyond.[113] Second, he had never been at all rich,[114] although all his life he had been accustomed to associating on a basis of equality with relatively wealthy men, so that he had as good an understanding of credit as of debt. Third, for reasons I cannot entirely understand, he was one of the least enthusiastic Larteh cocoa farmers I had ever met, trade not agriculture being his forte.[115] Fourth, as a widower of long standing, with no son, he seemed different from all the successful family men around him and could take an amused view. Fifth, he had known what it was to go broke: around 1929, some laborers had ruined him. And sixth, he was something of a politician, having been concerned with organizing cooperative groups of cocoa farmers designed to eliminate the "Lagosian" middlemen—though he readily admitted that the Lagosians were no more rapacious than other strangers who tempted innocent though wily cocoa farmers with large advances on crop.[116] As readers will appreciate from my tone of voice, I now regret that I failed to collect adequate biographical information from E. O. Walker until it was too late. However, I hope that the special quality of his detached objectivity is well conveyed by his comments on the cases that came before the Okorase tribunal. His memory was excellent,[117] his judgments always balanced, and his knowledge of human cunning profound.

That cocoa farmers, rather than cocoa buyers, were the "moneyed men" in Larteh (as in Akwapim generally) is conclusively proved by the list of those who subscribed the capital of as much as £1,072 for the building of the splendid Mmetiamu bridge.[118] Of course some rich farmers were also produce buyers (perhaps palm oil and kernels, as well as cocoa)—but the real métier of successful farmers was credit-granting, a professional occupation that greatly encouraged the "cocoa migration"; penniless farmers of known respectability were able to borrow considerable sums on reasonable terms in order to invest in cocoa land. Each of the nine named subscribers in the Mmetiamu list was "defined" as a cocoa farmer in terms of the location of his cocoa lands.

E. O. Walker introduced me to the son of James Ashong who subscribed £125 toward the building of the bridge.[119] Between 1894 and 1900 James Ashong,[120] together with his father, his elder brother (Israel Kwame) and a Larteh friend,[121] bought a cocoa land at Domeabra, near Mmetiamu, on the eastern bank of the Densu. From the proceeds of this land they soon bought another at Koransan[122] west of the river, so in due course there was need for a bridge. It was Israel Kwame who "called a meeting of the whole neighborhood and told them that owing to floods they often could not get back after they had gone to the other side of the river and that many women and children had lost their lives."[123] He it was who proposed that Jacob Isliker, a Swiss "building engineer," who had been employed by the Basel Mission, should be employed by the farmers to build a bridge.

E. O. Walker's memory of his early days was so excellent that, lacking further space, I content myself with relating a few scraps of early information. He left school at the end of 1913 and immediately joined Elisha Kwadjo's cocoa-buying "firm" as a weighing clerk, who bought and inspected cocoa and supervised laborers. So bored was Kwadjo, who was a very successful cocoa farmer, with the business of buying cocoa beans that he immediately turned that business over to his sister's son. Besides, the concern would have been bankrupt, had such a legal possibility existed: unlike the farmers he was *directly* at the mercy of European businessmen.[124]

Appropriately, E. O. Walker lived near the Mmetiamu bridge at this time, until, in 1915, he joined Ofori Bros. and was transferred to Koforidua. The three Ofori brothers in the business had all been teachers: a fourth brother was a Larteh minister; their father, who was of course a cocoa farmer, had provided the capital. The business flourished and E. O. Walker enjoyed buying cocoa beans and palm kernels in Krobo country; but in the slump following the postwar boom, Ofori Bros. collapsed. Penniless though he was, E. O. Walker decided to work for himself, but not for long. One way and another he suffered many ups and downs working in business until about 1934 when he returned home to Larteh, where he became a somewhat inactive food farmer, who employed no laborers.

On 27 November 1966 E. O. Walker addressed a letter to me in Cambridge referring mainly to some personal court cases involving cocoa lands, near Mmetiamu, that worried him greatly. He added that he knew Ivor Wilks very well ("one of the finest men in Legon") and he deplored the lack of funds at the Institute of African Studies.

Notes

1. Polly Hill, *Migrant Cocoa Farmers of Southern Ghana,* hereafter *MCF* (Cambridge, 1963), Appendix 8.3. This bridge over the Densu river (which was one of three) had been built by a Swiss contractor who had been hired by a group of Larteh and Mamfe farmers who had put up the capital; it was probably opened to foot passengers, who paid a third toll, on 24 April 1914. Despite being totally neglected, the bridge still stands sturdily; it ought to be one of the major tourist attractions of sub-Saharan Africa, but no Ghanaian government (least of all in colonial times) has ever shown the faintest interest in it.

2. Ghana would certainly not have achieved independence as early as 1957 had it not been for the unbridled enterprise of the migrant cocoa farmers, whose thinking and behavior was based on long-term considerations.

3. Hill, *MCF,* Appendix 2.9. A *huza* was both a land-purchasing group and the land it purchased. One of the main distinctions between the *huza* system and the company system of the patrilineal Akwapim farmers was that the Krobo state had expansionary *political* motivations, unlike the Akwapim state. In the geographical appendix of the first edition of Christaller's dictionary (see note 8) it was noted that Krobo country had "many plantations on and N. of the Akuapem range between Akuapem, Akem and Akwam[u]."

4. Marion Johnson, "Migrants Progress," pts. 1 and 2, *Bulletin of the Ghana Geographical Association* 9, no. 2 (1964); 10, no. 2 (1965).

5. The migrant cocoa farmers spoke of the trans-Densu lands as *asuogya,* which, in certain contexts, was a metaphor implying "going together over the water."

6. Johnson, "Migrants," pt. 2, 24–25.

7. Ibid., pt. 1, 16.

8. J. G. Christaller, *Dictionary of the Asante and Fante Language,* 2d ed. (1933),

272. In the first edition of this dictionary (1881) the word "slaves" was used in place of "laborers." In an appendix to this edition (which was, unfortunately, omitted from the second edition) it was noted that the Akwapim "townships" had "at shorter or longer distances . . . numerous villages in which some owners live part of the years, others the whole year, for their agricultural pursuits" (640); however, most of these villages lay in "valleys in the W. (or S.W. and N.W.)"; that is, not in the Densu valley. Unfortunately, no figure was given for the number of Larteh villages. Christaller attached much importance to his geographical appendices, partly because he was anxious that the "archaic elements" in place names should not be neglected.

9. *Grammatical Outline and Vocabulary of the Oji (Tschi) Language* (Basel, 1854)

10. Johnson, "Migrants," pt. 1, 8.

11. Ibid. 9. Even earlier, this tract had presumably been Akwamu country. In the geographical appendix of the first edition of Christaller's dictionary, it was observed that as the Akim people had "sufficient cultivable land in the neighbourhood of their dwelling places" they did not build villages for "agricultural purposes" (641). (Unfortunately, in *MCF,* I had overlooked this appendix in which it was noted that the "different places" belonging to each of eight "Akyem districts" were frequently separated by great distances, parts of other districts intervening, so that Apapam, for example, together with five other places, which were widely dispersed, belonged to Kukurantumi. Christaller offered no explanation for this "dispersal," which is relevant to the question of the incomprehensible scope and degree of control exerted over large tracts of southern forest by such sellers as Apedwa and Apapam; see Hill, *MCF.*)

12. See map i, "The great roads of Asante in the early nineteenth century," in I. Wilks, *Asante in the Nineteenth Century* (Cambridge, 1975).

13. Oral information that was not, unfortunately, recorded in Hill, *MCF.*

14. Amazingly, when at Okorase I had omitted to ascertain the identity of the original land vendor(s)!

15. Lying close to that fulcrum, the Mmetiamu bridge, not far from Koforidua, Okorase has for long been situated just to the west of the main Accra to Kumase road.

16. West of the river, where the migrant cocoa farmers were strangers, they seldom had their own tribunals. E. O. Walker listed five other tribunals one of which was, interestingly enough, at Asuboi on the road to Suhum; see appendix 5.3 of Hill, *MCF,* "The Akwapim/Akim Abuakwa Dispute over Jurisdiction."

17. The cases were heard by George Paul Kumi, chief of Okorase; most, though not all, of the records were kept by the court registrar Gechie Byron.

18. Such editing, which is indicated by ellipses, was, unfortunately, necessitated by the extremely repetitious nature of the proceedings, as always in courts of law. Also, a few obvious petty mistakes were silently rectified.

19. There was no indication that because events had occurred (say) ten to fifteen years ago, they might have been forgotten.

20. See Hill, *MCF,* 134, where E. O. Walker's views on the changes in inheritance systems resulting from the trans-Densu migration are recorded.

21. It is not clear whether land had been bought by one or two companies of Larteh farmers.

22. A well-known creditor, Asamoa Kumah, was one of those who subscribed toward the building of the bridge at Mmetiamu; Hill, *MCF,* 245.

23. E. O. Walker commented: "This is very bad: the land should have gone to Awusi's descendants."

24. Plantiff is arguing that defendant's mother would not have asked his permission to work the farm had she not known that it was his property.

25. It was not unusual for relatives or friends to receive a one-third (*abusa*) share of the cocoa in return for overseeing the farm, but it was only in special circumstances that a half share (*abunu*) went to the overseer.

26. Rightly or wrongly, Christaller defined the *ntome* (or *ntomme*) as a species of palm "the living stems of which may serve as posts in fences or for landmarks."

27. The symbolic significance of the *ntome* boundary plant was such that its "fixing" would have implied that defendant owned the land—a point that the tribunal appeared to ignore.

28. The Benkumhene's official treasurer.

29. The meaning is unclear as I was told in Larteh that companies did not have a "ward" or "brong" basis.

30. This would have been quite inappropriate insofar as he already "owned the farm"—but how had he acquired it if so?

31. Is a distinction being made between the land and the farm?

32. See Hill, *MCF,* for the system of measuring land in terms of "ropes." Although the rope was a standard length, it is certain that the farm was a large one.

33. Accounting would have been necessary had Awusi been alloted only a share of the cocoa instead of all of it.

34. Awusi had proposed to pledge the farm to the witness—as had been expressly forbidden.

35. This is unclear.

36. The Bight of Benin; namely, Nigeria, where many Gold Coast craftsmen, originally trained by the Basel Mission, sought work in the 1890s and earlier.

37. The railway reached Pakro in 1911 and it was probably not until a few years later that plaintiff returned. If he had gone away soon after the purchase of the land, he may have been away for nearly twenty years.

38. Defendant was reassuring plantiff that the land was "lying down for him," for use when required. (In the 1950s the migrant cocoa farmers used many metaphorical expressions conveying that land, like a person or animal, was awaiting its owner's return).

39. A locality west of Koforidua, near the well-known waterfall of that name.

40. This particular rope (see note 32) was 24 yards long; that is, 12 "armstretches" or *abasam.*

41. Put in pawn: the service of the pawn representing "interest" on the loan.

42. Defendant appears to have been asking plaintiff how he could think he had any claim considering that the £10 he had borrowed had been repaid by him (defendant).

43. It was important that the *guaha* ceremony should have been performed for this validated the sale of land; see Hill, *MCF.*

44. Ibid. Or, in other words, for permission to pay for the land over a period, as was usual.

45. Namely, the leader of the company that was formed in Larteh.

46. Defendant was here stating that the debt was due to be repaid within a year when the pawns would be freed.

47. Why should the freed pawns have been entitled to cultivate the land?

48. Robert Kofi was a trader in palm produce and cocoa at both Dodowa and Ayikuma (on the plain east of the scarp) where he was said to have had "storey-houses."

49. No doubt this was a retrospective rationalization.

50. Emmanuel Asiedu was a rich Larteh-Kubease man who owned more land than he needed at Okorase. According to E. O. Walker he was born in 1843 and died in 1899 and the land in question was presumably resold during his lifetime. He was a palm oil producer, having a plantation on the Akwapim upland between Larteh and the Mamfe junction; he was also a trader. He is thought to have been one of the first to glaze his windows in Larteh. One of his sons was Awua Asiedu, the Anglican priest.

51. In other words, he had paid defendant's bride price.

52. Presumably, this was because a bribe of £20 had been paid.

53. Who was, presumably, a company leader.

54. Otherwise Asamoa Kumah; see note 22. Presumably this was partial payment for a land bought through a company of which Asamoa Kumah was leader.

55. Possibly a locality near Tafo, farther north.

56. Akyremade was one of the Larteh-Ahenease wards.

57. They were half brothers with the same mother.

58. Yaw Kuma had bought a large area of land at Okorase, some of which he had resold to other Larteh men; see Hill, *MCF,* 220.

59. Awua Sono was another of those who had subscribed toward the building of the Mmetiamu bridge. Presumably plaintiff had borrowed from each of these men.

60. The width of the strips into which company land was divided was measured in ropes.

61. In other words defendant rendered accounts to his (also plaintiff's) mother and not to plaintiff direct.

62. Kwame was plaintiff's full brother.

63. See note 59.

64. E. O. Walker stated: "If a father dies any unmarried or widowed daughters should either get a share of the property or the inheritor should look after them. If the daughters are married then the inheritor should pay them something yearly from the father's property. If, say, the proceeds were £50 and there is no debt to pay, then he might pay them as much as £10 each. But if he is not a good man and they are away he may not send anything unless they come and demand it. If the brother refuses they might go to arbitration—but he is en-

titled to refuse if there are outstanding debts. It is for the women to choose whether they should have family or *brong* arbitration."

65. In other words, plaintiff had not been entitled to any share of the planted land but had been alloted a portion by courtesy of the rest of the family.

66. The wives of migrant cocoa farmers were usually much involved in cultivation.

67. Perhaps this meant that while there was no definite rule as to how land should be divided between the sons of different mothers, each of them was certainly alloted his own portion.

68. He had made fine cocoa farms.

69. As the son of the elder brother of defendant's late father, he would have been the inheritor; see Hill, *MCF.*

70. It is perhaps implied that "division between mothers" should have been equal.

71. In the deep hollow northwest of Larteh, by the Bompong stream. This family land would have been used for food farming and would have passed to the inheritor Yaw.

72. The inheritor Yaw was not entitled to any share of the cocoa land.

73. It is not clear whether this land at Okorase was "proper company land"; if so it would have been divided into strips, each farmer receiving his due share of the forest.

74. E. O. Walker pointed out that it was a general rule among the patrilineal farmers of Akwapim that the land alloted to the leader of a company should have lain on the extreme left of the baseline when facing the land, and this fact, which had previously been overlooked, is certainly confirmed by the farm maps in Hill, *MCF* (though, as Mr. Walker admitted, there were exceptions to this rule). If a group consisted of brothers, as in this case, the eldest of them would have had land on the left; as for the other brothers they might have been in any order except that it was usual for one of the more senior to have land at the extreme right. "The small children should be in the middle; if girls have any share [which is most unusual]they would be in the middle."

75. Again, this is unclear if the group had been a company proper that had bought forest land.

76. Schenk and Baker, a German firm of produce buyers.

77. He was a cocoa buyer at Asuoya, on the Accra plain beneath Larteh; he was a brother of Mr. Aborah; Hill, *MCF,* 243.

78. It is to be noted that when denigrating Kwame he referred to him as "plaintiff's brother."

79. That is Capt. Asare and other Africans.

80. He proposed to put them into servitude as pawns until the debt was repaid.

81. This is unclear but may imply that the potential pawns had lost all their land.

82. From this careless reference by defendant to his having pledged a farm that did not belong to him, it is not clear whether he intended to hold on to the farm when it had been redeemed.

83. John Anang was the leader of the Methodist Church in Larteh.

84. Does this suggest that defendant was proposing to restore the pledged farm to plaintiff?

85. The brothers would have been allowed to pluck the cocoa in a casual way, which was a common practice according to E. O. Walker.

86. Boys from both branches of the family.

87. If one is correct in assuming that sons were never members of their father's company, this judgment is ignorant.

88. Presumably the suggestion here was that defendant might have done some further planting on the new farm that plaintiff and the other boys were permitted to "enjoy."

89. In the 1950s farmers often spoke of clearing land as "plowing"—though they had never seen a plow.

90. Asamoa Yaw, who was Akrofi's creditor, was a rich trader who had a house at Ayikuma in the plains east of Larteh. He owned land on the Akim side of the river Densu, opposite the Mmetiamu bridge.

91. See Case A above.

92. See note 59.

93. Whether the land had been formally pledged to Asamoa Yaw is not clear. But he was familiar with the neighborhood and is accordingly referred to as "the leader."

94. Gyebi Kwame was the "land maniac"; see Hill, *MCF,* 205, who, in the opinion of his relatives was unable to desist from buying land; he was believed to have bought land for food-growing before 1890, but this was all east of Densu. E. O. Walker said he had been well known for rearing cattle on the Accra plains near the Shai hills.

95. E. O. Walker suggested that it was because the Benkumhene, as a high chief, was unable to leave Larteh to visit the forest, that Gyebi Kwame had bought the land on his behalf.

96. He was a close relative of Oheneba Awusi.

97. When a debtor died his creditors were apt to descend on his relatives, demanding immediate repayment.

98. Presumably the witness asked for land at the extreme right of the baseline (see note 74); perhaps he hoped to claim some adjoining forest.

99. Curiously, I had never heard that "certificates" were issued to land purchasers—presumably by the company secretary.

100. Again, the high status of creditors is to be noted.

101. Johnson, "Migrants," pts. 1 and 2. As already noted, she viewed the "cocoa migration" as part of a larger movement extending far back in time and in space.

102. Ibid., pt. 1, 18.

103. As it happens fieldwork on the ground (rather than in libraries, archives, or the imagination) would never have been Marion Johnson's forte and her account of Mankata is a little confused. Judging from a couple of expeditions we made together, I think that she was too kind to disbelieve her "informants" sufficiently. (One might say that she became the object of fieldwork by others.)

104. I was regarded as a "mere economist," who was too innocent to appreciate the sophisticated "fact" that land was never salable. (But that was before I joined the Institute of African Studies.)

105. The earliest map to which she refers in her migration articles was by the botanist Thonning (1802), from the Danish Royal Archives.

106. D. Henige and T. C. McCaskie, eds., *West African Economic and Social History: Studies in Memory of Marion Johnson* (Madison, Wisc., 1990).

107. Or should I say "West African"?

108. *Journal of African History* 7, no. 2 (1966): 197–214.

109. "The Cowrie Currencies of West Africa," *Journal of African History* 11, nos. 1, 3 (1970): 17–50, 331–50.

110. The coauthor was A. K. Quarcoo. *Baessler-Archiv*, n.s. 17 (1968): 47–88.

111. From an obituary notice by the economist Douglas Rimmer.

112. Readers will be glad to hear that this is as far as I am prepared to go in the direction of autobiography.

113. Plate 3 of Hill, *MCF*, shows E. O. Walker on his food farm at Larteh, with a view of the Accra plain 1,200 feet below.

114. This may have been connected with the fact that his father, C. D. Walker, who had been a catechist and a teacher, went to Calabar as a civil servant in about 1898, staying there for some seventeen years. Although he was said to have sent money from Nigeria to his wife and mother, to maintain his cocoa farm, his prolonged absence must have impoverished his family, both financially and emotionally.

115. His brother, the Benkumhene, was also little concerned with cocoa farming, his chief interest being in a distant land on the Afram plains, which he may never have visited.

116. "Lagosians" were, of course, Nigerians of any ethnic group.

117. Thus he could remember the selling of casks of cocoa (the larger being the "butt," the smaller the "puncheon") from Dodowa to Accra, a job that took two or three men two days. He could also remember being with his mother at a (long-extinct) market at Boafo, near Larteh, in about 1905, at a time when no food came there from across the Densu.

118. Hill, *MCF*, 245. (Cocoa farmers had also financed the building of inferior bridges at Mangoase and Bibianiha.)

119. Ibid., 244.

120. His capital was said to have come from making pottery and rearing pigs.

121. I find the composition of this group puzzling, being unaware of any similar case involving patrilineal farmers.

122. Hill, *MCF*, 18–19.

123. His capital in the Mmetiamu bridge was £103.

124. At one time Cadbury had briefly tried cultivating cocoa in the Gold Coast but had given up, owing to the bad practices of "native" farmers.

"When I die, I shall return to my own land": An "Amina" Slave Rebellion in the Danish West Indies, 1733–1734

RAY A. KEA

> Those who have suffered the sentence of history—subjugation, domination, diaspora, displacement.
> —Homi Bhabha

In March 1734 the colonial governor of the Danish West Indies wrote the following to the governor-general of the French West Indies several months after the outbreak of a slave insurrection on St. John: "No doubt you will have learned of the cruel catastrophe which we have suffered on our island of St. John, caused by a rebellion of our Mina Negroes, who, after having massacred 40 of our whites of both sexes, destroyed and burned all the plantation and sugar works of the said island."[1] Unfree, alienated labor moved from the margins of the social order to its center. A page of history turns. The St. John rebellion was the first successful islandwide slave revolt of the Danish West Indies. It lasted from November 1733 until June 1734.

Among the planters and civil authorities in the Danish Caribbean the "Minas" ("Aminas" or "El Minas") had the reputation of being the worst of their slaves, a reputation ascribed to the Aminas' presumed propensity to become maroons or runaways. One late seventeenth-century governor of the Danish West Indies reported that "not only are they the worst runaways of all Blacks, but they believe that at their death they return to their fatherland, or as they express it: '*mij dodte mij loppe in myn lande.*'" In translation this Dutch Creole expression reads "when I die, I shall return to my own land."[2] Death signified the end of the Amina slaves' absence from their homeland.

The essentialist and essentializing term "Amina(s)" generally signified Akan-speaking people from the Gold Coast. The St. John rebels were principally Akwamu men and women, most of whom had been sold to the trading agents of the Danish West Indies and Guinea Company between 1730 and 1733 following the military and political collapse of the Akwamu state in 1730. Their life experiences registered a catastrophic transformation: from the status of free, privileged members of one political community to the status of unfree, laboring nonmembers of another. The term was also used to include Adanme; that is, people of the La(doku) kingdom. Adanme men and women were actively involved in the insurrection.[3]

This essay is a preliminary inquiry into the course and development of the St. John uprising, preliminary in the sense that it marks an initial effort of investigation and is not the final result of a full-fledged research project. As the Amina insurgents had formerly lived in Akwamu, the study considers the rebellion in the context of Akwamu state-building processes. The rebels were located not just in the oppressive present of a plantation social setting but in an "archaeology"; that is, a history and a political and cultural existence on the other side of this setting. How do questions of structure, agency, autonomy, and identity pertain to the Aminas' insurrectionary situation? It is clear from the evidence that the rebels were not engaged in maroonage, (fleeing the plantations for the purpose of setting up permanent and autonomous settlements beyond the reach of the planters' authority).[4] As maroons they would have continued to coexist with the planters' regime. Their aim was a great deal more far-reaching, namely, to overthrow the rule of the planter class and to establish an *oman,* or polity, where the Aminas themselves would exercise an uncontested political suzerainty and social mastery over the island of St. John as a new planter class. In effect, the insurrection amounted to an effort at political revolution: slaves transforming themselves into slaveholders and planters. For the Aminas to attempt to build a new political organization, to imagine the creation of a new system of governance, implies that they were, in fact, drawing on their knowledge and experience of Akwamu statecraft.

The West African background of the Aminas—their socialization and interpellation as subjects of "real" historical relations—was formed in the political, cultural, military, and social milieu of the Akwamu state of the later seventeenth and early eighteenth century. Their social heritage was embedded in a complex history of state-building and diplomacy, urban and class formation, trade and wealth accumulation, and much more. In the insurrectionary actions of the Aminas—in that class struggle over the social relations and the means of production—we may discern the intersection of this heritage with the history of capital accumulation in the Atlantic world.

As the insurgents violently contested the hegemony of the Danish colonial plantation regime with its culture of forced labor, we can "position" them historiographically as subjects in history, as sufferers surely, but also as agents in the historical process. They existed in a milieu in which the unfree were to be created and represented as objects of the actions of dominant others—this domination being the very condition of such representation—but not as conscious subjects and historical beings.[5] This life condition of a commodifying plantation world the Aminas fought against. Their struggle was their *dasein,* or "being there," their "extreme situation," their rejection of the routines and practices of everyday plantation life. C. L. R. James explains the nature of *dasein:*

> Then there comes in the life of every person and every unit something that is called the *dasein*—"being there." At certain times in our lives we are there, in the world as it is, and we face the reality of our existence, and life becomes somewhat different. . . . [E]xistence becomes authentic. We have to come to conclusions, we have to make decisions ourselves, and we live an authentic existence. . . . The *dasein* means that you are involved. . . . An event can be seen properly historically in regard to what is expected to happen and in regard to what has happened in the past.[6]

The actions and decisions of the Amina insurgents were drawn from, and, in a sense, were situated within the remembered framework of Akwamu *oman* culture and an Akwamu social imaginary. The rebellion was an event in the sense described by James: there was a living memory (the past) of a dominant Akwamu sociopolitical system and there was an engaged effort (an expectation) to establish in the West Indies a new political order.

Both the Akwamu polity and the Danish West Indian plantation colonies were part of a larger, formative context: the polycentric world-system. The world-system concept offers a "space" for conceptualizing Akwamu history and the St. John insurrection as elements of a functioning Atlantic-based system structured by alienated forms of social labor, a circulating (merchant) capital, the macro-organization of surplus extraction, and primary capital accumulation.[7] Within this framework, the Akwamu political formation and merchant economy of the seventeenth and early eighteenth centuries can be described as a distinctive, autonomous, and functioning center of extraction/accumulation. It extracted surpluses from politically dependent economies; in turn, it supplied commodified surpluses to other economies: slaves to the Americas and gold and ivory to Europe. By the 1720s it had become, arguably, a "semi-peripheral" zone within the world-system. The Danish Caribbean islands, one of the markets for Akwamu slave exports, were the colonial possessions of the kingdom of Denmark, and were a "peripheral" zone of surplus value production and capital accumulation.

The source materials on the revolt can be divided into two broad categories:[8]

1. the sources generated at the time of the rebellion or shortly after its complete suppression, such as the official records and documents of the Danish West Indies and Guinea Company, and these would include, inter alia, the testimonies of captured Amina rebels;
2. writings by later authors who used the contemporary or near contemporary sources to produce accounts of the re-

volt. Included in this category is a 1975 historical novel about the rebellion entitled *Night of the Silent Drum,* by John L. Anderson.

The novel is based in part on official records and contains the names of a number of the participants in the rebellion (see section III below).[9] This study relies, primarily, on an examination, albeit limited, of the second category of sources.[10]

I

Historians' knowledge of seventeenth- and eighteenth-century Akwamu history owes much to Ivor Wilks's research and studies. In 1957 he published in the *Transactions of the Historical Society of Ghana* a seminal and pioneering essay on the rise of the Akwamu empire between 1650 and 1710.[11] Based largely on the archival records of the Danish, Dutch, and English chartered trading companies, the article constructed, in impressive detail, the late seventeenth- and early eighteenth-century political history of this expansionist polity when it emerged "as a coastal and imperial power" by 1710. Between 1680 and 1730, a period of some fifty years, the Akwamu kingdom dominated an extensive area along the eastern Gold Coast and the western Slave Coast and in the coastal hinterlands of these two areas.

What was the *longue durée* of Akwamu historical and political development? One reading of the normative history of this polity from a recent study offers this perspective:

> In the forest country [of modern Ghana] the earliest centralized kingdom was that of Akwamu. The seeds of the empire were sown in the early sixteenth century and the progress of the empire builders took some two centuries to reach fruition. A major reason for the territorial expansion of Akwamu was the desire to trade directly with the Europeans on the coast and eliminate the coastal people as [middlemen]."[12]

This (functionalist) interpretation attributes the political motivation for territorial expansion to the growing demands of the Atlantic trade. Wilks's study has shown that the Akwamu state represented a radical change in the geographical distribution of political power over a wide area. It also represented a distinctively new kind of polity on the Gold Coast and in Akanland: for example, with respect to its militarized political organization and its commitment to gunpowder warfare and its new apparatus and focus of authority.[13] However, the determining priority, the dominant structuration, was a new mode of organizing the interaction between the caravan-entrepot market of the merchants and the army-battlefield campaigns of the soldiers. The activities of and the resources necessary for warfare (military campaigning and territorial conquest) and commerce (exchange operations and credit transactions) were "combined" at the level of a new and different kind of state administration. The latter constituted a "site" where the relationship between the Atlantic-based world-system and the accumulation strategies of the ruling elite were mediated. The Atlantic trade was not an externality, but was inscribed in political and social relations as a shaping force.[14]

How is this development toward territorial and social expansion to be interpreted? I suggest that the growth of trade within the Atlantic world had the effect of expanding the sphere of commodity circulation (in the form of merchant and money-lending capital) and monetary relations in the Akwamu political economy. We may view the Akwamu "empire-building" process as an activity in the formation of merchant capital and in the reconstitution and reformulation of the means and methods of wealth accumulation. The historical basis for this activity can, perhaps, be located in the formation of a mercantile-military complex; that is, the creation of a sociopolitical alliance, a "power-bloc," of merchants (the caravan-entrepot: *abirempon*) and professional military men (the army of musketeers: *awurafram*).[15] New ways of organizing musketeers as the primary means of destruction, new ways of waging warfare, and the invention of military codes and a particular martial ethos served as strategic resources in the state-building process. The military, a hierarchical, disciplinary organization, was simultaneously a form of ideological training and a means of enrichment. It was an "enabling" institution within a regime of mercantile accumulation. All of this was part of a complex history that in certain respects can be interpreted (to rephrase Michel Foucault) in terms of the accumulation of men and women and of trading, on the one hand, and the creation of a particular kind of disciplinary order, on the other.[16]

The social and political "logic" of the trader-soldier relationship drew upon particular sixteenth- and seventeenth-century structural trends and elements. Under the conditions of expanding trade, local merchant capital within the hinterland of the Great Accra urban/entrepot complex, seeking to restructure and reconstitute the network of its circulation and the basis of its formation, formed an "alliance" with militarism. I propose that there existed a conjuncture between new forms of military organization and tactics and expanded commercial opportunities, as one set of bracketed features, and the concomitant growth of merchant and money-lending capital in new, emergent centers of trade and politics, as another set. The alliance, or power-bloc, was a social and political relationship structured by the circulation of goods, gold, labor, and prestations, on the one hand, and an expanding "monetarized" social milieu on the other. The conjuncture was formative of particular social relationships, established in the course of material reproduction, and personal identities and new kinds of cultural and symbolic "capital." An autonomous power-bloc of merchants and professional soldiers/mercenaries—specialist groups constituted within the economic space and the booming export gold trade of the Great Accra urban/entrepot complex—gradually emerged from positions of political subalternity to positions of dominance and imminence. The power-bloc was, in certain respects, a specific institutional definition of the means of access to the circulation and distribution of social wealth/capital. The alliance of trader and soldier was internal to the social history of Akwamu empire-building and the empire's military and political culture as well as its merchant and social economy.[17]

By the late seventeenth century the empire-building trading-military complex had established its circuit of exchange with the

Caribbean, Europe, and the American mainlands. The European trading stations in the various port towns along the Akwamu-dominated coast linked the Akwamu merchant economy and the larger Atlantic exchange system. The coastal Accra and Adanme middlemen and traders were the essential link between the commercial sector of the Akwamu economy and the mercantilism of the greater Atlantic world. A 1727 Danish report gives a brief description of the transactions within this sector:

> Those who are wholesale traders sell slaves to the Europeans for cowries and other goods, and with these buy slaves far in the interior; the rest of the people and the caboceers gladly buy what they need with cowries and sometimes gold; they purchase spirits, gunpowder, flintlock muskets, tallow, iron knives, flintstones, cotton cloths, [etc.].[18]

The circuit of capital in Akwamu assumed several forms: slaves, currencies (cowries and gold), and processed or manufactured goods. It was mediated by "wholesale traders," the exporter of slaves to the markets of the American plantation regimes. This trade economy was constitutive of the historical habitat of the Amina rebels in their Akwamu milieu.

To deepen its interaction with the factors of the different chartered companies and ships' captains and to consolidate the polity's complex "habitation" of space, late seventeenth- and early eighteenth-century Akwamu rulers attracted to the capital, Nyanaoase, and the royal court a wide range of different, specialized groups—mercantile, military, cultural, artisanal—of diverse social, cultural, and linguistic origins. These gained access to revenue flows, credit facilities, and war booty; they acquired possibilities for long-distance trade and secured employment in the military and the administration.

By the first decade of the eighteenth century the consolidation of state power had constituted and demarcated differing elements in a dense and complex "settlement" of territory on the Gold and Slave Coasts. These ranged from the material organization of production and exchange to the observance of annual ceremonies and daily rituals. The state capital was the privileged site of consumption and ceremonialism. It symbolized the wealth and prosperity of the realm as well as the political and sacral order of the king, his court, and his "grandees." Akwamu was simultaneously a military-political regime, a symbolic-cultural order, and a world of social and material relations. It was well defined by divisions and hierarchies between "things," groups and persons, and practices, and these were given symbolic and "metaphysical" order by dominant "regimes of truth." This, too, was the historical habitat of the Amina insurgents of St. John before their enslavement in the Danish Caribbean.[19]

During the reign of Akwonno (1702–25), the Akwamu state—in particular, the royal court and the households of the king's "grandees"—became heavily involved in money-lending as a matter of royal policy. Associated with its role as creditor, was its role as enforcer of the rights of the creditor. The *sika-den,* a special paramilitary unit and answerable to the king alone, was created to enforce the payment of debts. It could seize persons and/or confiscate property in order to settle outstanding debts, both within Akwamu and beyond its jurisdictional borders. In 1725, a new king (Ansa Kwao, 1725–30) decided to employ the *sika-den* solely within Akwamu "to rob and steal," as one account has it. Persons and property were sold to the European factors for trade goods, especially spirits. In the course of one year, the account continues, the king, his "great men," and his "sika-den" consumed spirits to the value of a couple of thousand people. This description may overstate the effectiveness of the *sika-den;* still, there is no question that the jural and armed intervention of the kingship into money-lending relationships expanded the accumulative possibilities of the ruler, his great men, and his armed retainers, especially during the 1720s.[20]

The surplus appropriation and accumulation strategies proved to be fatally divisive. They constituted a public "terrain" where oppositional ideas, relationships, and an alternative politics could emerge among disgruntled and disaffected urban-based traders, brokers, subordinate officeholders, and others. In 1729–30 the

Akwamu state faced a political and social crisis of unprecedented severity: a succession of uprisings generated by an uncompromising opposition to the political order's judicial and confiscatory practices. In an effort to transform and redress the state's policies and practices and, thereby, to reinscribe and reinterpret its "public sphere," the oppositional forces rebelled. They called themselves *akua apem,* "one thousand [military] companies." After some initial successes, they were put on the defensive by King Ansa Kwao's counteroffensive. However, the insurgents were able to solicit the material support of a powerful neighboring state, Akyem. In 1730 an Akyem army, together with the armies of its confederate allies, invaded Akwamu and completely overran its western and central provinces and districts. The major towns of the Akwamu heartland, including the state capital of Nyanaoase, were sacked.[21] This was a moment of "being there," of "authentic existence" for the *akua apem.* With strong external support, they were able to bring about a successful political revolution. Akwamu, the "sum" of certain historical processes, confronted the "sum" of the political, social, and material processes that brought about its destruction.

II

The defeat of the Akwamu military forces in 1730 and 1731 proved catastrophic for the supporters and adherents of Ansa Kwao's ancien régime. Describing the fate of the vanquished, one report gives this account:

> [After the defeat of Akwamu], the Adampes, Mountain-Blacks, and the Accras took as many as they wanted, and as it was the rainy season many thousands of Aquamboes voluntarily left the "bush" and surrendered themselves to the Accras; one can well imagine what they did with them as long as they could exchange one Aquamboe for a pot of spirits.[22]

A great many of these Akwamu were destined for the West Indies.

In July 1729 the Danish company's vessel, *Haabet Galley,* arrived in the Danish West Indies. Its enslaved "cargo" included 63 men, 45 women, 14 boys, and 4 girls. It is likely that among these persons were rebels against the Akwamu sovereign and, perhaps, debtors who had been seized and, subsequently, sold by the *sika-den.* The 126 slaves probably included Akwamu, Accra, and Adanme, all subjects of Ansa Kwao. Some of them participated in the 1733 uprising. In February 1731 the same vessel landed in the Danish Caribbean with a total of 55 persons: 21 men, 29 women, and 5 boys. All of the males, with the exception of two, were said to be Adanme, former subjects and retainers of a ranking Adanme officeholder. The latter was, perhaps, in Akwamu political service. The two non-Adanme were, very likely, Akwamu, and supporters of the political order. In June 1732 the *Countess of Laurwig* arrived in the Danish Caribbean with 115 slaves. The majority were Akwamu. In May 1733 the *Laarburg Galley* reached St. Thomas with 242 individuals: 124 men, 64 women, 26 boys, and 28 girls. Most of these slaves ended up on St. John. Nearly all were Akwamu. Among them was a man known on St. John as "King June" (*Kong Juni*); he was the main organizer and leader of the uprising. All of the above slaves were purchased at Christiansborg Castle in June 1732, and they probably represented the last-ditch stand of armed Akwamu opposition.[23] In 1732–33 Akyem military forces carried out a series of campaigns against scattered pockets of resistance and sold those captured to the Danes and other European traders.[24]

In 1733 the Danish West Indies comprised three islands: St. Thomas, purchased in 1672, but not developed into a regular plantation colony until 1688; St. John, purchased in 1675; and St. Croix, purchased in 1733.[25] It was not until 1715 that concerted efforts were made to establish plantations on St. John, and these continued throughout the 1720s. This activity depended on regular supplies of slave labor from the Guinea coast. The political revolution of the *akua apem* was, therefore, something of a boon to the St. John economy: it produced hundreds of potential laborers. By 1733 the island had 109 sugar plantations, a dozen or so sugar mills, 208 whites, and 1,087 slaves. St. John lacked towns. It had a small fort called Frederiksfort, or Fortsberg. According to Anderson, the St. John slave population included five princes, at least fifty "lesser noblemen," one princess, and one king. Most were Aminas. Before their defeat by the revolution of the *akua apem,* their careers and social identities had been one with a century-and-a-half-old state-building tradition and political culture. There were at least three maroon small settlements on the island. The maroons were Aminas.[26]

The plantation society into which the Akwamu and other slaves were forcibly delivered was a hierarchical, racialized, patriarchal class society with structured inequalities, exploitative social and material arrangements, and asymmetrical power relations.[27] Its political economy was dominated by structurally alienating commodity-producing relations. The labor force of enslaved men, women, and children were themselves commodities—legal, inventoried property—engaged in the production of commodities and surplus value. With its draconian slave codes and its culture of gallows, whips, and torture, the plantation order was the embodiment of internment and the expropriation of "personhood." The enslaved were inscribed in a world of "self-assured domination and violent repression," but also a world of an always contested and "imperfect" domination. The very fact of the 1733–34 rebellion attests to the existence on the "terrain" of the plantation itself of a separate political "domain" within the enslaved population that planter dominance and authority and the alienating effects of commodity production were unable entirely to eradicate, suppress, or supersede.

A coded system of interacting material and symbolic "spaces" mediated the social relationships among the slaveowners, the slaves, and the "free(d)."[28] These spaces were "overdetermined"; that is, they carried multiple meanings:

1. the "wilderness"/"impenetrable bush," where maroonage prevailed, symbolized disorder and chaos to the planters. This "site" was constituted by the runaways, or maroons, as an adversarial alternative to the plantation;
2. the plantation and its immediate hinterland, where slaves produced wealth/surplus value, were governed by decreed

codes, and here order and culture as defined by the planters prevailed;

3. the fort, the local seat of civil-military administration and the armory, was a symbol of the planters as a burgher militia.

The plantation and its attendant hinterland were the social space organized for the creation of surplus value and the constitution and reproduction of the communities of the enslaved. During the rebellion, it was the site of a fierce social struggle, where the rebels contested the hegemony of the planter class, as they fought to create a new political order on the entire island.

The slave population was not homogeneous: it was distributed across a number of cultural categories and occupational sites. The slaves came from different parts of western Africa; they had different linguistic and political cultures, ideologies, and histories. The slaveowners' discursive practices and systems of nomenclature were ideologically incapable of constructing complex representations of the unfree; they created fixed essentializing identities such as the following:

1. "bussals" (or "bosals"), slaves newly, or recently (i.e., within a year or so), arrived from Africa. A significant number of slaves on St. John were "bussal" slaves, many being employed in the eastern part of the island where, at the outbreak of the rebellion, plantations were still in the process of being established;
2. "creoles," slaves who had been born in the West Indies, or had long resided there. Creole slaves were concentrated in the northern and western parts of St. John; few of them participated in the uprising;
3. "maroons," slaves who had fled the plantations and had established autonomous communities for themselves in the remote and mountainous parts of the island. A maroon community was established on the island of St. Thomas at the end of the seventeenth century. This was the first to appear in the Danish-owned islands. Comparatively few of the St. John maroons joined the insurrection.

Another set of slave identities were linked to occupation and the plantation economy's division of labor: (1) the "royals," or "warehouse blacks," (2) the "house blacks," or household servants, (3) the "craft blacks," or artisans, and (4) the "kamina," or "field blacks." Most "bussals" were to be found in group 4, but some were also in group 1; creoles were, mainly, in groups 1, 2, and 3.[29]

There were other classificatory categories of subalternity: (1) "free man," a landless black who came to the Danish islands from elsewhere but not as a slave; (2) "free black," a manumitted slave who possessed a certificate of freedom; (3) "free slave," a black of local origin who had no certificate of freedom but was not legally the property of another. Hardly any free(d) persons from any of these groups participated in the rebellion. The various ideological categories of slaves and free(d) stood in different relationships to the material and symbolic spaces of the island.

Due to a succession of natural calamities, the year 1733 was one of subsistence crisis for the enslaved population. During the spring and summer there had been a long period of drought (in the 1720s drought had plagued St. John several times) followed in July by a destructive hurricane, that inflicted considerable damage on crops, buildings, and shipping. A plague of insects destroyed a substantial portion of the island's cash crops. Another storm struck in the early fall destroying the maize crop, the slaves' principal staple. The slaves were threatened with, or, in many instances, reduced to, famine and starvation. Indeed, in the long drought of 1725–26 many slaves starved to death and others survived by stealing provisions and committing other offenses against the planter establishment. Owners retaliated against this insubordination by executing seventeen slaves.[30]

In order to forestall disobedience, self-assertion, and rebellion among the slaves during this time of extremity, the governor of the Danish West Indies, Philip Gardelin, issued on 5 September 1733 a slave code (*straffereglement*) with nineteen regulations.[31] The governor, who accepted as an article of faith that God himself had made Africans slaves, was particularly worried about an outbreak of maroonage among the enslaved labor force, and therefore issued the slave code as an administrative means of enforcing the slaves' condition of subordination and their absolute obedience to their owners' authority. The code was to be proclaimed, to the beat of a drum, before the slave population, three times a year. A sampling of the regulations is listed below:

1. leaders of runaways or runaway blacks shall be pinched three times with redhot irons and then hanged;
2. accomplices in a conspiracy shall each lose a leg, unless the owner reduces the sentence to the loss of an ear and 150 lashes;
3. participants in a conspiracy, who fail to report it to a white, shall be branded on the forehead and receive 100 lashes;
4. slaves caught within eight days of having runaway shall receive 150 lashes; slaves caught within twelve weeks shall lose a leg; slaves caught within six months shall lose his life, unless the owner pardons him in which case he is to lose a leg;
5. slaves who receive stolen goods or protect runaways shall be branded on the forehead and receive 150 lashes;
6. The black who raises his hand against a white in anger or threatens him or speaks sharp words to him should without mercy be pinched three times with hot irons and thereafter hanged;
7. when a black meets a white on the road he should move to the side and stand still until the white has passed him, otherwise the white may give him a whipping;
8. when it is proven that a black has intentionally poisoned someone or intends to poison someone, he should be pinched three times with red hot irons, then broken on the wheel.

This hierarchical structure of command, with its objectifying discourse, did not have the desired effect: among many of the "bussals" it generated an oppositional sense of identity. Indeed, near the end of the rebellion one imprisoned insurgent stated that the incentive to revolt was initiated by Gardelin's policy of cutting off a leg of each captured maroon.[32] Here was no shared and unified culture, but accumulated oppression and alienation.

III

On 23 November 1733 the council meeting of the civil authorities of Charlotte Amelia, St. Thomas, was abruptly interrupted when a soldier from Frederiksfort burst into the meeting room and handed the governor a letter. Its contents were read aloud to the council:

> With distress, we wish to inform you that the Company's, Suhm's, Hendriksen's, Soedtmann's, and Peter Krueger's Blacks have seized the fort and killed all of the people together with Soedtmann's, Kint's, and Becker's children, Moth's overseer, Krueger's wife, and also many more. . . . We all are in danger of our lives, for they are drawing much nearer to us. We therefore implore you to send help as soon as possible; and we hope you will not leave us in anxiety; as we are in very great distress.
>
> NB. All of the men who could be assembled are gathered at Durlo's [plantation], where we await your assistance, and we have each killed one of the rebels."[33]

The insurrectionary die had been cast.

One valuable source of information on the early stages of the rebellion, from 23 November to 4 December 1733 is a report by Pierre J. Pannet, a French planter on the island of St. Thomas. He emphasizes that careful planning went into the execution of the rebellion: "The Negroes were meeting at night to plot at their ease, without anyone being able to stop them or to imagine that these meetings would lead to their [that is, the planters'] total ruin."[34] The general scheme was to take the planters completely by surprise, kill them, or drive them from the island, and then take control of it. Practically all of the insurgents were "bussals."

Who were the participants in the rebellion? Oldendorp relates that "the rebels came from the Amina tribe, whose numbers on the island amounted to many hundred."[35] Pannet also recognized that the rebels were mainly Aminas; however, he mentions none by name. The secondary sources either fail to identify any of them or identify only the leadership, usually by the names given to them by their owners. There are two exceptions, however. In his historical novel about the uprising, John Anderson identifies a number of the participants by their African names, and, in a similar vein, the Danish author Thorkild Hansen in his history of the Danish West Indies provides the African names of several of the insurgents.[36] The names of the men included:

1. "Abedo," an "Aquambo nobleman," on the Suhm plantation;
2. "Apinda" (or "Apinty"), a "nobleman," on the Carolina, or Company, plantation (owned by the Danish West Indies and Guinea Company);
3. "Aquashie," a "prince of the Aquambo tribe," on the Adrian plantation;
4. "Asari," or "Asarconssong," the eunuch;
5. "King Bolombo," or "King Claes," a king of the Adampe tribe in Africa, on the Suhm plantation;
6. "Kanta," a lesser nobleman of the Amina tribe, and an assistant foreman on the Carolina plantation;
7. "Odolo";
8. "Quassi" on the Susannaberg plantation;
9. "Quassi" on the Annaberg plantation;
10. "Cotompa";
11. "Asa, medicine man"/"witch doctor" and "kamina" slave on the Carolina plantation;
12. "Kompa," "medicine man"/"witch doctor" and "kamina" on the Carolina, or Company, plantation;
13. "Accra" (or "Acra"), on the Kroeyer plantation;
14. "Adu," on the Soedtmann plantation;
15. "Thiamba" (or "Tjamba"), on the Horn plantation;
16. "Bragatu," on the Carolina, or Company, plantation;
17. "Acubo";
18. "Bomboe";
19. "Sepuse," on the Soedtmann plantation;
20. "Otry" (or "Autria"), on the Suhm plantation;
21. "Coffy" (or "Coffie"), on the Runnels plantation.

The names of the women included:

1. "Breffu," on the Kroeyer plantation;
2. "Judicia, number two wife of Bolombo," on the Castan plantation;
3. "Aquashiba," an "Aquambo princess," on the Bewerhoudtsberg plantation;
4. "Brakka";
5. "Atou";
6. "Bua";
7. "Cuba."

The principal leader of the uprising, "King June," was said to have been a "chief in Africa." He was a "bussal" slave and a foreman on the Soedtmann plantation. Other leading figures in the rebellion included "Kanta," "King Bolombo," "Prince Aquashie," and "Breffu."

Can any of these persons be identified with the many Akwamu and Adanme who are mentioned in the Christiansborg records of the Danish West Indies and Guinea Company from 1710 to 1730? The question cannot be answered with confidence yet. The rebels, especially those described as persons of high status, would have been active in the various spheres of Akwamu social, cultural, and public life at the time. On the basis of the company's documentation, especially the references to Akwamu, Adanme, and other debtors in the debt-books, I attempt some tentative and speculative identifications. The Christiansborg records contain hardly any names of Akwamu or Adanme women, and so it is virtually impossible to assign identities to any of them. A thorough investigation and cross-referencing of the company's Christiansborg and St. Thomas records would certainly provide the evidence required for constructing more substantial and positive profiles of at least some of the rebels' lives in Akwamu than is offered here. Absolutely positive identifications for all of the Amina insurgents is most unlikely no matter how far-reaching the research, but, assuredly, for some of them it is possible to reconstruct their lives in Akwamu with some measure of confidence. The following efforts represent a mere step in that direction.

King June's Akwamu name was Jama (or Jamma). Gardelin, for example, uses both names in his reports on the uprising. Who was Jama (that is, Nyamma)? His name appears with some regularity in the Christiansborg documents of the 1720s.[37] He is always referred to as an important dignitary. The earliest reference to him appears in a 1725 document. There he is described as "the king's servant" (*Kongens Dreng*), that is, he was a member of the royal court. In other documents he is regularly described as a "cabuseer"; that is, an *obirempon,* a designation that indicates that he was a person of rank at the court. As a prominent royal servant, he had several responsibilities: he collected the monthly tribute as well as gifts that the Danish company paid to the Akwamu sovereign; he collected fines whenever the king imposed them on the different tributary coastal towns or the Danish trading stations; he served as the king's trading agent at Christiansborg Castle. He also traded at Christiansborg on his own account. When rebellion broke out in 1729–30, Nyamma commanded a military force of between 1,000 and 2,000 men in defense of Christiansborg. In his role as military commander (of the royal bodyguard?), he was described in one Danish report as one of the king's "most distinguished lieutenants." Presumably, he was an *owurafram* and held a command position in the Akwamu army. Along with his civil duties as a royal revenue-collector and royal commercial agent, he served the king as a military officer. It is possible he was an officer in the *sika-den.*

Were "Asari," or "Asarconssong," the eunuch, and "Assary Amanakung," (Asare Amanako) the same? The latter resided in the Akwamu capital, was the head of the royal hornblowers (presumably the *asokwahene*), and, like Nyamma, was a ranking officer of the royal court.[38] Amanako is never referred to as a eunuch, however. Anderson gives this description of "Asari": "A household slave of one of the Amina noblemen captured by a vengeful Aquambo, Asari was no Amina, but a Malagasy[!]"[39]

The "Malagasy" designation is fanciful. But it is possible that "Asari" was a non-Akwamu attendant, or officer, in the Akwamu royal court, or a retainer in the household of an *obirempon.*

The "Accra" of Kroeyer's plantation may be the "Accra," that is, the *Okra* (a title), who was described in 1729 as one of the Akwamu ruler's servants. In August of that year the *Okra* was seized by Accra rebels and, apparently, was sold later to the Danes.[40] In February 1731 there was a slave named "Accra" aboard a Danish ship that landed at St. Thomas, and this person was to play an important role in the uprising.[41] The assumption is that he was the *Okra.* Like Nyamma and Amanako, he was a royal servant, a courtier, who lived in Nyanaoase. Unlike Nyamma, he was not a "caboceer" nor was he a military officer; he was a slave attendant or page of the king. Nyamma, the *Okra,* and Amanako were members of the king's *gyaase* (household).

"Kompa," who was known as a "medicine man" on St. John, was, perhaps, an *okomfo* (priest) or an *obosomfo* (priest) when he lived in Akwamu. A certain "Quampa" (Okumpa) traded with the Danes at Christiansborg in the early 1720s, but the appropriate records provide no description of his position or general social situation.[42] That "Kompa" of St. John and "Quampa" of Akwamu were the same person is by no means unlikely, but, pending further research, is, for the moment, an open question. Kanta, one of the main leaders of the rebellion, does not appear under that name in the Christiansborg records in the period 1710–30. However, in 1703 there is a single reference to a certain "caboceer Akanta," (Okanta), a powerful, high-ranking (court?) official who seems to have lived in the capital.[43] Whether he is the same Okante who arrived at St. John in 1732 or 1733 is uncertain.

What of "Coffy" (Kofi) of Runnels plantation? The Christiansborg documents contain few references to any Akwamu men of this name. A certain "Ando Cophi" (also referenced as "Andi Coffi," that is, Ando Kofi), is mentioned in the period 1710–30.[44] He lived in the capital, but the references say nothing about his position in the court or state administration. Given the scale of his trade at Christiansborg between 1717 and 1725 it can be assumed that he was a man of means and of political and social weight.

Was "Prince Aquashie" the same as the "great caboceer Quassi Bribrie" (Kwasi Biribiri [or Biri])? In the second and third decades of the eighteenth century Biribiri was one of the senior officeholders (an *owurapon*) in the state organization, perhaps holding the position of *Twafohene.* He was a brother-in-law of King Ansa Kwao and from about 1714 until 1730 he served as the broker of James Fort, a trading station of the Royal African Company in the Accra town of Soko. He was an important and affluent trader as well. In the early months of 1730 he commanded a force comprising five subordinate officers and more than 2,000 musketeers that was dispatched to the coast to subdue the Accra rebels. Following the defeat of Akwamu, he was appointed by the Akyem victors in early 1731 to oversee and manage the resettlement of Akwamu survivors in and around the burned-out ruins of the capital and other destroyed towns. Instead, Biribiri organized, or at least openly assisted, a kind of resistance movement against the new political order. He was captured probably in late 1731, sold to the Danes, and transported aboard the *Countess of Laurwig* to St. Thomas, where he arrived in June 1732.[45]

The slave known as "Abedo" could be the same person as "Abiadu," an Akwamu who lived in the coastal of Kpone in the 1720s. This town was under Akwamu political/administrative control, and Abiadu was probably an official there. "Adu" of Soedtmann's plantation could be the same as the "Adu" who lived in the coastal town of Tema during the 1720s as one of its officials.[46] Like Kpone, Tema was under Akwamu administration. Both Abiadu and Adu traded at Christiansborg, principally in slaves and in 1725 both had outstanding debts at the fort. Abiadu's debt was to be repaid with one woman slave and one adult male slave. Adu had a debt amounting in value to sixty-four *rigsdaler* (or four ounces gold). Adu was very likely the same "Agdo," who is frequently mentioned in a Danish company trade journal for the years 1717 to 1721.[47] He was a major purchaser of merchandise.

"Otry" (or "Autria," that is, Okyere), could have been one of two persons mentioned in a Danish Company debt-book: "Ogri" or "Okre."[48] "Ogri" was described in 1725 as the son of Apem ("Apim"), the Akwamu ruler of Kpone from about 1710 to 1730. He resided in Kpone and in 1725 was in debt to the Danish Company to the value of two adult male slaves. "Okre" apparently lived in or near the capital and not on the coast. In 1725 his debt at Christiansborg was valued at one woman slave. His position is not identified but he might have been one of the court servants.

Anderson states that "King Claes," or "King Bolombo," was the "first-born of the Number One wife of a king of the Adampe nation."[49] There are no references to a "Bolombo" in any of the Christiansborg documents I have seen. Was he the son of the last ruler of an independent La kingdom, which was conquered by Akwamu in 1702? Or was he the son of "Aichu" (Ayeku), the ruler of Togbloku, the main commercial center in the lower Volta river basin and capital of a coastal tributary district, in the period 1710–30?[50] Togbloku was destroyed during the anti-Akwamu revolt, and "Bolombo," who was, perhaps, a loyalist, was captured in the fighting, sold to the Danes, and, subsequently, shipped to the Danish Caribbean in 1732 or early 1733.

Bolombo, Nyamma, and all of the others shared the same life experiences and immediate historical context: the dissolution of an imperial city-state formation and the removal of their identities and roles by this event. Yet, we may suppose, they retained a particular political and cultural vision of the world that was, doubtless, congruent with the social imaginary of Nyanaoase court culture and its state-building tradition.

IV

The first action of the uprising took place at three in the morning on 23 November on the plantation of Mr. Soedtmann, the ranking magistrate on the island. An hour later Frederiksfort was taken by the insurgents. "Then, the rebels, being masters of the fort, raised the flag and sounded the alarm with cannons to draw the planters to the fort in order to lead them into ambushes, which the rebels had laid along the way. However, several were warned by loyal Negroes, who saved them from this treachery."[51] Pannet continues:

> Through the capture of the fort, the massacre of several planters, and the plunder of the houses of those whom terror had forced into flight, the rebels had armed themselves with guns, swords, sabers, gunpowder, and lead, in addition to the cutlasses they had made out of iron hoops, and other weapons made of bills and axes.[52]

Thus armed, the twelve or fourteen rebels, led by the *bombas* (slave foremen), Claes and Kanta, reached the plantation of Peter Durlo on the island's west coast. According to Pannet, twenty-seven whites and twenty blacks "who appeared loyal to them" had sought refuge there. The first phase of the rebellion was going according to plan.

The rebels' initial objective was to seize control of the Suhm, Soedtmann, and the company plantations. These formed a half-circle on the plains facing the fort and Coral Bay. Control of them meant that the fort could be cut off from the rest of the island. While one group of rebels, under the command of King June, remained to hold the fort and to occupy the plantations around it, another group, estimated at three hundred by Pannet (or eighty according to another source), under the command of Kanta and Claes, was to move along the island's north coast, killing all they met and driving the survivors, including slaves who refused to join the uprising, to the Durlo plantation at the western end of the island.

To the planters the firing of the cannon was the general signal that a slave uprising had occurred and, according to prearranged plans, they were to arm themselves, form a militia, and go directly to the fort where they would place themselves under the command of the garrison. To the insurgents the cannon shots were a signal to all the slaves on the island that the revolt had begun. While the planters were on their way to the fort and, unknowingly, into an ambush laid by King June, the main group of rebels went from plantation to plantation, killing the unprotected women and children as well as any slave overseers and planters they could find. Their objective was to gain control of the plantations along the entire northern coast of St. John and then join forces with King June in the western interior of the island. A few maroons and some of the slaves from the plantations that had been attacked joined Claes and Kanta. King June, with a smaller but unspecified number of rebels, traveled westward along the island's principal road, the king's road, seizing all plantations en route; he was to meet Kanta and Claes at the Adrian plantation in the interior of the island. His plan was to have the Aminas occupy the two largest and richest of St. John's plantations, Adrian and Beverhoudtsberg, both of which were located in the western end of the island.

Suhm's plantation, situated due north of Frederiksfort, functioned as the main supply base and political seat of the rebels in the early days of the uprising. "It was there," Pannet reported on the basis of information received from captured insurgents, "lived the king, the queen, and the chief officers they had elected."[53] Unfortunately, he fails to identify any of these persons by name, although it is clear from other sources that King June, or Nyamma, the former royal servant, was made king. Nor does he provide any details about the kind of political arrangements the insurgents were setting in place. The assumption is that they were creating an *oman,* although under the circumstances not a full-fledged one. The uprising had a clear political aim. In an essay published a few years ago Wilks makes a necessary and compelling historiographical point: knowledge of Akan statecraft could survive the infamous Middle Passage.[54] The "instrumentalizing" of this knowledge can be documented in the St. John uprising.

Pannet presents a brief account of the Aminas' political intentions:

> These rebels had plotted to retain the island and they had divided the plantations among themselves, according to the rank and position which each was to hold. The Negroes from other nations were to be provided to them to do their labors and were to belong to them as

> slaves. This is the reason why they preserved all the sugar factories and other buildings.[55]

The infrastructure of the sugar-cotton economy was to be left intact: it was to be the material basis of the new political order. The means of production and slaves were to be possessed by officeholding *abirempon.* Wilful destruction of property was to be strictly avoided. The institution of slavery was to remain the principal means of labor control and surplus (value) appropriation in the new dispensation.

The rebels' plans were not limited to St. John, however. Pannet further reports:

> They had additionally resolved that, after succeeding with the St. Jean [St. John] revolt, they, in concert, with the Amina Negroes of this island [St. Thomas, four and a half miles west of St. John], would have brought about our complete ruin and would have then worked on that of Tortola [less than half a mile from St. John].[56]

The implication is that the St. John Aminas had somehow established contact with the Aminas of St. Thomas and Tortola, and were expecting their active support. Pannet does not say whether the expected support was to come from maroons or plantation slaves, or both. The three islands were to form the territory of the new *obirempon* regime. The rebels "carried" a political tradition and a political culture that had no territorial base. Their project was to reterritorialize them and to realize the political imagination of an earlier generation of *abirempon* and *awurafram,* an imagination that had "tamed" a world. But the Aminas were without the material resources and the backing of a Nyanaoase.

Toward the end of November, Governor Gardelin sent, from St. Thomas, a relief force of between forty-nine and fifty-one soldiers, planters, and creoles: thirty or so were to relieve the siege of the Durlo plantation and the rest were to retake Frederiksfort.[57] The rebels were successfully driven from the plantation, which, then, became the planters' base of operations against the insurgency. The fort was captured by the second relief force, after which it proceeded to attack the Suhm plantation and to drive King June and his officers from it. Nevertheless, other insurgents continued to occupy the surrounding plantations from which they conducted assaults along the northern and eastern coast. These compelled the relief force to abandon the Suhm plantation. Still, by early December, thirty-two of the rebels had been captured. Some, the presumed leaders, were immediately executed; others faced torture and a trial.

Lack of weaponry was an insurmountable obstacle for the insurgents. Already less than two weeks after the outbreak of the uprising there were problems. Pannet indicates what measures the rebels were prepared to take in order to deal with the shortage of ammunition:

> Today, on the 4th of December, 8 prisoners arrived from St. Jean. We learn that the rebels are assembled at Kroyer's [plantation on the eastern end of the island] and are beginning to lack ammunition. They offered to Captain Vessup [a large plantation owner] 10 Negroes for 10 kegs of powder. Two from among those who were present were willing to recognize him as their leader should he be willing to help them, with Robinson, to conquer St. Jean and St. Thomas. They made a good impression and received the Negroes on account and sent them here [to St. Thomas]. A general attack against the said Negroes is planned for tomorrow, if only they can be surprised in their encampment.[58]

The "10 Negroes," who were to have been exchanged for gunpowder, were, no doubt, non-Aminas; presumably, they were slaves, or, possibly free(d) blacks, who had refused to join the rebellion. Vessup never sent the gunpowder; however, the St. Thomas authorities believed the Aminas received muskets and gunpowder from an English planter.[59]

After losing their base at Suhm's plantation, King June, his court, and officers moved their headquarters southeast of Frederiksfort to Bourdeaux's plantation, which was located on the island's highest hill. This happened in late December and early January 1734. Within a short time a small settlement of about twenty to thirty large and small houses was built in a ravine at the foot of the plantation. The sources do not give the name of the settlement, which was, no doubt, to be the Aminas' capital; like Nyanaoase it, too, was "under" (*ase*) a hill. The location provided unobstructed oversight of the fort and its harbor as well as a commanding view of an extensive section of the king's road. In the meantime, the other rebel forces occupied plantations throughout the rest of the island, including the smaller and poorer plantations along the southern coast.

From December 1733 until April 1734 the Aminas effectively ruled St. John, exercising political, social, and institutional power over the island's population. How was the island governed and how were the plantations run? Did the new rulers have to contend with maroons and insubordinate slaves? The secondary sources are generally silent on these matters: for example, they say nothing about the general treatment of slaves on the plantation; nor what the Aminas relations with the maroon communities was; nor which Aminas were placed in charge of which plantations; nor is there anything about the passing of laws and the issuing of decrees. However, it is evident from the sources that the Bourdeaux plantation functioned as the principal center of food and livestock distribution; secondary food distribution centers were maintained at a number of plantations, especially in the northeastern part of the island.[60]

Although the planters of St. Thomas and St. John had at their disposal a well-armed military force of 250–300 men, it did not perform effectively against the rebels. Throughout the month of January the Aminas successfully beat off all Danish attempts to subdue them. In February 1734, they defeated an English militia of sixty men from the island of Tortola and in March they defeated another English force of fifty, this one from St. Kitts. As Westergaard points out, "stratagems, attempts at poisoning, and the armed forces of Danes and English had failed to dislodge or exterminate the desperate slaves." The insurgents' strategy was to occupy and maintain control of the plantations. They were not prepared to retire to the "wilderness" in order to become maroons. The general sentiment among the planters was one of resignation: they were ready to abandon St. John even though there were planters with their families and slaves and a relief force still holding out on the Durlo plantation.[61]

After failing to gain support from the English governor of St. Christopher, Gardelin, in desperation, appealed to the French governor of the island of Martinique for immediate military assistance in a letter dated 21 March:

> No doubt you will have learned of the cruel catastrophe which we have suffered on our island of St. John, caused by a rebellion of our Mina Negros, who, after having massacred 40 of our Whites of both sexes, destroyed and burned all the plantations and sugar works of the said island. I had thought that the planters with the assistance which we furnished them, might have prevailed over these rebels. We caught a few to whom I meted out sentences in conformity with their actions. The rigor which I employed did not intimidate them; to the contrary, their numbers have grown and they appear to be more resolute than ever. In the meantime, Monsieur, our planters, weary from a continued vigil and chase, have become infirm and incapable of serving further. . . . I feel that we are on the verge of some terrible happening unless you have the kindness to honor me with your assistance; I request it, Monsieur, in the name of the King, my master. Not only are you bound to save us because we are allies, friends and neighbors, but also because, as Christians, you cannot allow slaves to triumph over our weakness and to render us victims of their rebellion.[62]

This was sent in early April.

Before the arrival of the French force, forty rebels launched an attack on the Durlo plantation. But after destroying a storehouse, they were forced to retreat with casualties; in the ensuing weeks the Aminas' policy had changed. They resorted to a strategy of attrition, no doubt owing to their debilitating lack of gunpowder, muskets, and musket balls, which made it virtually impossible to secure the plantations against well-armed assaults. In fact, the only arms many of the rebels had in the final weeks of the insurrection were knives and bows and arrows. Plantation buildings and structures and fields were to be destroyed. By the time the St. John *oman* was overthrown, the Aminas had managed to completely or partially destroy no fewer than eighty-five plantations, leaving only thirty undamaged. A field of battle had become a field of ruins.[63] (Some of the plantations might have been destroyed by resentful slaves who opposed the Amina *abirempon* and their adherents.)

On 23 April two French ships carrying between two hundred and three hundred well-armed men—French and Swiss troops and a militia of "mulattoes and free Negroes"—reached Coral Bay. A small Danish force was sent from St. Thomas to join them. Military operations against the Aminas began immediately. The objective was clear-cut: "to exterminate these wretches to the last man." By mid-May the strength of the Amina regime had been broken and Danish planter rule restored. Around 4 May, one group of about eleven Aminas took their lives; another group of some twenty-five (including six women) did the same between 13 and 15 May. By taking their own lives, they avoided torture and gruesome deaths, but maintained their protest. Practically all of the leaders—King June, Kanta, Claes, Breffu, and others—were among those who committed suicide. With the revolt broken, the French ships returned to Martinique on 1 June.[64]

The prevailing opinion among the authorities was that the Amina "not only do not deserve the least bit of mercy, but . . . it is impossible to imagine a torment sufficiently great to be proportionate to their crimes." Thus, captured prisoners had to face the plantation regime's "theater" of torture and pain: some were tried and publicly tortured to death; others were immediately executed after being captured. A small group of about fourteen men and women (and a few children), under the leadership of "Prince Aquashie" (Kwesi Biribiri?), managed to remain at liberty for another two months, but as maroons, not as insurgents who had overthrown the ruling planter class and had established a new form of planter rule in its place. They were promised pardons if they surrendered. They did, whereupon they were quickly transported to St. Thomas where most of them were tortured to death; some were burned at the stake, others were sawed in half, and still others were impaled. "Prince Aquashie" was decapitated right after he surrendered.[65]

Two difficulties seriously affected the course of the rebellion: (1) the lack of firearms and ammunition; (2) the unwillingness of the majority of the slaves on the island to join the revolt. Of the 1,087 slaves on St. John, only ninety to one hundred joined, although some accounts place the number as high as three hundred or even more. One historian states that only about 146 men and women were involved in the rebellion from the beginning to the end, among whom were 35 slaves owned by the Danish company and 28 owned by Suhm, a former governor at Christiansborg Castle. These formed the core of the uprising.[66]

Writing in the second half of the eighteenth century, Oldendorp spells out what the lack of widespread support meant to the possible success of the rebellion:

> Had the spirit of the revolt spread to all the Negroes on the island, it is very possible that not a single white person would have survived. In reality, the rebels were only from the Amina Blacks who numbered several hundred on the island. Most of the creoles, however, remained faithful to their masters and defended them. Many other Negroes were neutral and looked upon the confusion as a favorable opportunity to remedy the extreme scarcity of things, goods and basic commodities, which weighed heavily on them at that time, by taking the provisions of the Whites.[67]

What was to have served as a focus for the political mobilization of both "bussals" and creoles when each had differing historical and cultural "profiles?" Oldendorp offers no clear answer. The slaves shared the same class relationship in terms of their relations of production. However, the "bussal" and creole slaves' social constructions were not the same: in part, because of their different locations in the social-occupational structure and, in part, because of their different social-cultural characteristics. These interactive differences produced uneven ideological effects and unequal social commitments, and the absence of a "spirit of revolt" on the island.

How are we to interpret the uprising and the struggle to establish an Amina political ascendancy on the three Danish islands? It was, manifestly, not a conflict between Copenhagen and

Nyanaoase over political control of territory in the Caribbean. Nor were the Aminas restoring the lost "silences" of earlier generations of unfree labor. They espoused a counterhegemonic political order, not as a desperate "sansculottes" seeking to liberate the enslaved population from its enslavement, but as a dispossessed and unfree political-military aristocracy aiming to establish its own sovereign autonomy. In the end their political revolution failed, but not before achieving mastery over St. John for a period of nearly six months. At least half of the insurgents took their own lives rather than face their enemies. "When I die, I shall return to my own land" was their expression of defiance and challenge. It was their way of "speaking" their own historical *dasein.*

Can we claim November 1733 to June 1734 a heroic yet contradictory moment of struggle and resistance in the African diaspora? In response, one can, perhaps, offer C. L. R. James's modern sensibility on death and history as a way of comprehending the Aminas' struggle and resistance:

> [T]he end of all historicity and temporality is the fact that we will die. . . . It is the one thing that nobody can do for us. We have to die for ourselves. The result is that when we become concerned about the *dasein* and really feel ourselves a part of the world every calculation of ours is concerned with the fact that we are going to be dead, that we have lived a certain life and that we have at last ventured and made an authentic contact with the world as it is.[68]

Notes

1. "Monsieur Gardelin, Governor of the isle of St. Thomas to Monsieur le Marquis de Champigny, Governor General of the French Windward Islands," in *The French Intervention in the St. John Slave Revolt of 1733–34,* trans. and ed. A. P. Caron and A. R. Highfield (Occasional Paper No. 8: Bureau of Libraries, Museums, and Archaeological Services, St. Thomas, USVI, 1981), 26.

2. Ibid., introduction, 8–9 and 51 n. 13.

3. For slave participants in the rebellion see the introduction in P. J. Pannet, *Report on the Execrable Conspiracy Carried Out by the Amina Negroes on the Danish Island of St. Jan in America 1733,* trans. and ed. A. P. Caron and A. R. Highfield (Christiansted, St. Croix, USVI, 1984), 2; T. Hansen, *Slavernes Oeer* (Haslev, Denmark, 1970) chaps. 1–5 passim; J. L. Anderson, *Night of the Silent Drums* (New York, 1975), passim.

4. For maroonage in the Americas and the Danish West Indies see R. Price, ed., *Maroon Societies: Rebel Slave Communities in the Americas,* 2d ed. (Baltimore, 1979); N. A. T. Hall, *Slave Society in the Danish West Indies: St. Thomas, St. John, and St. Croix,* ed. B. W. Higman (Baltimore, 1992), chap. 7. See also J. L. Thornton, *Africa and Africans in the Making of the Atlantic World, 1400–1680* (Cambridge, 1992), chap. 10.

5. For the ideological and social construction of slaves in the Danish Caribbean see Hall, *Slave Society,* chaps. 2 and 3.

6. C. L. R. James, "A New View of West Indian History," *Caribbean Quarterly* 35 (1989): 55–56. James is elaborating on Martin Heidegger's existentialism within the framework of West Indian history.

7. See A. L. Karras and J. R. McNeill, eds., *Atlantic American Societies* (New York, 1992); A. K. Smith, *Creating a World Economy: Merchant Capital, Colonialism, and World Trade, 1400–1825* (Boulder, Colo., 1991); E. Wolf, *Europe and the People Without History* (Berkeley and Los Angeles, 1982); I. Wallerstein, *The Modern World System: Mercantilism and the Consolidation of the European World-Economy 1600–1750,* vol. 2 (New York, 1980); A. G. Frank, *World Accumulation, 1492–1789* (New York, 1978).

8. For this classification of the sources see introduction in Pannet, *Report,* 3–6.

9. One assessment of the novel has this comment: "Although his work is not history in the strictest sense of the word, Anderson has remained surprisingly faithful to the historical sources, which he has evidently studied very close and in great detail"; Pannet, introduction to *Report,* 6.

10. Apart from Pannet's *Report* and *The French Intervention,* the following sources have been used: Hansen, *Slavernes Oeer,* chaps. 1–4; W. Westergaard, *The Danish West Indies Under Company Rule (1671–1754)* (New York, 1917), 167–78; Kay Larsen, *Dansk Vestindien, 1666–1917* (Copenhagen, 1928), chap. 4; J. O. Bro-Joergensen, *Dansk Vestindien indtil 1755 in Vore Gamle Trope-Kolonier,* ed. J. Broensted (Fremad, 1966 repr.), 1:216–37; P. Eilstrup and N. E. Boesgaard, *Fjernt fra Danmark. Billeder fra vore Tropekolonier, Slavehandel og Kinafart* (Copenhagen, 1974), 54–61; C. Degn, *Die Schimmelmanns im Atlantischen Dreieckshandel: Gewinn und Gewisswen* (Neumuenster, 1974), 39–41; G. G. A. Oldendorp, *History of the Mission of the Evangelical Brethren on the Caribbean Islands of St. Thomas, St. Croix, and St. John,* ed. J. J. Bossard, trans. A. R. Highfield and V. Barac (Ann Arbor, 1987), 235–36 (originally published in German in 1777).

11. I. Wilks, "The Rise of the Akwamu Empire, 1650–1710," *Transactions of the Historical Society of Ghana* 3, pt. 2 (1957).

12. J. Anquanda, *Rediscovering Ghana's Past* (London, 1982).

13. See Wilks, "Rise," 127–28; idem, "The Mossi and the Akan States, 1400 to 1800," in *History of West Africa,* 3d ed., ed. J. F. Ade Ajayi and M. Crowder (Harlow, Essex, 1985), 1:492–93; W. Rodney, "The Guinea Coast," in *The Cambridge History of Africa c. 1600-c. 1700,* ed. R. Gray (Cambridge, 1975), 4:301–2.

14. See R. A. Kea, "Administration and Trade in the Akwamu Empire, 1681–1730," in *West African Culture Dynamic: Archaeological and Historical Perspectives,* ed. B. K. Swartz Jr. and R. E. Dumett (The Hague, 1980), 371–92.

15. For the *abirempon* (*obirempon,* "a man of rank or distinction, a king, a hero") and *awurafram* (*owurafram,* "one who knows how to use his weapon") J. Rask, *Ferd til og fra Guinea, 1708–1713* (Oslo, 1969), 60–61, 103 (originally published in Danish in 1754). See also Kea, "Administration," passim; and idem, *Settlements, Trade, and Polities in the Seventeenth Century Gold Coast* (Baltimore, 1982), 69–73, 161–62, 275.

16. See *The Foucault Effect: Studies in Governmentality,* ed. G. Byrchell et al. (Chicago, 1991), esp. M. Foucault, "Governmentality," 87–104.

17. For a historical overview of the sixteenth- and seventeenth-century Gold Coast, see Kea, *Settlements,* passim.

18. *Rigsarkivet,* Copenhagen (hereafter *RA*). *Vestindisk-guineisk Kompagnie, 1671–1755* (hereafter *VgK*). *Breve og Dokumenter fra Guinea, 1722–1731.* To the Directors from H. Suhm et al., Christiansborg, 5 Mar. 1727. Also Kea, "Administration," 373–74, 383–89.

19. For an account of the political and social economies of Akwamu and its "habitation" of space see Kea, *Settlement,* 36, 125, 155, 162; idem, "Administration," *passim.*

20. For the *sika-den* (black gold) see L. F. Roemer, *Tilforladelig Efterretning om Kysten Guinea* (Copenhagen, 1760), 125, 143–44. Roemer does not refer to the *sika-den* as debt collectors. My interpretation of their role is based on *sika-den* debt-collecting practices in the second half of the eighteenth century in former Akwamu provinces.

21. *RA. VgK. Breve og Dokumenter fra Guinea 1722–1731. "Aarsagen og Oprindelse hvorfore vii herved Accra bliver saa opholdt udi Negotien,"* A. Waeroee, Christiansborg, 30 August 1730; and ibid., To the Directors from A. Waeroee, Christiansborg, 24 Dec. 1730; Wilks, "Rise," 130–31.

22. Roemer, *Tilforladelig,* 154.

23. For the various slave shipments to the Danish Caribbean, see Westergaard, *Danish,* 324–25; Anderson, *Night,* 69, 95–107; Hansen, *Slavernes Oeer,* 52–53; Larsen, *Dansk,* 82–83.

24. See, for example, *RA. VgK. Negotie-Journaler fra Guinea,* 1698–1721, 1723–1754, entries for 16, 26, and 30 December 1732.

25. For a recent historical study of the Danish West Indies see Hall, *Slave Society.*

26. Bro-Joergensen, *Dansk,* 217–22; Westergaard, *Danish,* 165–66; Larsen, *Dansk,* 80–81; Anderson, *Night,* 60, 110.

27. See Westergaard, *Danish,* chaps. 6–8.

28. See Oldendorp, *History,* 233–34. Also Degn, *Die Schimmelmanns,* 39; Hall, *Slave Society,* chap. 4; Hansen, *Slavernes Oeer,* 66–74; Larsen, *Dansk,* 81.

29. For slave classificatory categories see Oldendorp, *History,* 219–20, 225–26, 231, 233–34; Hansen, *Slavernes Oeer,* 66–74; Anderson, *Night,* 397; Hall, *Slave Society,* chaps. 4, 5, and 8.

30. Larsen, *Dansk,* 81–82; Westergaard, *Danish,* 164–67.

31. Introduction to *The French Intervention,* 14–15, 17; Westergaard, *Danish,* 166–68; Degn, *Schimmelmanns,* 39–40; Eilstrup and Boesgaard, *Fjernt,* 59; Hansen, *Slavernes Oeer,* 48–51; Hall, *Slave Society,* 56–59.

32. Hansen, *Slavernes Oeer,* 124.

33. Quoted in ibid., 57–58. Also Eilstrup and Boesgaard, *Fjernt,* 60.

34. Pannet, *Report,* 12.

35. Oldendorp, *History,* 235.

36. For the names of the Amina rebels see Hansen, *Slavernes Oeer,* 52–58, 78–139 passim; Anderson, *Night,* 403–5 and passim.

37. *RA. VgK. Forhoers og Domsakter fra Guinea, 1717–46. Kommissionens Forretning og Dom m.v. i Sag mod Kioebmand Christian Syndermann,* 1725–26; ibid., *Negotien-Journaler fra Guinea,* 1698–1721, 1723–1754, various entries for the years 1728–30; ibid., *Gaeldboeger fra Guinea,* 1723–1733, entries under "Aquando/Ensaanquau" and "Ensaanquau"; ibid., *Relationer om Forholdene i Guinea,* 1733–1746. To the Directors from J. Sparre, Copenhagen, 4 Feb. 1734.

38. See, for example, *RA. VgK. Sekretprotokoller, foert paa Christiansborg i Guinea,* 1723–1730. A. Wellemsen et al., Christiansborg, 22 Sept. 1727.

39. Anderson, *Night,* 64.

40. *RA. VgK. Negotien-Journaler fra Guinea,* 1698–1721, 1723–1754, entry for 10 Aug. 1729.

41. Hansen, *Slavernes Oeer,* 124–25; Anderson, *Night,* 71. According to Roemer (*Tilforladelig,* 244), an *okra* was a slave who was destined to die when the king died, "and therefore each of the king's subjects had to respect them and give them whatever they wanted." See also the Rev. H. N. Riis, *Grammatical Outline and Vocabulary of the Oji-Language* (Basel, 1854) 206.

42. See, for example, *RA. VgK. Breve og Dokumenter fra Guinea,* 1705–1722. *Specification paa hvad panter, guld, etc. som ved aabninge befandis i Mons. Peder Oestrups skriv schatol, kister, etc.,* David Herrn et al., Christiansborg, 28 Feb. 1722.

43. *RA. VgK. Dag-Journaler, foert paa Christiansborg,* 1698–1705, entry for 10 Nov. 1703.

44. See, for example, *RA. VgK. Breve og Dokumenter vedk.skifte og afregning efter afdoede kompagnitjenere i Guinea. Underretning om de Sortes Gield i Guinea vedkommende den indkomme extract af afgangne Knud RTostes Gieldbog;* ibid., *Gaeldboeger fra Guinea,* 1723–1733. Entries under *Ando Cophi udi Quambue.*

45. *RA. VgK. Breve og Dokumenter fra Guinea,* 1722–1731. *Aarsagen og Oprindelse hvorfore vii herved Accra bliver saa opholdt udi Negotien,* A Waeroee, Christiansborg, 30 Aug. 1730; ibid. *Relationer om Forholdene i Guinea,* 1733–1748. To the Directors from J. Sparre, Copenhagen, 4 Feb. 1734; *Algemeen Rijksarchief,* The Hague. *Archief der Nederlandsche Bezittingen ter Kust van Guinea* 97. Letter from J. de la Plange and Blittersdorp, Accra, 16 Nov. 1730; Kea, "Administration," 388; A. K. Quarcoo, "Museum Report," *Research Review* 2 (University of Ghana, Institute of African Studies, 1966): 51.

46. For Adu and Abiadu see, for example, *RA. VgK. Forhoers og Domsakter fra Guinea,* 1717–1746. *Kommissions Forretning og Dom m.v. i Sag mod Kioebmand Christian Syndermann,* 1725–1726; ibid. *Gaeldboeger fra Guinea,* 1723–1733, entry under "Christian Pettersen."

47. *RA. VgK. Negotie-Journaler fra Guinea,* 1698–1721, 1723–1754, various entries for the years 1717–21.

48. For these two persons see *RA. VgK. Gaeldboeger fra Guinea,* 1723–1733, entries under "Christian Pettersen."

49. Anderson, *Night,* 61.

50. For the 1702 Akwamu conquest of the La kingdom see Wilks, "Rise," 124–25. For "Aichu" of Togbloku see, for example, *RA. VgK. Gaeldboeger fra Guinea,* 1723–1733, entries under *Aichu udi Tuberkue.* See also ibid., *Relationer om Forholdene i Guinea,* 1733–1748. To the Directors from J. Sparre, Copenhagen, 4 Feb. 1734.

51. Pannet, *Report,* 12–13. Also Oldendorp, *History,* 235–36; Larsen, *Dansk,* 86; Bro-Joergensen, *Dansk,* 229–30.

52. Pannet, *Report,* 14.

53. Ibid., 17.

54. I. Wilks, "The State of the Akan and the Akan States: A Discursion," *Cahiers d'études africaines* 22 (1982): 243 and note 6.

55. Pannet, *Report,* 17.

56. Ibid.

57. Larsen, *Dansk,* 86–88; Bro-Joergensen, *Dansk,* 231–32.

58. Pannet, *Report,* 18. Also Larsen, *Dansk,* 88–89; Bro-Joergensen, *Dansk,* 232.

59. Bro-Joergensen, *Dansk,* 232.

60. For the Aminas' food supply centers see Hansen, *Slavernes Oeer,* 124. For their settlement see "Longueville to the Minister," 21 June 1734 in *The French Intervention,* 41, and Hansen, *Slavernes Oeer,* 115, 120–21.

61. Westergaard, *Danish,* 171–72; Larsen, *Dansk,* 89; Bro-Joergensen, *Dansk,* 232. Also Hansen, *Slavernes Oeer,* chap. 4 passim.

62. "Monsieur Gardelin, Governor of the isle of St. Thomas to Monsieur le Marquis de Champigny, Governor General of the French Windward Islands, St. Thomas, the 21st of March 1734," in *The French Intervention,* 26. See also Bro-Joergensen, *Dansk,* 232–33 and Anderson, *Night,* 362–75.

63. Westergaard, *Danish,* 177; Larsen, *Dansk,* 90–91, 92; Bro-Joergensen, *Dansk,* 233–34.

64. For the French defeat of the Aminas see *The French Intervention,* 27–49. Also Westergaard, *Danish,* 174–77; Larsen, *Dansk,* 91–92; Bro-Joergensen, *Dansk,* 234.

65. Westergaard, *Danish,* 176; Anderson, *Night,* 380–84.

66. Pannet, *Report,* 14; Oldendorp, *History,* 235; introduction to Pannet, *Report,* 2; Westergaard, *Danish,* 176; Bro-Joergensen, *Dansk,* 230.

67. Oldendorp, *History,* 235.

68. James, "A New," 56.

Early Asante: Is Wilks Right? PETER SHINNIE

I first met Ivor Wilks in 1958 when, as the newly arrived head of the Department of Archaeology at what was then the University College of Ghana, I went to Tamale for the Easter School of the Extra-Mural Department. I then realized that I was in the presence of a potentially distinguished scholar who needed only an appropriate academic position to make important contributions to historical studies. Shortly after, as director of the then very new Institute of African Studies I was able to get a research professorship for him and thus vicariously to play an important part in the furtherance of research into Ghana's history.

Much of Wilks's research has been concerned with the history of Asante and he is one of the very few who has tried to probe further back than the period in the late seventeenth century when the written records begin. Two important papers of his illuminate that period, which we might call the proto-historic, just before the formation of the Asante state when the Akan people were creating centers of permanent occupation in the forest area of Amansie and Adanse.[1] These papers make a very important contribution to the discussion of the origins of Asante and of agriculture in the forest, which Wilks rightly considers to be the formative factor in the development of settled life in the area: the formation of the matriclans, *mmusua,* and ultimately the Asante state.

Basing his argument largely on the number of generations between known historical figures and the supposed founding ancestresses of the matriclans reflected in the traditional stories, which are remarkably consistent and show four or five generations, he calculates the beginnings of settled life and agriculture to have taken place in the fifteenth century. The arguments presented are excellent and the reasoning is hard to fault even if those who have looked at agricultural origins in a wider context would have expected this important event in human history to have happened somewhat earlier.

Before written history it is only the traditional oral history and archaeology that can throw light on these rather murky corners of human development. The Asante oral histories are very difficult to use and the vagueness as to how they were collected makes it difficult to know how reliable the stories are. Henige has already pointed out some of the problems relating to the Asante stool histories and implies that no great reliance can be placed on them. As he says: "the entire fabric of early African history becomes suspect."[2] This may be too harsh a verdict for the Asante material, but it certainly suggests that much more care needs to be taken in interpreting the results.

One of the major weaknesses in the collecting of these texts is that almost none of them are available in the vernacular. It is a cardinal principle of scholarship that texts should be available in the original language; for example, no serious student of ancient Egyptian history would attempt to carry out research into the history and culture of ancient Egypt without a knowledge of the language even if he or she has access to excellent translations. Similarly, not to have the original Twi texts for Asante historical traditions is a disadvantage that I hope will be overcome in the material that I have assembled during the course of archaeological research.

Until the last few years very little archaeological work has been done in the forest regions of Ghana. For several years Oliver Davies toured the country making surface collections and writing notes that were published a few years ago by the Department of Archaeology of the University of Ghana; these notes are an excellent resource for anyone wanting a general survey of what can be found in Asante by surface collecting. The lack of archaeological investigation in the supposed homeland of the Asante has been a severe handicap, and what has been done has suffered from not being able to provide a chronology.

Now a new project that started in 1986 may throw light on the problem and provide some closer dating than has been previously possible and make it possible to look at the suggestions made by Wilks. This project, organized from the University of Calgary and financed by the Social Sciences and Humanities Research Council of Canada with help from the National Geographic Society, the Earthwatch Foundation, and the Asante Development Fund has had as its main aim an investigation of early Asante by archaeological means.

The project started by excavating for three seasons (1986, 1987, and 1989–91) at Asantemanso, considered in many Asante traditions to be the place of origin of the Asante people from where the ancestors of at least the Oyoko and Aduana *mmusua* came out of a hole in the ground. The place of this hole is still known and libations are poured to it on ceremonial occasions. As with so many traditions there are other contradictory ones: Adanse, further south, is also claimed to have been the original home of the Asante; and some versions say that Ankyewa Nyame, the ancestress of the Oyoko came from the sky, sometimes on a golden chain, at a place called Asiakwa before moving to Asantemanso. There are other variants. In spite of this Asantemanso is frequently referred to as an important and sacred site closely associated with the origins of Asante and the place from which they moved to Kwaman (later to be known as Kumase). How far back this tradition goes we cannot say, but Rattray in 1923 visited the site and says of it, "the site which the Ashanti [*sic*] perhaps hold to be the most hallowed spot in all their territory." The first European mention seems to be in 1831–32; a Dutch document reads, "where in former days Kumase krom (town) stood, according to the reports of the Asantes."[3]

There is no doubt of its sacred and historic character today; the sacred forest, described by Rattray, is still preserved and policed and the inhabitants of the now small hamlet are well aware of its historical importance. The queen-mother of Asantemanso, whose mother was the earlier queen-mother whom Rattray met, has a special place in the Asante hierarchy and is one of the few who have the privilege of standing in front of the Asantehene still wearing her sandals.

Survey and excavation at Asantemanso for the three seasons produced results that indicate earlier settlement in the forest than Wilks has suggested. Some of these results must be tentative until there has been further research on the materials, predominantly ceramic, but information already available suggests strongly that there was permanent settlement at Asantemanso as early as the last few centuries B.C. There is a considerable range of dates suggesting that the site has been occupied from its early beginning to the present day. The area in which evidence of human settlement has been found is considerably larger than that now occupied by the hamlet and it is possible to make a rough assessment of how the main focus of the settlement has changed at various periods (Fig. 1).

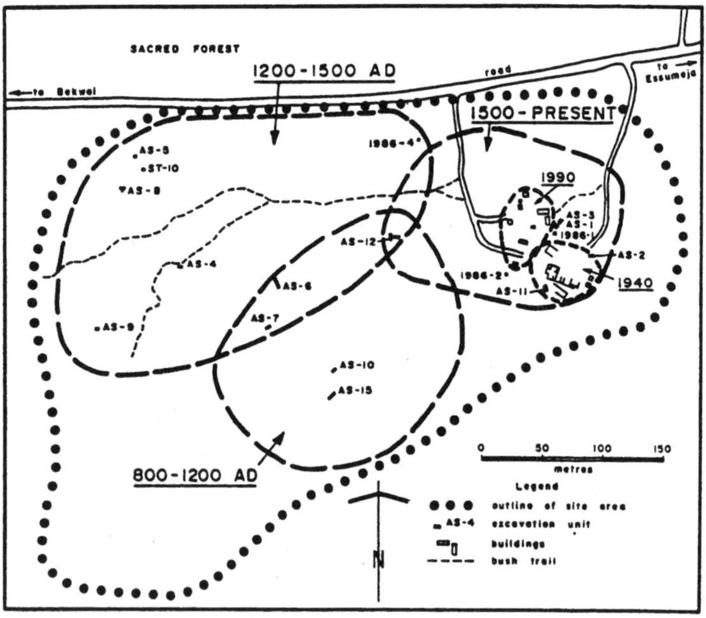

Fig. 1.—Asantemanso settlement locations.

The chronology is based, for periods prior to the appearance of tobacco pipes and European imports (ceramic and glass) entirely on radiocarbon dates derived from charcoal and are at present mainly available only in uncalibrated form. Archaeologists are well aware of the problems associated with using such dates, particularly when only a few have been obtained, but the number now available for Asantemanso and their internal consistency as well as the appearance of datable European imports in parts of the site where carbon dates are congruent suggests that a reasonable reliance may be placed on them. There may well be some aberrant dates and the normal way in which such dates are published (the laboratories give the results in years before an artificial present—actually 1950—indicated by the letters B.P.) is based on one standard deviation by which there are two chances in three that the date falls within the published range; what is often forgotten is that there is a one in three chance that it falls outside that range. This is why it is rash to use single dates from archaeological sites to draw far reaching conclusions. The non-archaeologist reader should note that bp;bc;ad are normally used for noncalibrated dates whilst B.P.;B.C.;A.D. are used when the dates are calibrated (that is adjusted for known aberrations) and assumed to be more accurate. The dates published here converted to uncalibrated bc/ad dates are listed in chronological order from earliest to latest. It should be borne in mind that the dates are derived from samples in various parts of the site and from different levels in the excavated trenches.

Although not calibrated for the period covered they give a reasonable indication of the date of the level and show clearly that there was occupation from before c. A.D. 1000; the earliest date (Beta-39075) of 4,160 +/− 60 bc is believed to be aberrant, but the excavators see no reason to dismiss the other early dates. There is strong evidence for occupation through the thirteenth to fifteenth centuries, and this continued through to the present day.

The implication of a largish town by as early as about A.D. 1200 (perhaps considerably earlier) with a population of a few thousand suggests that Wilks's date for the beginning of settled life in the forest is too late. What we cannot as yet say, and evidence for this remains elusive, is whether or not this was an agricultural society. A settlement of this size certainly implies a fixed population and from worldwide observation strongly suggests agriculture as the predominant mode of subsistence. What crops—in the absence of the now widespread New World cultigens—were grown is not yet known and evidence will be hard to find. We can suppose yams and plantains dominated. Other evidence for settled life is to be found in traces of iron production; no furnaces have been found, but slag is present from about A.D. 1000 or a bit earlier.

This is not the place to go into a detailed description of the archaeology of Asantemanso; suffice it to say that there is clear evidence, in the presence of artifacts, of human occupation for a long period, of a settlement large enough to have had a population of several thousand, and for a shift in the main area of occupation at different periods. Unfortunately the archaeological remains do not make it possible to say very much about the life or culture of the early inhabitants. It is difficult to find evidence for buildings since the normal building material, almost certainly of wattle and daub, would not leave any traces (though some evidence for floors has been found).

The story of Asantemanso has to be read mainly from its pottery and of this there is plenty, most of it still awaiting detailed study. What can be said at this stage is that two distinct pottery traditions can be defined; the earlier one usually, though not very happily, known as "Earthworks" pottery since it has been found in the region of the Birim valley earthworks where it was studied and discussed by Kiyaga-Mulindwa.[4]

"Earthworks" pottery has now been found in a number of places. It was first identified by Wild who associated it with what he called the "Nyame Akuma" people.[5] The fullest discussion is to be found in Bellis.[6] The work at Asantemanso confirms the opinion of earlier workers that this distinctive and easily identifiable pottery precedes in date what I call, for want of a better name "proto-Akan," the "Atweafo" pottery of Kiyaga-Mulindwa.

Precision in the dating of the change of pottery styles must wait for further study of the Asantemanso material, but it may be suggested that about the beginning of the eleventh century there was a considerable change in pottery styles.

What the evidence does not tell us is what caused this change. Was it merely a fashion change with the same people continuing a settled life in the forest? Or does it mark a more fundamental change with arrival of a new ethnic, and possibly linguistic, population? Nothing available at present can tell us this but it is tempting to think that there may have been Guan speakers in the forest before the coming of the Akan and that they were the makers of the "Earthworks" pottery. No potsherd can tell us what language its maker spoke, and it would be unwise to push this suggestion too far. However, such a marked change in pottery style suggests more than just a change in fashion, and the widespread evidence for the "Earthworks" pottery from Twifo Heman to the Birim valley and Amansie makes it clear that, whoever the people associated with it, they inhabited the central Ghana forest in the area where subsequently the main Akan states arose.

This essay has considered the views on the beginning of Asante proposed in the Wilks papers and to see to what extent archaeological work can help elucidate the important issue of the origin of Asante. Though the evidence from Asantemanso strongly implies an earlier date than that proposed by Wilks, there is nothing to suggest that the mechanism by which agriculture and the subsequent political and social developments of the proto-Asante was other than that which he proposes in his important papers.[7]

Table 1
ASANTEMANSO DATES

Laboratory Number	Uncalibrated Date
Beta-39075	4160 ± 60 bc
Gd-5804	530 ± 60 bc
Gd-5801	490 ± 60 bc
Beta-17652	ad 260 ± 110

Table 1
ASANTEMANSO DATES Continued

Laboratory Number	Uncalibrated Date
Beta-25573	ad 660 ± 80
Beta-25081	ad 880 ± 80
Beta-17648	ad 930 ± 130
Beta-25574	ad 970 ± 80
Beta-39071	ad 1040 ± 80
Beta-17651	ad 1100 ± 110
Gd-5806	ad 1140 ± 80
Beta-17647	ad 1220 ± 100
Beta-17649	ad 1230 ± 60
Gd-5807	ad 1240 ± 80
Beta-25092	ad 1250 ± 80
Beta-25088	ad 1250 ± 80
Beta-25087	ad 1260 ± 80
Beta-17650	ad 1270 ± 100
Beta-25090	ad 1280 ± 80
Beta-39072	ad 1280 ± 80
Gd-6331	ad 1310 ± 80
Beta-39070	ad 1320 ± 80
Beta-25084	ad 1350 ± 80
Gd-5803	ad 1360 ± 50
Beta-25567	ad 1370 ± 80
Beta-25089	ad 1400 ± 80
Beta-39073	ad 1420 ± 90
Beta-25086	ad 1450 ± 80
Gd-5802	ad 1477 ± 40
Gd-5800	ad 1480 ± 50
Gd-5806	ad 1510 ± 80
Gd-6327	ad 1530 ± 70
Beta-39076	ad 1540 ± 50
Gd-6326	ad 1540 ± 80
Gd-6327	ad 1540 ± 80
Beta-25572	ad 1550 ± 80

Table 1
ASANTEMANSO DATES Continued

Laboratory Number	Uncalibrated Date
Beta-25569	ad 1550 ± 80
Beta-17646	ad 1550 ± 100
Beta-25085	ad 1640 ± 80
Gd-5805	ad 1650 ± 50
Beta-25568	ad 1670 ± 80
Beta-25571	ad 1670 ± 80
Gd-6328	ad 1710 ± 70
Beta-25091	ad 1720 ± 80
Beta-25082	ad 1740 ± 80
Beta-25570	ad 1740 ± 80
Beta-25083	ad 1760 ± 80
Gd-4644	Modern
Gd-6329	Modern

Notes

1. Ivor Wilks, "Land, Labour, Capital and the Forest Kingdom of Asante: A Model of Early Change," in *The Evolution of Social Systems,* ed. J. Friedman and M. J. Rowlands (London, 1977); idem, "The State of the Akan and the Akan States: A Discursion," *Cahiers d'études africaines* 22, pts. 3–4 (1982): 231–49.

2. D. Henige, *Oral Historiography* (New York, 1985), 123–24.

3. Wilks, "Land, Labour," 509.

4. D. Kiyaga-Mulindwa, "The Earthworks of the Birim Valley, southern Ghana" (Ph.D. diss., Johns Hopkins University, 1979).

5. R. P. Wild, "The Pottery of the Nyame Akuma People. Part I," *Teachers' Journal* (Gold Coast) 9, no. 2 (1937): 94–99; "The Pottery of the Nyame Akuma People. Part II," *Teachers' Journal* (Gold Coast), 9, no. 3 (1937): 43–48; "The Pottery of the Nyame Akuma People. Part III," *Teachers' Journal* (Gold Coast), 10, no. 3 (1938): 249–55.

6. J. O. Bellis, "A Late Archaeological Horizon in Ghana: Proto-Akan or Pre-Akan?" in *The Golden Stool: Studies of the Asante Center and Periphery,* ed. E. Schildkrout (New York, 1987).

7. Wilks addresses some of the issues raised by Professor Shinnie in his "'Slavery and Akan Origins?' A Reply," *Ethnohistory* 41, no. 4 (1994): 657–65. *Eds.*

"It's mine" and "It's ours" Are Not the Same Thing: Changing Economic Relations between Spouses in Asante

VICTORIA B. TASHJIAN

Introduction

This essay[1] explores how economic changes taking place in Asante around the turn of the twentieth century affected the economic relationship between wives and husbands, and more particularly the way in which these changes affected the economic importance of conjugal labor. This period was characterized by the rapid expansion of cash cropping and, more generally, a significantly expanded monetization of the rural Asante economy. As a consequence of these events, both the value and the meaning of conjugally based labor—that is, labor performed jointly by husbands and wives, and any dependent children—changed quite dramatically. With this change in the significance of conjugal labor came a change as well in the meaning of the independent, individual ownership of property typical of marriage in matrilineal societies.

To backtrack just a bit, in marriage in matrilineal societies, property is generally owned by one spouse or the other, instead of being jointly owned by both. That is, any resources may be the property of the husband, or the property of the wife, but they are never jointly owned by the couple as a single conjugal unit. This circumstance derives in part from the fact that in matrilineal societies inheritance, like descent, is traced through the maternal line, and since marriage is exogamous—individuals must marry someone who is a member of a matrilineage other than their own—spouses can never inherit from each other. The assumption then follows that since spouses will not benefit from each other's toil, they should keep their resources separate.[2]

It is important to highlight a distinction that does not always emerge clearly from the many pronouncements that property is not jointly owned in these marriages: separate, individual ownership of property does not mean that considerable sharing of resources, of labor or money, does not occur between spouses. Indeed, in Asante, assistance to the enterprise of a spouse is common. One instance of such assistance is found in the primacy in Asante, at least from the eighteenth century, of conjugally based labor, that is, labor performed jointly by husbands and wives. This tended to flow from the wife to the husband: in Asante marriage, husbands have an unquestioned right to the labor of their wives, and they call on this right freely. Mingling of spousal resources also occurred when the money of one spouse was used to help develop the property of the other. This second common form of assistance was one that, in contrast to labor, more frequently traveled from husband to wife than vice versa.

The separate ownership of property generally found in marriages in matrilineal societies, then, does not imply complete economic independence in marriage; separate ownership of property does not mean a complete void of assistance, in the form of labor or money, from one spouse to the other. Rather, separate ownership means that any such assistance is recognized as assistance to an enterprise that is wholly owned by another, and that one's input of labor or money will not change this fact. This point is significant because only the owner of property is entitled to the profits it generates.

It is when these two practices—separate ownership of property within marriage, and sharing of spousal resources in marriage—are combined in a more fully monetized rural economy that the potential for conflict emerges. Unless husbands and wives contribute equally to the development of each other's newly valuable property (and in such a way that the assistance does not result in a transfer of ownership from one spouse to the other) one will not be fully compensated for his or her input of labor or money, since the income from a property accrues only to its legal owner. If unequal resource contribution occurs, there is then something of an economic contradication in marriage: individual ownership of property exists alongside the unequal use of joint conjugal resources.

An intensification of this contradiction is, in fact, what happened in Asante from the second decade of this century. The long-standing right of Asante husbands to the labor of their wives must be stressed, for this was a practice that caused conjugal labor to be disproportionately directed to the property of husbands. This was not particularly problematic in a subsistence economy, so far as can be determined from the incomplete historical record for precolonial rural Asante and from the statements of Asante who were born in the early twentieth century, before the advent of widespread cash cropping. But it did create increasingly unequal financial rewards for husbands and wives in a more fully monetized economy. These inequalities heightened as opportunities for working in the cash economy broadened, for men did not hesitate to make increased demands upon the labor of their wives. Cash cropping, and particularly the cultivation of cocoa, is not the only variable to consider (though it is perhaps the most thoroughly studied sector of the modern Ghanaian economy): income-generating opportunities also arose wholly separate from agriculture. Before examining the effect of twentieth-century economic developments on a husband's right to his wife's labor, I shall first consider this right in historical perspective.

Historical Overview of Conjugal Labor

The existence of conjugal labor from at least the eighteenth century is widely confirmed, and while data on the rural Asante economy before the twentieth century is limited, conjugal labor then seems to have been directed mostly to subsistence-level agricultural production. In a discussion of Asante farming practices before the changes wrought by rural capitalism, predating even the nineteenth century, Wilks notes that husbands and wives typically worked together, and even that male farmers most often sought labor assistance from their wives' relatives rather than from their own lineage. LaTorre, in his study of the eighteenth- and nineteenth-century Asante economy, concurs that the nuclear family was the standard work unit for cultivating food crops, while Arhin's article on the nineteenth-century Asante peasantry points out that conjugal labor was the norm and that, in direct contrast, "there was no matrilineally organized working group." Rattray identifies the ideology justifying conjugal labor; namely, that in marriage men had an undisputed right to the labor of their wives.[3] Without question, Asante spouses have long given each other significant assistance in food cropping, in spite of separate ownership of property in marriage.

The point made by Wilks, LaTorre, and Arhin, that conjugal and not kin-based labor had long been usual in Asante subsistence agricultural production, was seconded by Asante themselves, who said that in the first and second decades of the twentieth century, conjugally based agricultural production was the norm.[4] In the early years of this century, before the widespread commoditization of agriculture, what conjugal labor meant in practice was that spouses gave each other mutual assistance in cultivating their food farms. In the majority of marriages, men and women both had plots of family land on which they grew the staple root crops, plantains, and vegetables that formed the base of the Asante diet. Women had their food farms located on their family property, men had theirs on their family property, and spouses helped each other farm. (People tended to marry within their village, making this arrangement possible.) As one man who farmed with his wife on both his own and on her family land explained: "We grew cocoyam, plantain, it was later that cassava came on. . . . We didn't share the farms [that is, ownership of the farms' harvests] because if I went to the farm and there were foodstuffs and I got them, it was the whole children who enjoyed it, and when she also went and she got something, we all enjoyed it."[5] Since both spouses consumed produce from each other's farms, and also used jointly cultivated foodstuffs to help ensure a steady supply of food for dependent children, conjugal labor was mutually beneficial and simply made good practical sense. As another person said, "In the olden days, if the wife worked with the husband, they only worked and enjoyed what came out of it. . . . Each helped the other to farm on his or her land."[6]

A very practical reason for joint labor on food farms also existed, and derived from the nature of farming in the semi-deciduous rain forests of central Asante. Farming in tropical forests requires shifting plot cultivation because of the rapid depletion of soil nutrients that occurs when land is cleared and farmed. In Asante, cleared plots are cultivated for an average of one to three years before being fallowed for a minimum of five years, and usually considerably longer, while secondary growth reappears and the soil regenerates.[7] The need to let farmed land lie fallow, as well as the practice of starting new farms each year so as to have farms in various stages of cultivation at all times, requires new plots of land to be cleared for agricultural use on an annual basis. This is no mean task given the extraordinarily dense growth of tropical forests: Wilks has estimated the sheer weight of flora per acre of land at 500 tons for virgin forest and at forty tons for previously cultivated land that has been undisturbed for the average fallow of fifteen years.[8]

In terms of conjugal labor, the significance of rotating plot agriculture lies in that Asante of both sexes uniformly maintained that clearing virgin forest, as well as secondary growth on long-fallow land, was a task that could only be performed by men.[9] One woman described clearing virgin forest:

> The women were not weeding. It was the men who did the weeding, and the women did the sowing. . . . Some of the trees that we felled, if you stood behind it and raised your hand, they could not even recognize you. . . . Women could not weed by themselves, like the tree I was talking about. . . . If weeds develop on the ground the woman couldn't weed.[10]

Since clearing either virgin or long-fallow land was an annual task that women did not perform, women perforce had to have a man's assistance in this crucial stage of farming. And since the basic work unit was conjugal and not matrilineal, the man who cleared a married woman's land was her husband.

The fact of widespread conjugal labor in no way mandated the existence of jointly owned property, and indeed separate ownership of food farms by both spouses was maintained. But the preeminence of conjugal labor in subsistence agriculture does raise the question of why separate ownership of property in marriage existed.[11] The answer is found in Asante's practice of matrilineal inheritance, which meant that spouses would never inherit from each other. The inevitability of all marriages ending through either divorce or death was the major impetus for independent farm ownership, for as one informant pointed out: "Anything could happen in marriage. There could be divorce, so when we decided to cultivate on our family lots, both of them, and there happened to be a divorce, none could be a loser . . . when you have yours and there is divorce you won't be worried."[12] Given the frequency of divorce in Asante, as in most matrilineal societies, this was no inconsequential consideration.

Jointly produced but individually owned food farms, then, were the general extent of conjugal labor in rural Asante during the earliest years of the twentieth century and, so far as the sketchy precolonial record indicates, for the eighteenth and nineteenth centuries too. While producing a reliable source of foodstuffs was obviously important, nonetheless the economic significance of this conjugal labor was limited. If divorce came, as it frequently did, division of the property was a nonissue, since each spouse had benefited equally from the conjugal labor, and since each spouse retained possession of those of the farms located on his or her own family land. Additionally, the food farms they had created together were of limited value: first, the crops were produced primarily for consumption and not sale, and so did not have a significant monetary value. Second, the farms were of value over a limited period of time only, for the nature of tropical forest agriculture, with shifting plot cultivation, meant any particular farm was productive for a period of only one to three years before being fallowed. The massive expansion of cash cropping and the commoditization of a far broader range of goods that accelerated in Asante from the 1920s, however, brought about major changes in the significance of conjugal labor, both in agriculture and in the nonagricultural fields to which conjugal labor was rapidly applied. For as the value of labor increased exponentially, so did men demand an ever-larger portion of their wives' labor power, yet women did not share in the profits in a proportion commensurate to their labor inputs. I shall first discuss the effect of cocoa cultivation on conjugal labor, and then examine conjugal labor in a marriage in which the husband worked as a tailor.

Conjugal Labor and Cash Cropping

Cocoa was Asante's main cash crop, and one important aspect of cocoa cultivation was the need to travel in order to obtain land on which it could be grown, for all of the suitable lands in central Asante rapidly came under cultivation. With this travel, the balance and significance of conjugal labor changed dramatically. Spouses no longer resided in a village where both had access to family land, land on which they produced foodstuffs to which each alone held indisputable rights. Instead, the couple traveled to vacant land far afield and, once there, in the vast majority of instances only the husband obtained rights to land. In theory, both husband and wife could have gained access to separate plots of individually owned land (this was accomplished by paying an annual fee to the local ruler) and thus reproduced village property-holding patterns. In practice, however, this was not done, and overwhelmingly the husband was the only one who obtained use rights to land. This resulted in farms that belonged to him and him alone, but on which both he and his wife labored.

In this setting where both spouses did not retain rights to land, the right of a husband to his wife's labor took on entirely new meanings. The balance of conjugal labor described above—mutual assistance on each other's farms—did not here exist, and was instead replaced by a unidirectional flow of labor from wives to their husbands' farms. No longer was the woman's contribution reciprocated by her husband's labor on her farms, for she no longer owned any farms in the vicinity on which he might provide assistance.

Travel to a husband's distant cocoa farms also meant that a woman was unlikely to continue any income-generating activities of her own; cocoa cultivation is highly labor-intensive in its early stages and allows little time for other activities. Husbands had little compunction in demanding that wives direct their energies only to the needs of the young cocoa farms, and didn't hesitate to withhold trading money from their wives to pressure them into laboring on the farms.

Why did women, who could divorce easily, agree to this generally unfavorable change in their economic status? Most important, women generally wanted to be married while they were of childbearing age, and if a woman refused to accompany her husband to his farms, he was very likely to divorce her, since marriage conferred on him the right to her labor.[13] So even though women almost uniformly stated that it was good to have their own income-generating activity—a preference generally incompatible with accompanying a husband to his distant cocoa farms—if they wanted to remain married they had to accompany their husbands to these farms.

The priority given to the man's enterprise was clearly expressed by one woman who was asked whether she preferred farming on her own or her husband's land. She replied:

> It didn't happen that way, that we should make a choice as to whose land we would farm on first. If it happened that the man was insisting that I accompany him to his farm, and I also insisted that he accompany me to my farm, I would have forgone my farm and accompanied him to his. I would have since he is the man, and he takes care of you, even though [there is the saying that] "'It's mine' and 'it's ours' are not the same thing." I have to heed to what he says. Whether you like it or not, that was all that you were left with.[14]

If she didn't agree, divorce was likely to follow, as one man described: "All the wives helped me on the farms. I made farms for the first two wives and the third wife wanted to go and farm [for herself] at a certain place, but I would not agree, because I was still working on my farms, so we divorced. I wanted her to come and work on my farms. The first two wives understood me better."[15] In other words, an understanding wife was one who adhered to the expectation that she would contribute her labor power to her husband's enterprises, and the cost to a woman of choosing to work on her own property could well be divorce.

It is important to note, as the above quotation suggests, that women could and sometimes did choose divorce in preference to laboring on a spouse's farm; the ability of Asante women to divorce with few social, psychic, or material costs stood them in good stead. But more frequently, especially during the childbearing years, they would agree to work on their spouses' farms. It is also important to add that after menopause, women frequently divorced and at this stage became cocoa farm owners in their own right. But that is a different story.

The effects of this new pattern of conjugal farming were numerous and profound. First, unlike the case with conjugally produced food farms, the cocoa farms created through a couple's joint labor were not entities from which both necessarily derived benefits, for only the owner of a property had a right to its fruits. Thus, a woman had no incontrovertible right to even a share of her husband's cocoa farm or its profits. Additionally, cocoa farms were valuable in ways that food farms were not: cocoa was a cash crop, produced for the market, which had a monetary value, in marked contrast to the foodstuffs grown primarily for personal use. Also, cocoa farms were productive for many years more than were food farms, creating a long-term financial interest in these conjugally produced properties that simply had not been at stake with food farms. This led to obvious problems in the case of divorce: leaving a husband now meant a woman was walking away from properties of considerably greater value, and also properties of value over a substantially longer period of time, than had been the case with food farms.

Whether or to what extent women would be compensated for diverting their labor to their husbands' farms, then, became a major issue. Though the expectation was that women would be given a share of conjugally developed farms, husbands were under no absolute, enforceable obligation to share them out. As many people said, whether or not he did so was left to the man's discretion, a point phrased as follows: "They were doing whatever they pleased then. They were not compelled. It was dependent on the goodwill of the man." Or, "You will help him and when he likes, he gives you some. . . . If he loves you, he will give you some." And one man added, "in our time you gave the wife according to how you felt."[16] In other words, his responsibility to share the property was so nebulous as to be unenforceable.

Court records bore out men's limited responsibility in this regard, for the courts frowned heavily upon women's outright claims to ownership of any part of these farms, and invariably rejected any such ownership demand. Instead, they preferred to receive from female plaintiffs a more respectfully phrased request for a share of jointly produced farms. In stark contrast to conjugal foodstuff production, then, where each party had the right to the produce of his or her own farms, the proceeds of cocoa farms were the husband's property alone. I should add that this is in complete keeping with Asante principles of land tenure, and with Asante principles of property ownership: whoever owns the use rights to a property also owns the right to its profits. The point is, this system of property rights created conflicts once there was an increase in conjugal labor directed to the valuable property of one spouse alone.

Even when a man did agree to share any jointly produced farms with his wife, the question of what proportion of the farms would become hers remained. People uniformly said that a wife should be given one-third of the acreage though, as indicated above, both spouses had to give their full attention to the farm in its early years. It is interesting to note that the one-third share of the farm universally said to be due wives corresponds in ratio exactly to the one-third share of a harvest that was the normal compensation of the caretakers who actually plucked and harvested many cocoa farms, and who worked on a sharecropping basis. In terms of compensation, it seems that women were regarded, in essence, as the functional equivalents of overseers or caretakers on their husbands' farms. While the annual right of sharecroppers to a third of the yearly harvest differs in magnitude from the wholesale alienation of a third of a farm's acreage to a wife, there is a connection between these ideas of what constituted appropriate reimbursement. For, in each case the proper ratio of return was one-third of the entity that the laborer, sharecropper or wife, had helped to create. It is probable that as the use of unfree labor—pawns and slaves—declined, men relied increasingly upon the labor of both sharecroppers and wives, and remunerated them at parallel rates of return.

In any case, a woman's right to the one-third share was ambiguous and not easily enforced. In actuality, frequently a wife received a smaller share or nothing at all, for several factors influenced a woman's ability to affect her generally recognized right to a share of the farms. Cocoa did not produce a harvestable crop for a minimum of two to three years after being sown, and farms generally were not divided before they had matured to this stage. If a woman divorced her husband before this time, then, she received no share. Also, even in the absence of divorce, if the transfer of ownership was not completed before a husband died, his heirs were unlikely to honor his intention, and her share would never be realized.

There is no doubt that women were concerned about the uncertainty of the returns they would receive for labor expended upon a husband's cocoa farms. One woman, who had worked with her first husband on his farms, only to realize almost nothing in return, balked when asked by her second husband to accompany him to his farms. She said:

> I declined to accompany him. . . . I didn't want to go because of what I had experienced with the first man. If someone had cheated me before the first husband, I wouldn't have gone with the first husband, but it was because the first one cheated me, that was why I was reluctant to go with the second one. Once I have been cheated by an earlier marriage and divorced, if I happen to marry again and the

> husband wants to make farms with me, I will inquire, and if I sense cheating that will come from the man, I wouldn't go; I would rather divorce.[17]

This was all new terrain for women, for cash cropping on the farms of a husband created problems that simply had not existed with the conjugal farming on both spouses' farms that had been the previous norm. The sense, as in the instance just quoted, that women learned through bitter experience was expressed time and again. Another woman told me, "My father didn't give my mother anything but she had worked with him greatly. . . . It was after that that my mother thought of getting her own land."[18] As women became more familiar with the possible pitfalls of migrant cocoa farming on a husband's farms, increasingly they sought to protect themselves before committing to such work.

Even when women did agree to work on their husbands' cocoa farms, if after some time they sensed that they would not be adequately compensated for their labor, they might then opt for divorce. This option was superior to no remedy, for such a woman could then put her labor to her own enterprises. It was not a course of action that led to any compensation for the time and effort she had already put into a husband's cocoa farms, however; men were highly unlikely to give a share to a wife who was divorcing them. Thus, a woman's power lay only in her ability to remove herself and her labor power from her husband's control, and accept a loss for however many years she had labored for him without recompense.

Some men were not unwilling to exploit the fact that if their wives divorced them, even the tenuous obligation to give some portion, no matter how small, of jointly produced farms was no longer in force. Consequently, at the time when he would otherwise give a share of the farms to his wife (at the earliest, farms were shared out when the trees matured and bore fruit) husbands might behave in ways likely to encourage wives to leave them, as one woman described: "Maybe the time has come for you to give her some. Intentionally you decide to go for another woman so that it will anger her to leave. Some people will think of that and not leave. It is very frustrating and some women grow lean out of their brooding."[19] There could not be a more obvious difference between this situation and the description of divorce in the days before widespread cash cropping, for as was said of divorce when couples were only jointly working each other's food farms: "when we decided to cultivate on our family lots, both of them, and there happened to be a divorce, none could be a loser . . . when you have yours and there is divorce you won't be worried."[20] With cash cropping, divorce was no longer a circumstance in which "you won't be worried"; instead, divorce resulted in women who "grow lean out of their brooding." Given the frequency of divorce in Asante, this was far from an unimportant switch.

People recognized most directly the connection between cocoa and this change in the significance of divorce. One person said:

> Before cocoa [people] were farming, cultivating cassava, plantain and others, so they were helping their husbands still. They did it on a subsistence basis. Nobody would buy it if you decided to sell. . . . In those days when they cultivated foodstuffs and they ate the fruits of it, and the man decided to divorce her, each went his or her way. But when she helps him to cultivate cocoa farms, and she doesn't get anything out of it, then it means she has done a useless job.[21]

Without question, the ramifications of farming using conjugal labor changed profoundly with the switch from the production for use of food crops to the production for the market of the valuable cash crop cocoa.

Conjugal Labor and the Commoditization of Goods

Cash cropping was not the only offshoot of the economic changes occurring around the turn of this century; the movement to a more fully monetized economy also involved commoditizing a broad range of goods that then had to be produced and marketed. This development, like cocoa, affected the financial relationship between spouses. As with cocoa, one of the effects was the diversion of women's labor to their husbands' income-generating activities. This is illustrated by the case of a woman whose husband was a tailor, relying on his wife to help sell the clothing he produced. Before she married him she had been making clay pots, the income from which was her own, but after their marriage, she said, "He didn't allow me to make pots. [Instead], when he sewed uniforms, I took them around selling them. I went round the villages." She added that the money realized from the sale of the uniforms was his: "I gave him the money, all of it."[22] As with cocoa farming, her labor was shifted from her own enterprise to his, and her input of labor to her husband's work was not directly compensated.

Also as with cocoa, the commoditization of goods led to an increase in travel. Indeed, traveling to sell goods was a necessary part of most small-scale productive enterprises, for people involved in certain occupations, including specialists in skilled crafts, had little choice but either to relocate permanently in larger towns or cities, or to work as itinerant artisans visiting numerous small villages; the demand for their craft in any single rural village was simply insufficient to support them. For example, tailors found larger markets in Kumase; as the woman married to a tailor explained, Nkwanta, where they lived, "was a village, and people were not patronizing it, so he decided to take it to Kumase." She also described how relocating could be seasonal in nature: "We went around all the time to villages and at Christmas we would have gone to a village and be sewing. We were sojourning."[23] The increase in travel for trading purposes meant that women frequently were forced to leave behind whatever business activities they were independently engaged in, the profits of which had been theirs alone.

Conclusion

The issue highlighted here—the changed meaning of conjugal labor with, first, the growth of cash cropping and, second, the heightened commoditization of goods—is only one of many offshoots stemming from the changes affecting the economic world in which rural Asante moved in the early twentieth century, when opportunities to engage in agricultural production for the market and small-scale trade expanded. Factors affecting the ability of women and men to exploit the new economic opportunities range far beyond those identified here, but space does not allow me to do more than briefly mention them. One important variable in taking advantage of new economic opportunities was the ability to travel at will; yet women, and more particularly married women, faced unique constraints on their mobility, both because of their responsibility to provide domestic services in marriage, and more generally because of limitations placed upon all women's independent freedom of movement. Access to capital was a second important variable; here again men were in a more favorable position than were women, partly for the reason outlined above, that is, male rights to conjugal labor (which could result in a cash income) but also in part because of the differential in women's and men's average age of first marriage, which made it more difficult for a woman to build up capital for investment in various endeavors (she had no prolonged period of single adulthood in which to do this). That women lacked access to capital was reflected in the many observations that "it is men who have money." Third, men took on new responsibilities in marriage, or revised forms of older responsibilities, which could only be met in the cash economy. These financial obligations included providing larger amounts of chop money to wives, providing seed capital for petty trading to wives, and paying for their children's formal education. Not surprisingly, men did not feel that marriage represented an economic windfall, and as one man rather sourly observed of men's financial obligations in marriage, "Normally how much would a wife give to a husband? It is men who are stupid [and] who give their money to the wives."[24] But these are all matters for another discussion.

This essay has focused on the allocation of labor in marriage, an allocation that took place in marriages in which individual and not conjugal ownership of property remained the norm even in a time of greatly increased reliance upon conjugal labor, even in a system that gave men alone unfettered access to conjugal labor. This focus on conjugal labor gives a view of only one aspect of marriage finances; as a general rule, it was the case that men more frequently provided assistance to a spouse's enterprises in the form of money, and women more frequently provided assistance in the form of labor. With this caution, it can be said that in the narrow sphere of conjugal labor, informed as it was by the right of husbands to the labor of their wives, there is little doubt that the increase in production for the market more often represented a benefit to husbands than to wives. Rattray, who was in Asante in the early twentieth century just before the takeoff of cocoa farming, noted the right husbands had to the labor of their wives, but said of it, "such a right . . . in reality amounts only to the mutual assistance that persons living together and sharing a common menage would naturally accord to each other."[25] Without question, this reality changed with a more highly monetized rural economy: wives became, in essence, unpaid laborers for their husbands.

Notes

1. This essay, a draft of which was presented at the African Studies Association 1992 Annual Meeting in Seattle, Washington, is based on research conducted in Oyoko, Mamponten, and Kumase, Ghana, during 1990. The research was funded by grants from the John D. and Catherine T. MacArthur Foundation, the Graduate School of Northwestern University, and the Program on International Cooperation in Africa of Northwestern University's Program of African Studies. Far above and beyond the financial support of these institutions, I am deeply indebted to Ivor Wilks, whose unfailing encouragement and profound knowledge of Asante have made possible my nascent career as a scholar of Asante. This essay is presented to him with great gratitude and affection.

2. The Asante custom of separate property ownership in marriage is documented as far back as the turn of the nineteenth century, for Bowdich, who visited Asante in 1817, wrote that "the property of the wife is distinct, and independent of the husband." T. Edward Bowdich, *Mission from Cape Coast Castle to Ashantee* (London, 1819), 260.

3. Ivor Wilks, "Land, Labour, Capital and the Forest Kingdom of Asante: A Model of Early Change," in *The Evolution of Social Systems,* ed. J. Friedman and M. J. Rowlands (London, 1977), 492; Joseph R. LaTorre, "Wealth Surpasses Everything: An Economic History of Asante, 1750–1874" (Ph.D. diss., University of California–Berkeley, 1978), 29; Kwame Arhin, "Peasants in 19th-century

Asante," *Current Anthropology* 24, no. 4 (1983), 472; R. S. Rattray, *Ashanti Law and Constitution* (London, 1929), 25.

4. Two pieces of evidence for a sort of matrilineal work unit (other than the common grouping of maternal uncle and nieces and nephews) did come to light and are worth brief mention. First, young, unmarried women often traveled and worked with their older brothers. Second, there were a number of instances of brothers migrating en masse to farm in Brong Ahafo. The brothers all took their wives with them, however, and the work unit remained the nuclear family. These two examples of sibling migrations are perhaps the closest thing to a matrilineal work unit within one generation to exist, tempered though they are by, in the first example, their transitory nature and, in the second, a continued reliance on conjugal labor. They are really less evidence for a matrilineally based labor force than for a preference, when sojourning, to have members of the matrilineage in close proximity. Of course, outside of marriage relatives could work together, and in adolescence a young man frequently moved from working on his father's farm to that of his uncle (which he could inherit), while daughters might work with mothers (from whom they inherited). But while married, farming with one's spouse was most usual.

5. Interview 61, pp. 1–3, Kwame Asamoa, 9 Nov. 1990, Oyoko, Ghana.

6. Interview 54, p. 7, Efua Dufie, 31 Oct. 1990, Oyoko, Ghana.

7. Wilks, "Land, Labour, Capital," 492; LaTorre, "Wealth," 29–30. Wilks points out that the length of use before fallowing depends in part upon the crop being cultivated, as some but not all species can be harvested for more than one year. LaTorre and Wilks both make the point that the length of time a plot is allowed to lie fallow is affected not only by the amount of time necessary to restore the soil's fertility, but also by the degree of population pressure on the land. LaTorre adds that fertilizing with manure is not possible in Asante since the prevalence of trypanosomiasis in the rain forest makes large-scale animal husbandry impossible, though Wilks (citing the nineteenth-century traveler Dupuis) indicates that wood ash was used as a fertilizer. Wilks, "Land, Labour, Capital," 497.

8. Wilks, "Land, Labour, Capital," 501.

9. Sarpong notes that the responsibility men hold for clearing land is symbolically recognized at a male infant's naming ceremony. As part of the ceremony a cutlass is placed into the infant's hand, because "he is supposed to be able to clear the forest and cut down huge trees . . . hard work which alone will enable him to sustain his family." Conversely, at her naming an infant girl has a basket placed over her, since women bear responsibility for gathering and cooking foodstuffs. The Rt. Rev. Dr. Peter Sarpong, *Ghana in Retrospect: Some Aspects of Ghanaian Culture* (Tema, 1974), 91.

10. Interview 55, p. 3, Efua Fosuwa, 1 Nov. 1990, Oyoko, Ghana.

11. Turning this question on its head, one can ask too why, in a matrilineal society with matrilineal inheritance and separate ownership of property in marriage, conjugal and not kin-based labor ever became common practice.

12. Interview 51, p. 1, Akosua Nyantakyiwa, 24 Oct. 1990, Oyoko, Ghana.

13. The reasons for preferring marriage primarily involved a preference for

childbearing in marriage, and a belief in a spiritual protection women received from men via marriage.

14. Interview 12, p. 3, Akua Kyere, 8 Aug. 1990, Mamponten, Ghana.

15. Interview 5, p. 2, Opanin Kwabena Twetwe, 25 July 1990, Mamponten, Ghana.

16. Interview 55, p. 6; Interview 49, p. 4, Ama Akyaa, 23 Oct. 1990, Oyoko, Ghana; Interview 58, p. 2, Kofi Anto, 6 Nov. 1990, Oyoko, Ghana.

17. Interview 56, p. 5, Abena Kwa, 2 Nov. 1990, Oyoko, Ghana; Interview 63, p. 1, Abena Kwa, no. 2, 12 Nov. 1990, Oyoko, Ghana.

18. Interview 55, p. 6.

19. Interview 31, p. 4, Adwowa Fodwo, 1 Oct. 1990, Mamponten, Ghana.

20. Interview 51, p. 1.

21. Interview 49, p. 4–5.

22. Interview 57, p. 3, Aduaa Yaa Ama, 5 Nov. 1990, Mamponten, Ghana.

23. Ibid., 3–5.

24. Interview 46, p. 5, Barima Tawia, no. 2, 16 Oct. 1990, Mamponten, Ghana.

25. Rattray, *Ashanti Law,* 25–26.

Slavery and the State in Asante History

LARRY W. YARAK

I

While the major contribution of the work of Ivor Wilks is often considered to be his study of the politics and institutions of the nineteenth-century Asante state, best represented by his widely acclaimed *Asante in the Nineteenth Century,*[1] I have found myself increasingly drawn to his more recent analyses of the origins of the broader social, economic, and political order created by the Akan-speaking peoples of the West African forest. In particular, I regard his extended essay "Land, Labour, Capital and the Forest Kingdom of Asante"[2] as a work of the greatest importance. At once a specialized study of Akan environmental, social, and political history, this essay also makes a signal contribution to the general question of the origins of the state, a major theme in modern African historiography. It shows Wilks's analytical skills at their sharpest, weaving together the often thin strands of evidence for early Akan history to form an impressive tapestry, rather modestly termed a "model of early change." The analysis convinces less by means of an overwhelming deployment of oral and written sources—in the way that *Asante in the Nineteenth Century* does, for example—than by linking seemingly unrelated analyses derived from published studies of the Akan forest environment, agrarian systems, and social structure with fragmentary but highly suggestive references from Akan oral traditions and archives of diverse European provenance. A companion essay, narrower in scope, but equally important for understanding the origins of the underlying structures of the Akan political order, appeared several years later under the title "The State of the Akan and the Akan States."[3]

There are two key ideas that underlie these closely related works to which I draw special attention here. The first is Wilks's explicit rejection of a social evolutionary interpretation, such as that offered by R. S. Rattray, of the origins of the Akan sociopolitical order.[4] In "State of the Akan," Wilks describes his view as the "'big bang' theory of the origins of Akan society" (234), and this phrase conveys the idea perfectly. Wilks argues convincingly for the utter novelty of the Akan agrarian and political order that emerged in the forest during the fifteenth and sixteenth centuries: "Akan society, as it is known from the historic period, came into existence as a result of a change in the mode of production which involved a transformation in the economic base, a reorganization of the social relations of production, and the appearance of new political structures" (234).

The second point I highlight is the central role Wilks's analysis assigns to Akan involvement in the developing regional and ultimately global economy of the fifteenth and sixteenth centuries. As he shows, the crucial aspect of that involvement was the Akan export of gold, which ultimately found its way into the developing world economy, and the Akan importation of slaves from the West African regional economy. Slaves were employed most crucially in the labor-intensive task of clearing the forest for farming. Their assimilation into Akan society was facilitated by the development of the matriclan system of social organization, and on this socioeconomic base the rudiments of a hierarchical political order were established. Wilks's analysis thus clearly demonstrates the indispensability of a "world-time" framework for the reconstruction of early Akan history. Such a global perspective has in fact been characteristic of Wilks's work since the beginning of his career, and received its earliest general exposure in two influential articles published in 1961 and 1962 in the *Journal of African History*.[5]

These two ideas—an anti-evolutionary perspective and reference to the global system—I have found to be of the utmost utility as I have examined the literature regarding the significance of slavery in the Akan, and especially the Asante, political economy of the eighteenth and nineteenth centuries.[6] The study of precolonial African slavery has of course generated a substantial and at times disputatious literature. On the one hand, there has recently appeared a spate of general studies, such as those of Lovejoy and Manning,[7] which attempt to chart the rise and fall of African systems of slavery and the slave trade from a more or less continental perspective. On the other hand, there are a considerable number of narrower studies of individual African slave systems, most influential among which has been the collection edited by Miers and Kopytoff.[8] Strangely missing from this latter literature has been any extended study of Akan precolonial slavery, based on recent oral investigations among Ghanaian informants and the voluminous archival record.[9] An important exception is the work of Emmanuel Terray, whose studies of the Abron state of Gyaman, located on the margin of the Akan world, constitute a starting point for any serious analysis of Akan slavery. But it remains to be seen whether Terray's analysis of the sociopolitical order that arose in Gyaman has general applicability to the study of the Akan societies of the forest heartland. More important, can Terray's model bear careful scrutiny in the context of Wilks's view of the "big bang" origins of the Akan forest order, and does it make sense when viewed from a global history perspective, such as pervades Wilks's work?

2

It is difficult to do justice to the richness of Terray's analysis in a brief study such as this. His work explores the origins and nature of Abron society with a theoretical and empirical sophistication that arguably has no equal in Akan studies; for this reason it has rightly attracted wide attention. Here I focus only on Terray's general characterization of the precolonial Abron political economy, an analysis he feels is also valid for other Akan states such as Asante. In a pair of articles published in English in 1974 and 1975[10] Terray argues for the coexistence of two modes of production within the Abron social formation, a lineage and a slave mode of production; adopting an Althusserian mode of analysis,[11] he further argues that the slave mode was dominant. The slave mode of production was dominant because the social formation was organized around the need to reproduce the servile relations that maintained the supremacy of the Abron aristocracy:

> in Ashanti as in Gyaman, the earth was plentifully available; the instruments of production were made of materials—wood, iron—that could be obtained directly, easily or by exchange, and their simplicity meant the vast majority of people could make them themselves; also, the subjection of the producer was not able to be accomplished through the appropriation of the material factors of production, as was the case under feudalism with the ground, and in capitalism with machines. Consequently the establishment of bonds of direct personal dependence was the chief means of expanding control over men, and so of access to wealth. Now slavery and captivity were the most effective and rigorous forms of these bonds of personal dependence; that is why the functioning of the entire social formation was organised around them.[12]

The lineage mode of production prevailed in the free commoner villages, which were principally Kulango (hence ethnically distinct from the dominant Abron) and which nominally served the Abron state. Master-slave relations predominated between the Abron ruling class and the captives, whose labor provided for the subsistence needs of the aristocracy, transported its goods in long-distance trade, and produced the gold it used to purchase luxury goods and fresh slaves for its labor needs. Relations between the Abron and the Kulango—between the state and the free peasant producers—were those of taxation, but Terray hastens to point out that the tribute extracted from the free primary producers was "relatively light."[13] For him the defining feature of Abron society was the central role of servile relations in structuring the entire social formation:

> a mode of production is dominant within a social formation when it subjects the functioning of the other modes of production represented in this social formation to the requirements of its own reproduction. . . . [Thus] the functioning of dominated modes of production is modified and deformed by the action of the dominant mode

> of production. But conversely, the subordination of dominated modes of production to the requirements of the dominant mode in turn transforms the functioning of the latter.[14]

Despite this dynamic model of interaction between two modes of production, with one in a position of dominance, Terray takes pains in "Classes and Class Consciousness" to de-emphasize the significance of direct interaction between the Abron state and the (largely Kulango) free peasantry. "Abron hegemony," he writes, "had no consequences as far as the control and distribution of land are concerned" (114). Another important form of state intervention is taxation; that is, levies of goods or labor imposed by the state on primary producers. Terray stresses the "lightness" of such taxation in Gyaman. Taxes of a material nature were largely symbolic; the peasants' obligatory military service he terms "military assistance," as peasant soldiers shared in the spoils of victory. Consequently, he describes the relationship between the Abron state and Kulango peasants as one of "relatively peaceful . . . coexistence"; indeed, he writes, throughout most of the nineteenth century, "the Kulango bore Abron hegemony without too much difficulty" (119). Abron domination was thus merely "formal" in nature, and Kulango relations of production "remained unchanged" (120). The lineage mode of production in fact appears hardly affected at all by the Abron state.

The primary reason for this, Terray continues, lay in the Abron need to ensure Kulango "assistance" in war. War was the major means by which the Abron could obtain fresh inputs of captive labor, and overburdensome material exactions by the state might threaten the peasants' willingness to fight (126). Fresh infusions of captives were needed in turn because captives' descendents were constantly being assimilated to an economic status indistinguishable from that of free peasants. The Abron were powerless to prevent such generational assimilation, with the consequent severance of relations of servitude, because of the profound weakness of the state: its lack of a standing army and of elaborated institutions of political domination (127). Terray's analysis thus presents us with a paradox: while logically coherent, it counterintuitively assigns a place of "dominance" in the social formation to a mode of production (slavery) whose own functioning was constrained by the operation of the lineage over which it is supposedly dominant. Terray's evidence rather demonstrates the relative weakness of the Abron aristocracy as a class vis-à-vis free peasant producers and captives in the process of assimilation. One could perhaps argue more convincingly that peasant and slave resistance to the exactions of the Abron state and aristocracy played the truly "dominant" role in structuring the broad configuration of social relations in Gyaman.

It may be asked why Terray chose to construe the relationship between the lineage and slave modes of production in Gyaman as one of the dominance of the latter over the former. A partial answer is suggested by Terray's citation at the beginning of his 1974 article of the comments of Engels on the question of the origin of the state. Like Engels,[15] Terray seems to view the origin of the state as an essentially evolutionary question: since the state appears only with the development of exploitation to the point that economic classes could become "classes-for-themselves," the question really is, How did such class divisions emerge in a society originally organized by kin- and gender-based relations of production (where exploitation did not lead to the formation of "classes-for-themselves")? For Terray, "only a development internal to the productive forces . . . for example, through the introduction of slavery" could create the conditions necessary for the rise of the state.[16] Terray's analysis of the Abron social formation thus seems to have been shaped fundamentally by a desire to show how a true class society, and therefore the state, could evolve in what was pristinely a society dominated by the lineage mode of production. For Terray, as for Engels, slavery was the original, primitive form of class society, and its "introduction" gave rise to the state.[17] Surprisingly, this is a perspective similar to that developed by the non-Marxist anthropologist Rattray; as I noted above, Wilks's recent work has sought to refute such an interpretation, at least for the forest heartland of the Akan.[18] If Wilks is correct in rejecting on empirical grounds an evolutionary approach to the origins of the Akan state—in asserting the "big bang" origins of Akan sociopolitical order—then it would seem unnecessary to posit, as Terray does, a dominant slave mode of production in Gyaman in order to explain the origins of the state. An alternative model of a precapitalist class society could do just as well in analyzing the character of class domination in such a society, and it might provide a more useful tool of analysis in discerning the inherent contradictions of that society, its internal "laws of motion." I shall return to this matter below.

I have attempted so far to criticize Terray's argument on its own terms. In an essay published in 1979 Dumett subjected elements of Terray's analysis to a very different kind of critique.[19] This criticism subsequently elicited an interesting rebuttal from Terray.[20] Dumett's principal purpose was not to examine the general question of slavery among the Akan, but rather to focus more narrowly on the character of precolonial Akan gold production and its relation to the state. He necessarily had to contend, however, with Terray's assertions concerning the use of slaves in goldmining organized by the Abron state. Dumett argued that most gold was produced not by slaves in the service of their masters, but by "family groups" washing alluvial soil during the dry season.[21] But, as Terray notes in his rebuttal, Dumett seems to have confused Terray's contention that the slave mode of production was dominant in the theoretical sense outlined above with the idea that slaves produced most of the gold exported by the Abron; in other words, he seems to have misinterpreted a qualitative argument as a quantitative one.[22] Nevertheless, Dumett's essay performed the useful service of gathering together much empirical evidence concerning the organization of labor in Akan gold production, even if his critique of the "Terray hypothesis" was off the mark and his allegations of empirical error unsubstantiated.

More interesting is Terray's lengthy response to Dumett. Here Terray devotes much of his attention to defending the empirical rigor of his work. Only toward the end of his essay does he reiterate the qualitative nature of his argument, which is really the crux of the matter; that is, the central role of the slave mode of production is demonstrated not by its quantitative significance, but by its qualitative structuring of the entire social formation. However, Terray then concedes that Dumett's criticism had led him to reconsider his interpretation, at least with regard to extending it to nineteenth-century Asante. In a significant shift, he allowed that a "compromise" with Dumett might be warranted: his original view that the slave mode of production dominated the lineage mode should still be seen as valid, but only for eighteenth-century Asante; following the abolition of the overseas slave trade in the early nineteenth century, "state slavery" underwent a decline as a result of conscious state policy, and "domestic slavery" rapidly increased.[23] For a variety of reasons, however, such a change is not discernible in the history of the Abron kingdom of Gyaman, where, Terray argues, state slavery continued to dominate.[24]

Unfortunately, Terray's modified interpretation of Asante slavery leaves the situation more muddled than would a simple adherence to his earlier view. For, if the slave mode of production was no longer dominant in Asante after the abolition of the overseas slave trade, does this mean that the lineage mode of production was now dominant? Terray does not address this question with the theoretical rigor of his earlier work; the implication, however, is that this is what he has in mind.[25] But such a view has little of explanatory value in the study of the complex politics, shifting political economy, and changing structures of belief in nineteenth-century Asante, so vividly portrayed in Wilks's *Asante in the Nineteenth Century* and in the work of T. C. McCaskie.[26] In particular, the key event of that century before the imposition of colonial rule, the utter breakdown of the Asante political and moral order in the decade of the 1880s,[27] would be difficult to explain on the basis of an analysis of the Asante political economy in which the "dominance" of a lineage mode of production is posited. Though there is some dispute among historians about the roots of the 1880s crisis, none would argue that the contradictions in an "Asante lineage mode of production" had anything to do with it; this was a crisis of the state. A materialist approach to Asante history, such as that advocated by Terray, must provide us with the tools for comprehending such critical events in Asante history.[28]

3

A more useful model for analyzing the Asante political economy and the place of relations of servitude in it can be derived from the work of Chris Wickham.[29] A historian of medieval Europe and of the "other" transition—from antiquity to feudalism—Wickham has in common with Wilks an urge to view local developments in a global and comparative context. Like Terray, he adopts a materialist approach employing similar conceptual tools of analysis: a typology of modes of production and their articulation in specific social formations. Unlike Terray, however, his argument is premised on the view that the differentiating elements in "exploitative" (that is, class) modes of production are the "specific systems of the appropriation of the surplus" of the primary producers.[30] After investigating a selection of precapitalist class societies that appeared in both Europe and Asia over the last two millennia, Wickham argues that the most frequently encountered modes of production are "coercive rent-taking" (or "feudal") and "tax-raising" (or "tributary") modes. Of the "feudal" mode of production, he writes (adopting Hindess and Hirst):[31]

> feudal relations are represented simply by tenants paying rent to (or doing labour service for) a monopolistic landowner class; such landowners will always, while the system is stable, have the non-economic coercive powers necessary to enforce their control, whether informally or through the control of public or private justice, but these powers do not have to be formally codified in the seigneurie to exist.[32]

In contrast, the "tributary" mode of production involves the extraction of surplus from peasant producers through taxes, whether collected in money, goods, or labor. This mode gives rise to a "'state class' based on a public institution, with political rights to extract surplus from a peasantry it does not tenurially control."[33] Wickham argues that in many precapitalist social formations the rent-taking and tax-raising modes coexist in an antagonistic relationship, with the state and landlords competing for the surplus of the primary producers and landlords resisting the state's imposition of taxes on themselves.[34] The tributary mode, Wickham further asserts, is dominant "in most traditional state societies."[35]

The attraction of such a conceptualization of the tax-raising or tributary mode will be obvious to anyone with a cursory knowledge of the precolonial Asante political economy. But a further advantage of Wickham's approach, as I see it, lies in his emphasis on the *economic* relationships between surplus producers and surplus takers and his refusal to include the legal or ideological nature of their relations in the definition of the mode of production. This preference in fact lies at the heart of Wickham's rejection of the long-debated, so-called Asiatic mode of production and Perry Anderson's sophisticated analysis of the feudal mode of production,[36] both of which introduce (for different reasons) political or ideological superstructures into the definition of the mode of production.[37] Wickham's categories are therefore flexible enough to apply in a wide variety of social settings; at the same time, they can generate heuristic analyses of the historical dynamics of specific societies by impelling us to examine the ways in which multiple modes interact in a given social formation. Thus, for example, what distinguished medieval social formations of the West was precisely that the coercive rent-taking, or feudal, mode dominated the tax-raising mode. Conversely, in the Asian societies that Wickham examines, the tax-raising or tributary mode was dominant. I shall show that this was also the case in Asante.

A further advantage of Wickham's notion of the tax-raising mode of production is that it does not hinge on the ways that peasants organize their productive relations at the village level, any more than it depends on the way that tributes are raised in politically subject provinces:

> There can thus be a whole variety of types of co-operation persisting in such villages, arrays of organisation of production from the individual to the totally communal that could often have pre-existed class

exploitation, but are now systems in articulation with, and dominated by, the tributary state, as part of the whole social formation. The state does not need to control the economic and social lives of its subjects; it just needs the funding that enables it to pursue its chosen objectives. It is in these areas that we find class struggle between the state and its peasantry (and indeed its landowners): in the amount of tax payable, especially when it is felt that there are no adequate returns.[38]

The advantage of this formulation, as I see it, is that we are not led to pay an inordinate amount of attention to the supposed continued existence of the lineage mode of production in the peasants' villages. Once a tax-raising state is imposed on peasant producers, by whatever mechanism, it is difficult to see how any analysis can focus on the local kin- and gender-based relations of production as if they continued to exist in isolation. They do not; they have been transformed through the domination of the state. In any meaningful economic sense—that is, as a mode of production useful for analyzing the dynamics of the larger social formation—the lineage relations of production of the village cease to exist. Of course, in the case of the forest Akan, assuming Wilks is correct about the "big bang" origins of their sociopolitical order, they *never* existed autonomously prior to the rise of the tax-raising early Akan states.[39]

The presence of the tax-raising/tribute-collecting mode of production in eighteenth- and nineteenth-century Asante is readily documented. The basic impositions of the state on free citizens included death duties (*awunnyade*), war tax (*apeato*), and accession tax (*fotobo*).[40] In addition there is evidence that members of the ruling class were themselves subject to monetary taxes on the benefits they derived from their use of slaves.[41] Also, there is evidence that by the end of the nineteenth century the Asante state made attempts to rationalize these taxes into a single head-tax payable in gold.[42] Most important, however, all Asante citizens were subject to military service; as war played such a significant role in imperial strategy, in the imposition (or maintenance) of tribute payments from subject provinces and in the generation of captives, this state-imposed labor service seems to have been fundamental to the functioning of the tax-raising mode of production in Asante. It is not surprising that an elaborate ideology of warfare was developed to extol the virtues of individual and collective bravery in combat and to celebrate the achievements in war of past rulers. Arhin has devoted particular attention to this important aspect of Asante culture.[43] It would be extremely useful to quantify the level of taxation in nineteenth-century Asante, but given the lack of sources, we may never be able to do so. Nevertheless, the central role played by tax resistance (increasing from the 1830s) and by popular anticonscription movements (in the 1870s and 1880s) in the political conflicts that enveloped the late nineteenth-century Asante state, culminating in the profound crisis of the 1880s, should be enough to indicate that the tax-raising mode of production was very probably dominant.[44]

What then of slavery? Following Wickham's lead in focusing on the mode of surplus extraction from primary producers, rather than on legal status or ideology, what is striking in Akan slavery is the steady and relatively rapid assimilation of captives to an economic status approximating that of free citizens. Yet descendents of captives never attained full equality of economic status; they were always subject to the exaction of specific payments and labor service by the descendents of the masters who purchased their ancestors. Their access to land was mediated by their status as "adopted" members of free lineages; the land they worked remained the possession of the free members of the lineage to which they were attached, and it was controlled by the "chief," the occupant of the office (or "stool," in Akan locution) that exercised lineage leadership or held a position in the state's political apparatus. Among the Akan these descendents of captives are known as *gyaasefo* (people of the hearth): "The *gyaasefo* farmed for the chief, assumed responsibility for his debts and provided him with a wide range of personal services as his stool-carriers, drummers, hornblowers, umbrella-carriers, bathroom attendants, messengers, tradesmen, sextons, and so forth. The chief was heir to all of their property."[45] It would therefore seem appropriate to view such persons as in effect tenants, and those who occupied positions of authority in the lineage as in effect landlords.[46] This relationship thus constitutes a distinct mode of surplus appropriation in Asante, a "coercive rent-taking" or "feudal" mode of production that was subordinate to the tax-raising mode.[47] It is important to remember that *gyaasefo* as citizens remained subject to taxation by the state.

The process of incorporating captives into a relationship of tenantry seems to have been so powerful that it may make little sense to speak of a slave mode of production in Asante in any economically meaningful way. To be sure, captives, especially those newly acquired by war or purchase, were vulnerable to a host of legally sanctioned depredations: they could be (and many were) sold out of the country, in contrast to free Asantes and even the descendents of slaves; they could be (and some were) executed upon the death of their masters in order to serve them in the next world; they could be (and many were) given the most menial and dangerous labor, such as in the gold mines. This is all well known. But the critical question is, Did their legal status as slaves give rise to a distinct mode of surplus appropriation, and thus to a slave mode of production, separate from the feudal and tax-paying obligations of other primary producers? All the available evidence tells us no, although new research may force a modification of this view. In any case, an added advantage of focusing on the economic relations between captives and their descendents, on the one side, and masters and their descendents, on the other, is that we avoid the whole question of the legal definition of slave status that has so far dominated investigations of Akan slavery.[48]

If there was a distinct slave mode of production, based on newly acquired captives, it has had little demonstrable impact on the dynamics of Asante history as we currently know it. If there was too rapid a concentration of captives in one location, as seems to have occurred in the 1810s and 1820s when the Atlantic Slave Trade was suppressed, the possibility of a slave uprising was obviated by a policy of dispersal, as alluded to above in the examination of the work of Terray.[49] Otherwise, the major events in the nineteenth century are best examined in the context of two sets of contradictions: first, those inherent in the tax-raising mode of production—the struggle over economic surplus between the state and primary producers; second, those inherent in the articulation of the tax-raising and rent-taking modes of production, which led to competition for peasant surplus product between the state and "landlords." For example, by viewing stool occupants (chiefs)—both inside and outside the state's political apparatus—as antagonistically competing with the state for the surplus product of primary producers, we gain further insight into the tensions within the Asante state that I have examined elsewhere from a Weberian perspective.[50] On this basis, one can begin to construct a genuinely Marxist analysis of the Asante state.[51]

Not only do the analytical categories of the tax-raising and coercive rent-taking modes of production developed by Wickham provide us with useful tools for the examination of specific conjunctures in Asante history; they also allow us to situate Asante squarely within a broader comparative framework, a global historical context. I have pursued this line of analysis in keeping with a particular aspect of Ivor Wilks's work that has had considerable influence on my own. One has only to look at the treatment given Africa, usually truncated to "sub-Saharan" Africa, in most world history textbooks currently in print to see that much of the painstaking and sophisticated work done by Africanist historians over the last twenty to thirty years has scarcely begun to be heard beyond a specialized Africanist audience. Given the high quality and global significance of at least some of that work, well-represented by the contributions of Ivor Wilks, that is indeed a great pity. Viewing Asante in "world-time" has benefits not only for the localized study of the history of one African society; it will also influence (and, perhaps, change) the way that a growing generation of world historians views Africa.

Notes

I wish to thank James Rosenheim and Brenda Blair for reading and commenting on an earlier version of this chapter. I have also benefited from innumerable conversations with Jeff Rice about Asante history and from several discussions with Robert Resch about the use of modes of production analysis. I have only myself to blame for any errors that remain.

1. I. Wilks, *Asante in the Nineteenth Century: The Structure and Evolution of a Political Order* (Cambridge, 1975).

2. I. Wilks, "Land, Labour, Capital and the Forest Kingdom of Asante: A Model of Early Change," *The Evolution of Social Systems,* ed. J. Friedman and M. J. Rowlands (Pittsburgh, 1978).

3. I. Wilks, "The State of the Akan and the Akan States: A Discursion," *Cahiers d'études africaines* 22, nos. 3–4 (1985): 231–49. Since this chapter was written Wilks has published revised versions of these papers in his *Forests of Gold: Essays on the Akan and the Kingdom of Asante* (Athens, Ohio, 1993). The changes he has made do not affect the argument made here.

4. Wilks, "State of the Akan," 232–34.

5. I. Wilks, "The Northern Factor in Ashanti History: Begho and the Mande," *Journal of African History* 2, no. 1 (1961): 25–34; idem, "A Medieval Trade Route from the Niger to the Gulf of Guinea," *Journal of African History* 3, no. 2 (1962): 337–42. See also his more recent articles, "Wangara, Akan and the Portuguese in the Fifteenth and Sixteenth Centuries. I. The Matter of Bitu," *Journal of African History* 23, no. 3 (1982), and "II. The Struggle for Trade," *Journal of African History* 23, no. 4 (1982); revised versions in Wilks, *Forests of Gold.*

6. My current research entails the use of primarily Dutch archival sources—deriving principally from the Dutch recruitment effort on the Gold Coast and in Asante in the middle decades of the nineteenth century—in order to reconstruct the history of slavery and the slave trade. I hope shortly to return to Ghana to carry out work with oral informants on this project.

7. P. Lovejoy, *Transformations in Slavery: A History of Slavery in Africa* (Cambridge, 1983); P. Manning, *Slavery and African Life: Occidental, Oriental, and African Slave Trades* (Cambridge, 1992).

8. S. Miers and I. Kopytoff, eds., *Slavery in Africa: Historical and Anthropological Perspectives* (Madison, Wis., 1977).

9. R. Dumett, "Traditional Slavery in the Akan Region in the Nineteenth Century: Sources, Issues, and Interpretations," in *West African Economic and Social History: Studies in Memory of Marion Johnson,* ed. D. Henige and T. McCaskie (Madison, Wis., 1990), 8.

10. E. Terray, "Long Distance Exchange and the Formation of the State: The Case of the Abron Kingdom of Gyaman," *Economy and Society* 3, no. 3 (1974): 315–45; idem, "Class and Class Consciousness in the Abron Kingdom of Gyaman," *Marxist Analyses and Social Anthropology,* ed. M. Bloch (London, 1975).

11. For a recent cogent examination of Althusserian structural Marxism, see R. Resch, *Althusser and the Renewal of Marxist Social Theory* (Berkeley and Los Angeles, 1992), esp. chap. 2: "Modes of Production and Historical Development."

12. Terray, "Long Distance Exchange," 331.

13. Terray, "Classes and Class Consciousness," 128.

14. Ibid., 91. A similar argument is offered by G. E. M. de Ste. Croix, *The Class Struggle in the Ancient Greek World from the Archaic Age to the Arab Conquests* (Ithaca, N.Y., 1981) with regard to ancient Greek and Roman societies.

15. See F. Engels, "The Origin of the Family, Private Property and the State," in *Karl Marx and Frederick Engels: Selected Works in One Volume* (New York, 1968), 576–82.

16. Terray, "Classes and Class Consciousness," 97.

17. This is one reason, I believe, so many American Africanist historians have a difficult time accepting Terray's analysis. American scholars are accustomed to thinking of slavery in its New World guise; that is, as a decidedly *modern* form of class exploitation.

18. Wilks, "State of the Akan," 232–34.

19. R. Dumett, "Precolonial Gold Mining and the State in the Akan Region: With a Critique of the Terray Hypothesis," *Research in Economic Anthropology* 2, ed. G. Dalton (Greenwich, Conn., 1979).

20. E. Terray, "Gold Production, Slave Labor, and the State in Precolonial Akan Societies: A Reply to Raymond Dumett," *Research in Economic Anthropology* 5, ed. G. Dalton (Greenwich, Conn., 1983).

21. Dumett, "Precolonial Gold Mining," 45–47.

22. Terray, "Gold Production," 121–22.

23. Ibid., 119. Presumably the phrase "state slavery" refers to the slave mode of production; and "domestic slavery" to the assimilation of captives by commoner villages organized by lineage relations of production.

24. There are other reasons for hesitation in extending any model developed for Gyaman to the Akan states of the forest heartland, such as Asante. In Gyaman, the Abron ruled over a congeries of ethnically diverse peoples, while the forest Akan states were much more ethnically homogeneous. Further, the development of the institutions of the Abron state never achieved the level of complexity and sophistication as did the Asante state, a level of state development that, I have argued elsewhere, warrants examination on its own terms and for which Weber provides the most useful tools of analysis; see L. Yarak, *Asante and the Dutch, 1744–1873* (Oxford, 1990). Terray is clearly aware of these important differences between Gyaman and Asante, but he does not appear to believe that they constitute sufficient grounds for considering the Asante case as fundamentally different from Gyaman. I believe they do.

25. Terray, "Gold Production," 120.

26. See inter alia T. C. McCaskie, "Anti-Witchcraft Cults in Asante: An Essay in the Social History of an African People," *History in Africa* 8 (1981): 125–54; idem, "Accumulation, Wealth and Belief in Asante History. I. To the Close of the Nineteenth Century," *Africa* 53, no. 1 (1983): 23–43; idem, "Komfo Anokye of Asante: Meaning, History and Philosophy in an African Society," *Journal of African History* 27, no. 2 (1986): 315–39; idem, "Death and the *Asantehene:* A Historical Meditation," *Journal of African History* 30, no. 3 (1989): 417–44.

27. Wilks, *Asante,* chap. 13; McCaskie, "Accumulation, Wealth and Belief," 37–39.

28. Furthermore, the argument that "state slavery" declined and "domestic slavery" increased also runs counter to Lovejoy's and Manning's interpretations of the "transformation" of African slavery that took place during the nineteenth century. Both historians have advanced formidable arguments that a substantial

expansion in the scale of slaveholding and the economic use of slaves occurred in West Africa, as a result of the suppression of the transatlantic slave trade; see Lovejoy, *Transformations,* 276; Manning, *Slavery and African Life,* 49, 140; P. Lovejoy, "The Impact of the Atlantic Slave Trade on Africa: A Review of the Literature," *Journal of African History* 30, no. 3 (1989): 365–94. It should be noted that not all scholars agree with the views advanced by Lovejoy and Manning; see D. Eltis and L. Jennings, "Trade Between Western Africa and the Atlantic World in the Pre-Colonial Era," *American Historical Review* 93, no. 4 (1988): 936–59.

29. C. Wickham, "The Other Transition: From the Ancient World to Feudalism," *Past and Present* 103 (1984): 3–36; idem, "The Uniqueness of the East," *Journal of Peasant Studies* 12, nos. 2–3 (1985): 166–96. I am grateful to Robert Resch for having brought these works to my attention.

30. Wickham, "Uniqueness of the East," 167–68. Terray has explicitly defined a mode of production as "the combination of one fundamental productive relation and the ensemble of the conditions of its reproduction," thus tying relations of production to aspects of the political and/or ideological superstructure; see E. Terray, "On Exploitation: Elements of an Autocritique," *Critique of Anthropology* 4 (1979): 32. As Wickham has observed: "Modes of production are ideal constructs; the justification for particular definitions, as long as they have an internal logic and thus make sense, must be their usefulness" in historical analysis; Wickham, "Other Transition," 7.

31. B. Hindess and P. Hirst, *Precapitalist Modes of Production* (London, 1975).

32. Wickham, "Other Transition," 6.

33. Wickham, "Uniqueness of the East," 170–71.

34. Ibid. It is interesting to note that Wickham draws none of his examples from Africa.

35. Ibid., 175.

36. P. Anderson, *Passages from Antiquity to Feudalism* (London, 1974); idem, *Lineages of the Absolutist State* (London, 1974).

37. Wickham, "Uniqueness of the East," 166–71.

38. Ibid., 185.

39. Which Wilks quaintly calls "*obirempon*-doms"; "State of the Akan," 241–44.

40. Wilks, *Asante,* 69.

41. Ibid., 70.

42. Ibid.

43. For example, K. Arhin, "The Asante Praise Poems: The Ideology of Patrimonialism," *Paideuma: Mitteilungen zur Kulturkunde* 32 (1986): 163–98.

44. On tax resistance, see I. Wilks, "The Golden Stool and the Elephant Tail: An Essay on Wealth in Asante," in *Research in Economic Anthropology 2,* ed. G. Dalton (Greenwich, Conn., 1979), 22–23; idem, "Dissidence in Asante Politics: Two Tracts from the Late Nineteenth Century," in *African Themes: Northwestern University Studies in Honor of Gwendolyn M. Carter,* ed. I. Abu-Lughod (Evanston, Ill., 1975); revised versions in Wilks, *Forests of Gold.* On anticonscription movements, see Wilks, *Asante,* 504–9, 534–38.

45. Wilks, "State of the Akan," 243.

46. Here I want to avoid the essentially ideological question of how the Asante themselves understood land "ownership." The main issue is one of access to the main instruments of production, land, and tools; not how the producers and surplus takers rationalized and justified that access.

47. Wilks concurs in this interpretation of the "feudalizing tendency" of the relations between stool occupants and their *gyaasefo;* "State of the Akan," 245.

48. See A. N. Klein, "The Two Asantes: Competing Interpretations of 'Slavery' in Akan-Asante Culture and Society," in *The Ideology of Slavery in Africa,* ed. P. Lovejoy (Beverly Hills, Calif., 1981); Dumett, "Traditional Slavery."

49. Terray, "Gold Production," 118–19.

50. Yarak, *Asante and the Dutch.* It should be evident that I do not regard Weberian and Marxist modes of analysis as inherently in conflict; quite the contrary.

51. As Wilks once called for: I. Wilks, "What Manner of Persons Were These? Some Reflections on Asante Officialdom," in *The Golden Stool: Studies of the Akan Center and Periphery,* ed. E. Schildkrout (New York, 1987), 111. Cf. Yarak, *Asante and the Dutch,* 25–26. Curiously, in his most recent published work Wilks continues to express interest in applying Weberian categories of analysis to the Asante state; see I. Wilks, "On Mentally Mapping Greater Asante: A Study of Time and Motion," *Journal of African History* 33, no. 2 (1992), 188. Wilks has published revised versions of these papers in *Forests of Gold.*

Orality, Literacy, and Literature: A Comparison of Three West African Heroic Narratives

RALPH A. AUSTEN

West Africa has served for some time as a testing ground for the relationship between orality and literacy. This is a region where Islamic writing has been present for many centuries without, however, inhibiting the continued development of a very robust oral literature. On the basis of West African studies, Jack Goody, among others, has suggested that the shift from oral to written expression represents not only a major gain in the technology of communications but also as the marker (and perhaps cause) of critical shifts in general human cognition and culture.[1]

This essay proposes to pursue the questions raised by Goody and others through the study of three well-known West African narratives. The first and most famous is the Sunjata Epic, which recounts the deeds of the thirteenth-century founder of the Mali empire.[2] The second, somewhat more obscure work is a set of historical biographies collectively referred to as the Jabi Ta'rikhs because they relate the genealogy of the Jabi branch of the Jakhanke clerical lineages.[3] The third, *Infaku'l Maisuri* (The expenditure of what is easy), is the biography by Muhammad Bello of his father, Usman dan Fodio, leader of the nineteenth-century Fulani jihad in northern Nigeria.[4]

These narratives, taken in succession, illustrate rather neatly the categories Goody has laid out for the progression from orality to literacy: the Sunjata Epic is a work that reached its indigenous audience only through oral performance; the Jabi Ta'rikhs represent the sort of restricted Islamic literacy that Goody noted in his own earlier work in Northern Ghana;[5] and Muhammad Bello's book emerges from a much more fully literate culture. In the first section of this essay I shall apply my own version of Goody's evolutionist approach to the comparison of the three works as I believe it has a certain degree of historical validity and can also be linked to more general theories of literary history. In the second section, however, I shall question such a hierarchical comparison of the three works on both historical and literary grounds. These narratives did not, it turns out, come to life in a linear time series; rather, they are contemporaneous with one another and thus all participate in a common dialogue between oral and literary culture. Moreover their literary/aesthetic power, even when all three are written down seems to operate in inverse proportion to their degree of literacy.

In pursuing this analysis I shall be looking fairly closely at the works in question, although one obvious condition is that the Sunjata Epic exists in very many variants,[6] the Jabi Ta'rikhs have at least a few versions,[7] and *Infaku'l Maisuri* has a single canonical form. I shall return to this distinction later; for the present, I shall assume that there is a standard common core to the Sunjata Epic and that the variations in different versions of the Jabi Ta'rikhs do not matter too much.

From Orality to Literacy

The initial "evolutionist" comparison of the works will focus on three issues: (1) the literal medium of communicating the texts; (2) the representation of personal and social consciousness in the narratives; (3) the modes of reference to other texts.

The orality of "Sunjata" is most obviously indicated, as already noted, through the practice of its performance before a living audience by a bard who has himself learned the text from other oral performers. Thus any written version of the epic (and there are many by now) is ultimately derivative from, rather than constitutive of, its oral rendition.

The Jabi Ta'rikhs are found in both oral and written form, and their written versions vary from mere genealogical lists to very detailed accounts of at least some ancestors of this lineage. Here we are clearly on the boundary line between the written and the oral: not only do both forms of the same narrative coexist, but the one-page genealogical texts obviously serve as prompts for more extended oral narrations.

Ironically, we know less about the genesis of *Infaku'l Maisuri* than about the other narratives precisely because it is a written work preserved in a succession of copies rather than a text linked to any kind of observable oral performance.[8] However, from our knowledge of the jihad of Usman dan Fodio (conveyed via other written works) we can safely assume that this book was composed on paper rather than through the transcription of any prior oral version. There are numerous passages where Muhammad Bello cites speech (both formal and informal) as the source of his information or even the subject of his own discussion. But these passages constitute discrete elements of the work that are always framed within the dominant discourse of writing rather than oral performance.

The classic studies tracing the development in European literature from the ancient and medieval epic to the modern novel place considerable emphasis on changes in the representation of individual and social consciousness. In doing so they closely parallel Goody's arguments about the transition from orality to literacy and are particularly relevant to the present textual comparison. Thus for Bakhtin the epic presents its hero in a distant past "infinitely far removed from the discourse of a contemporary about a contemporary addressed to a contemporary";[9] for Auerbach, the epic hero is a fixed entity shown by a series of external actions and emotions rather than "the simultaneous existence of various layers of consciousness and the conflict between them"; he also functions as the "foregrounded" representative of a ruling elite unconcerned with the "background" of more complex and autonomous social reality.[10]

"Sunjata" fits easily into this model of the epic; it is set in an era separated by many centuries from that of the performer, and the language is always elevated in tone and style. The hero is particularly inhibited from revealing his inner consciousness by the

Mande cultural prohibition against public speech by noble figures, who are represented in this function by their casted bards (*jaliw*/griots), the same group that also performs the epic. The deeds in "Sunjata" are complex and subtle, involving, as Bird and Kendall have noted, far more searches for secret knowledge than the scenes of violent combat characteristic of Homer or Beowulf.[11] Nonetheless, these searches do take the form of confrontations of various kinds (exchanges of goods, seductions, rape, sacrifices, musical and artisanal performances) rather than individual self-questioning. Finally the realm of action is entirely that of male warriors and hunters. The latter are not an elite in European class terms, but they are a male society with affinities to certain special categories of women while completely removed from the quotidian domestic (and more feminized) domain of human and agricultural reproduction, a domain that is also conspicuously absent from the epic.

By the criterion of articulated consciousness, the Jabi Ta'rikhs are no less "oral" than the Sunjata Epic. The narrative focuses upon a hero, al-Hajj Salim Kassamba (also referred to as Karanmukhuba, "the Great Scholar") who lived more than a century before the present versions of the texts were composed; this seem to be distance enough to confine him to the elevated "epic discourse" defined by Bakhtin. The actions of al-Hajj Salim and the other major figures in the narrative consist mainly of learning various Islamic sciences, which certainly makes for less engaging reading than "Sunjata" (fortunately the narrative, in all known versions, is fairly brief). However, these deeds, as well as the more quotidian activities of "recitation and plowing" and even the few dramatic moments of fleeing local misrule and performing miracles are all presented very much from outside the consciousness of the hero, who remains the agent of locally interpreted Islamic principles rather than of his personal self-awareness. Moreover, the inclusion of agricultural labor in this account serves less to integrate its protagonists into the surrounding "pagan" Sudanic world than to isolate them in a sort of monastic discipline; "plowing" is always linked to "recitation [of Islamic liturgy and learning]."

We might expect even less self-reflective and social consciousness in *Infaku'l Maisuri*, which is very much a hagiography. Muhammad Bello literally considers his father to be a saint (*wali*) and even tells us about a mystical trance in which he encounters God (6). However, the fact that this is a work written about an immediate father rather than a distant ancestor does bring the text closer to "the discourse of a contemporary" ascribed by Bakhtin to modern literature. The narrative thus does penetrate from time to time beyond the public representation of the hero. In one oft-cited passage (8), Muhammad Bello takes us backstage at one of Usman's popular preaching sessions:

> I have noticed that when he wanted to go out to the people, he would stand quietly in the corner of the house, and say something, and then he would go to the people. I asked him about this, and he said: "I am renewing my enthusiasm, and making a promise to God of faithfulness to what I am going to do, and I ask of him that those present might understand what I am talking about. And this way, I would renew my enthusiasm in the gathering, and I would remember the promise."

The tone here certainly remains very pious, but there is an immediacy about the situation and a literal sense of Usman "psyching himself up" that we would not expect in a formal oral rendition of these same events. What the text is doing at this point is to incorporate informal "contemporary" speech into a formal written work and by this means at least suggesting something about Usman's inner state of mind. At the same time *Infaku'l Maisuri* does not tell us very much about the surrounding everyday world of Hausa and Fulani society except as it directly opposes the religious mission of Usman or, as will be seen below, it is represented in other Islamic texts.

Muhammad Bello's ability to portray elements of his father's inner life depends upon both the technology of writing and participation in a more fully literate culture than that of the Sunjata or Jabi Ta'rikh performers/authors. In the case of Sunjata it is impossible for anyone to have recorded the immediate speech, let alone the inner thoughts of the hero. In the case of Jabi hero Karanmukhuba, such an act is technically possible but culturally inconceivable as writing would not be used in his world for such mundane and intimate purposes.[12] We can get a fuller idea of the differing relationship of these three works to the culture of literacy by the way in which each of them makes reference to other texts.

If we can accept the term "text" for oral works, most performances of "Sunjata" are highly intertextual. They incorporate into their narrative core not only other stories but also other genres such as praise poetry, song, proverbs, and folktales. They also contain references to narratives known to the performers in part through their exposure to Islamic learning. Thus there are inevitably prologues dealing with Bilal (the alleged Ur-ancestor of Sunjata) in Mecca that include early episodes of classic Islamic history. Some versions of the epic also contain references to Dhu-'l-Qarnayn, the generic Mediterranean world conqueror (usually identified with Alexander the Great), known locally either through the Qur'an or written and oral Saharan epics.[13]

Yet the "literalness" with which other texts are quoted operates in inverse proportion to their intelligibility as prose narratives. Epic performances contain pieces of praise poetry that seem to have been memorized verbatim and may well have been preserved over many centuries.[14] But the condition of this preservation is a poetic density that obscures literal meaning, often to the point of unintelligibility. Indeed, the narrative portions of the epic may be seen as contemporary (and often quite varied) interpretations of the allusions embedded in the poetry.

The references in the epic to other narrative material, whether derived from Mediterranean/Islamic writings or local oral sources, consists mainly of the manipulation of motifs rather than the citing of specific texts. Thus while the oral bard is not free to reinvent his text at each occasion, as Goody and some "performance theorists" suggest or imply, he is not in immediate, "literal" dialogue with verbal formulations independent of his own utterances.

The Jabi Ta'rikhs, by contrast to "Sunjata," are replete with references to other books. Since much of the narrative concerns the itineraries of the Jabi ancestors from one teacher to another (each of whom is responsible for a particular book of Islamic learning) this work may be considered in one sense the most intertextual of all the accounts under consideration. Yet we can hardly speak here of a confrontation between texts since the content of the books learned by Karanmukhuba and others is never discussed in the Jabi narrative.

What we have here is, indeed, writing restricted—and simultaneously elevated—to a technology. The narrative is to a considerable extent an elaboration of each Jabi ancestor's diplomas, testifying to his mastery of the powers presumably embodied in the works of classic Islamic learning cited as well as the teachers who transmitted them. Some of this power is also represented through the brief references to miraculous occurrences (for example, moving a rock from its position blocking a river), but these echo very weakly the miracle stories associated with Islamic holy men in the Sahara and North Africa.[15] The texts give the sense that the authors hesitate to write down what may appear as "pagan folklore"; that is, that they restrict their textual horizons *to* orthodox written works just as much as their imagination is restricted *from* making any independent use of what may be in such books.

Paradoxically, in thus shying away from the motifs of oral literature the Jabi Ta'rikhs remain very close to some elements of its form. The "diploma" dimensions of the narrative are thus easily woven into the genealogical accounts that form the oral base of the texts. We also know that in the Sudanic learning of orthodox Islamic works orality may have been just as significant in it as writing; the pupil often acquired his own copy of a "book" only by literally writing it down at the feet (and voice) of his teacher.[16]

In contrast to the other two works *Infaku'l Maisuri* constantly quotes other Arabic (and possibly vernacular) texts. Many of these quotations are from the Qur'an and cannot be considered in any real dialogue with Muhammad Bello's own text. In many respects they resemble, both in their dense poetic form and their status, the praise poetry incorporated into the Sunjata Epic although they are, for the most part, far more distant from the biographical subject of the work at hand. Moreover, this work mentions fewer classic Islamic texts than the Jabi Ta'rikhs because Usman dan Fodio seems to have shifted at a relatively early age from the role of itinerant student to that of a popular preacher in his home territory.

We see the fully literate character of *Infaku'l Maisuri* rather in relationship to two types of less canonical external texts: the lives of real or alleged holy men and arguments about the legitimacy of jihad against Islamicized states of the Central Sudan. We have noted how the Jabi Ta'rikhs avoid any elaborate reference to the hagiography of deeds rather than learning because they apparently appear to associate such tales with the oral culture of surrounding non-Muslim societies. For Muhammad Bello, "evil mallams" and the miracles associated with them are the target of explicit and constantly repeated attacks, a posture that thus licenses him to tell their stories at great length. Another basis for such narrative emancipation, however, is the knowledge, through his own reading, that virtuous Muslim scholars before him have written such accounts; indeed some of Muhammad Bello's most extended tales of clerical corruption are quotations from the seventeenth-century Moroccan scholar, Hasan al-Yusi (10–11).

Muhammad Bello also cites the writings of several Muslim scholars who opposed jihad in the Sudan and his purpose here is to refute them. The most frequently cited passage from the *Infaku'l Maisuri* is the debate between Bello and Shehu el-Kanemi, the reformist Islamic ruler of Borno.[17] This is a very valuable document but could as easily be the inscription of a contemporary oral exchange as the reinscription of a written one. For Muhammad Bello, el-Kanemi was a voice he had to confront in his own time through whatever medium or mediation was current.

More interesting for understanding the literary culture in which this text is embedded is the argument with the long-deceased Ahmad Baba of Timbuktu, who had argued in the sixteenth century against attacks by other Muslim powers on the states of the Sudan. Muhammad Bello does not undertake the kind of historical analysis of Ahmad Baba's argument that we would expect from a modern scholar: he pays no attention to the Moroccan invasion of Songhai (and abduction of Ahmad Baba himself) that is the immediate context for his polemic.[18] Nonetheless, he does recognize (or is forced to recognize by the culture he lives in) that there is a text composed in another time and place that addresses his own circumstances and is known independently to his contemporaries, therefore requiring that it be answered rather than ignored or reinscribed in his own terms. Muhammad Bello thus summarizes this contrary argument and argues on a basis that might convince those who have also read Ahmad Baba of his own superior claims (19):

> As for what was said by Ahmad Baba when he responded that these countries, i.e. Borno and Katsina and some of Zaria, and the areas nearby, are Muslim countries, it is possible that they were Muslim in previous times, up to the time of Ahmad Baba, then they apostatized afterwards. Or it is possible that it is because he did not have any contact with them, and did not really know them, but decided based on what appeared to him to be so, and was commonly reported. Or it is possible that he was just looking at the proliferation of Islam among those other than the rulers. The second possibility is more likely, because if they converted to Islam and were faithful to their religion, it would have been heard and reported. But we never heard that they had quit the ways of their early heathen grandfathers up to our time, though they assisted Islam.

With this last passage we recognize in *Infaku'l Maisuri* the kind of text we still write today and therefore a fellow inhabitant of our side of the great divide that Goody has placed between the literate and nonliterate cultures. Muhammad Bello even produces, here and throughout all the Sokoto jihad literature, the kinds of "lists" that Goody insists are so characteristic of literacy.

This last and the other characteristics distinguishing *Infaku'l Maisuri* from the accompanying works on the present list are not trivial and demonstrate the power of the theories of literacy and literature developed by Goody, Bakhtin, and Auerbach, among others. But they are inadequate for understanding the historical relationship between orality and literacy in West Africa and thus their evaluation must momentarily be suspended.

Literature(s) in Dialogue

The treatment of these three texts as "stages" in a development toward full Islamic literacy runs the risk of reading into African literary history a meta-narrative of "modernization" very obviously derived from the way in which the Western Europe world (even through such a trendy and "eastern" figure as Bakhtin) has represented its own cultural trajectory. This problem is particularly acute for texts that derive from an African world not in close contact with Europe but in fact much more internally connected than the previous analysis of their distinction might suggest. Above all, we must take into account the fact that the works being compared here all derive from essentially the same period.

This last point may not seem obvious: the Sunjata Epic claims to speak in the voice of the medieval Mali empire; the Jabi Ta'rikhs are twentieth-century writings; and *Infaku'l Maisuri* was completed around 1812–13. Even if only this last work alone can be dated with some degree of precision,[19] it is also now generally accepted that the Sunjata Epic too was only composed in the latter eighteenth century, with much of its narrative development continuing through the nineteenth.[20] The present redaction of the Jabi Ta'rikhs is quite recent, which is not itself a problem for their contemporaneity with more advanced forms of literacy; but its focal hero, al-Hajj Salim Kassamba (Karanmukhuba), lived roughly at the same time as Usman dan Fodio (c. 1745–1836/7). All three of these works are thus stamped with the influences of a common historical period in West Africa and cannot be fully understood if we do not take into account their joint participation in a broad, intricate, and in many respects still ongoing dialogue between oral literary discourse and Islamic literacy. Moreover, in this dialogue the richest literary achievement does not always correlate with the highest level of literacy.

The case for "Sunjata" will be made briefly because it is the subject of other essays.[21] The epic is, in sum, an oral work composed in dialogue with a culture of literacy. What this means is that the specific components of the narrative and its performance owe no more to their coexistence with local Islamic written texts than has already been noted in the discussion of intertextuality. However, the most prestigious performers of "Sunjata" talk *about* the epic in ways that make it seem much more intimately bound up in Islamic literary discourse. The generic Mande terms for this kind of lengthy oral narrative are thus *tariku* (ta'rikh) and *maana* ("signification," a term probably derived from training in the exegesis of primal Islamic texts such as Qur'an and hadith). Some of these Malian bards also claim that the accuracy of their performance is controlled by a secret manuscript of the entire epic, although it is very unlikely that any local scholar, trained only in writing Arabic (or French) could transcribe such a lengthy Mande-language work.[22]

What is indicated by the Islamicizing references to "Sunjata" (along with the broader context of the Kamablon ritual in which the work presumably developed) is that the idea of putting together all the indigenous components of the epic into a single, coherent work owes something to the confrontation with Islam. Epics of this kind are not, after all, so very common in tropical Africa where praise poetry and informal oral history are the more prevalent modes of recalling heroic careers. The Sunjata Epic occupies a virtually unique place in the canon of African oral and, more recently, written literature precisely because it brings together poetry, history, folklore, and social commentary in a form accessible to both an indigenous and a universal audience and even questions the autonomy of "elite" male domains.[23] That achievement is possible because the epic was composed during the eighteenth and nineteenth centuries, long after the events it celebrates took place and because the *jaliw* had before them the general model of a master narrative derived from the more intense presence of Islam in West Africa during this period.

In a literal sense, the authors of the Jabi Ta'rikhs are far more aware of Islamic narrative models than the superficially Islamicized performers of "Sunjata." However, the story they tell eschews the archetype of the founding Prophet and universal ruler, reproducing instead the less compelling contemporary career pattern of submission to the disciplines of a well-established religious system.

The real drama in this text comes from a dialogue with alternative possibilities for accommodation between Sudanic culture and Islam. However, in accordance with the values of the Jabi clerics, these alternatives are never fully articulated and only become evident to a reader aware of the larger historical and cultural context within which the text is operating. This context includes the alternative literary genres represented by "Sunjata" and *Infaku'l Maisuri:* the first represents a use of Islam to develop indigenous cultural resources; the latter advocates a radical repression of all "pagan" local practices in favor of Islamic orthodoxy.

The Jabi Ta'rikhs appear on the surface to follow a weak version of the Muhammad Bello option; they present a negation of local culture only by default and a commitment to Islamic learning through nothing more than the formal statement of credentials. Yet a more subtle reading of the text reveals a good deal about the way Islam has integrated itself into Sudanic society by a complicated process of political renunciation, parallel syncretism, and ascetic economic entrepreneurship.

Political renunciation in several forms is made quite explicit in the text. We are thus told how Karanmukhuba refused a position of provincial rulership within the Futa Jallon state on the principle that "he would not accept political authority at all unless its existence was his own exclusive property" (442).

The possibility of establishing such authority through a jihad like that of Usman dan Fodio is never directly discussed although there is already considerable eloquence in silence when referring to a period where struggles of this kind were prevalent throughout the West and Central Sudan. In one ambiguous passage some of al-Hajj Salim's pupils do join a jihad in the Casamance region of Senegal, but it is not clear whether their master is encouraging them in this effort or repudiating them for doing so.[24]

The combination of withdrawal from local politics and dedication to formal learning creates the image of a clerical community practicing an extremely orthodox version of Islam. However, within the list of expected Islamic disciplines studied by Karanmukhuba—law, Qur'anic commentary, theology, Arabic grammar, the life of Muhammad—occurs one item that seems slightly out of place. This is geomancy (here called "the science of agreement," 441), meaning the mathematical manipulation of sacred texts for the discovery of hidden meanings that can then be used in divination and the construction of amulets.[25] I have labeled such a practice "parallel syncretism" because it does not formally compromise the dedication of Jabi clerics to Islam but rather constructs Islamic writing in such a fashion as to make it more widely functional in a Sudanic context. Goody may be correct in his contention that it is precisely this magico/religious treatment of literacy that is the key to its "restricted" role in precolonial West Africa, although it is not clear if the relationship is one of cause or effect.[26] But if our inquiry is shifted from the issue of literacy to that of literature, the reference to magic opens up the Jabi texts to reveal something of the way in which its protagonists actually lived the learning that the narrative otherwise presents only in catalogue form.

The somewhat antiheroic "quietist" position of Karanmukhuba and his followers provides another positive link to West African life through the success of the community as economic entrepreneurs. The text again mainly discusses this issue allusively with its frequent, almost casual, references to the connections between "reciting, plowing and pursuing legitimate ends" (443). However, in a passage that sounds as if it comes straight out of Max Weber's *Protestant Ethic,* we are told how the strength of the community is "owing to their wealth that ultimately derived from their renunciation of worldly goods, concern for the cultivation of their religion, and the amount of time that they devoted to religious observances" (443).

Like Weber's Calvinists and Quakers, the Jabi Jakhanke are "worldly ascetic" pioneers of local capitalism, a capitalism involving not only the trading functions usually associated with West African Islam but also intensive agriculture. This kind of enterprise appears to originate at the time of Karanmukhuba (or perhaps earlier) and has continued through the colonial era into modern times.[27]

The seemingly arid Ta'rikhs can therefore be read, with some interpretive effort, as a quite revealing account of Islamic involvement in the historical currents of eighteenth- and nineteenth-century West Africa. Their "restricted literacy" thus becomes more than a stopping point between oral "tradition" and fully literate "modernity." If economic development is the true key to success in the modern world, these texts may even represent a fuller modernity than such a work as *Infaku'l Maisuri.*

Muhammad Bello's work, once considered in a dialogic rather than an evolutionary relationship with the other two texts discussed here, does lose some of its literary stature. The weakness of *Infaku'l Maisuri* in this context derives precisely from its bold and successful break with the oral and indigenous culture it is confronting. The greater immersion of the author in a world of literacy allows him to provide a much fuller record of the individuals, events, ideological debates, and institutions of his time than do the other texts. But the work itself never takes on a life that transcends or transforms its subject matter.

One problem here is language. While the Sokoto jihad did much to transform both Hausa and Fulani into literary languages, Muhammad Bello chose to write this biography in Arabic; the result is an often cumbersome prose as well as the lack of an encompassing structure to the text, whose whole remains less than the sum of its many parts. *Infaku'l Maisuri* has thus become a work more consulted by scholars than read within its own culture.[28] Ironically, the most profound revelation in this text is the level of literacy attained by its author and his immediate community. However, as students of African orality have long contended, literacy and literature are not necessarily coterminous concepts.

Conclusion

The main purpose of this essay is not to rank "Sunjata," the Jabi Ta'rikhs, or *Infaku'l Maisuri* according to criteria of either literacy or literature. It is rather to explore the complex relationships between these aspects of West African narrative and to argue that any text from this region can be fully understood only by considering its explicit and implicit dialogue with other genres of verbal articulation. If the study were to be extended to the discussion of modern African literature, the inextricable cross-links of an oral literary heritage and a culture of fully developed literacy would be even more obvious.

However, I shall stop with the three more or less precolonial texts discussed here. Among them, only "Sunjata" (mainly in the somewhat "literacized" version of Niane) is widely read either within West Africa or outside it; precisely, however, because of its literary power, this work requires even more elaborate contextual analysis than the other texts. Nonetheless, the Jabi Ta'rikhs and *Infaku'l Maisuri* are equally precious as documents of the culture and history of the region. By exploring the relationship between such very diverse modes of formal narrative we can better appreciate both their differing achievements and the common African historical context that simultaneously creates this body of literature and is created by it.

Notes

1. Jack Goody, *The Domestication of the Savage Mind* (Cambridge, 1977).

2. D. T. Niane, *Sundiata; An Epic of Old Mali,* trans. G. D. Pickett (London, 1965); John William Johnson, *The Epic of Son Jara: A West African Tradition* (Bloomington, 1986).

3. Thomas C. Hunter, "The Jabi Ta'rikhs: Their Significance in West African Islam," *International Journal of African Historical Studies* 9, no. 3 (1976): 435–46; idem, "The Jabi Ta'rikhs" (unpublished, Committee on African and African-American Studies, University of Chicago, n.d.). Unless otherwise indicated, references are to the published version of Hunter although some important passages are contained only in the second composite translation.

4. References, unless otherwise indicated, are to a partial translation by J. B. Broderick (edited by Ralph A. Austen) of the C. E. J. Whitting edition of *Infaku'l maisuri* (London, 1951). A translation is available to anyone who sends me a blank diskette and a stamped, self-addressed return envelope.

5. Goody, "Restricted Literacy in Northern Ghana" in *Literacy in Traditional Societies,* ed. Jack Goody (Cambridge, 1968), 198–264.

6. For a discussion of these variants, see Stephen P. D. Bulman, "Interpreting Sunjata" (Ph.D. diss., University of Birmingham, 1990).

7. The basis for these "texts" reveals my debt to Ivor Wilks; my understanding of Sunjata is shaped by the November 1992 conference at Northwestern University that he helped to instigate and organize; Thomas Hunter, who translated and put together the two composite versions of the Jabi Ta'rikhs used here is our common student (one of the main manuscripts used by Hunter was collected by Ivor Wilks at Bobo Dioulasso).

8. For a brief discussion of the philology of this work see Murray Last, *The Sokoto Caliphate* (New York, 1967), xxx–xxxii.

9. M. M. Bakhtin, "Epic and Novel," in *The Dialogic Imagination*, by M.M. Bakhtin, trans. Caryl Emerson and Michael Holmquist (Austin, Tex., 1981), 13.

10. Erich Auerbach, *Mimesis: The Representation of Reality in Western Literature*, trans. Willard R. Trask (Princeton, 1953), 13, 21–23.

11. Charles S. Bird and Martha B. Kendall. "The Mande Hero: Text and Context," in *Explorations in African Systems of Thought*, ed. Ivan Karp and Charles S. Bird (Bloomington, Ind., 1980).

12. There is some argument among scholars about when and to what degree writing was even used for the commercial transactions of precolonial West African Muslim merchants; Ralph A. Austen, *African Economic History: Internal Development and External Dependency* (London, 1987), 43, 50.

13. H. T. Norris, *Saharan Myth and Saga* (Oxford, 1972), 26–71, passim.

14. Ivor Wilks, "The History of the Sunjata Epic: A Review of the Evidence" in *In Search of Sunjata: The Mande Oral Epic as History, Literature and Performance*, ed. Ralph A. Austen (Bloomington, forthcoming).

15. For good Mauritanian examples see H. T. Norris, *Shinqiti Folk Literature and Song* (Oxford, 1968), 124–52; it also appears, from the research experience of Suret-Canale, that the Jabi clerics include more elaborate miracle stories in the oral renditions of their history than are found in the written texts; Jean Suret-Canale, "Touba in Guinea—Holy Place of Islam," in *African Perspectives*, ed. Christopher Allen and R. W. Johnson (Cambridge, 1970), 61–62.

16. Thomas Charles Hunter, "The Development of an Islamic Tradition of Learning among the Jahanka of West Africa" (Ph.D. diss., University of Chicago, 1977), 328–39.

17. Thomas Hodgkin, *Nigerian Perspectives: An Historical Anthology* (London, 1960), 198–205; the passages here were translated from the Whitting edition of *Infaku'l Maisuri* by Charles/Abdullahi Smith; they are reprinted in David Robinson and Douglas Smith, *Sources of the African Past* (London, 1979), 146–48.

18. He also lacks the kind of critical distance from local texts that is characteristic of twentieth-century West African Muslim scholars who have traveled to the Middle East and developed greater command of Arabic and familiarity with alternative practices of Islam. For an excellent account of such "new literacy," see Robert Launay, *Beyond the Stream: Islam and Society in a West African Town* (Berkeley and Los Angeles, 1992), 91–103.

19. Last, *Sokoto Caliphate*, xxxl.

20. Ralph A. Austen, "The Historical Transformation of Genres: Sunjata as Panegyric, Folktale, Epic and Novel," in Austen, *In Search of Sunjata;* idem, "Elitism vs. Populism in the West African Epic: The Politics of 'Sunjata,'" His-

tory Workshop Conference, University of the Witwatersrand, South Africa, July 1994.

21. Austen, "Historical Transformation of Genres."

22. If the manuscript does exist, an explanation consistent with accounts of how it is used may be that it contains little legible information but serves as a name list and/or mnemonic talisman for the *jaliw;* Wilks has described a manuscript of this kind shown to him by a Kamagate scholar from Bonduku (transcript of 1992 Northwestern University Sunjata Conference Proceedings, copy on deposit at Northwestern University Library and Program on African Studies, 62).

23. Austen, "Elitism vs. Populism."

24. This passage from the *Ta'rikh al-Jabi* is found only in Hunter, unpublished.

25. It is surprising to find such a mention in the text since the very process of acquiring *batin* (esoteric) knowledge is usually kept secret by the Jakhanke; see Hunter, "An Islamic Tradition of Learning," 10–14, 340–402.

26. Goody, "Restricted Literacy," 226–37, 241.

27. For a discussion of the links between Islam and entrepreneurship in modern West Africa see Donal Cruise O'Brien, *The Mourides of Senegal* (Oxford, 1970).

28. Thus the praise of the book as a historical source in Last, *Sokoto Caliphate*, xxxii.; a similar fate seems to have befallen the Kano chronicle (John Hunwick, private communication; see "A Historical Whodunit: The So-Called Kano Chronicle and Its Place in the Historiography of Kano," *History in Africa* 21 [1994]: 127–46).

Borgu in the Cultural Map of the Muslim Diasporas of West Africa

PAULO FERNANDO DE MORAES FARIAS

In his work Wilks has repeatedly called attention to the "Suwarian" tradition in West African Islam.[1] This tradition has as its putative fountainhead of teaching authority the figure referred to as *Al-Ḥājj* Sālim Suwārī, who has been tentatively dated by modern scholars either to the late fifteenth century,[2] or to several generations earlier.[3] From the Middle Niger and the headwaters of the Niger and Senegal, exponents of this tradition spread across West Africa, to the Volta basin and to the east of it, in the wake of the Wangara trade diaspora. They carried with them Manding patronymic-group names, and a distinctive understanding of the way in which Islam could, and should, be lived *in partibus infidelium*. Wilks has described this understanding as "an ideology of pluralism," to be contrasted with "the ideology of *hijra* and *jihād*," and as "a praxis to enable Muslims to function within essentially non-Muslim societies." He sees it as "a delicate balance of priorities" that pursued cooperation with unbelievers and refrained from proselytizing them, but that tenaciously worked for *tajdīd;* that is, for the maintenance and renewal of the specific cultural identity of the Muslim communities themselves.[4]

In the interaction with non-Muslim communities, the Suwarian tradition and other homologous Muslim traditions helped to create cultural practices that recur with similar characteristics across the linguistic map of West Africa, and that involve non-Muslims as well as Muslims. Hence Muslim traditions of this type are relevant not only to the history of Islam in the strict sense, but also to the history of the construction of the West African cultural panorama over and above religious differences. Yet this wider constructive role runs the risk of being overlooked and obscured from opposite sides.

First, from the intellectual stance adopted by the African Muslims who claim the *jihād* tradition as their own, Suwarian and similar traditions can be perceived as ideologies of ignorant, or unprincipled, accommodation and "mixing." Therefore, these traditions may be seen as part of a lower stage in the history of Islam in West Africa, not worthy of the same admiration and research attention as are lavished on the West African *jihād* movements.

Second, and by contrast with the first point of view, from other modern African intellectual stances Islamic culture can be perceived as irremediably alien to African authenticity. Hence not only *jihād* movements, but also Muslim traditions of the Suwarian type, tend to be seen as unmitigatedly negative. According to this line of thinking, the history of the relations between Muslims and non-Muslims has been, inevitably, a history of "resistance" to Islam, in which Muslim communities have made no constructive contributions to the culture of non-Muslim populations.

To avoid both these extreme views, I shall apply Wilks's insights to aspects of the contemporary culture of Borgu, a region divided by the border between Nigeria and the Republic of Bénin, and in which Muslims and non-Muslims have a long history of cultural exchanges, kinship linkages, and political solidarity. I shall focus on two yearly Borgu festivals, with particular reference to their celebration in the kingdom of Nìkì (Nikki on most maps) and the chiefdom of Bānīkpààrù (Banikoara), both of which are situated in the Béninois part of Borgu. I shall situate these two festivals within the general map of the historical expansion of Muslim long-distance trade. But I shall also discuss the specific role played by one of them—the *Gaani* festival—in the local culture of Borgu.

The Historical Construction of Borgu's Cultural Space

Borgu was shaped, and given a degree of historical coherence, not only by its network of kingdoms and chiefdoms,[5] but also by the network of Muslim trader communities distributed over both Béninois and Nigerian Borgu. Cultural exchanges and mutual accommodation took place where nodal points of the two networks coincided, and it is to this that is owed much of the special flavor of Borgu's traditional culture, as can be clearly seen in the yearly *Gaani* festivals and other festivals.

The two major languages of Borgu's precolonial kingdoms and chiefdoms are Bààtɔ̀núm (a Gur language that is the majority language of Béninois Borgu, and that is also spoken in parts of Nigerian Borgu) and Boko-Busa (a Mande language known as Boko or Bo'o in Béninois Borgu). By contrast, in those Borgu communities that owe their origin to long-distance trade, Dèndí (a variety of the Soŋoy or Songhay language) became established as the commercial lingua franca, and as the medium of their resident Muslim culture.[6] These communities were created during the expansion of a Soŋoy-speaking trade network over vast areas of West Africa, an event that has been dated to the fifteenth, or perhaps the fourteenth, century.[7] They mostly lived in wards separate from the (non-Muslim) royal and chiefly wards.[8] The wards originally established by Muslim traders were, and still are, called *Maro* (in Bààtɔ̀núm), *Fárándí* (in Dèndí), or *Wangara* (a more general term for trading diasporas, current across language divisions in several regions of West Africa).

Given their origin in foreign trade, the Dèndí-speaking communities of Borgu are traditionally called *sɔɔbu* (sing. *sɔ̄ɔ̄;* "foreigners") in Bààtɔ̀núm. It has been assumed by some observers that the Wasangari aristocracy of Béninois Borgu (the region with which the present paper is mostly concerned) did not intermarry with the *sɔɔbu,*[9] partly because the Muslim traders supposedly displayed strict adherence to Muslim law in not allowing their women to marry "pagan" Wasangari men.[10] However, as concerns present times, it is clear that the Wasangari not only give their daughters and sisters in marriage to men of the *sɔ̄ɔ̄* communities, but also marry Muslim women from these communities.[11] Furthermore, marriage exchanges between the Wasangari and the *sɔbu* clearly go back a long way in time.

Actually, the Dèndí-speaking *Maro* communities are closely connected with the traditional rulers of Borgu from the very beginning. The economic and ritual activities of Muslims contributed to the power of chiefly and kingly lineages virtually from the start. In the case of the Nìkì polity, this transpires not only from traditions collected among the Muslims of the Nìkì-Maro ward,[12] but also from other—Wasangari-centered—traditions. Gεsεrε royal traditionists insistently state that slaves were first traded in exchange for horses by *Sùnɔ̀* Dobidia, who is represented as the second ruler of the Nìkì kingdom and founder of its capital, and as the king under whom Wasangari power first became effectively established in the area.[13] It is also said that during his reign Muslim traders settled in Nìkì, *Kpāgu Yɔbu* (the *Yākpāgu* or *Kpāgu* market) was established there, and the first Gεsεrε praise-chanters (who are generally believed to have come to Borgu from Soŋoy or Songhay) were brought to the court.[14] It is stated that one of the wives of *Sùnɔ̀* Dobidia was the daughter of a Hausa trader, who is sometimes described as of Katsina, or alternatively of Zaria, origin.[15] She is said to be the mother of King Kpee Laafia or Kpee Daafia, and as such the ancestress of the Yari-Laafiaru or Yari-Daafiaru, one of the royal-lineage segments that compete for the Nìkì kingship.[16] In this competition, the Yari-Daafiaru have traditionally drawn on the support of the Muslims of the Nìkì-Maro ward.[17]

Another early king, represented as a son of *Sùnɔ̀* Dobidia by another wife, and as the ancestor of another of Nìkì's royal-lineage segments, is depicted as having benefited by his association with Muslims at a crucial moment in his career. He was Kpee Gunu *Kaba Wuko* ("Kpee Gunu who cleared away the grass," or "who cleared the ground"). It is said that Nìkì had been abandoned during wars following the death of *Sùnɔ̀* Dobidia, but was reoccupied (or founded a second time) by Kpee Gunu *Kaba Wuko,* after its site was cleared of overgrowth[18] with the ritual help—said to have included the sacrifice of a white cock—of a Muslim divine, who had to be brought in from outside because the Muslims of the first Nìkì had dispersed during the wars. In the reestablished Nìkì, Kpee Gunu *Kaba Wuko* is said to have established new Muslims bearing the patronymic-group names Taruwεrε and Ture.[19]

An early beginning for Muslim long-distance trade across Borgu is also suggested by other evidence. The mid-seventeenth century *'Aṣl al-Wanqariyyin* (an anonymous document on the history of the Wangarawa of Kano) mentions the presence of Wangara traders in "Barghū" and "Busa," possibly with reference to the fifteenth century.[20] The fourteenth- and fifteenth-century Arabic epitaphs at Kukiya (modern Bentiya), an old Soŋoy center in the territory of the Republic of Mali, near the border with Niger, are likely to reflect the presence of traders engaged in contacts with areas further to the east and the south, including Borgu.[21] In fact, c. 1664, but most probably drawing on earlier information, one of the Timbuktu chronicles describes B.r.ku" (Barku or Borgu) as a source of excellent cola nuts.[22]

The Perception of "National" Festivals in Recent Discourses of Borgu Identity

Since the late 1970s, an intense interest in history and cultural identity has flourished among Bààtɔ̀núm-speaking and Bo'o-speaking members of the intelligentsia of Béninois Borgu. This interest has nurtured a discourse of ethnic identity that endeavors to ground a sense of Borgu nationality on a pristine pre-Islamic, and pre-Christian, past. But though in principle this discourse equally rejects Islam and Christianity as alien, in fact it borrows abundantly from misperceptions of the history of Islam current among Christian missionaries and European writers during the colonial period in West Africa.[23]

The *Gaani* festival is regarded as the quintessential encapsulation of the unique character of Borgu culture, which is said to be fundamentally alien to anything Islamic. But actually the name and certain characteristic features of the *Gaani,* and also of the *Dɔ̀ɔ̀ Kɔ̃ru* ("Fire Throwing") festival, which is celebrated earlier than the *Gaani,* at the beginning of the lunar year, follow patterns that are widespread in West Africa. Moreover, neither the *Dɔ̀ɔ̀ Kɔ̃ru* nor the *Gaani* of Borgu can be understood without taking into account Islamic cultural idioms, and the way in which these idioms have been made to operate within local non-Muslim culture.

Both festivals recur yearly according to a computation of lunar months and days of the week modeled upon the international Islamic calendar. There are twelve lunations in this calendar of festivals. As with Islam-derived calendars elsewhere in West Africa, the names of the lunations refer to the preparation, celebration, and aftermath of rites that coincide with high points of the Islamic year. The high points referred to in this particular calendar of festivals include the fasting during the ninth month (*Ramaḍān*) of the Islamic year, and the Ibrāhīmic/Abrahamic sacrifice of a sheep at the *'Īd al-Kabīr* festival, on the tenth day of the twelfth month of the Islamic calendar (*Dhū 'l-Ḥijja*). However, in this paper we need mention only the names of the first lunation, *Dɔ̀ɔ̀ Kɔ̃ru* (named after the festival), the second lunation *Dɔ̀ɔ̀kɔ̃ Wonnɔ̃* (the junior brother of *Dɔ̀ɔ̀ Kɔ̃ru*), also known as *Gaani Gōbī Kaso* (preparing money/resources for the *Gaani*), the third lunation (*Gaani*), and the fourth, *Gaani Banna,* defined as the aftermath of *Gaani.*[24]

The *Dɔ̀ɔ̀ Kɔ̃ru* (Fire-Throwing) Festival

The name of this festival is formed with the Bààtɔ̀núm words *dɔ̀ɔ̀* (fire) and *kɔ̃ru* (the act of throwing). It is celebrated throughout Borgu, and descriptions of it are available from Nìkì and Bānīkpààrù (Banikoara).

In Nìkì, as in Bānīkpààrù and elsewhere in Borgu, *Dɔ̀ɔ̀ Kɔ̃ru* is the New Year festival. It falls on the tenth day of the first lunation, which begins—in accordance with the Islamic calendar—at sunset, in the evening of what would still be the previous (ninth) day if the modern Western calendar were being used. The *Sìnà Boko* (king) goes in procession to the west of the city with lit straw torches, and throws them there.[25]

In Bānīkpààrù, the *Bara Sùnɔ̀* (the head of the drummers) plays in the early evening before the palace of the *Nā Sùnɔ̀* (the traditional chief of Bānīkpààrù, who—atypically in Borgu—combines his chiefly authority with the function of supreme earth priest in the area). Later in the evening, the *Nā Sùnɔ̀* goes with a large following to a point situated to the west of the town, to throw torches—a ritual exorcism of evil influences. The procession then returns to the palace, before which a dance connected with the cult of twins is performed. The following morning, the local Muslims under the leadership of their *Imām* (called the *Bàà Deman* in Bààtɔ̀núm) come to visit the *Nā Sùnɔ̀* to recite from the Qur'ān, and to predict the important events of the year. Later, dignitaries and male and female descendants of the *Nā Sùnɔ̀* visit his palace, and his "grandsons" and "grand-daughters" enjoy the license to openly criticize decisions taken by him. Music playing, singing, and dancing continue in the following days.[26]

These descriptions of the *Dɔ̀ɔ̀ Kɔ̄ru* of Nìkì and Bɔ̄nīkpààrà (Banikoara), in the Béninois part of Borgu, demonstrate beyond doubt that this festival belongs in the same category as several other West African celebrations of the new lunar year. They also point to links with North Africa.

Evidence from Morocco and Tunisia shows that water and fire rites, associated with the "death" of the elapsed solar year and the beginning of the new solar year, were detached from the seasonal cycle and fitted on the Islamic lunar calendar. They were made to move over the seasons in association with the first festival of the Islamic year. This is the *'Āshūrā'* festival, which is the New Year festival for Muslims, and which is celebrated on the tenth day of *Muḥarram,* the first month of the Islamic calendar. North African purificatory rites during *'Āshūrā'* include the fumigation of houses and animals with lit branches.[27]

On another side of Africa, in Somalia, the New Year festival of *Dab-shid* (Kindling Fire) also includes fire rites. It is alternatively referred to as *'Īd Fara'ūn,* "the Festival of Pharaoh."[28] Conceivably, this Arabic name could indicate that the festival is perceived to have non-Islamic roots. But it is likelier that the name simply refers to the association, which is not exclusive to Somalia, of the festival of *'Āshūrā'* with the commemoration of the death by drowning of Pharaoh and his armies.[29]

In Iran and elsewhere, Shī'ite Muslims commemorate at this time of the year the martyr's death of Ḥusayn, grandson of Prophet Muḥammad, in 61 A.H./680 A.D. or, alternatively, commemorate together his death and those of his brother Ḥasan and his father ʿAlī. Though Morocco now has no significant Shīʿite population, Moroccan lore also uses the pre-Islamic idiom of celebration of the death of the year to commemorate the death of figures of early Islam. Thus Moroccan celebrations of *ʿĀshūrāʾ* are associated with the mourning for ʿAlī's sons, and sometimes also with the mourning for Prophet Muḥammad's own death (though classical Muslim authorities place his death at a different time of the year, the date accepted by most of these authorities being the twelfth or the thirteenth day of *Rabīʿ al-awwal,* the third month of the Islamic year).

The linkage of fire rites with the *ʿĀshūrāʾ* festival was probably carried by North African Muslims to West Africa. Alternatively, or perhaps additionally, seasonal fire rites practised in West Africa before the arrival of Islam in the region were amalgamated with *ʿĀshūrāʾ* south of the Sahara.[30] Whichever the case, evidence of such syntheses of different idioms is reported from New Year festivals in different West African cultures. While some of these cultures (Hausa, etc.) have a long tradition of Muslim rulers, others (v.g. Dāχomὲ or Dahomey, Mamprugu) do not.

In Hausaland, *ʿĀshūrāʾ* is celebrated in Kano as the Islamic New Year. One of the Hausa names for the month of *Muḥarram* is *Watan Wowwo* (the lunation of burning), because on its nineteenth day boys throw torches at one another.[31] Nadel recorded that, among the Nupe, the rites of the Islamic new year involve "play with lit torches and bonfires."[32] Actually, the first lunation of the Nupe Muslim calendar is called *Etswà Nạvùṇ,* "the lunation of torches."[33] In Abomὲ or Abomey, the capital of the precolonial kingdom of Dāχomὲ (Dahomey), the night of the New Year celebrations introduced by Muslims became known in the Fõ or Fɔ̃ language as *È ñi zò,* "one throws fire."[34] In Dagbon or Dagomba, in the north of the Republic of Ghana, *ʿĀshūrāʾ* is known as *Bugum* ("fire," in the Dagbani language). On its night, torches are lit in Dagbon's capital Yendi, and are taken to a place to the west of the town, where they are thrown.[35] Still in northern Ghana, among the Mamprusi—the inhabitants of Mamprugu—one of the twelve lunations of the year is equally called *Bugum*, a word that also means "fire" in their Mampruli language.[36] The rites of the Mamprusi *Bugum* festival, which is celebrated during this lunation, are centered on the throwing of torches, which in the capital—Nalerigu—are lit from a torch held by the *Nayiiri* (the overall traditional ruler of Mamprugu); in other areas they are lit from a torch held by the local chief. These Mamprusi rites also include drinking and sprinkling water in which Muslim prayers written in chalk have been dissolved. Local Muslims regard this festival as the beginning of the lunar year.[37]

All this attests to the pervasive role of Islamic, nonseasonal, calendrical idioms in the reorganization of the order and layers of institutional time, in societies that nevertheless were dependent on careful seasonal distribution of their economic activities.[38] Such reorganizations of calendrical time were not necessarily geared to the recurrence of Muslim long-distance caravans, nor to the specific customs of local Muslim minorities. Rather, as we will see in the case of the *Gaani* festival, they often had much to do with reconceptualizations of the position of local non-Muslim rulers.[39]

After *'Āshūrā'*, the next festival in the international Islamic calendar is the *Mawlid al-Nabī* (Prophet Muḥammad's birthday) on the twelfth of *Rabī' al-awwal*, the third month of the Islamic year. In Borgu, it coincides with the *Gaani* festival.

The Gaani Festival

The *Gaani* is a traditional festival not only in Nìkì, but also elsewhere in Nigerian and Béninois Borgu, in large polities such as Busa,[40] and Kpãne or Kpande,[41] and in smaller chiefdoms such as Bānīkpààrù and others.[42] It is the most conspicuous Borgu festival.[43]

In the colonial period, two opposed ways of explaining the *Gaani* were proposed by European observers. The colonial administrator Bramoulle, when he was the head of Nìkì's administrative *sous-division*, categorized both the *Dɔ̀ɔ̀ Kɔ̄ru* and the *Gaani* as nothing but transposed and distorted Islamic festivals.[44] By contrast, Lombard has stated, with reference to the *Gaani,* that the coinciding Islamic festival was nothing but a pretext for the celebration of a "tribal" and "animist" festival. However, neither of these explanations is tenable. First, the *Gaani* is not centered on Islamic worship but on the celebration of kingship. It makes no place in its rites for the commemoration of the birth of Prophet Muḥammad. But, second, though the *Gaani* is not an Islamic festival, it is precisely its calendrical link with the *Mawlid* that enables it to be purely a kingship festival. This calendrical link is not a mere pretext. Rather, it is an essential part of the *Gaani.*

As we have written elsewhere,

> [by] being attached to the Muslim calendar, which moves over the seasonal year, the *Gaani* severs any links it may have historically had with seasonal rites. In other words, it has been freed from other functions and concentrated entirely on kingship *qua* kingship.[45] It is a striking example of the usefulness of the Muslim calendar for non-Muslim rulers.[46]

Neither Lombard nor other European observers have provided any detailed ethnographic description of the *Gaani.* I recorded aspects of the Nìkì *Gaani* on video in October 1990, and later provided a description of some of them in writing.[47] But it is actually to Borgu scholars that we owe the first preliminary descriptions of this festival.[48] These scholars have found in the *Gaani* what is, in their view, a most perplexing Muslim presence. Being too honest to suppress this evidence, they have tried to explain it away within the parameters of the particular brand of cultural nationalism that brands Islamic culture as essentially alien to Borgu.

In the case of Nìkì, the festival has been described as having a first phase that runs over three days, and a second phase that takes place seven days after the end of the first. According to this now received description, the first phase consists of a so-called *Gaani* eve (allegedly the "first" day), followed by the *Gaani* day proper (*Gaani Tōri*), which is then followed the next day (known as the *Kaayesi*) by other ceremonies centered on kingship. The second phase, known as the *Yɔ̄ɔ̄ Kɔ̄ɔ̄gii Gaani* (the *Gaani* of the *Yɔ̄ɔ̄ Kɔ̄ɔ̄gii*) is said to happen a week after the final day of the first phase.[49] The *Yɔ̄ɔ̄ Kɔ̄ɔ̄gii,* a title that approximately means "the female elder in charge of the [sacred] razors," occupies an office of royal rank.[50] She must not be appointed from the same royal-lineage segment as the one to which belongs the reigning *Sìnà Boko* (king). Her role in the *Gaani* consists in initiating the ritual shaving of the heads of the young Wasangari princes and princesses, and giving them new, princely names. Without having been through this *rite de passage,* none of the new male princes will be allowed to compete later for the kingship of Nìkì.

However, some inaccuracies have crept into the received description of the *Gaani.* First, the beginning of each of the two phases of the festival corresponds, respectively, to the commemoration of Muḥammad's birthday on the twelfth of *Rabīʿ al-awwal* (the third month of the Islamic calendar), and (judging from comparative evidence from other parts of West Africa) to the commemoration of Muḥammad's naming day (his *ʿaqīqa*) on the nineteenth of the same month. Hence, in the past, the *Gaani* of the *Yɔ̄ɔ̄ Kɔ̄ɔ̄gii* appears to have been scheduled for the seventh day after the beginning of the *Gaani* proper or *Gaani* of the king, not for the seventh day after its end.[51] (At present, however, both in Nìkì and in Bānīkpààrù—where the office corresponding to that of the *Yɔ̄ɔ̄ Kɔ̄ɔ̄gii* of Nìkì is called *Bana Kura*—the giving of princely names begins on the day of the *Kaayesi;* that is, on the final day of the *Gaani* proper.)[52]

The Islamic celebration of the naming day (the *ʿaqīqa*) is the sacrifice of umblemished sheep or goats (two for a boy, one for a girl) accompanying the first haircut of a newborn child. Usually it takes place on the seventh (or the sixth) day after birth and coincides with the name-giving.[53] In Nìkì the *Gaani* of the *Yɔ̄ɔ̄ Kɔ̄ɔ̄gii* borrows from the *ʿaqīqa,* but the borrowings are adapted to a different social purpose and displaced to a different stage in the life of the individual. The points of contact between the two ceremonies are obvious: the *Gaani* of the *Yɔ̃ɔ̃ Kɔ̃ɔ̃gii* involves shaving and naming, and closely follows Prophet Muḥammad's birthday. But the shaving and (re)naming of the Wasangari princes is a collective, yet socially restricted, rite specifically linked to aristocratic status; generally princes and princesses undergo it when they are about seven years old, rather than on the seventh day after their birth.[54]

A second misunderstanding embedded in the received description of the festival is the notion of the alleged "eve" of the *Gaani*.[55] Properly speaking there is no such "eve." What actually happens is that, following the Islamic computation of time, the first day of the *Gaani* begins in the evening of what would still be the previous day, if the modern "Western" or "Christian" calendar were being adhered to. To clinch this point, it is worth noting that whenever the *Gaani* falls on a Friday, it is postponed to Saturday,[56] so as not to coincide with the Muslim Friday rites, and with the parallel homages to kingship that recur every Friday as a matter of routine (showing once again that ritual manifestations centered on kingship tend to gravitate to Islamically significant days). Yet, in 1989, according to the Western calendar, the so-called eve of the *Gaani* fell "on a Friday," yet the festival was not transferred to the following day—obviously because it had begun on what was already Saturday according to the Islamic calendar.

In Nìkì, in the afternoon of the first day of the *Gaani*, the *Sìnà Boko* (king) goes out of the palace in procession for ritual visits to a number of stations along a prescribed itinerary.[57] Most of these stations are traditional shrines. But the king's first two visits are, respectively, to the *Bàà Deman*'s mosque (the only place at which the king dismounts during the procession), and then to the compound of the *Bàà Deman*'s deputy. In 1990, it was the *Bàà Deman* who closed the *Kaayesi* ceremonies the following day; on this occasion he and his deputy were allowed to come closer to the person of the king than any other officeholder.[58]

In Bānīkpààrū, in the afternoon of the first day of the *Gaani*, the *Nã Sùnɔ̀* goes in procession to the *Idi gĩgire* (festival praying area), a name derived (through Dèndí) from the Arabic word *'Īd* (festival) and from the Dèndí word *jìngàrâì* (mosque, praying area).[59] The ruler's procession goes round the *Idi gīgire* three times, and then moves on to visit a series of traditional shrines.[60]

Those who still see Islamic culture as essentially alien to Borgu regard this high profile of Islamic elements in the *Gaani* festival as no less than "embarrassing,"[61] and "paradoxical."[62] But their perplexity is born from a historical misconstruction that sees the presence of Muslims and Islamic cultural idioms in Borgu as a result of what is referred to as "invasions" by "jihādist" armies.[63] This is of course a reductionist approach that ignores the process of peaceful penetration of Islam through trade that characterizes the history of many regions of West Africa, and of Borgu in particular. It is part of an ideology that has been widespread in West African—and in Africanist—historiography since the colonial period.[64] This ideology reduces all patterns of the propagation of Islam in Africa to the pattern embodied in the warlike exploits of the Sokoto *jihād* (which indeed sent armies into Borgu), and of other West African *jihād* movements. In the specific case of Borgu, this anachronistic confusion of peaceful penetration with armed invasion also found a champion in Frobenius.[65]

This misconstruction overlooks the political solidarity of Muslim communities with non-Muslim rulers that has consistently characterized the history of Borgu. But, actually, though some traditions state that, in the 1830s, under the influence of Ìlọrin, a *jihād* war was organized against Nìkì by the Dèndí-speaking Muslims of Gawdebɛrɛ (Godeberi, in the Nigerian part of Borgu), the same traditions also state that this *jihād* movement was defeated precisely because the Dèndí-speaking Muslims of Nìkì preferred to side with Nìkì's king and princes, with whom they shared political and economic interests and kinship networks.[66]

Prevented by their own presuppositions from grasping these solid historical linkages between Borgu Muslims and Borgu non-Muslim rulers, some modern cultural nationalists try to interpret away the Islamic threads woven into the fabric of the *Gaani*, by highlighting certain would-be explanations obtained from contemporary informants. Some of these alleged explanations state that the *Gaani* is celebrated on the twelfth and thirteenth day of

Rabīʿ al-awwal, the third month of the Islamic calendar, in order to commemorate the joy experienced by the people of Borgu at the news of Muḥammad's death (on the thirteenth), which supposedly liberated them from Muslim pressure.[67] Alternatively it is stated that during the legendary "Kisira" migrations,[68] Kisira and his followers were pursued by hostile Muslim armies, but these armies stopped to commemorate the birth of the Prophet on the twelfth of *Rabīʿ al-awwal,* which gave Kisira's party the opportunity to escape and reach Borgu, where they were able to continue to practice their traditional non-Muslim cults.[69] It is then concluded that the coincidence of the *Gaani* with the *Mawlid* must be a commemoration of the lucky escape from the danger of enforced Islamisation.[70] Yet, nothing in the public *Gaani* rituals of Nìkì and Bānīkpàárù suggests commemoration of resistance to Islam, or of joy for Muḥammad's death (as nothing in them suggests commemoration of joy for Muḥammad's birth either).[71]

Another demonstrable misconstruction affects the attempts to explain the origin of the name *Gaani.* Lombard, and recent Borgu authors, are aware that the word *Gaani* is homophonous with the Dèndí word *gàanì,* which means "dance" (the main Bààtɔ̀núm word for "dance" is *yāàbù*).[72] However, Lombard dismisses this Dèndí etymology, on the assumption that "dancing" cannot have been the original meaning of the name of the festival. As to Borgu's contemporary cultural nationalists, some of them have strenuously searched the Bààtɔ̀núm and Bo'o languages for etymologies for the name of the festival.

On the Bo'o-speaking side, *Gaani* has been said to derive from the expression *gañili-lɛ dakpɛ,* in which *gañili* means the wooden structure of the horse's saddle, *lɛ* means "to hit," and *dakpɛ* means "feast"; hence "the feast in which the saddle's wooden armature is hit."[73] In this view, after escaping the pursuing Muslim armies, the Bo'o-speaking party led by Kisira decided to commemorate the event by shows of horsemanship, during which the saddles were rhythmically hit.

On the Bààtɔ̀núm-speaking side, this Bo'o etymology has been rejected, and a derivation from the Bààtɔ̀núm verb *gane* (to ward off, to prevent) has been proposed, in accordance with the presupposition that the *Gaani* commemorates the prevention of militarily enforced Islamization.[74]

It is hence clear that the proposed Bo'o and Bààtɔ̀núm etymologies are closely connected with basic historical and ethnographic misapprehensions about the *Gaani.* In fact, these over-ingenious etymologies are totally unnecessary. Why the *Gaani* bears this name is fairly clear. If one plots on the map of West Africa the available evidence about the commemoration of the *Mawlid,* it is easy to recognize two internally consistent families of African names for this Islamic festival, and for the African rites coinciding with it. Each of these families of names is distributed over a wide geographical area. In one area the names are Manding or derived from Manding languages, while in the other area they belong to the Soŋoy or Songhay language or are derived from it.

Throughout both areas, dancing seems to have a historical association with local commemorations of, or during, the *Mawlid.* Actually, in the Middle East too, the *Mawlid* has been traditionally associated with music, dance, and merrymaking; this is one reason why its celebration has been regarded with mistrust by many Muslim jurists, and why it is forbidden in Saudi Arabia.[75]

Turning to the more westerly of the two areas, one finds that among the Mandenka or Malinke of the Republics of Mali and Guinea-Conakry the *Mawlid* is known as *Dõmba* or *Donba,* meaning "Big Day [of festivity]," a name also given to the month in which the *Mawlid* is celebrated, while the month preceding it is known as "the month before *Donba.*"[76] The same name occurs among the Juula or Dyula of the northern Côte d'Ivoire, among whom dancing was associated with the *Mawlid,* although dancing during this festival is now frowned upon by local Muslim scholars.[77] North of the Republic of Ghana, among the Dagomba, the *Mawlid* covers the commemoration of Muḥammad's birthday, on the twelfth of *Rabīʿ al-awwal,* and of his naming day on the nineteenth of the same month. This is a pattern repeated in other West African cultures, including Borgu in the past.[78] The *Mawlid* is commemorated with dancing by the Dagomba, who give it the (clearly Manding-derived) name *Damba.*[79]

BORGU

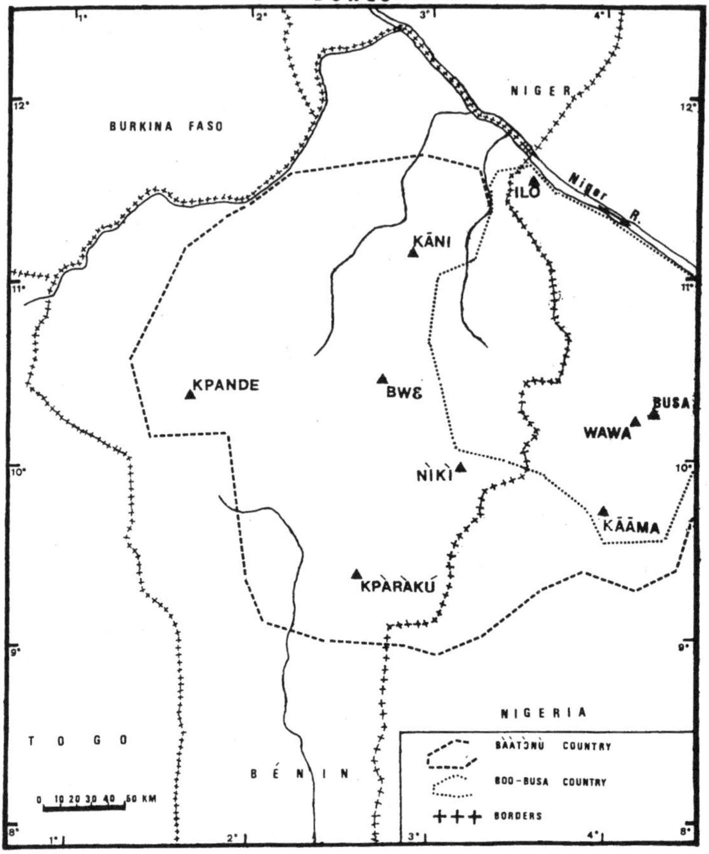

In the other geographical area, local names for the *Mawlid,* or for other celebrations coinciding with it and dated according to the Islamic calendar, come from the Soŋoy words *gáàn* (to dance), and *gàanì,* which literally means "dance," and which at one level continues to be linked, in Soŋoy-speaking cultures, to the possession cult of the *Hɔ̀lláy* or *Hóllé̀y* deities.[80] Among most of the Soŋoy themselves, both the *Mawlid* festival and the lunar month in which it occurs are generally called *Gàanì.* In Timbuktu, however, the festival bears another Soŋoy name, for the following reason. Soŋoy newborns have their head shaved at their naming ceremony, which takes place seven days after birth, and which follows the pattern of the Islamic ceremony of *ʿaqīqa* already described in the present paper. Timbuktu's *Mawlid* celebrates not the Prophet's birthday but his naming day, on the nineteenth of the month of *Rabīʿ al-awwal.*[81] Hence in the Soŋoy spoken in the city the festival is called *Kyebu* ("Shaving"), a name cognate with those given to both the act of shaving and the naming ceremony in the forms of the Soŋoy language spoken much farther to the southeast: *Cébú* in Soŋoy-Kaado and Zarma, and *Cábú* in Dèndí.[82]

Thus the homology between Nìkì's *Gaani* of the *Yɔ̃ɔ̃ Kɔ̃ɔ̃gii,* the *Kyebu* of Timbuktu, and the *Cábú* of Dèndí-speakers (one of the linguistic communities of Borgu), and the Islamic *ʿaqīqa,* is once more made clear. The borrowing of *ʿaqīqa* rites for ceremonies connected with access to chiefship and kingship is, of course, not exclusive to Borgu: the *Zarmakoy* of Dosso has his head shaved eight days after his installation.[83]

Given the vast extension of the Soŋoy-speaking trade diaspora,[84] and also the powerful and widespread political influence of the Soŋoy empire in the fifteenth and sixteenth centuries, the Soŋoy festival name *Gàanì* was directly or indirectly transmitted to several other West African languages and populations, more often than not in connection with the *Mawlid.* In the light of the currently available evidence, at the western extreme of this area is the Pullo (Fulɓe or Fulani) population of Liptaaku, in Burkina Faso, which gives the name *Gaani* both to the *Mawlid* and to the lunation in which this festival is celebrated.[85] At the eastern extreme is the Kanuri-speaking population of Borno.[86]

In regions farther north the same festival name is employed for the *Mawlid* in the Ăgădez area,[87] and by the Tuăreg Kăl-Ferwan and other Tuăreg of the Ayəṛ (Aïr or Ahir) region.[88] In this region the lunation in which the festival takes place is also called *Gaani.*[89] Two litanies chanted in Tayəṛt (the language of the Ayəṛ Tuăreg) in honor of Prophet Muḥammad, during the *Gaani,* have been published.[90] South of the Ayəṛ, in Hausaland, the month of the *Mawlid* (*Rabīʿ al-awwal*) is also known in Kano

(Nigerian Hausaland) as *Watan Gane* or *Watan Gani* (the lunation of *Gani*). The festival celebrated during it in honor of the birth of the Prophet is often referred to as *Sallar Gane* or *Sallar Gani* (the *Salla* of *Gane,* or *Gani; salla* being the Hausa word for "Muslim prayer" and "Muslim festival"). It takes place on either the twelfth or the nineteenth of the month.[91] A similar usage has been reported from the "Francophone" part of Hausaland within the borders of the Republic of Niger.[92]

Much farther south, in the area of the confluence of the Niger and Benue, at Lokoja, Idah, Okene, and so forth, up to 1952 the *Mawlid* was referred to as *Gani Gani,* and its celebration included drumming, singing, dancing and, in some places, masquerades. But after that year, under the influence of the branch of the Tijāniyya *ṭarīqa* paying allegiance to *Shaykh* Ibrāhīm Nyass, which devotes special attention to the commemoration of the birthday and the naming day of the Prophet (on the twelfth and nineteenth of *Rabīʿ al-awwal,* respectively), the character of the celebration changed, with emphasis being now placed on the teaching of Islam.[93]

To the northwest of the Niger-Benue confluence, in Nupeland, the name *Gànì* has been reported to occur both as the name of "a certain heathen dance where men and women dance together" and in the denominations of the second and third lunations of the Nupe Muslim calendar, respectively *Etswa Bawà Gànì,* "the Moon Before *Gànì,*" and *Etswa Gànì,* "the Moon of *Gànì.*"[94] Also relevant to the arguement of this paper is Nadel's description of a *rite de passage* in the Nupe system of age-grades. According to him, this rite included borrowings from Muslim tradition and took place only every six years. When its celebration occurred, it associated itself with the annual *Gànì* ceremonies. Still according to Nadel, the *Gànì* ceremonies had been introduced from Borno, by Muslims, but in Nupeland they featured a considerable degree of sexual license.[95] Unfortunately Nadel did not sufficiently clarify the relationship between the *Gànì* ceremonies performed every year and those performed only at six-year intervals, nor between the various aspects of the annual *Gànì* and the Muslim calendar.[96] Nevertheless, and without losing sight of the obvious differences, Nadel's *rite-de-passage* evidence (taken together with the evidence about the *Kyebu* of Timbuktu and the *Cábú* of Dèndí-speakers) bears an analogy with the promotion of children of the Wasangari aristocracy to full princely status in the *Gaani* of Borgu. In addition, Nadel's references to sexual permissiveness are not without analogy to an old custom, no longer practiced in Nìkì but still referred to in oral lore. According to local informants, in olden days, during the *Kaayesi,* restrictions regarding access to women were transgressed on behalf of the king of Nìkì. His senior wives went out to capture young women to be added to the number of the royal wives. Great shame was thus caused to the young men to whom the kidnapped women had already been promised, which is said to have led some of those men to commit suicide.[97]

After one has plotted on the map of West Africa the two geographical areas in which the names given to the commemoration of the *Mawlid* (and to performances of other rites timed so as to coincide with it) are traceable to Manding names (in one area), and to Soŋoy names (in the other area), it becomes clear that the evidence from Mamprugu, the country of the Mamprusi (in the north of the Republic of Ghana), displays an overlap and mutual interference of those two patterns of names. This probably mirrors a historical and geographical overlap of the cultural influences spread by the Manding-speaking and the Soŋoy-speaking trade networks.

In Mamprugu, the first and second lunations after *Bugum* (the Festival of Fire) are respectively called *Damma-Biraa* (the companion [or, the junior brother, the slave] of *Damma*) and *Damma* —a name cognate with the Manding-derived name (*Damba*) used for the *Mawlid* by the Dagomba. The *Damma* lunation of the Mamprusi contains the festival of the same name, which is the most important of the Mamprusi annual festivals, and which coincides with the *Mawlid* of the Muslim calendar. It displays some significant similarities with the *Gaani* of Borgu through its emphasis on local political rituals centered on rulership. However, the Mamprusi also use the partly Soŋoy-derived calendrical terms *Gaani-Biraa* and *Gaani* for two of the lunations computed in the year. But their *Gaané* lunar month does not coincide with the *Mawlid* lunation (*Rabīʿ al-awwal*) of the international Islamic calendar. Instead, *Gaani-Biraa* and *Gaani* have been, so to speak, displaced along the line of calendrical succession. They have become the names used (in alternation with other names) for, respectively, the first and second lunations after *Damma.* These two lunations contain no festivals of their own, but Mamprusi informants state that *Damma* "may continue" during them, and sometimes describe them as "slaves of *Damma.*"[98]

Concluding Remarks

The *Gaani* festivals of Borgu neither commemorate resistance to Islam nor display acceptance of Islam. Rather, they make use of the Islamic calendar for the purpose of celebrating kingship and chiefship, and for ritually representing the relationships between traditional rulers and different sectors of society, among them the historically close relationship between rulers (most of them non-Muslim) and Muslim communities. In Nìkì, the historical center of western and southern Borgu, the holders of the office of *Bàà Deman* or *Imām,* and other leading figures of the Muslim community, fulfill crucial functions in the *Gaani* ceremonies, which are made to coincide with the *Mawlid* of the Islamic calendar in order to set them apart from seasonal festivals. But the public celebration of the birthday and naming-day of the Prophet Muḥammad is replaced by the public celebration of kingship. It is as if the festival had to be emptied of any Islamic content and yet Muslims had to be given a very conspicuous place in it (which they gladly accept). In this the ambiguities of Borgu's traditional political culture are superbly represented. But these ambiguities are constructive: they are constitutive properties of that political culture. They are not "paradoxical," even though they may seem to be so when viewed through the lens of contemporary Bààtɔ̀núm-speaking, and Bo'o-speaking, cultural nationalism.

The *Gaani,* the *Dɔ̀ɔ̀ Kɔ̄ru,* and other culturally complex features of Borgu history and contemporary life, shed light on the mechanisms that allowed diaspora Muslims not only to play a "consular" role within non-Muslim societies, but also actively to contribute to the maintenance and reproduction of these societies.

Oral Sources (Interviews)

1. His Highness *Alhaji* Musa Mohammed Ki-Gera III, the Emir of Borgu, interviewed in his palace in Busa (January 1990, Nigerian Borgu).
2. *Alhaji* Ahmadu Aliyu, a retired traditional ruler of Wawa (January 1990, Wawa, Nigerian Borgu).

3a, b, c. Sābî Maamaa, better known as Bààbu Adam, a senior Gɛsɛrɛ traditionist of the Bàà Maro lineage living in the Gàá ward of Kpàràkú ("Parakou"), in Béninois Borgu, interviewed in his compound in (a) April 1988 and—(b) and (c)—twice in January 1990.

4. The *Bààbà Damagii,* a senior traditional officeholder in Kpàràkú ("Parakou"), interviewed in his compound in the Sìnà Gūrù ward of that city in April 1988.
5. The *Bàà Deman* (the *Imām*) of Nìkì, interviewed in the Nìkì-Maro ward (January 1990, Béninois Borgu).
6. Iburaima *Bàà Gɛsɛrɛ,* the *Bàà Bwɛɛ* (head of the Gɛsɛrɛ traditionists of Bwɛɛ or "Bouay"), interviewed in his compound in that town (January 1990, Béninois Borgu).
7. Abudu *Gɛsɛrɛ Magasi,* the head of the Gɛsɛrɛ traditionists of Kāni or Kandi, interviewed in his compound in that town (January 1990, Béninois Borgu).
8. *Àrùfá* Mohammed Goh, interviewed in the town known as Desa or Lesa in Bààtɔ̀núm, and as Ilẹ́ṣà Ìbàrìbà in Yorùbá (summer of 1969, Nigerian Borgu).
9. The *Yɔ̄ɔ̄ Kɔ̄ɔ̄gii* (the most senior female officeholder) of Nìkì, interviewed at her palace in Nìkì-Dāāri (January 1990, Béninois Borgu).

10a, b. *Wōrū Tokura* Bukari, the elderly head of the Gɛsɛrɛ traditionists of Nìkì (Béninois Borgu), interviewed in the Nìkì-Wɔɔre ward (April 1988 and January 1990).

11. The *Bàà Wàràkpe* of Nìkì, interviewed in the Nìkì-Maro ward (January 1990).
12. *Alhaji* Adamu Kilishi, private secretary to the emir of Borgu, interviewed in Busa (Nigerian Borgu) (January 1990).

Interview 8 was conducted by my late friend and student Musa Baba Idris, a young scholar from Kããma ("Kaiama") who died in a car accident on the Zaria-Kano road in 1973, before completing his Ph.D. thesis at the Centre of West African Studies of the University of Birmingham.

Interviews 4 and 10a were conducted by Mr. Obarè Bouroubin Bagodo (a lecturer in the Department of History and Archaeology, Université Nationale du Bénin, and member of the Sous-Commision nationale de linguistique baatɔnu), Dr. Solomon Oyèéwọlé Babáyẹmí (then of the Institute of African Studies, University of Ìbàdàn, now *Oba* Akínrìnọ̀lá I, the *Olúfì* of Gbọ́ngán in Ọ̀sun State, Nigeria), and myself.

Interviews 1, 2, 3b, 6, 7, 10b, and 12 were conducted by Mr. O. B. Bagodo, Mr. Oumarou Banni-Guénné (lecturer in history and geography at the C.E.G. of Pobɛ or "Pobé," then secretary general of Bénin's Commission nationale de langue Boo), and myself.

Interviews 3a, 3c, 5, 9, and 11 were conducted by Mr. O. B. Bagodo and myself.

Video. In this essay I also draw information from my video of aspects of the *Gaani* festival of Nìkì in early October 1990. The recording was made with the valuable assistance of my Béninois friend and colleague O. B. Bagodo.

Notes

1. Ivor Wilks, "The Transmission of Islamic Learning in the Western Sudan," in *Literacy in Traditional Society*, ed. J. Goody (Cambridge, 1968); "The Suwarians. Laissez-faire, laissez-nous faire?" Paper presented to the Conference on Is-

lam in Africa, Northwestern University, 28–31 March 1984; *Wa and the Wala: Islam and Polity in Northwestern Ghana* (Cambridge, 1989).

2. Wilks, "Transmission," 196; T. C. Hunter, "The Development of an Islamic Tradition of Learning among the Jakhanka of West Africa" (Ph.D. diss., University of Chicago, 1977).

3. L. O. Sanneh, *The Jakhanke* (London, 1979).

4. Wilks, "The Suwarians"; *Wa.* 98–100, cf. 112–15.

5. The main traditional polities of Borgu are, in Nigeria (from north to south), Ilo (Illo on most maps), Busa (Bussa), Wawa and Kã̄ãma (Kaiama); and in the Republic of Bénin (from north to south), Kãni (Kandi), Kpãne or Kpande (Kouandé), Nìkì and Kpàràkú or Kɔ̀rɔ̀kú (Parakou). The chiefdom of Bānīkpààrù (Banikoara), which is also referred to in this essay, is located to the northwest of Kãni.

6. Awaou Bachabi, "La Constitution du groupe Dendi de Zougou-Wangara. Approche historique" (Mémoire de Maîtrise, Université Nationale du Bénin, Ecole Normale Supérieure, 1980); Nassirou Arifari Bako, "La Question du peuplement Dendi dans la partie septentrionale de la République Populaire du Bénin; le cas du Borgou" (Mémoire de Maîtrise, Université Nationale du Bénin, Faculté des Lettres, Arts et Sciences Humaines, Département d'Histoire et Archéologie, 1989).

7. P. Lovejoy, "The Role of the Wangara in the Economic Transformation of the Central Sudan in the Fifteenth and Sixteenth Centuries," *Journal of African History* 19, no. 2 (1978): 178–93.

8. Wawa was one of the exceptions to this rule: according to its traditions, it was founded by Beri-Beri (Kanuri) trader-clerics and has had a Muslim dynasty from its inception (interview 2). Another exception was Gwadebɛrɛ or Gbere Bɛrɛ (Gòrò Bééri or Gordo Bééri in the Déndì language), a now ruined Muslim commercial town in the Bààtɔ̀núm-speaking area of Nigerian Borgu, south of the Moṣi river (interview 8).

9. J. Lombard, *Structures de type "féodal" en Afrique noire. Etude des dynamismes internes et des relations sociales chez les Bariba du Dahomey* (Paris and The Hague, 1965), 119, 172.

10. N. Levtzion, *Muslims and Chiefs in West Africa* (Oxford, 1968), 176.

11. Interviews 9 and 11.

12. Interview 5.

13. Musa Baba Idris, "Political and Economic Relations in the Historical Study of a Plural Society" (Ph.D. diss. left incomplete at the author's death, University of Birmingham, Centre of West African Studies, 1973), chap. 6; Obarè Bouroubin Bagodo, "Le Royaume Borgou Wasangari de Nikki dans la première moitié du XIXème siècle: Essai d'histoire politique" (Mémoire de Maîtrise, Université Nationale du Bénin, Faculté des Lettres, Arts et Sciences Humaines, 1978), 34, 39–40, 52.

14. Interview 3b; see also Idris, "Political and Economic Relations," chap. 8.

15. Idris, "Political and Economic Relations," chap. 8; Koumanyo Bio Guene, "La Généalogie des rois de Nikki de Sunon Séro à l'invasion coloniale française (1897)" (Mémoire de Maîtrise, Université Nationale du Bénin, Faculté des Let-

tres, Arts et Sciences Humaines, 1978), 92; Bagodo, "Le Royaume Borgou," 50–51.

16. Interviews 90 and 10b.

17. Interview 9.

18. Bagodo, "Le Royaume Borgou," 48 n. 1.

19. Interview 10a.

20. Muhammad al-Hajj, "A Seventeenth-Century Chronicle on the Origins and Missionary Activities of the Wangarawa," *Kano Studies* 1, no. 4 (1968): 8–10, 20; Lovejoy, "The Role of the Wangara," 180.

21. P. F. de Moraes Farias, "The Oldest Extant Writing of West Africa: Medieval Epigraphs from Ǝssuk, Saney, and Egef-n-Tawaqqast (Mali)" *Journal des africanistes* 60, no. 2 (1990): 65, 68, 104–5.

22. *Ta'rīkh al-Fattāsh,* ed. and trans. O. Houdas and M. Delafosse (Paris, 1964), 93 (Arabic text), 67 (trans.).

23. P. F. de Moraes Farias, "The Oral Traditionist as Critic and Intellectual Producer: An Example from Contemporary Mali," in *African Historiography: Essays in Honour of Jacob Ade Ajayi,* ed. T. Falola (London, 1993), 16–17.

24. Robert Orou Yorouba, "La Gaani et ses implications socio-économiques" (Mémoire de Maîtrise, Université Nationale du Bénin, Faculté des Lettres, Arts et Sciences Humaines, 1982), 18–20.

25. Interview 3a; Orou Yorouba, "La Gaani," 10.

26. Katigui Bani Bandiri, "Catalyse n^{0} 4: Quelques fêtes et cérémonies dans la chefferie traditionelle de Banikoara" (cyclostyled and distributed by the author, 1989).

27. E. Westermarck, *Ritual and Belief in Morocco,* 2 vols. (London, 1926), 2:65–67.

28. J. Spencer Trimingham, *Islam in Ethiopia* (Oxford, 1952), 267.

29. M. Gaudefroy-Demombynes, *Mahomet* (Paris, 1957), 397.

30. J. Spencer Trimingham, *Islam in West Africa* (Oxford, 1959), 76.

31. R. C. Abraham, *Dictionary of the Hausa Language,* 2d ed. (London, 1962), 933; P. E. Starratt, "Oral History in Muslim Africa: Al-Maghili Legends in Kano" (Ph.D. diss., University of Michigan, 1991), 144.

32. S. F. Nadel, *Nupe Religion: Traditional Beliefs and the Influence of Islam in a West African Chiefdom* (London, 1954), 244–45.

33. A. W. Banfield, *Dictionary of the Nupe Language,* 2 vols. (first published Shonga, northern Nigeria, 1914–16; repr. Westmead, Farnborough, Hants., 1969), 144, 353; S. F. Nadel, *A Black Byzantium* (London, 1942), 409.

34. B. Maupoil, *Contribution à l'étude de l'origine musulmane de la géomancie dans le Bas-Dahomey* (originally a Thèse complémentaire pour le Doctorat des lettres) (Paris, 1945), 79–80.

35. P. Ferguson, "Islamization in Dagbon: A Study of the Alfanema of Yendi" (Ph.D. diss., Cambridge University, 1972), 121.

36. S. Drucker-Brown, "Mamprusi Installation Ritual and Centralisation: A Convection Model," *Man,* n.s. 24 (1989), 488.

37. S. Drucker-Brown, "Calendar and Ritual: The Mamprusi Case," *Systèmes de pensée en Afrique noire* 7 (1984): 72.

38. Moraes Farias, "Oldest Extant Writing," 95–96.

39. Of course, the festivals dated according to this Islamic calendar move over the seasons and are independent of the seasonal cycle. There are, however, other festivals that are linked to seasonal events such as the harvest of crops (interview 3a). In Borgu, chiefs and kings play central roles in the seasonal festivals. Traditionally, however, chiefs and kings have also been at the center of ceremonies coinciding with at least some of the Islamic-calendar festivals.

40. R. Faurite, "Le Royaume de Busa dès ses origines médiévales à 1935" (Thèse de Doctorat de troisième cycle, Lyon II, 1987), 151–55. However, a recent visitor reports that public commemorations of the *Gaani* in Busa are now rather muted (personal communication from Mr. Richard Kuba, University of Bayreuth, February 1993).

41. Madeleine Akognon, "L'Organisation du pouvoir politique Wasangari à Kpandè (Kouandé) au XIXème siècle" (Mèmoire de Maîtrise, Universitè Nationale du Bénin, Ecole Normale Supérieure, 1980), 6; Orou Yorouba, "La Gaani," 22.

42. Bandiri, "Catalyse."

43. Lombard, *Structures de type "fèodal,"* 330–40.

44. A. Bramoulle, "Les Redevances coutumières dans le cadre de la chefferie supérieure de Nikki" (unpublished) (Porto-Novo, library of the Centre Béninois de la Recherche scientifique et technique, uncatalogued).

45. Cf. Drucker-Brown, "Calendar and Ritual," 79.

46. P. F. de Moraes Farias, "Praise Splits the Subject of Speech," in *Power, Marginality and African Oral Literature,* ed. G. Gurniss and E. Gunner (Cambridge, 1995).

47. Ibid.

48. Orou Yorouba, "La Gaani"; CEAP–Borgou, *Table ronde sur les origines de la Gaani, fête traditionelle des Baatombu (Baribas)* (Parakou, 1986); Bandiri, "Catalyse."

49. Orou Yorouba, "La Gaani," 29, 53, 71; CEAP–Borgu, *Table ronde,* 26.

50. Interview 9; Lombard, *Structures de type "fèodal,"* 282–83. 296–97.

51. Lombard, *Structures de type "fèodal,"* 339.

52. Interview 9; Bandiri "Catalyse."

53. On this, see N. J. G. Kaptein, *Muhammad's Birthday Festival* (Leiden, 1993), 57; Annemarie Schimmel, *Deciphering the Signs of God* (Edinburgh, 1994), 100.

54. Normally, it is between the ages of six and ten that the Wasangari child receives his or her princely name; see Lombard, *Structures de type "fèodal,"* 297, 301.

55. Cf. Lombard, *Structures de type "fèodal,"* 337–38.

56. Orou Yorouba, "La Gaani," 22ff.

57. Orou Yorouba, "La Gaani," 22ff.; CEAP–Borgou, *Table ronde,* 28–31.

58. Moraes Farias, "Praise Splits the Subject of Speech."

59. See N. Tersis, "Le Dendi (Niger)," *Bulletin de la Société pour l'Etude des Langues Africaines* 10 (1968): 73; S. Reichmuth, "Songhay—Lehnwörter im Yoruba und ihr historischer Kontext," *Sprache und Geschichte in Afrika* 9 (1988): 275–76.

60. The ruler does not join the rites of collective Muslim prayer either during the *Gaani* of Nìkì or the *Gaani* of Bānīkpààrù. His Highness *Alhaji* Musa Mohammed Ki-Gera III, the Emir of Borgu, told us that the old rulers of Busa also did not pray in public during the *Gaani* (interview 1). See also Bandiri, "Catalyse"; P. F. de Moraes Farias, "Ọ̀rànmíyàn's Frustrated War on Mecca: Reflexes of Borgu Ritual in Johnson's Yorùbá Narratives," in *Pioneer, Patriot, and Patriarch: Samuel Johnson and the Yoruba People,* ed. T. Falola (Madison, Wis., 1993), 124.

61. Orou Yorouba, "La Gaani," 73.

62. CEAP–Borgou, *Table ronde,* 28–29.

63. Orou Yorouba, "La Gaani," 32, 72–73; CEAP–Borgou, *Table ronde,* 25.

64. P. F. de Moraes Farias, "Yorùbá Origins Revisited by Muslims: An Interview with the *Arọ̀kin* of Ọ̀yọ́ and a Reading of the *'Aṣl Qabā'il Yūrubā* of *Al-Ḥājj* Ādam al-Ilūrī," in *Self-Assertion and Brokerage: Early Cultural Nationalism in West Africa,* ed. P. F. de Moraes Farias and K. Barber (Birmingham, 1990), 129.

65. P. F. de Moraes Farias, "A Letter from Ki-Tooro Mahaman Gaani, King of Busa (Borgu, northern Nigeria) about the 'Kisra' Stories of Origin (c. 1910)," *Sudanic Africa* 3 (1992): 113–15.

66. Interview 8, conducted by the late Musa Baba Idris in 1969.

67. Bandiri, "Catalyse"; Léon Bani Bio Bigou, *La Gani à Nikki* (Parakou, 1990), 4.

68. Moraes Farias, "A Letter from Ki-Tooro," and "Ọ̀rànmíyàn's Frustrated War."

69. Orou Yorouba, "La Gaani," 10–11, 72; CEAP–Borgou, *Table ronde,* 23.

70. CEAP–Borgou, *Table ronde,* 13–14.

71. It was in Busa that an ambiguous (and now discontinued) ritual of warlike challenge to Islam was performed during the Gaani; see Moraes Farias, "A Letter from Ki-Toro," 114. There is no vestige of similar rituals in Nìkì and Bānīkpààrù. As to joyful commemorations of the *Mawlid* as a Muslim festival, they may be conducted by Nìkì Muslims among themselves, but their public participation in the *Gaani* is focused not on the Prophet, but on kingship.

72. Lombard, *Structures de type "féodal,"* 335 n. 1; Orou Yorouba, "La Gaani," 31; CEAP–Borgou, *Table ronde,* 19.

73. Commission de Langue Boo, *Premier Séminaire national (4–8 septembre)* (Kalalé, 1985), 19.

74. CEAP–Borgou, *Table ronde,* 19–20.

75. Kaptein, *Muḥammad's Birthday Festival,* 44–45.

76. See M. Delafosse, *La Langue mandingue et ses dialectes (Malinké, Bambara, Dioula),* 2 vols. (Paris, 1929–55), 2:128–29; and the version of the Sunjata Epic by the *jeli* Fa-Digi Sisòkò recorded by Charles S. Bird at Kita (1968), and published as *The Epic of Son-Jara: A West African Tradition,* trans. J. W. Johnson (Bloomington, Ind., 1986), 105, 132–33. The word *dõ* or *don* means "day" or, with different tonality, "dance."

77. R. Launay, *Traders without Trade* (Cambridge, 1991), 7, 10.

78. See what has been said in this essay about the *Gaani* of the *Yɔ̃ɔ Kɔ̃ɔgii.*

79. Levtzion, *Muslims and Chiefs,* 98; Ferguson, "Islamization in Dagbon," 117.

80. P. Stoller, *Fusion of the Worlds: An Ethnography of Possession among the Songhay of Niger* (Chicago, 1989), 118, 231; P. Stoller and C. Olkes, *In Sorcery's Shadow: A Memoir of Apprenticeship among the Songhay of Niger* (Chicago, 1987), 234; Bernard Surugue, *Contribution à l'étude de la musique sacrée zarma songhay (République du Niger)* (Niamey, 1972), 4, 5.

81. A. Prost, "Supplément au dictionnaire soṅay-français," *Bulletin de l'Institut Fondamental d'Afrique Noire* 39:b:3 (1977): 606.

82. A. Prost, *La Langue soṅay et ses dialectes* (Mémoires de l'Institut Français d'Afrique Noire 47) (Dakar, 1956), 461; J.-M. Ducroz and M.-C. Charles, *Lexique Soṅey (Songay)–Français* (Paris, 1978), 55; Tersis, "Le Dendi (Niger)," 72.

83. J.-P. Olivier de Sardan, *Concepts et conceptions songhay-zarma* (Paris, 1982), 82–83, 281.

84. Lovejoy, "The Role of the Wangara."

85. P. Delmond, "Dans la Boucle du Niger: Dori, ville peule," *Mémoires de l'Institut Français d'Afrique Noire* 23 (Dakar, 1953), 97; and anon., "No Liptaaku Jooɗorinoo Arannde" (How the situation was in Liptaaku long ago), oral information collected in Doori (1967) by Amadou Bokoum, and published in *Jangen fulfulde* (Fulfulde readings), ed. Alfâ Ibrâhîm Sow (Alfaa Ibraahim Soo) (Niamey, 1970), 2:39–45, esp. 44. Among the Fulɓe of Borgu, the *Mawlid* is also called *Gaani.*

86. Trimingham, *Islam in West Africa,* 78 n. 1.

87. Y. Poncet, *La Région d'In Gall—Tegiddan Tesemt: Programme archéologique d'urgence* (Niamey, 1983), 78.

88. "Tuāreg" is of course a name used by outsiders; I employ it here solely for the sake of convenience. It is a European derivation from the dialectical form "Təwāṛəg" of Saharan Arabic. In their various dialects, when distinguishing all their different groupings from other categories of population, the "Tuāreg" call themselves Kăl-Tămašăq or, in other regions, Kəl-Təmajəq, Kəl-Tamahaq, and so forth; that is, "those of [the] tămašaq/təmajəq/tamahaq [language]."

89. D. Casajus, *La Tente dans la solitude: La Société et les morts chez les Touaregs Kel Ferwan* (Cambridge, 1987), 140, 372.

90. M. Albaka and D. Casajus, *Poésies et chants Touaregs de l'Ayr* (Paris, 1992), 105–9, 275–86.

91. Abraham, *Dictionary of the Hausa Language,* 296, 771; Starratt, "Oral History in Muslim Africa," 144.

92. See the oral history of Dawraa by Ibiraa, *Sarkin Makaɗaa* (head of the drummers/traditionists) of the Kance (Kantché) chiefdom, published by Issaka Dankoussou, *Histoire du Dawraa: Traditions historiques par Sarkin Makadaa Ibiraa de Kantché,* ed. and trans. Issaka Dankoussou (Niamey, 1970), 62–63.

93. Ahmed Rufai Mohammed, "Niassan Influence in the Niger-Benue Confluence Area of Nigeria (Paper delivered at the Conference on Islamic Identities in Africa, organized by the Center for the Study of World Religions, Harvard University, and the School of Oriental and African Studies, University of London, at London, 18–20 Apr. 1991), 22. This information was left out of the printed, shorter version of the paper: A. R. Mohammed, "The Influence of the Niass Tijaniyya in the Niger-Benue Confluence Area of Nigeria," in *Muslim*

Identity and Social Change in Sub-Saharan Africa, ed. L. Brenner (Bloomington, Ind., 1993), 116–34.

94. Banfield, *Dictionary of the Nupe Language,* 144, 177.

95. S. F. Nadel, "The Gani Ritual of Nupe: A Study in Social Symbiosis," *Africa* 19, no. 3 (1949): 177–86; Nadel, *A Black Byzantium,* 20, 23, 395–96.

96. But see also Nadel, *A Black Byzantium,* 409.

97. Orou Yorouba, "La Gaani," 29, 68.

98. Drucker-Brown, "Calendar and Ritual," 77.

Islam and Identity in the Kumase Zongo

ROBERT S. KRAMER

The year 1990 was a time of considerable conflict in the Kumase Zongo, involving groups of Muslims identifying themselves variously (and according to circumstances) as "Tijani," "Sunni" (Ahl al-Sunna), "Hausa," "Dagomba," "Gonja," "Asante" and "Ghanaian." Sometimes, as in an incident at Effiduase in June over property ownership, fighting broke out and people were hospitalized. The Kumase *Pioneer* of 8 June carried an article headed "Muslims Clash, Some Injured," followed immediately by the paper's "Thought for the Day," which happened to be a quote from the Qur'an and which both sides could have endorsed: "In the name of Allah, the Compassionate, the Merciful. Allah's curse is on the wrong doers who debar others from His path and seek to make it crooked, and who deny the life to come" (11:19). On other occasions, as in August in Aboabo, the conflicts concerned the right to preach in public; or, as in October in Old Zongo, the activities of the Asante Regional Islamic Education Unit. Reasons given for the conflicts by the parties involved ranged from the defense of Divine Truth to social justice to patriotic duty. Many of these conflicts are still being waged today. What is important for our present purposes, however, is not the conflicts themselves, but what they indicate about how members of the Kumase Muslim community identify themselves and their interests; and how Islamic ideologies can intersect with ideas of ethnicity to create new social and political dynamics.

Before turning to a discussion of the contemporary discourse, it is important to repeat and emphasize certain points raised by Enid Schildkrout in her book *People of the Zongo.*[1] To begin, Schildkrout makes the point that ethnic identity among Zongo residents has often been a matter of choice and circumstance. For example, nineteenth-century migrants to Kumase from the More-Dagbane-speaking states in the north might identify with other More-Dagbane speakers, such as the Dagomba or Mamprusi, or else with the Hausa or Wangara if they were originally descended from those peoples (74). In the early twentieth century, many non-Hausa migrants were identified as Hausa, and successive generations have continued to identify themselves as Hausa. Mainly this has been due to "the high value placed upon being Hausa among most Muslim groups," since Hausa identity has been associated with high social status, wealth, and Islamic orthodoxy. Moreover since the Hausa controlled certain sectors of trade, the claim to Hausa status carried with it obvious economic advantages (83–84). In some areas of the Zongo, Schildkrout states, it is difficult to tell if people are Hausa by "virtue of their parents' assimilation or by descent"; while the growth of the Zongo during this century has led to "internal segmentation," so that many people who "formerly might have identified themselves as Hausa" have become Mossi, Grusi, Dagomba, etc. (85). In short, it needs to be emphasized that identity in the Zongo has been both voluntary and situational.

A second and important point is that it has never been uniformly understood who exactly constitute the people of the Zongo: while the Asante might simply refer to the stranger community as a whole ("all northerners who were recent migrants, and who therefore were strangers vis-à-vis the Asante"), Hausa residents would more specifically refer to the Muslims among the migrants. Like ethnic identity, affiliation to the Zongo might change over time or with circumstance, and is also both voluntary and situational (85–87).

Finally, Schildkrout notes that something like a "common immigrant culture" has emerged in the Zongo, expressed in the use of Hausa as a lingua franca, the adherence of most migrants to Islam, the settlement patterns, cultural habits and economic activities practiced by the people, and also the profound sense of being aliens and strangers in a larger Asante community (86–88). Of paramount importance to the integration of migrants has been the practice of Islam, and specifically its "common norms": its "common cultural codes" that provide a value system and prescribe a way of behaving. Due to the historical association of Hausa people with the religion, it is of course a highly "Hausaized" version of Islamic culture that is practiced; in some instances the lines between Hausa authenticity and Islamic orthodoxy are entirely obscured. And yet this Islam, manifested in various institutions and associations, has helped to create a "sense of common culture." As the Islamic culture has developed, the appeal to its norms has served to break down the bonds of the Zongo's specific ethnic groups. The result in recent years has been the growing influence and authority of individuals other than the ethnic/tribal headmen—for example, religious scholars—and the rise of "multiethnic Islamic associations" in the Zongo's political affairs (90–94).

As we might expect, the presence of a common Islamic culture in the Zongo has not entirely minimized ethnic disputes, though it has provided the means for their mediation in the person of various Imams. Each of the thirty-plus ethnic groups in the Zongo appoints its own Imam, to whom disputes involving other Muslims are taken in the first order. In the event of an Imam's failure to resolve a case, the dispute might be taken either to the Asante Regional Chief Imam or to the Hausa chief (Sarkin Zongo); otherwise a complaint may be filed with the local police.[2] Given the great importance and prestige attached to the position of Asante Regional Chief Imam, it is not surprising that appointment to this office has occasioned some of the most bitter rivalry among the Zongo communities. One dispute in particular, involving the appointment to Chief Imam of a Dagomba, Muhammad Muntaka, in 1968, continues as a point of contention to this day.[3] Schildkrout notes that in this instance "most Dagombas maintained that, as Ghanaian citizens, they were not part of the zongo, which they defined in this situation as a community of non-Ghanaian strangers under the informal ritual leadership of the Hausa. . . . [Muhammad Muntaka] attempted to identify himself with a national Ghanaian Muslim community and tried to disqualify the

Hausa candidate on the grounds of citizenship, claiming that the Hausa were indisputably aliens, since their place of origin was outside Ghana."[4] The present Chief Imam, al-Hajj Ahmadu Chiroma, is Hausa and the son of an earlier Chief Imam.[5] He describes the dispute as follows: The Chief Imam is appointed by a committee composed of the Sarkin Zongo and a number of "elders." After the death of Imam Muhammad Chiroma in 1968, he was succeeded by his assistant, a Hausa named Abu Bakr ("Girba") Hakim. However a number of "Ghanaian" Muslims, composed primarily of Dagomba, Gonja, and Asante Nkramo, began to complain loudly about the Hausa domination of political and religious office in the Zongo. They organized themselves into a group called the "Muslim Mission," which included all "Ghanaian" Muslims and was set up to compete for offices against the Hausa. These people were well organized, with a chairman and secretary and complete administration. They began to apply the name "Muslim Community" to the "non-Ghanaian" (that is, Hausa) Muslims, to distinguish them from the Ghanaian Muslim Mission, though this was not a term used or recognized by the Hausa, who simply regard themselves as Muslims. By way of resolving the conflict, the Hausa and the Muslim Mission came to an agreement on sharing power: the deputy Chief Imam would henceforth be chosen from the group not occupying the Chief Imamship; upon the death of the Chief Imam, his deputy would most likely (though not necessarily) succeed him. Accordingly, after the death of the Hausa Imam Abu Bakr Hakim, he was followed in office by the Muslim Mission candidate, the Dagomba Deputy Imam Muhammad Muntaka. Muhammad Muntaka was succeeded in office by his deputy, the present Hausa Imam Ahmadu Chiroma, who presumably will be succeeded by his deputy, the Gonja Imam Musa. Significantly, what allowed this arrangement to be acceptable to both parties was their differing interpretations of ethnic identity: Muhammad Muntaka was regarded by the Hausa as a Hausa, as his father allegedly had been Hausa; the Dagomba meanwhile considered him a Dagomba, since his mother had been of that people and he had been raised by his mother's family. Imam

Chiroma closed by saying that the matrilineal practice is "not a part of Islam" but rather a Ghanaian tradition, but that it conveniently served the needs of the moment by satisfying both parties as to their share of power.[6]

Ultimately politics and social practice are not so simple as Imam Chiroma made them out to be. Members of the Gonja, Dagomba, and Asante Nkramo communities all insist that Muhammad Muntaka had been a full-blooded Dagomba and that the arrangement for sharing the office of Chief Imam is inviolable, not subject to the whim of the Sarkin Zongo and his "elders." One Dagomba, al-Hajji Mustafa Kessi, stated that Muhammad Muntaka's father had been the Imam of the village of Sabala near Yendi and al-Hajji had known him well. Muntaka had been "the only Ghanaian to be an Imam, all the others had been aliens, Hausas and Kotokolis and others." Muntaka had also been "the best of Imams, and the first Imam to be invited to Mecca by the Saudi king." Moreover, Muntaka's predecessor as Chief Imam, Abu Bakr "Girba" Hakim had not himself been entirely Hausa, but rather half-Gonja. "Ghanaians would not have allowed a non-Ghanaian as Chief Imam," al-Hajji assured me; "a government report had found Girba to be Ghanaian, and Girba himself strongly claimed to be Gonja."[7] The present Deputy Chief Imam, the Gonja Imam Musa, concurs with this view, stating that Girba Hakim had been a "Beriberi" from Nigeria on his father's side and a Gonja on his mother's side, while Muhammad Muntaka had been Dagomba on both sides. Imam Musa also insisted (and of course he has an obvious interest in this matter) that the arrangement worked out during the dispute of 1968 had specified that the "Muslim Community" and the "Muslim Mission" would share in turns the office of Chief Imam. It was modesty only that prevented him from acknowledging that he himself will become the next Chief Imam upon the death of Ahmadu Chiroma.[8] By way of a retort to these views, the Hausa assistant (*mutawalli*) to the Sarkin Zongo informed me that Muhammad Muntaka had actually been Hausa: his biological father had been Hausa but had died when Muntaka was young, and Muntaka's mother remarried a Dagomba who helped raise the boy. "But in fact Muhammad Muntaka was considered a Hausa." As to the sharing of power, the *Mutawalli* argued that the original agreement had been for the Muslim Community (Hausas) to get only the Chief Imamship, while the Muslim Mission (Ghanaians) would get only the Deputy Imamship. Hence "there is no legal basis for a member of the Muslim Mission to serve as Chief Imam, and this in fact breaks the agreement." What is really going on, the *Mutawalli* assured me, is that the Dagombas and Gonjas are using the Muslim Mission against the Hausa for political gain, which is why the Muslim Mission never appoints a member of the Asante Nkrämo as an Imam.[9] Finally, to round out the testimony, there is the opinion of Shaykh Adam Apiyadu, director of the Islamic Secondary School in Kumase (Suame district) and founder of the Muslim Mission in Kumase in 1963, to "spread Islam among the Asante and perform services." Shaykh Adam is a leader of the Asante Nkramo community and is himself the son of a Hausa father, though his identity is clearly Asante. In his view, Girba Hakim was born of a Hausa father and a Gonja mother, while Muhammad Muntaka was born of two Dagomba parents. (Muntaka's biological father, in fact, was said to be still alive and living in Kumase!) Shaykh Adam acknowledged that the opposing parties view identity differently: the Hausa insist that identity and succession should follow Hausa/"Islamic" practice, while the Muslim Mission wants an Imam from among the "Ghanaians," following "Ghanaian matrilineality." Ultimately, however, what determines succession to the Imamship is not agreement about a candidate's identity (which has never happened) or qualifications (which no one has ever questioned), but rather the desire to avoid conflict between Hausa and "Ghanaians." This arrangement, Shaykh Adam insisted, is followed only from fear of conflict and is not set in law; moreover the Deputy Imam is not always the most qualified to become Chief Imam. Shaykh Adam holds out the possibility that an Asante from the Muslim Mission might well become Chief Imam in the near future.[10]

The possibility of a Chief Imam from the Asante Nkramo is not one that the Hausa at least are willing to entertain very seriously. Such an arrangement, the *Mutawalli* insisted, would be "illegal." Somewhat ironically however, the *Mutawalli* offered that the main problem in the Zongo relates to the politics of identity: the Ghanaians refuse to accept the Hausa as Ghanaians, calling even the third-generation residents "strangers" (*Ahoho*). The Ghanaians do not realize that it is possible for the Hausa to have "dual citizenship" ("dual identity" is perhaps what he intended), and the problem is really one of tribalism.[11] Of course "tribalism" and the politics of identity are not specific to any one group. And while the appointment of an Asante to the office of Chief Imam may not be immediately likely, the Muslim Mission has managed to obtain legal recognition for its half-ownership of the Kumase Central Mosque. The chairman of the Ghana Muslim Mission, al-Hajji Ibrahim Baayeh, a member of the Nkramo community, warned that any decision made affecting the mosque without the consultation and consent of the joint owners "would be in contempt of the judgement of February 1970 by Justice D. F. Annan, now a PNDC member." Al-Hajji Ibrahim's attempt to discuss this issue with the Sarkin Zongo in May 1990 failed when the latter refused to meet with him.[12]

Adding to the conflict created in the Zongo by ethnic rivalry is an ideological schism that divides the Muslim community into two groups, each claiming ultimate authority in its interpretation of Islam. I am referring of course to the decades-old struggle between Muslims of the Tijaniyya Sufi order and those self-styled the "Ahl al-Sunna" or "Orthodox."[13] The Tijaniyya—by far the larger and better-established of the two—claims as its adherents most Hausa and northern Ghanaian Muslims of the Zongo, while the "Sunnis" appear to be a mixture of Asante Nkramo, Hausa, and other groups. Neither faction is ethnically specific however; nor is every Muslim necessarily a member of one faction or the other.[14] Exposure to the Tijaniyya takes place early in the life of many Zongo children: most private Arabic schools are run by members of the Tijaniyya who, while they do not instruct the students in Sufism, fully expect them to join the order eventually. Public preaching of the Tijani beliefs is a common occurence in the Zongo, and it is the duty of preachers to contact students after they have finished their schooling—when they have reached the age of *'aql* or "understanding things"—and bring them into the order.[15] Moreover, entry into the Tijaniyya is an easy affair: the Tijaniyya is set up, one preacher explained, to encourage its adoption by the people, and nothing outside the realm of normal Islamic practice is required.[16]

Contrary to the pattern of many Sufi orders, the Tijaniyya at least does not appear to be organized along distinctly hierarchical lines. While each region of Ghana has its own Tijani leader, there is no leader of the order in Ghana overall, and in fact "leadership" is relative to one's ability to propagate the order.[17] Tijani preachers travel frequently, speaking before the public and explaining the spiritual benefits of membership in their order. Frequently this brings them into direct contact—and conflict—with the Sunni group, which, influenced by the puritanical Islam of Saudi Arabia, has denounced the Tijaniyya as an "evil innovation" (*bid'a*). Physical violence between members of both groups is not uncommon, particularly when the Sunnis have attempted to preach in public against the Tijaniyya in the Zongo. In an exchange of epithets, the Sunnis have called the Tijanis "unbelievers" (*kuffar*)—and denounced anyone who prays with the Tijanis in the Central Mosque as an unbeliever—as well as "polytheists" (*mushrikun*); while the Tijanis for their part have labelled the Sunnis "Wahhabis" (this is meant as a pejorative) and "rejectors" (*munkirun*), in the tradition of those who rejected and opposed the prophecy of Muhammad. In October 1990 the two groups were in conflict over control of the Ghanaian Islamic Education Unit: the chairman of the Unit is allegedly a virulent anti-Tijani and sought to locate his office on the mosque grounds "in order to influence Tijani worshippers." He was opposed—for the moment successfully—by Tijani members of the board.[18] What elevates this conflict to something more than a local dispute is the patronage each side has received from outside, competing powers: the Tijanis have received funding on occasion from the

Islamic Republic of Iran,[19] while the Sunnis are almost entirely educated in and financed by Saudi Arabia. The likelihood of this ideological conflict continuing into the future is impossible to determine, as it is dependent to an extent upon continued Saudi financing of the Sunnis, and perhaps also a continued spirit of reform in the Islamic world. For the present, the Tijani-Sunni rift serves to mitigate other, ethnic tensions in the Zongo. Even as they have been competing over access to religious and political office, Tijani Muslims have in the last four years organized two conferences in the Central Mosque on the theme of Islamic unity. The failure of the Sunnis to disrupt these proceedings are seen by Tijanis—Hausa, Dagombas and others—as evidence of God's will to preserve the unity of the Zongo Muslim community.[20]

Notes

1. Enid Schildkrout, *People of the Zongo* (Cambridge, 1978). Subsequent page references are to this text.

2. According to the current Hausa chief, Abu Bakr b. 'Ali, the Zongo "stool" is reserved for the Hausa, as they are the predominant tribe in the Zongo. It is the Sarkin Zongo who "crowns" the Asante Regional Chief Imam and it is to the Sarkin Zongo that all cases go for final appeal (interview, 3 Sept. 1990, Kumase). Contrary to this, a Dagomba informant claimed that disputes involve the Sarkin Zongo only when one of the parties involved is Hausa, and that it is the various community headmen and Imams who must resolve a case. Interview with Hajji Mustafa Kessi, 20 Sept. 1990, Kumase.

3. On this dispute, see Schildkrout, "Islam and Politics in Ghana: An Analysis of Disputes over the Kumasi Central Mosque," *Anthropological Papers of the American Museum of Natural History* 52, no. 2 (1974): 113–37.

4. Schildkrout, *People of the Zongo,* 87.

5. Imam Muhammad Chiroma, reg. 1952–68.

6. Interview with Imam Ahmadu Chiroma, 17 Oct. 1990, Kumase. Of course it remains to be explained when exactly the northern Ghanaians (Dagombas, Gonja, Mamprussi) began to follow a matrilineal succession. If this was not historically part of their cultural tradition, is the practice then an innovation borrowed from the Asante host community? In this regard, we might note the current office of Zongo queen mother, known as the "Magajiyya queen mother," an obvious assimilation of the Asante queen mother and the Hausa Magajiyya. (For the Hausaland Magajiyya or "Queen of Prostitutes" see Mary Smith, *Baba of Karo* [New York, 1964], 63–64, 136, 229–30.) The Zongo Magajiyya is a more respectable version of the original, being concerned with the educational needs and civic responsibilities of local women. Interview with al-Tayyib Muhammad Tanko, 24 Nov. 1990, Kumase.

7. Interview with al-Hajji Mustafa Kessi, 24 Oct. 1990, Kumase.

8. Interview with Imam Musa, 14 Nov. 1990, Kumase.

9. Interview with al-Tayyib Muhammad Tanko, 14 Nov. 1990, Kumase.

10. Interview with Shaykh Adam Apiyadu, 22 Nov. 1990, Kumase.

11. Interview with al-Tayyib Muhammad Tanko, 1 Dec. 1990, Kumase.

12. *The Pioneer* (Kumase), 6 Aug. 1990.

13. This schism is discussed in detail by Mervyn Hiskett in "The Community of Grace and Its Opponents the Rejectors: A Debate about Theology and Mysticism in Muslim West Africa with Particular Reference to its Hausa Expression," *African Language Studies;* 17 (1980): 99–140.

14. For instance, Shaykh Adam Apiyadu of the Asante Nkramo, while sympathetic to the reformist tendencies of the Sunnis ("discouraging innovations and corruptions"), criticizes their extreme methods as poor strategy. The "brothers from Saudi" continue to perpetuate conflicts through their tactlessness, when what is needed is not to insult the Tijanis by calling them *kuffar* (unbelievers) but rather to reform them slowly by "creating good examples for the Tijanis to emulate." Interview with Shaykh Adam Apiyadu, 22 Nov. 1990, Kumase.

15. Interviews with Tayyib Abu Bakr Salu, Madrasat Imamiyyat al-Rashidiyya, 4 Sept. 1990, Kumase and Muhammad Sanni Muhammad Nasr al-Din, Madrasa Nasriyya, 4 September 1990, Kumase.

16. Interview with 'Abd' al-Wudud b. al-Hajj Harun Muhammad, 21 Sept. 1990, Kumase.

17. Ibid.

18. Interview with al-Tayyib Muhammad Tanko, 24 Oct. 1990, Kumase. In an attempt to prevent factional violence and ensure public safety, the Manhyia district police established a schedule for public preaching by the Tijaniyya and Sunnis in Aug. 1990. It does not seem to have succeeded in lessening tensions; indeed, both groups are now better informed about their rival's activities.

19. Interview with al-Hajji Mustafa Kessi, 20 Sept. 1990, Kumase. For example, Iran has subsidized a community toilet, women's quarters at the central mosque, funds for Zongo funeral arrangements, lights and fans in the central mosque, Qur'an reading competitions, and two seminars on the theme of Islamic unity.

20. Interview with al-Hajji Mustafa Kessi, 6 Aug. 1990, Kumase.

La Trahison des Clercs? The "Collaboration" of a Suwarian 'Ālim

ROBERT LAUNAY

The relationship between French colonial administrators and the *ulama,* Muslim clerics, in West Africa has of late come under close scrutiny.[1] The French attitude was characterized by periodic bouts of paranoia, an almost visceral fear of *le péril de l'Islam*—the peril of Islam[2]—that sometimes led them to perceive particular Muslim religious leaders as enemies, purveyors of pan-Islamic propaganda, and ready to incite revolt. This is not, by any means, to say that the French treated all Muslim clerics as enemies, or even as potential enemies. Rather, as early as the nineteenth century,[3] they were concerned with identifying the "friends" as opposed to the "enemies" among the *ulama.* To this end, they kept meticulous tabs on all Muslim clerics, minor as well as major. It was largely thanks to these files that Paul Marty, a scholar-administrator, was able to compile his massive, thirteen-volume survey of Islam in A.O.F.[4]

In spite of this undercurrent of distrust, it is remarkable that many members of the *ulama* proved to be quite willing to cooperate with the French authorities. In fact, as Louis Brenner has pointed out,[5] such an attitude was so widespread that any refusal to cooperate actively with the French was interpreted as a gesture of open and seditious hostility. It was on precisely such grounds that the French exiled Sheikh Ḥamallah of Nioro and pursued his quietist disciple Cerno Bokar Saalif Taal.

Retrospectively, it is tempting to characterize the policy of the majority of the *ulama* as a form of "collaboration," in the worst possible sense of the word. The implication is that, in a totally self-serving manner, Muslim clerics placed themselves at the disposal of their colonial masters, shamelessly and cynically contributing ideological support for the perpetuation of colonial domination. Indeed, such accusations were formulated quite openly in the 1950s by anticolonial Muslim militants, such as Cheikh Touré, a leader of the Union Culturelle Musulmane in Senegal.[6] Now, thirty years after independence, the issue of "collaboration" is certainly less acrimonious. Even so, the behavior of many of the *ulama* is seemingly, if not a blot on the historical record, at the very least an embarrassment.

The actions and positions of the clerics might seem to boil down to a question of motives. Were they acting out of narrow self-interest, or on behalf of the Muslim community as a whole? There are several objections for phrasing the issue in terms of such alternatives. First of all, it assumes an intrinsic conflict between "self-interest" and "the common good," implying that scholars profited at the expense of other Africans, and in particular their own followers. Ultimately, this concern with motives, if it does not serve specifically as a basis for ad hominem attacks on specific clerics, informs an implicit if not explicit critique of an entire "class" of Muslim clerics and a whole style of Islamic leadership. Such clerics are characterized, if not as outright reactionaries, then as "a conservative 'right wing.'"[7] This kind of characterization is, at best, inappropriate, at worst wildly anachronistic.

More crucial, a concentration on motives assumes that the significance of the actions of clerics is ultimately transparent. The relevant question is not, "Why did the clerics do as they did?" but rather, "What did they (and their constituents) think they were doing?" Such questions need to be answered in terms of specific cultural contexts. We need to know, in other words, about the "role" of Muslim clerics at specific times and places: What was expected of them? What kinds of behavior was considered appropriate or inappropriate? I suggest that, in some cases at least, Muslim clerics, by declaring their open and enthusiastic support for their French colonial masters, were behaving in a fully "appropriate" and sanctioned manner, exactly as their followers expected, indeed, desired them to behave.

As a case in point, let us consider a letter addressed to the people of Mecca from "the Muslims of Korhogo," written in 1916 by a Muslim cleric by the name of Mamadou Soumare, published in an appendix to Marty's volume on Islam in Côte d'Ivoire.[8] The original text of the letter, we are told, was in Arabic, but the French translation is also the author's; grammatical errors and nonidiomatic turns of phrase are deliberately reproduced in the text:

> The present document, written by Mamadou Soumare, son of Brahima Soumare, of Korhogo, is destined to be sent to the Muslims of Mecca through the intermediary of the Governor of Ivory Coast, so that they understand that we, the Muslims of the Post of Korhogo, are very happy to hear that they are now allied with the French to fight the Germans.
> Moreover, we are very unhappy to see the Germans make war on the French.
> Whoever does not wish to see the French in our colony (Ivory Coast) is also held in contempt by us Muslims, since our prosperity depends entirely on the arrival of these latter in our colonies.
> It is moreover thanks to the French that we are spare the ravages and pillages of Samory, slavery, and wars between one village and another.
> At present, we are free, we can live, work in peace, and perform our prayers in tranquility.
> Since we have learned that all the Muslims of the Holy City have allied themselves with the French against the Germans, our concern has been to pray to God that the Allies annihilate Germany.
> Let Germany be annihilated.
> Let the Germans (poor, rich, princes, kings) surrender and submit themselves to the French.
> We note that the French race is better than all the others.
> When you give a chicken to a Frenchman, he pays you the price of a sheep; one day of work for him is paid by a month's salary (unlike other races).
> Which explains why we consider His Excellency the Governor as our father and mother . . .

> Needless to say, these words are not of our own invention, but follow qur'anic rules and the point of view of Islam.
> Moreover Muhammad (our master), during his existence in the Holy City, was very fond of the French race. This explains why we Muslims should continue to love the French as he did . . .
> . . . we will always take the good will to exhibit a great burst of patriotism.

Marty included in another appendix a second, similar, letter,[9] written a year earlier by Kounandi Timite, imam of Bondoukou, "who had a long record of pro-French activity."[10] Fortunately for Almamy Timite, his command of French was decidedly inferior to Mamadou Soumare's, and so he apparently made no attempt to translate the letter into French himself. Consequently the French translation is somewhat—but only somewhat—less unidiomatic. At any rate, Mamadou Soumare's letter was not an isolated case. The colonial administration actively and systematically solicited such letters as part of the war effort; initially, they had feared that West African Muslims might sympathize with the Ottoman empire and thus with France's enemies, although these fears turned out to be groundless.[11] Soumare's letter alludes to the Arab rising, under the aegis of the Sherif of Mecca (with the support and encouragement of France and Britain), the news of which the French broadcast to their subject Muslim populations as part of their propaganda effort. Even so, it is of some note that Soumare alludes to the Meccans as allied with the French against the Germans, without even mentioning the Ottomans. Plausibly, the French, once convinced of the total absence of pro-Turkish sentiments among their West African Muslim subjects, preferred to downplay the Ottoman question altogether.

The publication of such letters during the war, as propaganda, comes as no surprise. Still, it is striking that, six years after the war's end, Marty chose to reprint them in their entirety. Their purpose, no doubt, was to demonstrate the loyalty of Muslim clerics to France, particularly to those French administrators who might still have lingering apprehensions about the "Muslim peril." With three-quarters of a century's hindsight, modern readers, I suspect, cannot but find them embarrassing. The rhetorical terms in which the French masters are praised is admittedly excessive by almost any standard. One might be tempted to characterize the tone as either the abject fawning of a toady or the hypocrisy of a cynical opportunist. One way or the other, is this not outright "collaboration," in the worst sense?

It is, of course, well-nigh impossible to rule out a cynical interpretation of Mamadou Soumare's motives. We can glean a little bit about him from Marty and from other colonial sources. According to Marty,[12] he and his father Ibrahim were the most learned Muslim clerics of the town and indeed of the region. His father had immigrated from the Bakel region in the Sahel around 1860, so the family was not native to the region. A cousin of Mamadou's, one Souleyman Soumare, was an interpreter for the colonial administration—which might support a cynical construction of Mamadou's behavior, or at least indicate a link between the cleric on one side and the colonial administration on the other.[13] A subsequent survey, completed in 1931, notes that Mamadou Soumare left Korhogo for the capital in 1927.[14] Unlike other scholars in Korhogo mentioned by Marty,[15] natives to the region in one sense or another and whose descendents are still to be found in town, he seems to have left little trace in the collective memory of Korhogo's Muslim community, on whose behalf, after all, he dispatched his missive.

In a fundamental way, however, Mamadou Soumare's motives, and the extent of his sincerity—or lack of it—are beside the point. His letter was sent on behalf of the Muslim community of Korhogo. The critical question is whether he was justified in doing so. Before answering, we must first examine who the Muslims of Korhogo were at that time. Before the colonial period, and throughout the early years of colonial rule, there was a close correspondence between religion and ethnic identity, not only in Korhogo but throughout northeastern and north-central Ivory Coast. Muslims in this region called themselves, and were called,

"Dyula."[16] The name "dyula" means "trader" in the Manding language, and the ethnic Dyula of northern Ivory Coast enjoyed a monopoly over long-distance trade throughout the region. They were part of a vast network of Mande traders involved in the exchange of goods from the confines of the desert to the north to the confines of the forest to the south. For the most part, Dyula lived as an ethnic, linguistic, and religious minority in various states and chiefdoms of northern Ivory Coast.

Korhogo was the seat of one of these chiefdoms, a relatively small one before the colonial period. The majority of the chiefdom, including its rulers, were native speakers of the Tiembara dialect of Senufo. The chiefdom, as well as the village of Korhogo itself, also included a minority of speakers of Fodonon, another dialect of Senufo that native Tiembara speakers cannot understand. In addition, there were hereditary groups of artisans—sculptors, blacksmiths, brass casters, leatherworkers—who have usually been called "castes" and who were, in any case, socially distinct from other Senufo.[17] Within this rather intricate ethnic and linguistic mosaic, Dyula Muslims constituted a distinct category, with their own religious practices, their own language, and their own professional monopolies, on weaving as well as on long-distance trade. According to the first colonial census, in 1908, the Dyula accounted for about 16 percent of the population of the chiefdom as a whole. This figure needs to be taken rather loosely, but clearly they were a sizable minority, and one whose presence in the region dates back to the seventeenth century if not earlier.

Precisely because the Dyula were members of a vast interregional network of Muslim traders, individuals were constantly moving in and out of the community, both in the short and in the long terms. Clerics, weavers, and traders might choose to settle wherever economic prospects seemed more attractive, attaching themselves as "strangers (*lunanw*) to a local "host" (*diatigi*).[18] Such moves were not necessarily made over long distances, and most groups and individuals in Korhogo's Muslim community maintained close ties with "home" communities relatively nearby.

On the other hand, Muslim traders from quite far away were integrated as "strangers" just as readily; Mamadou Soumare's father was by no means an isolated case. When the letter was written, the family had been established in Korhogo's Muslim community for about half a century. Indeed, the entire Muslim community of Korhogo consisted of "strangers," of groups descended from various individuals who had at one time attached themselves to one local "host" or another. The Soumare may have been relative latecomers to the region, but it would be highly misleading to label them "outsiders" in any definitive sense.

The Muslim community of Korhogo differed from its neighbors, not only in religion, but in language, occupations, and in many aspects of culture. These neighbors were somewhat disparagingly labeled *banmana* (pagans). In spite of these differences, a network of close ties bound the Muslim community to the local "pagans." The Senufo were, in the first place, consumers of cloth, whose weaving remained a Dyula monopoly. The cloth was used, not primarily for clothing, but as an item of value and as an essential component of funeral ceremonies, where large quantities were buried with the deceased.[19] The Senufo were also a market for tobacco, which the Dyula grew and processed, and for luxury goods such as salt and cola nuts, which were staple items in long-distance trade passing through the region. In turn, the Senufo produced foodstuffs for the market that Dyula could buy with the proceeds of their commercial activity rather than having to grow it themselves. The "pagans" even constituted an important market for Muslim clerics, whose livelihood depended in part on the sale of amulets. Clerics were often clients of local chiefs, who might, for example, request their services to pray for prosperity, for victory in war, and so forth. In short, Muslims enjoyed a variety of monopolies: over long-distance trade, over weaving, over tobacco, over Islamic scholarship. For these very reasons, chiefs and local notables were often interested in attracting them as clients.

The maintenance of close ties between Muslim communities and their "pagan" neighbors, especially chiefs, was hardly unique to Korhogo or to the Dyula; very similar patterns of cooperation characterized much of the Volta Basin region, to the east of Korhogo.[20] This region was characterized by a specific tradition of Islamic learning, tracing its origins to the teachings of al-Ḥajj Salim Suware, a fifteenth-century Mande cleric.[21] Though none of his writings survive—plausibly because he preferred to transmit his teachings orally rather than in written form—virtually all scholars in the region trace their learning back to him, in their *isnads,* pedigrees stating the names of their teacher, their teacher's teacher, and so forth.[22]

One critical feature of this tradition is the deep-seated notion that "religion" and "politics" are two separate domains that should remain unmixed.[23] Among the Dyula, this distinction was embedded in the division of local Muslim society into two hereditary categories: *mory* and *tun tigi,* which might be glossed respectively as "scholars" and "warriors." These labels applied, not to individuals, but rather to entire clan wards (*kabilaw*). The religious practices of "warriors" and "scholars" were distinct. "Scholars" were expected to follow the strictures of Islamic ritual and moral behavior reasonably conscientiously, at the very least praying five times a day, fasting during the month of Ramaḍan, abstaining from alcohol. To prepare them for a life as pious Muslims, boys were generally taught at least the rudiments of Arabic. This instruction consisted initially in memorizing passages from the Qur'an, and ultimately the entire book. The memorization of the entire Qur'an, was celebrated in an important rite of passage, the *kurana jigi,* "putting down the Qur'an." Individuals whose study had advanced this far were able to recite fairly easily from a written text, though they did not necessarily have a very clear understanding of what they were reciting. Many "scholars" never pursued their education beyond this stage. In Korhogo or in any other Dyula community of comparable size, there were always a few "scholar" lineages who specialized in scholarship, and whose sons regularly pursued their education at an advanced level.[24] However, any free Dyula male (and conceivably some slaves) was free to pursue his studies at any time and at any level appropriate;

it was by no means unusual for middle-aged or elderly men to decide to resume their studies, especially if they had amassed enough wealth to dispose of the necessary leisure time to devote to such an obviously meritorious activity.

"Warriors," on the other hand, were not expected to live up to the same standards of piety or of learning. They might pray irregularly, omit the fast during all or part of Ramadan, and indeed openly drink alcoholic beverages.[25] Essential training for young males consisted, not in a Qur'anic education, but rather in initiation into a *lo* (secret) society. Initiation rituals among Dyula Muslim "warriors" resembled those of their avowedly "pagan" neighbors. Ceremonies took place in a sacred grove, a specially preserved enclave of virgin forest, involving a variety of masks (often indistinguishable from the masks of their Senufo neighbors) and entailing a variety of blood sacrifices to sundry spirits. Individually, "warriors" might choose to adopt "scholarly" standards of piety and indeed give themselves up to study of the Qur'an, though generally only after reaching middle age.

These broad categories of "warrior" and "scholar" in no way determined the actual occupations of most individuals. Older "warriors" might devote themselves to religious learning, while "scholars" might engage in warfare and even in outright brigandage. However, positions of leadership in the community were systematically associated with either "warrior" or "scholar" status.[26] In principle, only "warriors" were chiefs, either of villages or of chiefdoms. Such office was not open, of course, to any "warrior," but was in any community the preserve of a specific chiefly clan ward. The exercise of chiefly office was connected to the possession of hereditary powers of witchcraft (*subagaya*). Malevolent witches might be male or female, "warrior" or "scholar," but only male "warriors" might openly claim to use the powers of witchcraft for socially sanctioned purposes, either as chiefs or as recognized "anti-witches" whose personal knowledge of witchcraft allowed them to unmask their evil colleagues. The participation of chiefs in *lo* initiation societies was also instrumental to the exercise of chiefly power: first, because the *lo* societies, like witches, wielded deadly occult powers; second, because direct or indirect control over the initiation societies afforded a powerful instrument of political persuasion, at least among other "warriors."[27] "Scholars," on the other hand, were qualified for positions of recognized religious leadership. Such leadership included the office of imam, an office that was more influential in some communities than others, and minimally so, as it happens, in Korhogo. More important than any office per se was the recognized status of "cleric," or *karamogo.* Only a *karamogo* had the right to take students. This status of *karamogo* was ceremoniously conferred on an individual in a rite of enturbanment, after he had been duly examined by local scholars and deemed fit to be included in their ranks. Clerics, like chiefs, wielded their own occult powers, linked to the knowledge of written magic charms (*sebe*).[28]

Ultimately, the distinction between these two kinds of leaders, chiefs and clerics, was even more fundamental than the global division of local Muslim society into "warriors" and "scholars." The real political power wielded by specific chiefs was, after all, highly variable. Individual "scholars" and indeed whole "scholar" clan wards frequently constituted serious political rivals to the chief in struggles for effective authority in any village or chiefdom. At the end of the nineteenth century, admittedly in extreme circumstances, a "scholar" replaced a "warrior" as chief of the chiefdom of Kadioha, near Korhogo.[29] Conversely, individual "warriors" might accede to the status of "cleric" as long as they possessed the requisite learning. Rather, the exercise of political power (*fanga*) and Islamic learning (*karamogoya*) were antithetical activities. Specifically, clerics had no business meddling in politics.

The extent to which this was—and remains—a fundamental ethical precept among Dyula Muslims was impressed on me in the course of a casual conversation with a friend of mine in 1984. I had mentioned, in passing, an event that was currently in the headlines of international news, the murder of a Polish priest by the secret police of that country. My friend's immediate reaction was to ask me whether the priest had been engaging in political activity. Before waiting for an explanation, he remarked that this must necessarily have been the case; the secret police of any country was hardly likely to murder a priest without any cause. He concluded that the priest had gotten exactly what he deserved; anyone holding religious office has no business in politics.

At one level, the notion that clerics should stay away from politics was a question of common sense and expediency in Korhogo and in other similar Muslim communities. More often than not, Muslims were locally outnumbered by "pagans" and under the authority of "pagan" chiefs. Such a state of affairs was, as we have seen, not necessarily to the disadvantage of local Muslim communities; quite the contrary. Muslims, not least the clerics themselves, enjoyed a variety of economic monopolies and often profited from the patronage of their chiefs.[30] Consequently, clerics were for the most part quite unconcerned with converting their "pagan" neighbors to Islam; Marty even cites a story, perhaps apocryphal, about Muslim clerics to the west of Korhogo who convinced a chief recently converted to Islam to revert to his traditional "pagan" ways.[31] In fundamental ways, local society was based, not simply on the mutual tolerance of different religious practices, but indeed on the principle of socioreligious pluralism. With the exception of Muslim "scholars" (but not "warriors"), groups who were socially, occupationally, and/or politically distinct initiated their adolescent males in separate initiation societies; in a sense, the Qur'anic education of young scholars was functionally equivalent to initiation. By maintaining this principle of complementarity, each group could protect its own particular prerogatives.

It would, of course, be misleading and naive to paint a picture of perfect harmony and complementarity. Just as "scholars" might be political rivals of their "warrior" chiefs, so specific Muslims might constitute, under various circumstances, a political threat to the authority of local "pagan" chiefs. Muslims might back rival factions of chiefly lineages, or even attempt to seize power in their own right. However, it was equally true that Muslims were often loyal clients of their "pagan" chiefs. Quite specifically, the Dyula of Korhogo relate a number of incidents where they fought on the side of their chief against other Muslims, as well as against other "pagans." However, it mattered little that specific Muslims might threaten the power of particular "pagan" chiefs; other "pagans," after all, constituted at least as great a menace. What mattered, rather, was that Muslims as a religious community were not perceived as a political threat. This was the specific danger that any clerical participation in politics might entail. If opposition to any chief were to be formulated by clerics, in religious terms, then all Muslims would be automatically suspect; all might suffer the repercussions of any uprising that any Muslims might undertake. On the other hand, as long as it was clear that the political choices of individual Muslims were unrelated to their religion, the religious community of Muslims was not in any way threatened by the actions of specific members.

While there were sound practical reasons underlying the notion that clerics should never meddle in politics, it is important to bear in mind that this was ultimately a moral principle, and not simply a question of expediency. This "apolitical" morality, however, must not be confused with quietism, with the notion that clerics ought necessarily withdraw from the world, avoiding contact, not only with power, but with the persons of the powerful. On the contrary, many Dyula clerics maintained close links with local rulers, links that were in no way construed as "political." The services of clerics were often in demand with local rulers; clerics were seen as manipulating powerful occult forces, both through written magic charms and from a knowledge of petitionary prayers (*duau*) and offerings (*saraka*). It was perfectly acceptable for clerics to provide such services to rulers, not only for the benefit of the village, chiefdom, or state as a whole, but even for the personal benefit of the ruler, or for that matter of other clients. Such services could be readily purchased. More exactly, the client of a cleric was responsible for rewarding him, particularly if his advice or remedy proved successful, in keeping with the importance of the service rendered and the client's ability to pay. In any case, it would have been foolhardy to reward stingily a cleric who wielded occult powers. Rulers were, in any case, well capable of being generous, and had every interest in doing so in order to be able to rely on the occult services of the most powerful clerics under their jurisdiction.

In short, clerics who made their services available to local rulers, and indeed who enjoyed their patronage, were not perceived as engaging in "politics." The provision of such services amounted to a sort of declaration of loyalty, not so much to the individual person of the ruler, or even to the office of chief, but rather loyalty to reigning authority in whatever form it took, provided that this authority did not interfere with Islamic worship or the integrity of the Muslim community. By offering their assistance to chiefs on one hand, and abstaining from any explicitly political discourse that might cast doubt on the legitimacy of local rulers on the other, clerics ensured that Muslims as a religious community would be accepted, if not in some cases welcomed, by local authorities.

Of course, even before the French, the clerics or the Muslim community at large were not only concerned with relations to local authorities. Throughout the second half of the nineteenth century, Korhogo was in the sphere of influence of, if not directly subject to, one foreign power or another. For most of the duration of this period, the chiefdom of Korhogo allied itself with the Tarawele (Traore) rulers of Kenedugu, in Sikasso, only a few days' march to the north, and far and away the dominant power in the region.[32] Samory also had a considerable impact on Korhogo and its hinterland. The young chief of Korhogo, Peleforo Soro (alias Gbon Coulibaly), recently installed by Babemba Tarawele of Sikasso, astutely led a delegation from the region in order to submit to Samory's authority when he realized the balance of power in the region was shifting in favor of Babemba's archenemy.[33] In fact, this strategic alliance spared Korhogo from "the ravages and pillages of Samory," which Soumare mentions in his letter. When slaves were freed by the French in 1908, and allowed to return home, colonial administrators noted how very few came back to the Korhogo region—only eleven from Baoule territory, and none from the Gouro—in sharp contrast to other regions where slaves had been heavily raided.[34] Indeed, Korhogo turned out to be a very strategic ally of Samory's, supplying his army both with foodstuffs and with soldiers, "pagan" Senufo as well as Muslim Dyula.[35]

For obvious reasons, the Samorian period in Korhogo reinforced, rather than challenged, the notion that Muslim clerics should remain "apolitical" by expressing their unqualified support for whoever was in power. After all, the "pagan" chief of Korhogo, their immediate superior, was an ally of the dominant Muslim power in the region. In any case, it must be stressed that this separation of religion and politics applied only to Muslim clerics as such, and not more generally to the *mory* (the "scholar" clan wards) as opposed to *tun tigi* (warriors). Indeed, Samory himself was a *mory* (as his name implies). In Kadioha, a Dyula chiefdom not far to the southwest of Korhogo, the Samorian forces installed a *mory,* Sabati-ba Cisse, as chief, over and above the "legitimate" Wattara *tun tigi* claimants.[36] However, Sabati-ba was chosen because of his effectiveness as a military and political leader, and not on any religious grounds whatsoever. Predictably, the Muslim clerics of Kadioha professed their loyalty both to Samory and to Sabati-ba. Thus Marty says of Ba Karamoko Keita, imam of Kadioha at the time, that "he lived on good terms with the representatives of the despot, to whom he supplied food, but he always subsequently denied having been devoted to Samory, alleging that he only acted accordingly under constraint."[37] In fact, when Samory's forces retreated from the region, many of Kadioha's Muslim clerics followed, fleeing with the Samorians to the Worodugu, where Samory was ultimately captured.[38] Even this clerical exodus cannot be taken as evidence of unqualified support for the Samorians, but stemmed rather from fears of reprisals from neighboring Senufo, whose revolt against the allied forces of Samory and Kadioha had been crushed shortly before, in 1896.[39] The Samorian presence had diametrically opposite effects in the chiefdoms of Kadioha and of Korhogo, exacerbating the opposition between Muslim Dyula chiefs and "pagan" Senufo subjects in the former while reinforcing the loyalty of Muslim

Dyula subjects to "pagan" Senufo chiefs in the latter. However, in both cases, the local chiefs were staunch allies of Samory; both had every reason to expect the "collaboration" of Muslim clerics, and all the evidence suggests that they were not disappointed. Even so, the rather disingenuous claim of the imam of Kadioha that he had acted "under constraint" is only partially misleading; the collaboration of the region's Muslim clerics with the Samorian forces was not, I would suggest, necessarily an expression of deeply felt convictions—political or religious—but rather a feature of the clerical role itself.

Peleforo Soro, the astute chief of Korhogo who had switched allegiances from Sikasso to Samory at just the right moment, showed signs of equal flair at the approach of the French, submitting to their authority and showing in general that he was capable of making himself useful.[40] His gambit paid off; in 1903, the administrative headquarters of the Cercle du Bandama were moved to Korhogo, which was effectively to become the "capital" of northern Ivory Coast.

Early French accounts of the Korhogo region describe the attitude of the Muslim community as one of *réserve méfiant,* (distrustful reserve).[41] Within less than ten years, the region had been occupied by three colonial armies. Rumors that French dominion, in its turn, would be short-lived, that yet another army would arrive and take its place, were far from implausible under the circumstances. One way or the other, the region offered virtually no active resistance to the French. Arguably, "distrustful reserve" was as characteristic of the French attitude toward the local Muslims as of Muslim feelings about the French.

It would certainly have been out of keeping for Muslim clerics who had long been loyal subjects of "pagan" chiefs suddenly to declare opposition to the rule of French "infidels" on religious grounds. However, it was impossible for clerics to relate to French administrators in the same way as they had interacted with African rulers. Clerics, after all, had been patronized by chiefs, and were both willing and able to offer them a variety of services, providing them with written charms (*sebe*) or powerful blessings (*duau*), for example. French administrators were simply not interested in these kinds of services. The kind of cooperation that the colonial authorities actively sought involved paying taxes and especially providing porters for French military convoys, a task that, not surprisingly, the locals avoided whenever possible.[42] Muslim clerics were hardly in a position to offer French administrators any assistance in these matters.

Ultimately, the only "service" that clerics could provide the French were public declarations of loyalty. Until the outbreak of the First World War, French administrators in Ivory Coast had little reason to solicit such declarations very actively. They had to cope with considerable armed resistance to colonial rule in the southern—and least Islamized—half of the colony, especially among the Baule and Guro. Such all too real revolts overshadowed any specter of a Muslim revolt that showed no tangible signs of materializing. However, such declarations could serve a useful purpose during the First World War. The French were demanding more and more recruits for the army, and forced labor to support the war effort in one way or another. Any rebellion in the colonies would have been doubly threatening, tying up as it would military resources that otherwise could be devoted to the war effort. Last but not least, as we have seen, Turkey, the major Muslim power in the world at the time, was an enemy of France.

Mamadou Soumare's letter was only one of many Muslim declarations of loyalty to the French. Paradoxically, by the standards of the Muslims of Korhogo, the French had finally solicited of their subject clerics the kinds of services that rulers had a right to—and were expected to—demand: the intervention of clerics by the means at their disposal (magic, prayer, blessing, or, in this case, letter-writing) for the victory of the ruler's army. By proclaiming not only his own loyalty but the loyalty of the entire Muslim community of Korhogo to the French cause, Mamadou Soumare was arguably behaving exactly as a Muslim cleric in Korhogo might have been expected to behave, providing useful services to the reigning powers that be. The tone of the letter, with its excessive praise of the French rulers, seems to us simultaneously naive and cynical. In fact, it is not necessarily either. The letter stresses the fact that the French have restored order to a politically troubled region—a true enough statement, given the turbulence of the last decade of the nineteenth century in the region—and that they permit Muslims to worship in peace and tranquillity. The point of the letter is that the author accepts the political legitimacy of French rule in religious terms—a true statement given the Dyula (and Suwarian) ideology of the separation of the religious and political domains. As long as the French did not interfere with worship, Dyula clerics could freely maintain that French rule was acceptable on religious grounds. Indeed it was in everyone's interest that clerics make this point as clearly and forcefully as possible. That such declarations might also profit the cleric who supplied them—much as the provision of charms and prayers on behalf of chiefs in the past—was a matter of course.

If anything, the French, and not the Muslim clerics, were guilty of naïveté. The fact that such letters were reprinted suggests that the authorities understood them as declarations of political support, hoping if not expecting that they might help win the political allegiance of the Muslim community as a whole. Such expectations betrayed a fundamental misunderstanding of the role of clerics in the Muslim community. Declarations of loyalty from clerics to those in power, whomever they might be, were not political statements; on the contrary, they were an expression of their "apolitical" status. Such texts underscored the notion that Muslims ought not oppose the French on religious grounds, but could not address the issue of whether or not the French should be opposed or supported on purely political grounds. How could clerics judge such a matter when, by their very nature, they were expected to abstain from any "political" involvement? Clerical declarations of loyalty left ordinary Muslims free to support or to oppose the French as they saw fit. Of course, it served the interests of both the clerics and of the Muslim community at large if the French gave more credence and attached more importance to such declarations of support than was warranted. After all, the French were right on one score: the clerics were not at all inclined to call for a revolt against the French in the name of Islam. However, all this entailed on the part of the clerics was effective neutrality, and in no way affected the loyalty of Muslims at large. Indeed, after the Second World War, many Dyula Muslims in Korhogo were active in the independence movement, which at the time was militantly anticolonial. But the independence movement was "politics," and no business of clerics!

Mamadou Soumare's letter is particularly interesting because it is addressed by a member of one culture (the Muslims of Korhogo), ostensibly to a second culture (the Muslims of Mecca), but in reality as a declaration to representatives of a third culture (the French). The text meant different things to members of different cultures. Conceivably, Soumare played on and manipulated these meanings, intentionally conveying a different message to the French and to his fellow Muslims. For the French, the letter was a declaration of loyalty and as such an essentially political statement. For the Dyula, the letter was a service that a Muslim cleric, as a nonrebellious subject, ought to render the local ruler, a service whose aim was, inter alia, to keep the Muslim community as a religious community in the good graces of the powers that be. That a cleric might ingratiate himself in this way to the local authorities, and consequently benefit from their patronage, was all for the better; in this way, the cleric could also serve as an intermediary between the rulers and the Muslim community at large. Nevertheless, this kind of service was construed as essentially nonpolitical. To read the document as a political statement is to read it with the eyes of the French, but not of the local Muslims of Korhogo. This applies just as well to modern readers, who might be inclined to categorize Soumare and his colleagues as "collaborators," as individuals who, by serving the interests of foreign rulers, were betraying their communities of origin. Arguably, the very reverse is true. Mamadou Soumare, by providing the French authorities with the letter they requested, was indeed acting on behalf of the Muslim community of Korhogo, as the heading of the letter indicates, and in a way that very community could recognize as legitimate.

La Trahison des Clercs?

It would, of course, be hazardous to overgeneralize on the basis of this one example. Certainly, other scholars steeped in the Suwarian tradition—Almamy Kunandi Timite of Bondoukou, for one—were acting under virtually identical assumptions, understood as such in their home communities. By no means were all of the clerics willing to express their support for the French colonial regime, Suwarians; Seydou Nourou Tall is the obvious example. In any case, the point is hardly to characterize traditions of Islamic scholarship in West Africa in crude terms, as "jihadist" or "quietist." The task is rather to understand, as best we can, how clerics and their followers conceived their relationship to their rulers, precolonial, colonial, and postcolonial.

Notes

1. Donal Cruise O'Brien, "Towards an 'Islamic Policy' in French West Africa," *Journal of African History* 8 (1967): 303–16, is a seminal article on the subject; some of its conclusions have been questioned by David Robinson, "French 'Islamic' Policy and Practice in Late Nineteenth-Century Senegal," *Journal of African History* 29 (1988): 415–35. Christopher Harrison, *France and Islam in West Africa, 1860–1960* (Cambridge, 1988), devotes an entire book to the subject. See also Jean-Louis Triaud, "La question musulmane en Côte d'Ivoire (1893–1939)," *Revue française d'histoire d'Outre Mer* 61, no. 225 (1974): 542–71.

2. This is the (ironic) title of a book by Louis Binger (Paris, 1906); Binger was trying to dispel such alarmist notions; Harrison, *France and Islam,* 32–33.

3. Robinson, "French 'Islamic' Policy," esp. 421–23, detailing the steps taken by Faidherbe to implement such a policy.

4. On Marty's writings and career, see Harrison, *France and Islam,* 105–36.

5. L. Brenner, *West African Sufi: The Religious Heritage and Spiritual Search of Cerno Bokar Saalif Taal* (Berkeley and Los Angeles, 1984).

6. Christian Coulon, *Les Musulmans et le pouvoir en Afrique Noire: Religion et contre-culture* (Paris, 1983), 121–25. On the Union Culturelle Musulmane, see also Lansine Kaba, *The Wahhabiyya* (Evanston, Ill., 1974), 234–52.

7. Mervyn Hiskett, *The Development of Islam in West Africa* (London, 1984), 299. "There were Muslim groups that saw their best interests served by a policy of conservatism" (ibid., 300; my emphasis). The characterization of Muslim clerics as "conservatives" and "progressives" is implicitly teleological. For a critique of such teleological approaches to the study of Islam in West Africa, see Robert Launay, *Beyond the Stream: Islam and Society in a West African Town* (Berkeley and Los Angeles, 1992).

8. Paul Marty, *Etudes sur l'Islam en Côte d'Ivoire* (Paris, 1922), 486–87.

9. Ibid., 488–89.

10. Harrison, *France and Islam,* 122.

11. Ibid., 118–26, discusses France's wartime policy toward West African Muslim clerics in some detail, citing a number of other letters that were published in the *Revue du monde musulman* in 1915.

12. Marty, *Etudes,* 174.

13. Souleyman Soumare was still active as an interpreter in Korhogo in 1940, amassing considerable wealth and power in his role as a broker between the French colonial administration and the local population, as documented in Nancy Ellen Lawler, *Soldiers of Misfortune: Ivoirien Tirailleurs of World War II* (Athens, Ohio, 1992), 43.

14. Archives Nationales de Côte d'Ivoire, IV–40/3.

15. Marty, *Etudes,* 174–77. Marty mentions by name the first three imams of Korhogo, whose names are still remembered in the community: "Sye gbe" (white-haired) Suware (whose nickname Marty erroneously mentions as "Segue" and glosses as "shaykh"); Karamoko Ali Fofana; and Mustafa Cisse. Even though Sye gbe's descendents still live in Korhogo, after his death in 1913, the imamate passed definitively into the hands of the Fofana and Cisse, who jointly possess rights to the office to this day. Marty also mentions Anzoumana Diane; the Diane clan ward still has a reputation for specializing in Islamic scholarship.

16. For a detailed description of the Dyula of Korhogo, see Robert Launay, *Traders Without Trade: Responses to Change in Two Dyula Communities,* (Cambridge, 1982).

17. On "castes" in Korhogo, see Robert Launay, "The Dieli of Korhogo: Identity and Identification," in *Status and Identity in West Africa: Nyamakalaw of Mande,* ed. David Conrad and Barbara Frank (Bloomington, Ind., 1995).

18. On the host/stranger relationship, see Robert Launay, "Landlords, Hosts and Strangers among the Dyula," *Ethnology* 18 (1979): 71–83.

19. See Robert Launay, "Transactional Spheres and Inter-Societal Exchange in Ivory Coast," *Cahiers d'études africaines* 18 (1978): 561–73, for an account of trade between Dyula and Senufo in Korhogo.

20. Nehemia Levtzion, *Muslims and Chiefs in West Africa: A Study of Islam in the Middle Volta Basin in the Pre-colonial Period* (Oxford, 1968).

21. See Ivor Wilks, "The Transmission of Islamic Learning in the Western Sudan," in *Literacy in Traditional Societies,* ed. J. Goody (Cambridge, 1968), 162–97; "The Suwarians: Laissez-Faire, Lassez-Nous Faire?" Paper presented to the Conference on Islam in Africa, Northwestern University, Evanston, Illinois, 1984; *Wa and the Wala: Islam and Polity in Northwestern Ghana* (Cambridge, 1989), 98–100; and Lamin Sanneh, *The Jakhanke* (London, 1979), on the teachings and influence of al-Ḥājj Sālim Suware. Sanneh argues for an earlier, thirteenth-century, date.

22. See also Robert Launay, "Pedigrees and Paradigms: Scholarly Credentials among the Dyula of Northern Ivory Coast," in *Muslim Travellers: Pilgrimage, Migration, and the Religious Imagination,* ed. D. Eickelman and J. Piscatori (London, 1990), 175–99.

23. See Wilks, "Transmission of Islamic Learning," 25, who characterizes the Suwarian tradition as "pacifist in rejecting *jihād* as an instrument of political

change; quietist in rejecting active proselytism, urging that true conversion must occur not in man's but in God's time; and accommodating in that it permitted the coexistence of believers and unbelievers in so far as the religious obligations of the former were not jeopardized." I have some reservations about the appropriateness of the terms "pacifist" and "quietist."

24. The content of this advanced curriculum is discussed in Wilks, "Transmission of Islamic Learning."

25. See Louis Binger, *Du Niger au Golfe de Guinée* (Paris, 1892), 1: 298, where he divides the Muslim inhabitants of Kong, in northern Ivory Coast, into three classes: "les musulmans lettrés," "les musulmans non lettrés, mais stricts observateurs des préceptes du Coran," and finally "les musulmans qui boivent du dolo," (the local beer).

26. Several *mory* informants in the village of Kadioha confided to me that their ancestors had systematically engaged in pillaging caravans and enslaving travelers.

27. See R. Launay, "Warriors and Traders: The Political Organization of a West African Chiefdom," *Cahiers d'études africaines* 18 (1988): 355–73.

28. Cf. Jack Goody, "Restricted Literacy in Northern Ghana," in Goody, *Literacy in Traditional Societies,* 199–264.

29. For an account of this "scholarly" coup d'état, see R. Launay, "Sabati-Ba's Coup d'Etat: Contexts of Legitimacy in a West African Chiefdom," in *State Formation and Political Legitimacy* (*Political Anthropology,* vol. 6), ed. Ronald Cohen and Judith Toland (New Brunswick, N.J., 1988), 45–67.

30. Rene Caillié, passing through Tingrela, northwest of Korhogo, remarked that "they [the "Bambaras," that is, the Senufo] might, owing to their superiority of numbers, molest them [the Muslim "Diaulas or Jaulas"] if they chose, yet they refrain from doing so, and go to their villages to sell them the superfluous produce of their harvest." *Travels Through Central Africa to Timbuctoo* (London, 1830 [reprinted 1968]), 1: 376.

31. Marty, *Etudes,* 152.

32. The alliances of the chiefs of Korhogo in the second half of the nineteenth and the first half of the twentieth centuries are thoroughly described in Tiona Ouattara, "Les Tiembara de Korhogo, des origines à Peleforo Gbon Coulibaly (1962)" (Ph.D. diss. [3e cycle], History, Paris 1977). Ouattara's discussion of the earlier history of Korhogo is far less reliable. See also Yves Person, *Samori: Une révolution Dyula* (Dakar, 1975), 3: 1561–63.

33. Ouattara, "Les Tiembara" see also Person, *Samori,* 3: 1570–71.

34. Archives Nationales de Côte d'Ivoire, Rapports Politiques, Cercle du Bandama, 1913.

35. For example, Samory's military commander in Wa was one Fanyinama from Korhogo; Wilks, *Wa and the Wala,* 121.

36. Launay, "Sabati-Ba's Coup d'Etat."

37. Marty, *Etudes,* 177.

38. This is apparent from the file on Muslim clerics compiled in 1931; Archives Nationales de Côte d'Ivoire, IV, 40/3.

39. Launay, "Sabati-Ba's Coup d'Etat"; Person, *Samori,* 3: 1746–47.

40. Peleforo switched allegiances one last time, eventually backing the RDA and Houphouet-Boigny without entirely losing the confidence of the French. He died in 1962. Looking at history Korhogocentrically, French colonial rule was just a long episode of Peleforo's reign!

41. Archives Nationales de Côte d'Ivoire, Rapports Politiques, Cercle du Bandama, October 1901.

42. Convoys from Korhogo were likely to head due south through Baoule territory, where resistance to French rule lasted until 1911 and where they were consequently under real danger of attack; see Timothy C. Weiskel, *French Colonial Rule and the Baule Peoples* (Oxford, 1980).

Islam and the Idea of Asylum in Asante

DONNA J. E. MAIER

The phenomenon of fugitives seeking sanctuary at religious shrines and politically symbolic sites from vengeance or persecution is well recorded in ancient, Middle Eastern, Asian, and Western histories. Asylum is also documented in precolonial African society. I have written elsewhere about the comparative historical background to the idea of asylum and demonstrated that in West Africa the practice differed in no significant manner from other societies, though details varied.[1]

In Asante certain traditional religious shrines were widely recognized as places of asylum, especially for escaped slaves. One can hypothesize that mosques and Muslim quarters in Asante also could have served as sanctuaries for fugitives and dissidents, as they did in some other parts of West Africa. The position of Islam in Asante, however, presents special problems. Ivor Wilks has argued that Islam developed there along lines of the Suwarian tradition (of the fifteenth-century West African scholar al-Hajj Salim Suwari); that is, in a mode of acquiescence to the non-Muslim state structure, awaiting God's time for the conversion of the rulers rather than proselytizing and adopting jihad to foment change.[2] An examination of the degree to which the Islamic community in Asante exhibited the privileges that the shrines of traditional religion enjoyed as fugitive sanctuaries will expose one more facet of the ambiguous role of Islam in Asante.

A comment on terminology is appropriate here. The English word asylum comes through Latin (*asylum*) from the Greek word *asulon,* meaning "inviolable," or "without right of seizure."[3] The word "sanctuary" comes from the Latin *sanctus,* meaning sacred. Places offering asylum are often but not always religiously sacred.

Thus while previous researchers and contemporary authors, including myself, often use the words interchangeably, asylum is really a more exact, and thus preferred term.

The Significance of Place

Asylum is almost always associated with a place. Place is of course physical, and asylum seekers historically needed to achieve the physical site of protection, be it an altar, a temple, a statue, a palace, a priest's compound, or even a sacred object or person. Generally, place was so important that its circumference was specifically delineated; should an asylum seeker leave the place by accident or design, he/she could be slain or captured with impunity.

Place has physical, social, and supernatural elements to it. Socially speaking, a place of asylum is almost always the manifestation of an institution that is competitive with or an alternative source of power to the prevailing political structure. Thus one of the most common generalizations arising from asylum studies is that the more a state or society is centralized, powerful, and capable of delivering a legal system, the weaker or less tolerated the practice of asylum becomes.

Religion is frequently a parallel power structure in society; beyond this, however, a religious place also embodies a supernatural or metaphysical value. Places of asylum are often sites of religious shrines, buildings, and communities not only because they are competitive foci of authority to the state, but because appeal to the protection of the supernatural, over and above the physical and social, can be a key feature of asylum. Fear of divine retribution of some sort, and not merely social censure, is a common (though hardly a sole) reason for the ability of asylum to function in a society.

The idea of asylum extends at least back to early biblical, Greek, and Roman times, and places of noted asylum ranged from shrines, to whole towns, and to even the emperor's statue. In late Roman and medieval times churches also became key centers of asylum. The comparative cross-cultural significance of asylum in these historical cases has been discussed elsewhere.[4] Research on the practice of asylum in Islamic society is not so fully developed.

In the case of Islam, the mosque is clearly a potential location for asylum. C. Glasse maintains that "mosques everywhere have been used as sanctuaries inviolable to pursuit," and adds one specific example: "In the Mawlay Idris Mosque in Fez there is a room accessible from a narrow passageway which has been used as a haven by fugitives."[5] Mosques in Islam can of course be as simple as a circle of stones but it is probable that places such as these are never perceived as serious asyla.

In Iran there has been a carefully articulated practice of asylum. The Persian word *bast* is used for the idea of asylum (not to be confused with the Arabic word *bast,* a technical term of the Sufis referring to a spiritual state of exultation). *Bast* refers to "certain places which were regarded as affording an inviolable sanctuary to any malefactor, however grave his crime."[6] As with almost all places of asylum, *bast* did not provide permanent refuge but merely a place from which to negotiate with the fugitive's pursuers. Under the Safawids, the royal stables ("the wrong-doer could claim sanctuary by standing either at the horse's head or at its tail"), the neighborhood of artillery, and even at times the royal kitchen constituted *bast.* The residences of mudjtahids, the mosques, and most important the tombs of Shia saints (*imamzada*), especially that of Shah Abd al-Azim, were all important places of *bast.* The *imamzada* of Shah Abd al-Azim is most famous, "owing to its proximity to the Kadjar capital [so that] those who were protesting against the actions of the government frequently took refuge there in the late nineteenth and early twentieth century."[7]

J. Hunwick has documented for West Africa during the Songhay empire some cases of mosques, and specifically the mosque of Gao, used as places of asylum. He refers to the plaintiff as seeking the *hurma* of the place, and the *hurma* of the imam, khatib, or qadi associated with the place. *Hurma* he defines as "a state of being forbidden, sacred or inviolable, entitled to respect, reverence, honour."[8] L. Sanneh also identifies the scholarly Muslim towns of Diakhaba and Gunjuru in Mali that were so holy they provided refuge from the central government.[9]

Asylum is consistently, though cursorily, documented in non-Islamic precolonial African society. T. Elias, writing on African law, asserts that in practically all African societies "sanctuaries" existed for accused persons fleeing from the immediate retaliation of an angry crowd. The asylum could be

> a sacred grove or king's palace, chief's or councillor's residence, pending the hearing of the case against [the accused]. . . . Once a supposed or even actual criminal has sought the refuge of a sanctuary—be it ever so ramshackle as a flimsy grove of bare thatch—none of his pursuers dare touch him. . . . Of course it is otherwise if the criminal were caught by the injured party and/or his sympathizers before reaching the security of a sanctuary.[10]

In West Africa, traditional religious shrines and priests' compounds have often been recorded as serving as asyla. M. Kingsley observed the phenomenon in Calabar and the French Congo, while R. Nassau commented on it in Gabon, both in the late nineteenth century. S. Johnson, writing of the Yoruba in 1897, noted that the house of any official "who must die with the king" in funeral ceremonies "is a sanctuary of safety and reprieve for all criminals condemned to death, if they can escape thither." The recollections of the slave Osifekunde relating to Yoruba in the 1820s referred to certain places, perhaps whole towns, specifically Makun and Mahin, where criminals and other refugees in Ijebu could flee and "where [the guilty party] cannot be reached."[11]

Similarly in areas around Asante and Akan territories, all traditional religious shrines apparently had the potential to provide some form of asylum, especially for slaves. T. E. Bowdich simply observed, when discussing the wealth of shrines, that "a slave flying to the temple, may dash or devote himself to the fetish." A. B. Ellis recorded in regions around the Volta that "any slave who takes refuge in a temple and dedicates himself to the service of the god, cannot be reclaimed by his owner." R. S. Rattray, referring to Asante, noted that "a slave could run away and seek sanctuary by throwing himself on the mercy of a god (e.g. Dente), or the *'samanfo* (ancestral spirits) at some Barim (mausoleum)."[12]

The Danish official Isert provided a very specific example, probably the earliest documentation of the practice, in 1784. He noted that the town of Mlefi (Lower Volta), "is also famous because of its fetish temple since any slave who can succeed in reaching there gains his freedom. I have had some experience of this myself on one occasion and to my vexation."[13] Dutch officials in the early nineteenth century also noted traditional religious shrines that became quite wealthy by gathering in escaped slaves, and the Ghanaian geographer K. Dickson observed that "lands around [all] major fetish centres like Prampram, Mlefi, Asentema in Akwapim, and Krachi were extensively cultivated by slaves liberated according to the age-old custom whereby a slave automatically became free once he took refuge in a fetish temple."[14]

With such a tradition of asylum in West Africa, one would hypothesize that in the case of Islam in West Africa, within and on the periphery of Asante, mosques were potential sites of asylum. They represented a separate place, a sacred place, and one supported by an authoritative, intellectual, and legal system separate from the traditional power structure. The case of the great mosque at Kong even suggests that mosques could co-opt and carry on the supernatural element of the traditional religious realm that they sought to supersede, for the Kong mosque is said to be built over the powerful *djo* (fetish or sacred object) of the last non-Muslim ruler of Kong. The *djo* was captured from said ruler by Seku Watara, a Muslim warrior who seized control of Kong about 1730; on Seku Watara's orders the *djo* was buried by Imam Baro. The mosque was then built over it.[15]

In fact, however, until at least the late 1840s, when Asantehene Kwaku Dua formed an official imamate in Kumase, there is no record of a formal or Friday mosque, *jami,* in Kumase, the capital of Asante, at all. Bowdich and Dupuis, who were interested in architecture and Islam respectively, among other things, described none. The Muslims of Kumase in the early nineteenth century lived close, even physically close, under the control of the Asantehene. The Muslim population of perhaps one thousand resided in the center of town along a street immediately next to the Asantehene's palace. Hutchison, who accompanied Bowdich, described them praying only on skins for prayer mats, in the home of the head of their community, Muhammad al-Ghamba, also known as Baba.[16] It was not until 1948 that the Muslim community obtained a plot of land in Kumase from the Asantehene and began the construction of a large central Friday mosque.[17]

There were Friday mosques in some Muslim towns on Asante's northern periphery by the early nineteenth century, but it would appear not many. The Friday mosque of Salaga was built shortly after 1807 by Sheikh Malam Cediya of Katsina, following a jihad that caused many of Katsina's citizens to emigrate.[18] Traditions from Wa describe a phase of mosque building that began in Kong about 1785 and reached Wa, where the first "true" mosque, rather than an area marked by stones, was built around 1801. Other Wa traditions maintain however that the first large Friday mosque of Wa was not constructed until 1885.[19] There are traditions that refer to the existence of a very old mosque at Gbuipe: J. A. Braimah wrote that "Jakpa [the legendary founder of Gonja, though probably the ruler Lanta, d. 1673] marched to [G]Buipe and rebuilt the mosque that was in ruins. He was buried in the mosque and the tomb is worshipped annually to this day."[20] The earlier mosque would be early indeed, perhaps the 'premier' mosque in Gonja. In two versions of the *Kitab Ghanja* a note indicates that the Gonja ruler Manwura (d. 1601) built the first Gbuipe mosque. The editors of the chronicle comment,

> We interpret this to mean that Manwura built the mosque at the grave of his predecessor, Namba. . . . [It] is still highly revered in Gbuipe. It is, significantly, referred to as the *mishiri,* compare Malinke *misiri,* Arabic *masjid,* "mosque." Wilks visited the grave in 1963. . . . The mosque had long crumbled, but . . . the location of the *mihrab* was still discernible in the middle of the eastern wall, and that of the minaret at the north-western corner. . . . The people of Old Gbuipe formed ranks within the ruins and were led in prayers for "Jakpa." Manwura's mosque at Gbuipe was presumably the premier mosque in Gonja.[21]

Whether Namba's tomb/mosque in Gbuipe was ever used as a place of asylum is not mentioned, but one would venture that if it is revered to this day, it may well prove upon future research to be a place of asylum. On the other hand, in the recent translation of *Tarikh Ghunja,* Wilks and Levtzion argue that Jakpa Lanta is probably the ruler said to be buried at Jakpasere, near Kpembe, and of that tomb there is indeed reference to its use as a place of asylum, as one informant related. "The Ghunja revere his [Jakpa's] tomb [at Jakpasere]. Anyone who sought refuge at it for protection would have been left alone. I even saw one of his descendants who killed someone flee there and he was left alone. But as a punishment they denied him [any claim to] chieftaincy (*wilaya*)."[22]

Nevertheless, in most of Asante and many of even the major Muslim towns of Gonja and the northern periphery, there was no Friday mosque until the 1880s. Binger, in 1888, visiting the town of Karaga in Dagomba, noted that "the majority of the people are Muslims . . . but there is no mosque. I have been told that in all that region there are mosques at Yendi and Kompoungou [Kumbungu] only." According to Levtzion, the Friday mosque at Kumbungu to which Binger referred was only built around 1875, by al-Hajj Ishaq, a Wangara, who visited Kumbungu and found there "a large Muslim community without a mosque."[23]

The absence of spatially ostentatious mosques in and around Asante may be attributable to a deliberate Asante policy of preventing their construction in an effort to check the Muslims' development of a physical base and presence. But an explanation may also lie in the ideology of the Suwarian tradition advocated by many of the ulama in the region. This tradition has been more eloquently discussed by others.[24] Suffice it to say here that it was a philosophy of accommodation and cooperation between Muslim and local non-Muslim communities and states in West Africa. It did not advocate proselytization or denunciation of the unbelievers that surrounded the ulama and Muslim trading communities in the southern regions of West Africa. Places where this ideology dominated are historical evidence supporting the gradual spread of mixed Islam rather than the "contrapuntal paramountcy" also seen in some parts of West Africa.[25]

The Suwarian tradition stood in sharp contrast to the jihad tradition of the late eighteenth and nineteenth century, which viewed much of West Africa as *dar al-harb,* and advocated *hejira* (withdrawal) and *jihad* (crusade) against unbelievers. Any compromise or cooperation of Muslims with non-Muslim rulers was unjustifiable and even apostasy to those of the jihad tradition. It is therefore perhaps not only metaphor that when the reformer al-Hajj Mahmud Karantaw of the upper Volta region returned from pilgrimage to Mecca in the mid-nineteenth century, and announced his intention to launch jihad in the territories north of Asante, he promised that "he would conquer his country and build a mosque in every town."[26] To a Muslim of Suwarian tradition, the building of a large Friday mosque would have been unnecessary provocation, sure to threaten one's non-Muslim hosts. To a jihadist the absence of mosques in the region was visible evidence of the weakness of Islam, and the building of them an essential religious statement.

Given the dearth of large mosques in Asante, it is difficult to document their usage for asylum. Nevertheless, with the prevalence of asylum-seeking at traditional religious shrines, and the respect shown by Asante for the religious abilities of Muslims, for their amulets, and for their prayers and sacrifices for the military success of the Asante,[27] one would expect to find some examples of the use of mosques as asyla. In the cases to be cited below (Wa and Kong) it is at least clear that assaults on mosques were considered shocking and unjustifiable by many Muslims in West Africa.

Limits to and Violation of Asylum

Asylum only functions successfully for a petitioner if everyone concerned agrees or acquiesces to it, including the government and individuals of the society involved. In fact rarely is asylum respected by everyone and it is more often honored in the breach. Individuals especially, and the government frequently, show no fear of the religious or social punishments that might rain down upon them for violating sanctuary. Examples from ancient and medieval history abound.[28] In modern times perhaps the most notorious example of violation of asylum is the invasion of the Golden Temple of the Sikhs in Amritsar by, first the British, and then sixty years later, by the Indian army.

Islamic sanctuary also clearly has its limits. In Iran in 1891 the famous reformer Djamal al-Din al-Afghani was allowed *bast* by the government for seven months in the *imamzad* of Shah Abd al-Azid. But the Qajar ruler Nasir al-Din changed his mind and sent five hundred horsemen to evict Djamal al-Din forcibly and expel him from Iran.[29] Perhaps more shocking but less publicized is of course the penetration by troops of the Grand Mosque in Mecca when armed fundamentalist radicals in 1979 sought to disrupt the pilgrimage, failed, and took refuge in the mosque. Of course, the appropriate *fatwas* were obtained by the Saudi authorities before the final assault began. In West Africa, Hunwick has observed that Askiya Musa of Songhay generally refused to recognize the asylum requests of Muslim holy men interceding for fugitives, while his father and his successors had recognized many.[30]

On the Gold Coast, Isert, who, it will be recalled, lost his slave when the latter rushed into a shrine for safety, employed a typical technique to recover him. He sent his baptized mulatto soldier into the shrine, who then pulled the poor chap out again. Bowdich observed in Asante that "by paying a fee of two ounces of gold and four sheep, any person shuts the door of the fetish house against all his run away slaves." And similarly Ellis, writing about southern Ewe in the late nineteenth century, noted that when a slave fled to a shrine for asylum, "by paying a fee to the priests, the owner can close the doors of all the temples in the neighborhood to his fugitive slaves, [thus] this provision of an asylum for an ill-treated slave is more apparent than real."[31]

A more common failure of asylum was when war refugees fled from the war zone to a shrine or town that they hoped would be safe, only to have the army pursue them to the gates of the place of refuge, and demand and receive their surrender. Many examples of this exist in European history, but three examples from West Africa are as follows. First, refugees fled from the Asante army to Kong in the eighteenth century but were surrendered by Seku Watara to prevent the town being sacked.[32] Second, in the 1740s, some Basa refugees fled to Krakye "seeking protection from Odente the far-famed fetish of the place," pushed by the conquering armies of Asantehene Opoku Ware. The Asantehene's son Adu Kwanfeni, Konadu Anim, and the Dwaben linguist Damang Safo negotiated their surrender in exchange for not attacking the town.[33] Third, Fante refugees fleeing the invasions of Osei Bonsu's army sought protection under the walls of the British fort at Cape Coast in 1807. The British commanding officer eventually surrendered half of them to the Asantehene and sold the other half into slavery rather than have the fort taken.[34]

Again there is scant information about mosques in the region of Greater Asante and even beyond, except when sources lament their destruction. Thus the new Friday mosque at Wa (built c. 1885) was destroyed in 1887 by Babatu when a group of Muslim resisters to his warring in the region took refuge there. Babatu, at first in alliance with Wa, turned on the town when its leaders refused to provide him with a payment of slaves he requested. While Babatu was looting Wa, a group of about one hundred people took refuge in the mosque, and Babatu then attacked and burned the mosque as well. This, a British observer noted, "gives Babatu a bad name with many Mohammedans in the Hinterland."[35] Samori also is most bitterly remembered for destroying the great mosque at Kong in 1897, supposedly slaughtering Muslims on its very steps, and Ahmadu Lobbo destroyed the great mosque at Jenne. In all three cases the Muslim communities were sufficiently shocked that we can infer a belief in mosques as at least a theoretical place of asylum.

Those Who Seek Asylum

In the comparative literature, asylum seekers generally fall into roughly five categories: (1) accidental murderers, fleeing blood vengeance; (2) escaped and abused slaves and wives; (3) debtors; (4) political dissidents; and (5) war refugees. J. H. Driberg, C. Dundas, and Elias, all writing on traditional African law, and all drawing primarily on East African examples, maintained that protection from malicious pursuit or excessive physical retribution in the case of accidental or unpremeditated murder or injury, and the consequent "free or frequent indulgence in vendetta by the populace," was "the chief social function" of asylum in African societies.[36] In West Africa the option for asylum seems to have been primarily taken by escaped and abused slaves, as Bowdich, Ellis, Isert, Rattray, and Kingsley all observed.

It is not clear that, historically speaking, political dissidents ever received much asylum at sacred places within their own countries. Certainly the process is not documented and regularized the way cases of manslaughter and debt were in biblical, Greek, and medieval European studies. Treason was specifically excluded from right of sanctuary in medieval England. *Bast* in Iran did function for political dissidents but only to a point, the example of Djamal al-Din al-Afghani being only the most famous. Hunwick on the other hand cites an example of a certain Sa'id Mara seeking (and receiving) asylum in the Gao mosque after participating on the losing side of the 1588 civil war in Songhay.[37] In West Africa, Smith refers to a Muslim "master of many war boys," who was expelled from Ijebu for the treasonous selling of munitions to Ibadan and who found sanctuary, "isi asala" at Ijebu Ife.[38] Political dissidents from Asante also sought refuge on its periphery. Thus many dissidents fled to the British-controlled Gold Coast in the nineteenth century, and others fled to the Volta region just outside Asante control after 1874.

However, the Muslim community in Kumase rarely took a position of opposition to the Asantehene's government. In fact in the early nineteenth century its members were chiefly occupied in making amulets and prayers for the support of the government. Thus they had no need to seek asylum in a mosque or in another Muslim community. When they were out of favor with the court it appears that they merely remained confined to their own small portion of Kumase. In the one case when Muhammad al-Ghamba chose to desert the Asante army on campaign in Gyaman —an act of political dissidence if ever there was—he returned to

Kumase rather than fleeing to Muslim communities in the north.[39]

In contrast, a state might be willing to provide asylum to particular groups of persons, even dissidents from another state, with an eye to gaining the benefit of their skills or their numbers. Romulus is said to have allowed escapees of all sorts to settle in Rome when first building it. English kings had sanctuary towns for archers to keep them from fleeing to France should they have committed a crime, and the Israelites allowed fleeing slaves of any sort from anywhere to settle in ancient Israel, presumably because it perceived a need for increased population. Frederick William issued the Edict of Potsdam within days of the revocation of the Edict of Nantes, thus to provide French Huguenot asylum in Prussia.[40]

Asante in the late eighteenth and even nineteenth century seems regularly to have spared learned Muslims in war zones in order to bring them back to Kumase for their skills. For example Abu Bakr Bamba was brought to Kumase as a captive in the 1770s from a campaign in Gambaga, and Uthman Kamagatay brought in 1844 after a campaign in Gonja.[41] Both were eventually promoted to high positions in Asante government. There is a reference by Bonnat that Asante extended this type of asylum to traditional religious priests taken in war as well.[42] Bowdich's information regarding Muhammad al-Ghamba states even more definitively that the latter "presented himself to solicit an asylum in Coomassie," in 1807, "having been driven from Gamba [Gambaga] by the rapacity of the King, his near relative," and the Asantehene gave him asylum in return for prayers and amulets for war.[43]

Government Power and Termination of Asylum

Most of the scholarship on the practice of asylum in places other than Africa concludes that as governments become more centralized, and develop a strong political structure, they seek to eradicate, or exploit and control, the practice of asylum. Sanctuary often exists because a government may be too weak in the face of an alternative social institution (especially organized religion) to break up a place of asylum or to prevent refugees from fleeing there. In other cases, a government may be weak enough that it cannot eradicate asylum by providing a full range of courts and legal recourse for its citizenry, but strong enough that it chooses to coordinate with and even authorize the practice of asylum within an alternative institution. As Bellamy argues, the English royal judges "viewed sanctuaries as liberties where the king's writ did not run, and therefore as something to be gradually eroded," as the monarchy grew more powerful.[44]

All governments, however, eventually act to restrict and eradicate most forms of asylum when they can. We might hypothesize then that as Asante "bureaucratized," strengthened, and expanded its political structure, it too would attempt to limit or proscribe the practice of asylum. Indeed, in 1804 Asante moved to abolish asylum in its coastal periphery province around Accra. In that year four Asante commissioners were sent to Accra by the Asantehene to tighten control on the area. They promulgated a new ruling that

> in the Asante King's name proclaimed that all swearing by the King's name should be discontinued; that theft shall be punished with threats, restoration or compensation and nothing further, and also that all slaves who place themselves in fetish shall be immediately handed over, or the fetish priest will be punished as a thief.[45]

Another example of the Asante state moving to limit asylum is found in the case of the rebellious province of Wassa. It agreed in 1816 to sign an agreement of submission with Asante that included a promise not only to pay tribute, but "that fugitive slaves shall be given back and murderers shall be delivered up without any further palavers."[46]

Similarly one would not expect to see the Asante state tolerating the use of mosques for asylum in its central territories. Indeed, as suggested above, it is possible that Asante did not even allow the building of a Friday mosque within the capital in the nineteenth century. Furthermore, there was no distinct advantage for individuals to seek protection under Islamic rather than traditional notions of justice. Both Muslim law and Asante law viewed murder as a tort and not a criminal offense; hence there was no particular advantage to a Muslim to claim some kind of "benefit of clergy" so as to be brought under Sharia rather than Asante customary law. Because both groups recognized slavery, there was no manumission in Muslim quarters merely because one claimed to be Muslim, as there was later for Christian converts when missions served as places of asylum and escape for slaves. Similarly, women in Asante society, because it is matrilineal, probably had a better opportunity in Asante courts than Muslim ones to argue for property ownership, compensation, inheritance, and custody of children.[47]

Nevertheless there is some evidence that various Asantehenes felt that Muslims, and especially literate Muslims, should be treated with some deference and leniency, at least partly due to what was perceived by Asante to be their spiritual abilities. When a Gyaman rebellion at the beginning of the nineteenth century was put down by Asantehene Opoku Fofie, more than five thousand Muslims were taken prisoner, but "in no instance were these people subject to the penalty of death, as many of the heathens were, neither were they sold into slavery."[48] Asantehene Osei Bonsu in 1804 went so far as to free all Muslim slaves in Asante. This was done partly on the advice of the Muslim clerics as described in a letter by Muhammad al-Ghamba:

> Bewail what has occurred in the land of the unbelievers, Asanti, by Allah's verdict and the rightness of the Muslims. Allah plunged them into misfortune, discord, calamity, unheard-of things and a disgraceful situation. It appeared in their land because of the affairs of the Muslims. QRNTN [Koranten] with the Sultan, his mother Qunadu, and all the elders said: "These calamities came to our land and spoiled it. Let us free the Muslims—Men and women, young and old—all the Muslims that had been captured and enslaved, to send them back to their land."[49]

Indeed Dupuis noted that Muslim prisoners of war enjoyed a sort of refugee status for they were "never put to death [by the Asantehene] like infidels; on the contrary they were well used and generally transferred to the eastern division of the Volta." When in 1818 Muhammad al-Ghamba, leader of the Kumase Muslim forces accompanying the Asante army marching against Gyaman, a pagan state but one with a large Muslim population, deserted and (rather oddly) returned to Kumase, the Asantehene swore that "had he not been a holy man I would have had him executed." But in fact Baba merely "fell out of favor."[50] In another case, in 1839, the "shaykh" of the Kumase Muslims, who had become involved in a military coup attempt, was merely made "a prisoner in his own house, chained to a log of wood," while the Asante plotters he conspired with, including Gyaasewahene Adu Damte and some sixty of his followers, were all executed.[51]

Thus the Muslim community in Asante as a whole enjoyed some protection from egregious violence, and there was a sense in Asante that literate Muslims were protected by their religion and their separate social standing: elite Muslims were not executed even for treason, Muslim slaves were all manumitted in 1804, and often Muslim prisoners-of-war were not sold into slavery. On the other hand Asante Muslims in the early nineteenth century were in a spatially circumscribed neighborhood of Kumase, and kept physically close to the Asantehene's place of power. Even Muslim prisoners of war were carefully settled in designated parts of (northeastern) Asante.

However, if the Muslim community were able to expand its independence of visible space and its social and spiritual separateness from the Asante government, it could potentially become an arena within Asante where "the king's writ" did not run. Indeed in the mid-nineteenth century the Muslim community of Kumase became larger in numbers, more dispersed physically throughout Asante, in possession certainly of some sort of physically visible mosque (with the creation of the Imamate in 1844), more powerful and independent economically, and apparently more politically seditious. At this time the Asante ruling class began to perceive a greater threat to its control of power than any benefit from skills that might accrue. Thus around 1850 the Muslim community was once again severely restricted. By the 1850s,

Hausa (Muslim) traders were no longer allowed to travel freely to Kumase so that Muslim scholars in the border towns of Salaga and Kete Krakye became less knowledgeable about central Asante. Al-Hajj Umar of Kete-Krakye (d. 1934) simply stated:

> My knowledge of Asante is not great, but I know it to be true that there was not one zongo in the whole land of Asante until Kumase was conquered at the time of the sultan of Asante, Karikari [1874]. Up to that time the land of Asante was closed. No Hausa entered it, and no-one else except slaves who the Asante bought.[52]

This state of affairs remained until British rule revoked such immigration restrictions after 1896.

Conclusions

The use of traditional religious shrines for asylum was a well-established practice in nineteenth-century West Africa, and Asante and its periphery were no exception. Comparative historical examples and analysis demonstrate that asylum, as observed in West Africa, functioned in no significantly different manner from other societies, though details varied. Mosques and the homes of Muslim holy men in West Africa served as locations of asylum from time to time as well. However, in the early nineteenth century, Muslims in central Asante were too close to Asante government to represent an alternative power source and hence presented little threat as a focus of asylum within the state. Asante Muslims produced amulets and said prayers for the government. At various times they had representation on the Asantehene's council. They served as secretaries to government officials, were attached to embassies, and helped negotiate treaties. They accompanied Asante to war. As Dupuis said, they "espoused court politics in public life." Asante recognized and solicited Islamic skills for the benefit of the government and consequently provided Muslims some reprieve from the harshest aspects of Asante law (execution). There was without doubt a certain status immunity allowed Muslims in central Asante. This could have been translated into a sufficiently competitive focus of power such that the

Islamic community might have become a spatial point of sanctuary. However, the community was physically limited and had no Friday mosque in Kumase until a very late date. The Asante government generally made efforts to restrict the movements of Muslims and to preempt the use of Islamic law, religion, and mosques for use as asylum, in contrast to the privileges of asylum that traditional religious shrines enjoyed. Thus the issue of asylum reveals Islam existing in a delicate relationship of balanced tension, though not harmony, in nineteenth-century Asante.

Notes

1. See D. Maier, "Working Paper on the Idea of Asylum at Mosques and Traditional Shrines in Asante and Its Periphery," presented at the African Studies Association Annual Meeting, 1992.

2. See I. Wilks, "The Suwarians," paper presented at the Conference on Islam in Africa, Northwestern University, March 1984; *Wa and the Wala* (Cambridge, 1989), 25, 98–100, 202–3; "The Transmission of Islamic Learning in the Western Sudan," in *Literacy in Traditional Societies,* ed. J. Goody (Cambridge, 1968), 177–80. See also L. O. Sanneh, *The Jakhanke* (London, 1979) for an analysis of this quietist spread of Islam in other parts of West Africa.

3. See T. J. Mazzinghi, *Sanctuaries* (Stafford, 1887), 9, for a discussion of definitions.

4. There is some discussion in the comparative literature concerning scholars who have tried to distinguish between "religious" asylum and "territorial" asylum, the former evolving not out of the aura of a place but of persons, especially Christian saints. See C. Riggs, *Criminal Asylum in Anglo-Saxon Law* (University of Florida Monographs 18, 1963), 4, 22, and 54 n; Mazzinghi. *Sanctuaries,* 110–11; and I. Bau, *This Ground Is Holy: Church Sanctuary and Central American Refuges* (New York, 1985), 132. The distinction seems forced to me as all places of asylum require the aura of some intercessionary person to help the case along. J. Hunwick in "Piety and Power: Relations between the Religious Estate and Ruling Estate in Songhay under the Askiyas" (unpublished paper, 1993), 7, implies, however, that the sanctity and inviolability of a Muslim holy man constituted his intercessionary powers and made his home a potential though hardly guaranteed place of asylum.

5. C. Glasse, *The Concise Encyclopedia of Islam* (New York, 1989), 333.

6. R. M. Savory, "Bast," in *The Encyclopedia of Islam* (Leiden, 1965), 1:1088.

7. A. K. S. Lambton, "Imamzada," in *The Encyclopedia of Islam,* 2:1170.

8. Hunwick, "Piety and Power," 7 n and 11.

9. Sanneh, *Jakhanke,* 27ff.

10. T. O. Elias, *The Nature of African Customary Law* (Manchester, 1956), 215–16.

11. M. Kingsley, *Travels in West Africa* (London, 1897), 466; R. Nassau, *Fetichism in West Africa* (New York, 1904), 314; S. Johnson, *History of the Yoruba* (London, 1921) 57; P. C. Lloyd, "Osifekunde of Ijebu," in *Africa Remembered,* ed. P. Curtin (Madison, Wis., 1961), 285–86.

12. T. E. Bowdich, *Mission from Cape Coast Castle to Ashantee* (London, 1819), 265; A. B. Ellis, *The Ewe-Speaking Peoples of the Slave Coast of West Africa* (London, 1890), 220; R. S. Rattray, *Ashanti Law and Constitution* (Oxford, 1929), 42.

13. S. A. Winsnes, trans. and ed., *Letters on West Africa and the Slave Trade: Paul Erdmann Isert's Journey to Guinea and the Caribbean Islands in Columbia* (1788) (Oxford, 1992), 82.

14. J. Verveer, letter to Minister, dd. Elmina 25 Dec. 1836, No. 9, Algemeen Rijksarchief, The Hague, Archief van het Ministerie van Kolonien, 1087; K. B. Dickson, *A Historical Geography of Ghana* (Cambridge, 1961), 121. See also D. J. E. Maier, *Priests and Power: The Case of the Dente Shrine in Nineteenth-Century Ghana* (Bloomington, Ind., 1983), chap. 2.

15. K. Green, "Dyula and Sonongui in the Region of Kong," in *Rural and Urban Islam in West Africa,* ed. N. Levtzion and J. Fisher (London, 1987), 106.

16. Bowdich, *Mission,* 129, map facing 323, and 405; J. Dupuis, *Journal of a Residence in Ashantee* (London, 1924), 71–72.

17. E. Schildkrout, "Islam and Politics in Kumasi: An Analysis of Disputes over the Kumasi Central Mosque," *Anthropological Papers of the American Museum of Natural History* 52 (1974): 126.

18. N. Levtzion, *Muslims and Chiefs in West Africa* (Oxford, 1968), 27; I. Wilks, *Asante in the Nineteenth Century* (Cambridge, 1975), 262; *Ghana Notes and Queries* 3 (1961): 28.

19. Wilks, *Wa,* 77 and 109.

20. Levtzion, *Muslims and Chiefs,* 60, quoting J. A. Braimah, "A History of Gonja," unpublished manuscript.

21. I. Wilks, N. Levtzion, and B. Haight, *Chronicles from Gonja* (Cambridge, 1986), 113.

22. Ibid., 163.

23. L. Binger, *Du Niger au Golfe de Guinea par Le Pays de Kong et le Mossi* (Paris, 1892), 2:65; Levtzion, *Muslims and Chiefs,* 117.

24. Again, see Sanneh, *Jakhanke,* and Wilks, *Wa,* and "The Suwarians," referred to in note 1 above. See also T. C. Hunter, "The Development of an Islamic Tradition of Learning among the Jakhanka of West Africa" (Ph.D. diss., University of Chicago, 1977).

25. See M. Hiskett, *The Development of Islam in West Africa* (London, 1984), 78; and F. Fuglestad, "A Reconsideration of Hausa History before the Jihad," *Journal of African History,* 19, no. 3 (1978): 319–39.

26. Wilks, *Wa,* 101.

27. For discussion of these activities in service of the Asantehene, see D. Owusu-Ansah, *Islamic Talismanic Traditions in Nineteenth-Century Asante* (Lewiston, Pa., 1991), 1–40.

28. See J. Bellamy, *Crime and Public Order in England in the Later Middle Ages* (London, 1973), 107–8; and N. Trenholme, *The Right of Sanctuary in En-*

gland (Columbia, Mo., 1903), University of Missouri Studies (1901), vol. 1, no. 5; and the Rev. J. C. Cox, *The Sanctuaries and Sanctuary Seekers of Medieval England* (London, 1911).

29. I. Goldziher, "Djamal al-Din al-Afghani," in *Encyclopedia of Islam*, vol. 2 (Leiden, 1965), 418.

30. Hunwick, "Piety and Power," 4 and 10.

31. Winsnes, *Letters*, 81; Bowdich, *Mission*, 265; Ellis, *The Ewe-Speaking Peoples*, 220.

32. Green, "Dyula and Sonongui," 104.

33. C. C. Reindorf, *History of the Gold Coast* (Basel, 1895), 88.

34. Ibid., 140.

35. D. Mackworth, "Report on Wa," Great Britain, Public Record Office, co879/52, African (West) no. 549, 356; Wilks, *Wa*, 107.

36. J. H. Driberg, "The African Conception of Law," *Journal of Comparative Legislation and International Law*, 16 (1934): 241; C. Dundas, "Native Laws of Some Bantu Tribes of East Africa," *Journal of Royal Anthropological Institute* 51 (1921): 236; Elias, *Nature of African Customary Law*, 216.

37. Hunwick, "Piety and Power," 11.

38. R. Smith, "Nigeria-Ijebu," in *West African Resistance*, ed. M. Crowder (New York, 1971), 180.

39. Dupuis, *Journal*, 98.

40. Trenholme, *Right of Sanctuary*, 203 and 29; Mazzinghi, *Sanctuaries*, 83–85; A. Grahl-Madsen, *Territorial Asylum* (Stockholm, 1980), 3.

41. Wilks, *Asante*, 246–47, 278.

42. J. Gros, *Voyages, Aventures et Captivité de J. Bonnat chez les Achantis* (Paris, 1884), 232.

43. Bowdich, *Mission*, 240.

44. Bellamy, *Crime and Public Order*, 111.

45. R. Kea, "Four Asante Officials in the South-east Gold Coast (1808)," *Ghana Notes and Queries* 11 (1970): 43.

46. Wilks, *Asante*, 157.

47. See I. M. Lewis, "Islamic Law and Customary Practice," in *Islam in Tropical Africa*, ed. I. M. Lewis (Oxford, 1966), 45–57.

48. Dupuis, *Journal*, 246–47.

49. Wilks et al., *Chronicles*, 215–16.

50. Dupuis, *Journal*, xxx–xxxi, 38–39, 98–99. W. Hutton, *Voyage to Africa* (London, 1821), 323–24.

51. Beecham, *Ashantee and the Gold Coast* (London, 1841), 93; Wilks, *Asante*, 488; I. Wilks, "Asante Policy Towards the Hausa Trade in the Nineteenth Century," in *The Development of Indigenous Trade and Markets in West Africa*, ed. C. Meillassoux (Oxford, 1971), 135.

52. Wilks, *Asante*, 267.

"They Have Become Privileged of God and His Prophet": Maḥram and Zāwiya in Sudanic Africa

R. S. O'FAHEY

In certain states across Sudanic Africa documents have been preserved that record the granting of immunity from taxation and other state exactions to Muslim holy men by their rulers. The authenticity of any particular piece of paper may be in question, the nature of what was granted may be obscure, but the underlying principle is accommodation. The ruler seeks to accommodate what are usually immigrant communities by defining their status within his state—a status both subordinate and privileged.

Since the language of the documents was Arabic and the holy men in question Muslim as were in varying degree the rulers themselves, the documents recording these transactions are couched within an Islamic framework. The commonest terms used to describe such grants are *maḥram, jāh* or *ḥākūrat al-jāh.*

Here, at the outset there is an interesting puzzle. There is little doubt that the dominant school of law brought to the region since "the coming of Islam" was the Mālikī School; neither is there much doubt that the two principal law manuals—in practice, the only two—available to those who wrote the documents or judged the disputes recorded in the *sijills* or court records were the *Mukhtaṣar* of Khalīl b. Isḥāq (d. 776/1374) and the *Risāla* of Ibn Abī Zayd al-Qayrawānī (d. 386/996). Very few other lawbooks are noted as being used in the region. But the terms *maḥram, jāh* and *ḥākūra,* are not to be found in either work. Conversely, such terms as *iqṭā'* or *waqf,* which are found in the manuals and are the common legal terms for an assignment by a ruler for some purpose or an endowment "for the sake of God," are either not used at all or else appear only very late and in different contexts.

Arabian Antecedents

> Have they not seen that We have appointed a sanctuary secure (*ḥaraman amīnan*)?
>
> —Qur'ān, 29:67

In Arabia, the notion of privilege or exemption (*jāh*) or sanctuary (*ḥaram* or *ḥawṭah*), whether applied to people or places, is much older than Islam. Serjeant has linked the concept of holy man and sanctuary to Muḥammad and the Meccan *ḥaram* and has documented modern examples from South Arabia that show continuities with early Islam and before.[1] Here the initiative comes from the holy man who "will declare a certain piece of land a *ḥawṭah* . . . the essential principle is that security under God's law is established and the saint recognised as His representative by the tribes, in administrative control."[2] The consent of the surrounding tribes is required and such *ḥawṭahs* often became important market and meeting places. The privileges of the lord of the *ḥawṭah* and his successors (who are known as *manṣab*) are called *jāh* and are guaranteed in writing by the surrounding tribes or their sultans; "they guarantee exemption from customs duties and even exemptions from certain categories of taxation for persons under the *Manṣab*'s protection though living outside the *ḥawṭah*."[3] Although this notion of sanctuary was and is a numinous and on occasion a politically fraught concept in Islam, not least as it relates to the mosque (as the Iranian revolution has shown), it never became codified as such in the lawbooks.

Maḥram and Jāh

At first sight, the oldest corpus of such charters of immunity or privilege that survive from Sudanic Africa are the so-called *maḥrams* from Kanem/Borno. The problem is that with one or two exceptions, all the forty or so documents we have were copied in northern Nigeria in 1918 by the Bornāwī scholar, 'Abd al-Raḥmān

b. Muḥammad al-Sanūsī, for the British official and amateur historian, H. R. Palmer.[4]

This uncertainty about their authenticity and provenance has led D. Lange to comment,

> D’ailleurs, même si quelques maḥram contiennent des passages anciens, il est devenu impossible de rétablir leur version originale en raison de manipulation répétées et indiscernables. Il convient donc de traiter la plupart des maḥram comme des traditions orales; en tant que telles ils conservent une certaine valeur.[5]

Lange’s reservations undoubtedly apply to the “earliest” charters allegedly issued by *mai* Ḥummay (c. 1086–97) to Muḥammad b. Mānī and his descendents and to the Masbarma holy clan.[6] With the thirty or so charters issued by the *mais* and later the Kānimī *shehus* of Borno, we undoubtedly have reasonably accurate copies of original documents.

Maḥrams were granted in return for spiritual services rendered or to come, a theme implicit, and often made explicit, in all Sudanic grants of privileged status; the alleged *maḥram* for Muḥammad b. Mānī can serve as an exemplar:

> King Bulu read with Muḥammad b. Mānī from *tabaraka alladhī biyaddih al-mulk* down to *min al-jinnati wa’l-nās* (i.e. from sūra 67 to the end of the Qur’ān). Bulu gave his teacher fifty camels and read from Yāsīn (sūra 36) to *wa’l-nās* and gave him sixty camels.[7]

In the later *maḥrams* privilege is often said to have been granted in return for prayers of intercession, *du‘a,* or to holders of religious office; thus in 1206/1791–92 *mai al-ḥājj* Dūnama b. ‘Alī granted privileged status to the “*‘ālim, faqīh, walī, shaṭṭīma* [a Kanuri religious title] Kakūduma” who had been appointed leader of the Friday Prayers. The taboo aspect of immunity is vividly described: “He has rendered unlawful their property just as the flesh of the swine and the shoulder of the monkey [are unlawful].”[8] The charters issued by the *shehus* of the al-Kānimī dynasty in the late nineteenth century are rather more prosaic; thus Abū Bakr b. ‘Umar al-Kānimī (1881–85) issued a charter in 1299/1882 for the descendents of Muḥammad b. Mānī,

> [Abū Bakr] has deigned out of his wide liberality and copious generosity to render the descendants of the imām Muḥammad b. Mānī privileged and to render privileged their properties, just as his later father[9] had favoured them in the same manner. He has exempted their properties from the itinerant officials (*al-sā'iḥīn*) and others. He has placed them in the ranks of the privileged (*silk al-muḥarramīn*), [from] whom there is [due] nothing from both the secular taxes and the sultanic imposts.[10]

The *maḥrams* of Kanem/Borno may well represent the oldest tradition of such grants in Sudanic Africa, whatever the actual date of the surviving documents. But the same ambiguity surrounds a charter of privilege alleged to have been issued in 913/1507 by *askiya al-ḥājj* Muḥammad of Songhai for the descendents of Mori Hawgāro.[11] "We have relieved them of all obligations (*waẓā'if*) [owed to] the sultanate and all of its dues (*gharāma*). Let no one, therefore, ask anything of them—even hospitality (*ḍiyāfa*)." "Hospitality," the provision of food, fodder, and shelter for the great ones of the state and for their retinues and animals were among the most onerous burdens falling on local communities.

In structure and wording, this *kitāb ḥurma* as it is called in the chronicle in which it is embedded, the *Ta'rīkh al-fattāsh,* is very similar to both the *maḥrams* and the *jāh*-charters of Darfur and the Funj Sultanate.

Of the charters of privilege from Sinnār and Darfur, a substantial number have by now been published; there is a considerable literature about them in the context of discussions about the *ḥākūra* or estate system in the two sultanates.[12] Here we are dealing with authentic documents that have survived, usually in the hands of the descendents of those to whom they were first given. The *ḥākūra* as it developed in Sinnār and Darfur into an elaborate system of landed estates granted as *mulk* or freehold property seems to have grown out of the earlier *jāh* stage. However, it is, for example in Darfur, by no means certain that *jāh*-rights were granted only to holy men. It may be that as *mulk*-right estates became the norm from about 1800, *jāh* simply became an omnibus term for grants of patronage over groups; for example, of herders of a nobleman's herds or of his maternal kin. This notion of a progression from *jāh* to *mulk* may be too deterministic a view, but there does seem to have been a move of some sort, certainly in Darfur, away from collective rights of immunity from taxation that were not specifically tied to land toward very precisely defined estates granted to an individual and his immediate kin.

Along the Nile such grants of privilege were being made already in the seventeenth century; a description of a community of holy men at al-Dabba on the Nile from 1700 clearly implies that they held privileged status: "Because of the *fuqarā'* this place has full immunity, and by royal decree no court official may come within several miles, or remove a wrongdoer."[13] A charter issued by the Funj ruler, Bādī IV (1724–62) in 1145/1732–33 confirms privileges first granted at least fifty years before:

> This is the grant (*jāh*) which I have written for Faqīh Bishāra b. al-Faqīh 'Alī b. Bursī, so that no one shall trouble him, his brothers, his sons, his relatives by marriage, his family, and all who are his kinsmen or who attach themselves to him. Let none of the *'ummāl* (i.e. officials) who are in the land trouble him. I, Sultan Bādī b. al-Sulṭān Nōl, have confirmed what Sultan Bādī b. al-Sulṭān Irbāṭ (ruled, 1644/5–1681] did in his grant.[14]

The earliest Darfur charters of this type are not much later in date, the earliest being issued by Sultan Muḥammad Dawra (c. 1720–30), but possibly in the lifetime of his father, Aḥmad Bukr (c. 1700–20). One grants privileged status in return for *dhikr* recitations; that is, the public remembrance of God and His Prophet.[15] Later the formula became standardized: "They have become privileged of God and His Prophet (and privileged of the sultan and are as cripples to the dīwān [i.e. the tax officials]." Among the synonyms for *jāh* used in the Darfur charters are *ḥurma, karāma,* and *ḥurriyya.*

In between Sinnār and Darfur, in Kordofan lay the kingdom of Taqalī, where Dr. Janet Ewald found and photographed a sequence of such charters issued by the Taqalī kings.[16] These are simple in structure, with a heading *jāh Allāh wa'l-rasūl,* and with the opening formula, *hādhā 'l-jāh al-kāmil al-mutamm . . .*, followed by the ruler's name and that of the grantee and a brief list of the taxes from which he was exempted.

The purpose of this survey of this type of document, from Songhai to Sinnār, is to suggest that there was very long period of gestation during which these formulae and the ideas behind them grew. In one sense, the ideas and the number of ways of expressing them in Arabic are limited enough to make the notion of Kanem, for example, or Songhai as another, the original exemplars unnecessary. Even less am I suggesting *jāhiliyya* Arabia or the Wādī Ḥaḍramawt as necessary sources. But the emergence within Sudanic Africa of original institutions and a local Arabic terminology to express the relationship between ruler and holy man other than the conventions found in the lawbooks at least suggests that we should avoid too mechanical and too chronologically foreshortened an understanding of the coming of Islamic Law.[17] The formulas also make clear, both implicitly and explicitly, that privilege or immunity was an act of grace and favor from the ruler to a subject, whether a saint or a clerk. By the beginning of the nineteenth century, the balance had changed: in Kanem/Borno and further west, the holy man was making himself the ruler; in the Nile Valley, with the destruction of the old order by colonial conquest under the Egyptians (but continuing a process begun before), a new type of holy man exploited the new situation.[18]

Zāwiya and Estate

The characteristic mosque/school establishment both along the Nile and in the savannas—*masīd, khalwa,* and *zāwiya* (although the latter is a later term and more specific to organized Sufism)—has been well described in the literature.[19] What is interesting is that from the early nineteenth century one can discern a new type of mosque/school community emerging in areas where they appear not to have been present before, where in these cases the initiative arose not so much out of an interaction between ruler and holy man, but from a new type of holy man operating either under a colonial umbrella or within a new political dispensation created by likeminded leaders.[20]

A striking phenomenon thoughout the region from about 1800 was the introduction of new Sufi brotherhoods—Sammāniyya, Khatmiyya, Tijāniyya, and many others—or the tighter organization of previously loose affiliations (Qādiriyya and Shādhiliyya). Behind this impulse lay a new type of international Sufism, usually called neo-Sufism, propagated by such figures as Muḥammad al-Sammān (d. 1777), Aḥmad b. Idrīs (d. 1837), and Aḥmad al-Tijānī (d. 1815).[21]

To illustrate this transition, I conclude with a brief discussion of the lodges or mosque/schools established by the followers of Aḥmad b. Idrīs. The Idrīsī-inspired orders followed two different patterns of expansion; in Libya and Somalia, both essentially nomadic societies, the characteristic pattern was the establishment of lodges (Ar. *zāwiya;* Somali, *jamaaca*) at the invitation of the local tribe on land donated by them. The most famous example in the literature is the spread of the Sanūsiyya order in Cyrenaica and throughout the central Sahara, a *ṭarīqa* or brotherhood established by Ibn Idrīs's principal student, Muḥammad b. 'Alī al-Sanūsī (1787–1859).[22] Although al-Sanūsī was a very different figure from the holy men of the Sudanic belt, in style the difference was not so marked; thus he was careful to ensure that the initiative to establish a lodge amongst them first came from the local community, as he himself explains in a letter dated 1849,

> Our followers . . . that are of the place of Tazar [Tazerbu in Kufra] . . . have come to us and have repented at our hands and have asked us to build a lodge in the aforesaid Tazar. And we intend it to be close to you and teach you, you and your children, the Book of God Most High and the Sunna of His Messenger Muḥammad, may the blessings and peace of God be upon him, and to make peace between you and those beduins who are jealous of you and who take your children and property, working in accordance with the words of God Most High, "If two groups of believers fight, then make peace between them (Qur'ān: 49,9)."[23]

Al-Sanūsī elaborated on the practical implications in another letter in 1855 about the building of the *zāwiya* of Msus,

> He says that he is sending to them Brothers to construct the buildings and that he has instructed them to build an annex which he can use

> as a resthouse when he visits the zawiya, though this is not to be built till the zawiya is completed. There will be builders and carpenters among the Brothers and all that is required of the tribal Shaikhs is selection of the site and supervision of the work. He points out to them that the work is for their benefit, in that they and their sons will receive in the zawiya an education, especially in the Koran and in the laws of Islam, and will be able to worship there. The Grand Sanusi cites passages from the Koran and the Hadith commending religious benefactions. Finally he prays God to assist those engaged in the building and those who have made themselves responsible for the upkeep of the zawiya. God helps those who help others. A man reaps what he sows.[24]

Although Evans-Pritchard, or rather his Italian source, calls such grants of land *waqf* or pious endowment, the other term he uses, *ḥaram* or, as he translates it, "inviolable," is probably more accurate, although the latter, as noted above, is not a formally recognized legal concept in the Sharia. The land, as would not technically be the case with *waqf,* remained the property of the tribe but was alienated and made inviolable (in the sense of "sanctuary") for a specifically religious purpose. As in Darfur and the Funj Sultanate, such grants were apparently written down; Evans-Pritchard gives a précis of such a document,

> In it the tribal sections of the Baraghtha, Tursh, Dinal and Shilmani place themselves under obligation, through signatories to the deed, to pay the zawiya of Taukra alms on flocks and crops, to supply camels to carry supplies to Jaghbub, and to help the zawiya in sowing, building, excavations, and other works. Subject to the penalty of paying double alms they will not, without the permission of the Shaikh of the zawiya, render like services to other zawiyas. They promise also to defend the zawiya and to respect those who live in it, or who are its guests, and agree that those who fail to do so may be punished in body or in estate. Each will be for the zawiya and the zawiya for each. God is greater than any man. Those who are obedient will be recompensed by Him. Peace be to those who follow the right path.[25]

He also gives a physical description,

> Some of the Cyrenaican lodges were larger than others but they all had the same features, a straggling warren of stone buildings compris-

ing a mosque, schoolrooms, guest-rooms, apartments for the Shaikh of the zawiya and his family, rooms for teachers and pupils, and houses for the Brothers, clients, and servants, and their families. Many had small gardens nearby and the local cemetary was usually adjacent to a lodge. Jaghbub, where several hundred persons lived, was the largest of such communities.[26]

The genius of al-Sanūsī, upon which his successors built and expanded, thus created in Cyrenaica a network of institutions that in design and function were totally new to the society in which they were implanted.

A similar network of religious lodges was established by the Idrīsī-inspired orders in Somalia. Obviously, they invite comparison with the Sanūsiyya lodges of Cyrenaica and the central Sahara. Indeed, the earliest such community within the Idrīsī network may be the Baardheere *jamaaca* on the Juba River in southern Somalia established in 1819 or 1821 by Shaykh Ibrahim Hassan Jeberow. There is, however, some uncertainty as to whether Shaykh Ibrahim was in fact initiated by Ibn Idrīs. What is interesting about the Baardheere *jamaaca* is that it initiated a *jihād* through which it was eventually destroyed.[27]

The descriptions of the settlements given by Cerulli, Lewis, and Cassanelli emphasize their economic role in opening up new agricultural land along the riverbanks,[28] land granted by the local clan elders. Cerulli describes the process of opening up new land,

> "The black lands [so described because of the soil]" along the Shabella's valley, the best for agriculture but formerly undervalued by Somali Bedouins only applied to cattle rearing, were in many territories the goal of the Ṣāliḥiyyas's aim and they were skilful enough to take advantage of contests between the tribes or other political circumstances and thus they tried to get granted to them by the tribes the best zones for agriculture.[29]

Cerulli further stresses that these were new foundations in previously undesirable areas: "Anzi tutto si può osservare come, fondate di solito in località prima disabitate, le nuove jamaʿat che assumono ben presto di villagi hanno un proprio nome, imposto ad esse dal fondatore."

The lodges' names could be significant; Muḥammad Gūled (d. 1918), a key figure in the diffusion of the Ṣāliḥiyya, an order deriving from Ibn Idrīs' Sudanese student, Ibrāhīm al-Rashid (d. 1874), in Somalia came from a servile community at Sidla on the Ethiopian borderlands. His first settlement was called Mecca; when he moved south to Aguran, he called his second lodge Medina, but when he moved back to Sidla, he called his final community Miṣr (Cairo). The significance of the first two names is obvious; the reason for the third is not.[30]

Like their earlier counterparts, these new communities could act as useful buffers, "In other instances, the settlements occupied border territory disputed by two neighbouring clans and thus provided a solution acceptable to both parties."[31] Cassanelli gives a general description of the settlements' membership,

> Membership in the religious settlements typically consisted of the shaykh and his adepts, who devoted themselves to farming and to teaching and prayer, and a larger number of participants from nearby clans who might take part in Friday worship and in periodic religious celebrations. Although structurally distinct from the clan, a settlement sometimes drew a majority of the members of a neighbouring clan into its religious activities; more commonly in the years before 1900, two or three *jamaacooyin* [pl. of *jamaaca*] representing different tariiqas competed within a single district for adherents.[32]

Lewis gives a concrete description of a Dandarāwiyya settlement at Sheikh as it was in 1955. The community had been founded in about 1885 by Shaykh Aadan Ahmed of the Habar Awal clan who had studied in Mecca with Muḥammad al-Dandarāwī (d. 1909), a student of Ibrāhīm al-Rashīd and the founder of the Dandarāwiyya, a particularly vigorous offshoot of the Idrīsī tradition that has spread widely in Egypt, the Sudan, Syria, Malaysia, and southern Thailand. The economic basis of the community, with 280 members and run by a *majlis* led by a descendent of the founder, was cattle nomadism and sorghum cultivation when the rains made the latter feasible. Religiously, the adherents living in the community were expected to follow the rules of the Dandarāwiyya *ṭarīqa* more rigorously than those outside; women were expected to wear the veil, and men wishing to marry into the community were examined as to their suitability.[33] Each member had to pay a monthly sum in addition to *ṣadaqa* and *zakāh;* these revenues went to a central treasury that was used to feed the poor, pay for hospitality, maintain the mosque and the tomb of the founder, and pay for the annual feasts in memory of the saints.

Lewis notes that membership in the lodge cut across tribal boundaries although the brethren were still liable for blood-compensation involving their clan. However, the lodge, as did similar institutions in the Sudan, played an important role as a sanctuary, "In which men could find refuge from their own agnates provided they were considered suitable for admission to the tariiqa." Internal quarrels were punished by fines for men, "While quarrels between women may be punished by the disputants being plastered with cow-dung": "The final sanction is expulsion from the community with loss of cultivating and grazing rights in its fields."[34] Lewis makes the point that *ṭarīqa* affiliation tended generally to override tribal identity and that since they possessed "a more developed system of authority and sanctions" the *ṭarīqa*-shaykh tended to exercise political authority.

The *jamaacas* of the Ṣāliḥiyya and Dandarāwiyya in Somalia appear to follow a similar pattern to the *zāwiyas* of the Sanūsiyya, although the latter seem to have been the most highly-structured of all the orders within the Idrīsī tradition. The Sanūsī brethren, supported partly by the adherents outside and partly by their own labors (al-Sanūsī prohibited begging), lived a quasi-monastic life and prayer, meeting for the silent *dhikr* each Friday and Monday evening—here one is much closer to the Anatolian or Iranian *khānqah* than the Sudanic *khalwa.* But it was not all work, study, and prayer at a Sanūsī lodge; the brethren at Jaghbūb played two types of ballgame, "as they are known among the beduin."[35]

A second pattern of expansion was by the incorporation of pre-existing religious centers, the older *masīd* and *khalwa,* into a new supracommunity *ṭarīqa* network. In the northern Sudan on the banks of the Nile where new settlements were in any event hardly possible since there was no unused land, this was the pattern followed by the Khatmiyya, Idrīsiyya, and Rashīdiyya. An example is Karrar's account of the history of the Naḍīfāb community of Abū Rannāt Island.[36] From the late seventeenth century, the Naḍīfāb have functioned as a community of religious teachers, specializing in teaching the seven forms of Koranic recitation. They were incorporated into the Khatmiyya at the time of the first journey through the northern Sudan in the years 1815–19 of Muḥammad 'Uthmān al-Mīrghanī (1793–1853), student of Ibn Idrīs and founder of the Khatmiyya brotherhood; al-Mīrghanī "appointed them *khalīfas* without actually meeting them," although they were placed under the jurisdiction of another nearby holy family. Thereafter, the ties of the Naḍīfāb with the Mīrghanī family were close, although the latter's local representative had to intervene fairly forcibly to prevent the community bifurcating in the mid-nineteenth century. The economic basis of these Sudanese riverain communities was somewhat different from the pattern described above—their ecological circumstances were very different—they relied especially on pious donations (*ṣadaqa*) of a date palm or piece of land here and there.[37] By such means communities like the Naḍīfāb were able to accumulate considerable wealth; thus in 1848, the then *khalīfa* and head of the community in his will,

> transferred the rights to his share in a considerable number of date palms scattered among different *sāqiyas* (agricultural units) in the region in order to use their produce to meet some of the expenses of accommodating guests and students. He continued by endowing the mosque with a number of date palms, "For the sake of God and His Prophet."

Cassanelli points to some aspects of the failure of these religious settlements to achieve and maintain leadership within the wider community; that religious leaders such as Muḥammad Gūled and the Qādirī, Uways b. Muḥammad (d. 1909) of Barāwa on the southern Somali coast, "came from client agricultural communities rather than powerful nomadic clans," that they were in some ways alienated from the main currents of Somali society.[38]

The distinction between "old style" and "new style" was never of course clear-cut and there is a very real continuity between the world of the *maḥram* and the "new internationalism" of Ibn Idrīs and his followers.[39] It was the Meccan arrogance of al-Mīrghanī that aroused the hostility of the "traditional" Sudanese holy man, but ardent propagator of Ibn Idrīs's teachings, Ibrāhīm al-Rashīd. The latter accused al-Mīrghanī of wanting to establish a *dawla:* a "state." The "new" Islam could now serve a multiplicity of interests, but the old political order had definitively lost out.[40]

I have described here only one thread in the complex interaction between African states and cultures of the region and Islam. Without subscribing to too evolutionary a perspective, it is possible to perceive a gradual change, whose momentum greatly accelerated in the nineteenth century, whereby the initiative passed from local ruler to both local and immigrant religious leaders. How effective the new lodges and settlements and the brotherhoods that bound them together were to prove may be seen in the resistance of the Sanūsiyya to the Italians, French, and British; the career of the "Mad Mullah" alias Muḥammad 'Abdille Ḥasan in Somalia, and the enduring role of the Khatmiyya and other orders in the politics of the Sudan.

Notes

An earlier version of this paper was presented to the symposium, "State, Land and Society in Sudanic Africa," held at the University of Illinois at Champaign-Urbana, April 1993.

1. R. B. Serjeant, "Haram and Hawtah, the Sacred Enclave in Arabia," in *Mélanges Taha Husain,* ed. Abd al-Rahman Bedawi (Cairo, 1962), 41–58. Serjeant discusses modern South Arabian examples in "Two Tribal Law Cases (Wāḥidī Sultanate, South-West Arabia)," *Journal of the Royal Asiatic Society* (1951): 33–47 and 156–69.

2. Serjeant, "Haram and Hawtah," 43.

3. Ibid., 45.

4. The discussion that follows here is based on work on an edition and translation of the extant *maḥrams* that I am undertaking together with J. O. Hunwick and Hamidu Boboyi. For an earlier discussion, see my "The Maḥrams of Kānem-Borno," *Bulletin of Information, Fontes Historiae Africanae* (hereafter, *BIFHA*) 6 (1981): 19–25.

5. *Chronologie et Histoire d'un Royaume Africain: Le Dīwān des Sultans du*

[Kānem-] Bornu (Wiesbaden, 1977), 5. But see now Hamidu Bobboyi, "Relations of the Borno *'ulamā'* with the Sayfawa rulers: the role of the *maḥrams*," *Sudanic Africa* 4 (1993): 175–204.

6. See H. R. Palmer, *Sudanese Memoirs*, 3 vols. (Lagos, 1928), 3:3–5, and idem, *The Bornu Sahara and Sudan* (London, 1936), 16.

7. Palmer, *Bornu*, 14.

8. Ibid., 48–49.

9. 'Umar b. Muḥammad al-Amīn al-Kānimī, who ruled 1837–81. 'Umar evidently issued a charter that appears to be no longer extant.

10. From the Arabic text in H. R. Palmer's Papers, Jos Museum, Nigeria.

11. The following is derived from John O. Hunwick, "Studies in the *Ta'rīkh al-Fattāsh* II: An Alleged Charter of Privilege issued by Askiya al-ḥājj Muḥammad to the descendants of Mori Hawgāro," *Sudanic Africa* 3: (1992): 133–48. Hunwick hedges his bets on the question of authenticity, but concludes that a real document probably lies behind the text given in *Ta'rīkh al-Fattāsh.*

12. The two main collections are *Public Documents from Sinnār,* ed. Jay Spaulding and Muḥammad Ibrāhīm Abū Salīm (East Lansing, Mich. 1989), and R. S. O'Fahey and M. I. Abu Salim, *Land in Dār Fūr. Charters and Related Documents from the Dār Fūr Sultanate* (Cambridge, 1983). Of the former work, there is a slightly different version published as Muḥammad Ibrāhīm Abū Salīm and Jay Spaulding, *Some Documents from Eighteenth-Century Sinnār* (Khartoum, 1992). More recently, some relevant documents have been published in *Sudanic Africa: A Journal of Historical Sources,* vols. 1–5 (Bergen, 1990) (continuing). A study of the *ḥākūra* system in Darfur is G. M. La Rue, "The Hakura System: Land and Social Stratification in the Social and Economic History of the Sultanate of Dar Fur (Sudan), ca. 1785–1875" (Ph.D. diss., Boston University, 1989).

13. From Jay Spaulding's unpublished translation of Theodoro Krump, *Hoher und fruchtbarer Palm-Baum des Heiligen Evangelij* (Augsburg, 1710).

14. See Jay Spaulding, "A Charter of Sultan Badi b. Nol of Sinnar, 1145/1732–3," *BIFHA,* 9–10 (1984): 5, 8–11.

15. See R. S. O'Fahey, "Two Early Dar Fur Charters," *Sudan Text Bulletin* 1 (1979): 13–17.

16. See Janet Ewald, "Speaking, Writing and Authority: Explorations in and from the Kingdom of Taqali," *Comparative Studies in Society and History* 30, no. 2 (1988): 199–224, and idem, *Soldiers, Traders and Slaves: State Formation and Economic Transformation in the Greater Nile Valley, 1700–1885* (Madison, Wis. 1990), 113 and 214–15, n. 119.

17. A comparable complexity and originality may be found in the *sijills* or records of court hearings. The court procedure—the hearing and oathing of witnesses, the role of plaintiff and defendant, the way the judgment is given—usually follow Mālikī Law. The substantive law administered was that of the sultans.

18. For the transition in the Nile Valley, see Jay Spaulding, *The Heroic Age in Sinnār* (East Lansing, Mich., 1985); Ali Salih Karrar, *The Sufi Brotherhoods in the Sudan* (London, 1992), and Neil McHugh, *Holymen of the Blue Nile: Religious Leadership and the Genesis of an Arab Islamic Society in the Nilotic Sudan, 1500–1850* (Evanston, Ill., 1994).

19. In addition to the references given above, one may add the substantial recent study of al-Ṭayyib Muḥammad al-Ṭayyib, *al-Masīd* (Khartoum, 1991). Al-Ṭayyib's study includes several original documents.

20. Interestingly in Darfur, which neither experienced a "Fulani *jihād*" nor Turco-Egyptian colonialism, there is a marked "*faqīh*-isation" of the rulers, to coin a term, from Sultan ʿAbd al-Raḥmān (ruled 1787/88–1803) onward. See both my *State and Society in Dār Fūr* (London, 1980), and Larue, "Hakura System" for interpretations of this change.

21. There is a vast literature on this subject; for an introduction, see R. S. O'Fahey and Bernd Radtke, "Neo-Sufism Reconsidered," *Der Islam* 70 (1993): 52–87; and O'Fahey, *Enigmatic Saint: Aḥmad ibn Idrīs and the Idrīsī Tradition* (London, 1990), for northeast Africa especially.

22. On his career, see Knut S. Vikør, "Sufi and Scholar on the Desert Edge. Muḥammad b. ʿAlī al-Sanūsī (1787–1859)" (Ph.D. diss., University of Bergen, 1991). On the role of these lodges in trans-Saharan trade, see Dennis Cordell, "Eastern Libya, Wadai and the Sanusiya: a tarîqa and a trade route," *Journal of African History* 18 (1977): 21–36.

23. Muḥammad al-Ṭayyib Idrīs al-Ashhab, *al-Sanūsī al-kabīr. ʿArḍ wa-taḥlīl li-diʿāmat ḥarakat al-iṣlāḥ al-Sanūsī* (Cairo, n.d.), 151.

24. E. E. Evans-Pritchard, *The Sanusi of Cyrenaica* (Oxford, 1949), 73–74.

25. *Sanusi of Cyrenaica,* 76. I have given these quotations at length because examples of original documentation appears not to be accessible. See further, the interesting discussion in Michel Le Gall, "The Ottoman Government and the Sanusiyya: A Reappraisal," *International Journal of Middle East Studies* 21 (1989): 97–99.

26. Ibid., 74.

27. See further my "Aḥmad ibn Idrīs and Northeast Africa," *Islam et sociétés au sud du Sahara* 2 (1989): 72–73.

28. The theme of "opening up" new land (legally *iḥyāʾ al-mawāt,* "the revival of the dead") also appears among religious communities who received *jāh*-rights under the older dispensation; see, as one example, my "Dār Fūr in Kordofan: The Sultans and the Awlād Najm," *Sudan Texts Bulletin* 7, (1985): 43–63.

29. E. Cerulli, *Somalia: Scritti Vari Editi ed Inediti,* 3 vols. (Rome, 1957–64), 1:151; see also ibid., 3:168–71, where he estimates that there were 53 Ṣāliḥiyya, 27 Aḥmadiyya (Idrīsiyya), 12 Qādiriyya and one Rifāʿiyya *jamaaca* in Somalia.

30. Ibid., 1:191 and 189.

31. Lee V. Cassanelli, *The Shaping of Somali Society* (Philadelphia, 1982), 194.

32. Ibid., 194–95.

33. The Khatmiyya rule is that an adherent must ask his shaykh for permission to marry; Aḥmad b. ʿAbd al-Raḥmān al-Raṭabī, *Minḥat al-aṣḥāb li-man arāda sulūk ṭarīq al-aṣfiyāʾ wa ʾl-aḥbāb,* in *al-Rasāʾil al-Mīrghaniyya* (Cairo, 1399/1979), 66.

34. I. M. Lewis, *A Pastoral Democracy* (London, 1961), 96–100.

35. al-Ashhab, *al-Sanūsī al-kabīr,* 49.

36. *Sufi Brotherhoods,* 144–50; this account is based on both oral sources and a body of documents in the National Records Office, Khartoum, Miscellaneous

1/27/261 to 488. There is additional documentation in Bergen, NO126.6/1 to NO144.6/19.

37. Thus, as examples, a half-plot of date palms was given in 1869, and a similar donation in 1883 (NRO, Miscellaneous 1/27/411 and 416). Both donations are described as *waqf,* although they are legally *ṣadaqa* to the local *khalīfa.* Evans-Pritchard, *Sanusi,* 76–77, describes similar donations, as does Lewis, *Pastoral Democracy,* 98. Translations of such documents from Cyrenaica are given in Massimo Colucci, *Il Regime della Proprietà Fondiaria nell'Africa Italiana,* (Bologna, 1942), 424–31. Colucci stresses the interaction between local law and Sharia in the establishment of such grants.

38. *Shaping of Somali Society,* 236–37; hence also, the tendency for such communities to seek for and receive the patronage of the Italian administration, 232, 237, and 286.

39. Ibn Idrīs was not an establishment figure; he avoided al-Azhar and the like. In a letter from his Yemeni years, he writes to a local ruler instructing him to restore to one of his followers the latter's *ḥawṭah* and reproving the ruler for changing established ways: see *The Letters of Aḥmad ibn Idrīs,* ed. Einar Thomassen and Bernd Radtke (London, 1993).

40. For a subtle delineation of these cross-currents, see Albrecht Hofheinz, "Encounters with a Saint: Al-Majdhūb, al-Mīrghanī and Ibn Idrīs as seen through the Eyes of Ibrāhīm al-Rashīd," *Sudanic Africa: A Journal of Historical Sources* 1 (1990): 19–60.

The Asante Nkramo Imamate: Conflicting Traditions

DAVID OWUSU-ANSAH

Introduction

The creation of an Asante Nkramo imamate by Asantehene Kwaku Dua Panin (1834–67) was part of an overall plan by that monarch to regulate Asante political society. McCaskie and Wilks[1] have discussed the impact of this reorganization on the Asante decision-making process. With specific reference to the position of Muslims in the Kumase administration, I have argued elsewhere that, by placing them permanently within the *Nsumankwaa* (the royal physicians corps), and by describing these Muslims as Asante Nkramo, the position of the royal Muslims became "traditionalized or institutionalized."[2]

It will be remembered that prior to Kwaku Dua Panin's reign, Muslim functionaries in Kumase had been perceived as non-Asante citizens—who were, however, sought after by virtue of their skills to address specific needs and preoccupations of the state. Some of these Muslims had direct access to Asante kings and thereby influenced certain national policies.[3] There were, nonetheless, those instances when some Asante rulers observed that such Muslim functionaries could not be trusted totally to identify their interests with those of the state. Many such Muslims returned to their home territories when their positions in Kumase became threatened.[4]

If Asante had to depend on Muslim services—to produce Islamic charms and amulets and also to communicate with significant individuals in its northern territories where Muslim traders and scholars operated—there was then the urgency to create a permanent Asante Muslim group or an Asante Nkramo imamate whose interests, as citizens, could be identified with those of the state. Furthermore, through the imamate, services of Muslims outside the group could be sought and regulated to suit administrative purposes. There is no evidence to suggest that Asantehene Kwaku Dua Panin logically articulated these arguments to justify his creation of the Asante Nkramo group in Kumase. However, it is evident by the functions and administrative position assigned the Asante Nkramo that the king's general goal of establishing "law and order" was served.[5]

The imamate of the Asante Nkramo has been well established and its members have been known, even by other Muslims, to serve solely the interests of Asante rulers. This relation of the Asante Nkramo to the Kumase administration was aptly expressed by Al-Hajj Liman Abu Bakr Adam, Imam of the *Zongo* (foreign Muslim) community of Kumase: "As for the Asante Nkramo Kumase is their town. . . . The Imam of the Asante Nkramo is the head of *all Muslims in Asante and he is the link between the Muslim communities in all Asante and the king of Asante*" (my emphasis).[6] Thus, the influence and prestige enjoyed by the Asante Nkramo people came from their permanent association with Asante royal power.

Interviews conducted with members of the imamate suggest that its composition is not monolineal. The Suame (Kumase) Asante Nkramo people who trace their patrilineal links to 'Uthman Kamagatay of Guipe and Daboya recognize themselves as the original royal Muslims.[7] Imams of the royal Muslim group have been selected from the Suame unit since the 1840s. An Nkenkaasu Asante Nkramo group of the 'Ali Kunatay lineage also exist within the royal Muslim corps. Although their settlements remain fifty miles outside Kumase, the Nkenkaasu Muslims are also recognized as part of the Asante Nkramo. In conversations with Asante officials in Kumase and with members of the Suame Muslims, the Nkenkaasu Nkramo were often defined as being "the same people as" or "brothers of" the Suame group. Such descriptions, the Nkenkaasu Muslims vehemently reject. In fact, the impression is clearly given in the Nkenkaasu Muslim traditions that the Suame Muslims usurped the leadership position of the

Asante Nkramo unit.[8] Such accusations notwithstanding, all scholarship on the royal Muslim corps conclude that 'Uthman Kamagatay and his people at Suame are the original Asante Nkramo.[9] What, then, is the nature of the Nkenkaasu Muslim tradition that leads historians to reject their claim as the original royal Muslims?

Analysis of Nkenkaasu Asante Nkramo Traditions

Fundamental to the Nkenkaasu Asante Nkramo tradition is the claim that their patriarchs, especially 'Ali Kunatay and his son Sulayman, were the Muslims most actively sought by Asante rulers in the formative years of the Asante Nkramo imamate. According to this tradition, 'Ali Kunatay was invited to Kumase by Asantehene Kofi Kakari (r. 1867–74). The monarch charged the *kramoko* (Muslim scholar) to make "war medicine" for victory in the eastern Volta expedition (1867–71)[10]—an engagement in which Asante forces under the command of Gyaasewahene Adu Bofo halted Ada and her British allies from expanding their interests on the Volta. Frederick Boyle, in his accounts of the 1874 expedition, also identified Sulayman b. 'Ali as the other Nkenkaasu Muslim notable in an Asante delegation charged with the unsuccessful mission of using charms to effect the retreat of British forces from the Pra.[11] This same Sulayman, according to the Nkenkaasu Muslims, was again solicited in 1892–93 by Asantehene Prempe I in an expedition against a rebellious Nkoransa.[12]

To be sure, Asante history in the period after 1867 was filled with foreign policy issues of grave consequences. Fundamental to the crisis was Asante understanding of British strategy on the Gold Coast. As Wilks has pointed out, a "state of undeclared war had existed between the British and Asante since the second half of 1866" when the former made efforts to restrict, and if possible, to cut off the flow of war materials entering Asante and the hinterlands.[13] For the British, the most effective way of achieving that goal was to increase their presence at the eastern and western regions of the "Protected Territory" by aiding independent-minded Asante tributaries.

It must be pointed out that the death of Asantehene Kwaku Dua Panin in 1867 had marked the ascendancy in Kumase of those in the Asante government who favored military action to redress grievances arising out of that nation's foreign relations. It was, therefore, not surprising that a "hawkish" response was advocated for the solution of the "British Problem."[14] It is also important to emphasize that it was understood in Kumase that attempts to seek redress by military means were very dangerous unless victory could be guaranteed. For this reason, Asante authorities solicited "powerful" religious personages whose prayers and charms were perceived as efficacious in influencing the outcomes of such engagements.

According to a tradition of the Nkenkaasu Muslims, the charms of their patriarch, Kramoko 'Ali Kunatay, positively affected the outcome of the eastern Volta expedition. For those who ascribe to this account, proof of the efficacy of Kramo 'Ali's charms was publicly demonstrated even before Asante forces took to the field:

> [Before Kramo arrived in Kumase], the king of Asante had already built a room in which he had a white cow; the doors to the room had been sealed. He [the king] instructed that the person who could tell the content of the room would be made responsible for making charms for the war and those . . . who could not predict the content of the room were killed. One Okomfo Denkyere from Wenchi predicted that the content was a four-legged animal, it was big and its color was white. This was a good prediction as it described [what the king had put in the room]. . . . Kramo 'Ali however made a different prediction that the content was a big animal, four-legged, and its color was pure black. Initially he was accused of lying, but when he insisted that the door be opened, to the amazement of the people, indeed there was a black cow when the Asantes knew that they had put a white cow in the room. This was a demonstration of Kramo 'Ali's medicine to change things, so the king of Asante asked the Kramoko to prepare the battle for him.[15]

It is generally agreed by historians of Asante that the eastern Volta expedition was very successful. This was evidenced by the numerous slaves returned to Kumase and the great durbar organized to welcome Gyaasewahene Adu Bofo, the commander of the expedition. It was in this expedition that Ramseyer and Kühne of the Basel mission in Anum and the French businessman, Bonnat, were taken prisoners. These Europeans, especially Ramseyer and Kühne in their *Four Years in Ashantee* (1875), wrote about the position of Muslims in Kumase. Some of their records may contribute to this evaluation of the Nkenkaasu Muslim tradition.

As Christian missionaries, Ramseyer and Kühne were struck by the "dirty red-yellow" Arabic-ornamented charm-garments that Gyaasewahene Adu Bofo and his captains wore for their protection during the expedition.[16] Later in Kumase, the Europeans were further impressed by the popularity of Islamic charms in the Asante capital. Asantehene Kofi Kakari, for example, was said to have possessed a pair of sandals inscribed with Arabic writings, which the monarch described as his talisman.[17] It was from the perceived efficacy of these charms among the Asante that Ramseyer thought the influence of Muslim dignitaries in the capital stemmed. For all the time spent in Kumase, during which they had many occasions to preach and record conversations with people, Ramseyer and Kühne heard no mention of the accounts of the episode in which *Kramoko* 'Ali was said to have publicly dazzled Asante officials with his magical powers. Given their apparent scorn of Muslim influence in the Asante capital, the European Christian missionaries would likely have recorded the tradition had they been aware of it. While Ramseyer and Kühne's records argue for a presence of an influential Muslim group in Kumase, there is no other information, either in Asante traditions or from *Nsumankwaa* histories, to serve as confirmation of the episode, which is fundamental to the claims of the Nkenkaasu Muslims.

In the conflict of 1873–74, however, Sulayman b. 'Ali (the son of Kramo 'Ali) was identified as the Muslim entrusted by Asante authorities to make charms to effect the retreat of the Europeans from the Asante interior.[18] Having secured the western approach to the Gold Coast in another 1867 expedition, Kumase did not see its territories on the coast threatened until after the ratification in 1872 of a Dutch-British arrangement to exchange possessions along the Gold Coast. The particular concern of Asante officials was the British interpretation of the status of Elmina, over which Kumase believed itself to have control as a result of its historic defeat of Denkyira in the early eighteenth century.[19] The ensuing war between the British and the Asante in 1873–74 proved crucial to the economic survival and political integrity of the Kumase government.

British mobilization for the engagement against Asante was extensive. Forces under the command of Sir Major-General Garnet Wolseley have been recorded to include more than "2,500 soldiers of the Black Watch, Royal Welch Fusiliers, Rifle Brigade and Naval Brigade; about 2,000 of the West India Regiments and Sierra Leone and Nigeria Colonial forces," and several thousand auxiliaries from the protected territories of the Gold Coast.[20] By January 1874, the British expeditionary forces had crossed the Pra and their commander, Garnet Wolseley, was in no mood to negotiate peace. Faced with this gloomy situation, Asantehene Kofi Kakari mobilized Muslim holy men whose magical powers he thought could effect the retreat of Wolseley's forces.[21]

The Muslims consulted included those Maurice described as "Moorish necromancers and fetish priests" of the northern hinterland.[22] Ramseyer and Kühne also wrote about the commission granted the Muslims in Kumase for the production of a "wonderful Mohammadan charm which with a mere shake of the hand was to have the effect of causing [Wolseley] to go back."[23] In Boyle's 1874 account, "the great prophet of [Asante], Sulayman," was identified as the leader of a Muslim group sent from Kumase to the Adansi Hills on an abortive mission to confront General Wolseley with a charm that was to effect his retreat to the coast.[24] Recognition is also given in the Suame Asante Nkramo traditions to a Nkenkaasu patriarch who was brought to Kumase to help in the preparation for the battle of 1873–74.[25]

The Sulayman referred to by Boyle was identified by al-Hajj Muhammad Sofa of Wa, a former resident of Buna, as the same

Sulayman b. 'Ali who the Nkenkaasu Muslim tradition lists as an ancestral grandfather.[26] In their tradition, however, no mention of his participation in the 1873–74 expedition against the British is expressed. As for the more senior patriarch, 'Ali Kunatay, whose charms and prayer aided Asante victory in the eastern Volta expedition, he was placed in Gyaaman territory where he had returned to continue his education. In his stead in the Asante capital was one Abu Bakr (a Suame Asante Nkramo) who, according to the Nkenkaasu tradition, was temporarily to fill the position of royal imam. Thus, while exonerating their patriarchs from any responsibility in the 1873–74 Asante loss, their own "eminent" position as royal Muslims was maintained in the tradition.

Various sources indicate that the 1874 sack of Kumase was soon followed in eastern Bron by anti-Asante rebellions that ultimately resulted in an alliance between the priest of Dente and the British. The dwindling Asante influence in her distant territories was evident also in Gyaaman's successful entry into a treaty of protection with the British in 1889. As a result, Kintampo and Atebubu markets in Nkoransa territory became too important to Asante officials. Conflicts in the region were, therefore, not to be tolerated in Kumase. According to Wilks,[27] the confrontation with Nkoransa arose from the secessionist platform of Nkoransahene Kofi Fa and his refusal to return Asante rebels held in his country to Kumase. Kofi Fa had also refused to take the oath of allegiance to Agyeman Prempe I, the then Asantehene. In fact, the Nkoransahene had even attempted to ally himself with British interests.

Asante responded to the Nkoransa ploy by dispatching troops in 1892 for the invasion of the town. Kofi Fa was successfully defeated and his town sacked by mid-1893. It has been argued in the Nkenkaasu tradition that this Asante victory was due partly to the efficacy of charms and prayers made by Sulayman b. 'Ali. As related in their accounts,

> after Kramo 'Ali's studies at Banda and a brief stay at Kintampo, he died there and his son Kramo Sulayman b. 'Ali Kunatay took over his business at Kintampo. He stayed at Kintampo for sometime before he moved to Wenchi. When the Asantehene heard that Kramo Sulay-

> man wanted to settle at Wenchi, the king sent some *Nsumankwaa* people to inform the ruler of Wenchi that Kramo Sulayman was the Asantehene's Muslim. It was because Kramo Sulayman was the son of Kramo 'Ali and had inherited the books from his father that the Asantehene asked him to make charms for him in another war against Nkoransa. Kramo Sulayman was successful in this [especially when he] moved to Nkoransa to make charms that defeated the *jinn* of Nkoransa before the actual battle was fought.[28]

The Nkenkaasu Muslims keep as evidence of their role in the Nkoransa expedition, a palanquin sent from Kumase to carry the incapacitated Kramo Sulayman b. 'Ali to the location where he made charms and prayers for "the defeat of Nkoransa *jinn.*"

Accounts of the death of Kramo 'Ali Kunatay at Kintampo and the solicitation of Sulayman b. 'Ali in the Nkoransa expedition of 1892, would leave Abu Bakr b. 'Uthman Kamagatay of the Suame Muslim unit in Kumase for about twenty years as temporary imam of Asante. But, Abu Bakr b. 'Uthman Kamagatay was one of the three Muslims (including Kramo 'Ali Kunatay and Sulayman b. 'Ali) who al-Hajj Muhammad Sofa of Wa remembered meeting at Buna in 1887/88.[29] If these Muslims were at Buna for any length of time—probably for studies as the Nkenkaasu tradition suggests—who in Kumase assumed responsibility of Asante Nkramo imam?

Conclusion

Examination of the various sources suggests that an Asante Nkramo unit had existed in Kumase since 1844 and 'Uthman Kamagatay was its original imam. Questions emerging from the analysis of the Nkenkaasu traditions confirm Wilks's conclusion that 'Uthman Kamagatay, as imam of the Asante Nkramo, lived in Kumase and served Asante rulers with his prayers and charms. As Asante Nkramo imam, however, it was expected of him to collaborate with other powerful holy men whose knowledge could have enhanced Asante chances in the conflicts in which it became entangled.[30] To be sure, a similar collaborative function was even expected of the Nsumankwaahene of Kumase who, "as the chief doctor of the Asantehene . . . was to seek help from other *abosom* (gods) in the performance of difficult tasks." Nsumankwaahene Baffour Domfe Gyeaboo III expanded on the nature of this office: "I can even go to the grassland country to seek the help of Muslims."[31] It was in relation to this Asante interpretation of the role of both the Nsumankwaahene and the Asante Nkramo imam that the relationship between them was described as one of "friendship" in the service of the king.[32]

The possible presence of Kramo 'Ali Kunatay in Kumase during preparations for the eastern Volta expedition in 1867, as the Nkenkaasu traditions suggest, was therefore not in conflict with the functions of 'Uthman Kamagatay as imam of the Asante Nkramo. The coming of Sulayman b. 'Ali to aid in the 1873–74 engagement against the British was equally acceptable. Al-Hajj Muhammad Sofa of Wa was then right to report that 'Ali Kunatay, Sulayman b. 'Ali, and Abu Bakr b. 'Uthman Kamagatay all worked for the Asantehene.[33] The conflicts in the oral traditions, especially of the Nkenkaasu unit, must have emerged after the deaths of both 'Uthman Kamagatay and Kramoko 'Ali Kunatay in the 1890s. As contemporaries, and having a record of service in matters affecting the interests of Asante, Sulayman's settlement at Nkenkaasu (about fifty miles from the Asante capital) must have alienated him from the position of prestige that the new Asante Nkramo imam, Abu Bakr b. 'Uthman Kamagatay, assumed. But as it was explained to this writer in Kumase, the Asante Nkramo imamate is an *mmammadwa* to be inherited only by the sons of their original holders.[34] Thus, notwithstanding Sulayman b. 'Ali's active participation in the affairs of the Asante Nkramo, he could not attain the position of Asante *Nkramo* imam—a position Abu Bakr b. 'Uthman of the Suame group inherited. The recognition of the Nkenkaasu Muslims as "the same as" or "brothers of" the Suame Muslims is, however, an affirmation of the historic duties of the former to the Asante state.

Notes

1. Thomas McCaskie, "The Paramountcy of the Asantehene Kwaku Dua 1834–67: A Study in Asante Political Culture" (Ph.D. diss., Cambridge University, 1974); "Office, Land and Subjects in the History of the *Manwere Fekuo* of Kumase: An Essay in the Political Economy of the Asante State," *Journal of African History* 21 (1980): 189–203; Ivor Wilks, *Asante in the Nineteenth Century; The Structure and Evolution of a Political Order* (New York, repr. 1989), 488–92.

2. David Owusu-Ansah, *Islamic Talismatic Tradition in Nineteenth-Century Asante* (Lewiston, Queenston, and Lampeter, 1991), 173–83.

3. Thomas Bowdich, *Mission from Cape Coast Castle to Ashantee* (London, 1819), 53; Joseph Dupuis, *Journal of a Residence in Ashantee* (London, 1824), 98; David Owusu-Ansah, "Power or Prestige? Muslims in 19th Century Kumase," in *The Golden Stool: Studies of the Asante Center and Periphery,* ed. Enid Schildkrout (New York, 1987), 80–92.

4. Owusu-Ansah, *Islamic Talismanic Tradition,* 88.

5. See Wilks, *Asante in the Nineteenth Century,* 488–92.

6. Owusu-Ansah, *Islamic Talismanic Traditions,* 181.

7. The complete record of interviews conducted with Suame (Kumase) Muslims can be found in my "A Talismanic Tradition: Muslims in Early Nineteenth Century Kumase" (Ph.D. diss., Northwestern University, 1986).

8. See Ivor Wilks, Field notes, interview with Malam Ya'qub Kunatay dd. Nkenkaasu, 23 June 1966; Wilks and al-Hajj 'Uthman b. Ishaq Boyo, Field notes, interview with Nkenkaasu Imam Sa'id dd. Nkenkaasu, 16 Sept. 1968. I am thankful to Ivor for granting me free access to these materials. My own interview with elders of the Nkenkaasu Asante Nkramo in 1989 confirmed information collected earlier by Wilks. See Owusu-Ansah, Field notes, interview with Liman Sa'id, Nkenkaasu Asante Nkramo Imam dd. Nkenkaasu, 18 Dec. 1989.

9. Wilks, *Asante in the Nineteenth Century,* 278; Owusu-Ansah, *Islamic Talismanic Traditions,* 173–83.

10. See Owusu-Ansah, Field notes, interview, 1989.

11. F. Boyle, *Through Fanteeland to Comassie: A Diary of the Ashantee Expedition* (London, 1874), 293–94.

12. Owusu-Ansah, Field notes, interview, 1989.

13. Wilks, *Asante in the Nineteenth Century,* 224.

14. Ibid., 235–42.

15. Owusu-Ansah, Field notes, interview, 1989.

16. F. A. Ramseyer and J. Kühne, *Four Years in Ashantee* (New York, 1875), 20.

17. Ibid., 124 and 140.

18. F. Boyles, *Through Fanteeland to Coomassie,* 293–94.

19. Larry Yarak, *Asante and the Dutch 1744–1873* (Oxford, 1990), passim; Wilks, *Asante in the Nineteenth Century,* 231–32.

20. Ibid., 238.

21. Ibid., 240.

22. J. F. Maurice, *The Ashantee War* (published anonymously, 1874), 16.

23. Ramseyer and Kühne, *Four Years in Ashantee,* 220–11, 263–67, 271.

24. F. Boyle, *Through Fanteeland to Coomasie*, 293–94.

25. Owusu-Ansah, Field notes, interview, 1986.

26. Wilks, *Asante in the Nineteenth Century*, 316.

27. Ibid., 279–82, and 296–99.

28. Owusu-Ansah, Field notes, interview, 1989.

29. Wilks, Field notes, interview with al-Hajj Muhammad Sofa dd. Wa, 16–18 Apr. 1964.

30. Wilks, *Asante in the Nineteenth Century*, 278.

31. Owusu-Ansah, "A Talismanic Tradition," 1986, 403–4.

32. Ibid., 407.

33. Wilks has explained the historic position of Muslims in Asante on the basis of what he described as the "Suwarian traditions." Further investigation would be needed before the spiritual and/or economic base of the "Suwarian" culture and the manner it affected the role of the Asante *Nkramo* can be assessed. For materials on Wilks's discussion of the "Suwarian traditions" see Wilks, "The Transmission of Islamic Learning in the Western Sudan," in *Literacy in Traditional Societies*, ed. J. Goody (Cambridge, 1968), 176–81; "Old Wine in New Bottle: The Asante Factor in Wangara Historiography," paper presented at the African Studies Association Annual Meeting, Seattle, Washington, 20–23 November 1992.

34. Owusu-Ansah, "A Talismanic Tradition," 396.

Politics and Poetry: Mohammed Rashid Shaaban's "History of Kumasi"

ENID SCHILDKROUT

It was obvious to those of us doing research in Ghana in the decade immediately after independence that this was a time of great intellectual ferment among West African intellectuals, both Muslim and non-Muslim. In the 1960s, Ivor Wilks, Jack Goody, Thomas Hodgkin,[1] and others were demonstrating that Ghanaian Muslims, while barely noted in the standard histories of colonial and postindependence Ghana, were very important in framing the discourse of the independence movement. They articulated political and spiritual goals—in speeches, conversations, correspondence, and petitions, as well as in organized political meetings, court cases, and literary texts. Although they were never able to fully realize their goals, they were an influential force in shaping the politics of independence.[2] Their position in the colonial and postcolonial independence movements was not very different from what it had been for three centuries in Asante.[3] As Wilks has so brilliantly demonstrated, the essence of their position has always been to hold on to the basic tenets of their faith, while living in *dar al-harb*.[4]

This essay is a very preliminary contribution to the analysis of the role of Kumasi Muslims in framing the discourse of independence.[5] It is a summary and description of a literary text written by Al-Hajj Mohammed Rashid Shaaban, a Kumasi-born Muslim who is a member of the Yarse ethnic group and a follower of the Tijaniyya.[6] While Shaaban actually lived in Suame, an area of Kumasi that he described to me as "formerly for slaves of the Asantehene," he considered himself a member of the Mossi community of Kumasi Zongo. He was a Muslim teacher by profession, and at the time he wrote this history he was the secretary of the Mossi Youth Association. Today, in 1994, he is assistant imam of the Mossi community in Kumasi and still resides in Suame.

I begin this paper with a description of the history of the document and a confession about why it has never been described before. This involves a discussion of the changes in the way scholars have approached the study of history and anthropology in the past three decades. The second part of the paper is a summary of the document. I include the table of contents as an appendix to give readers a better idea of the whole document than can be gained from my own still cursory description.

While doing predoctoral field research in Kumasi between 1965 and 1968, I worked with Ghanaian Muslims as "informants";[7] not knowing Arabic, however, I made minimal use of their libraries or literary resources. The research techniques I used as a graduate student in social anthropology at Cambridge were mainly "participant observation" supplemented by formal and informal interviews. These interviews and conversations, conducted in Hausa, focused on life histories, economic activities, local politics and history, migration patterns, social organization, ritual, and even people's dreams. I used questionnaires, filled out by myself or an assistant, to gather data about economics and kinship. I attended countless meetings, took minutes, and recorded, transcribed, and translated the proceedings with the help of two field assistants. As for field techniques, I recall Meyer Fortes saying that whenever I found an idle moment I should count: "anything and everything"—chickens, children, bags of grain, books in peoples' libraries. My *People of the Zongo: The Transformation of Ethnic Identities in Ghana* (Cambridge University Press, 1978) contains a wealth of quantitative data supporting my claims about changing patterns of ethnic identity in Ghana.

The written sources I utilized were mainly archival and in English or French: government records found in Kumasi, Accra, London, and local newspapers.[8] Nevertheless, this was the same period when Wilks, Goody, Hodgkin, Levtzion, and Martin were collecting and starting to study West African Islamic literature. Although I was aware of the plethora of Arabic literature that existed in the Zongo, not knowing Arabic, and having another focus for my research, I gave it only cursory attention. A reexamination of my field notes confirms frequent discussions of Islamic theology and philosophy[9] and many notations about the contents of books people were reading and discussing. I also held many conversations with the then ailing al-Hajj Baba al-Wa'iz, the author of *Kanz al-Mufīd li'l-murīd al-ṣādiq* and other books published in Cairo.[10] In fact al-Hajj Baba al-Wa'iz's brother, 'Abdu Rahman, who eventually succeeded his father as Mossi Chief in Kumasi, appears on the cover of *People of the Zongo.*[11] And Baba al-Wa'iz had been involved in a dispute with Rashid Shaaban, the author of the subject of this paper.[12]

In 1967 Rashid Shaaban presented me with a handwritten manuscript, written especially for me, concerning the history of Kumasi Zongo. The content was prompted, in part, by my presence and my research agenda, since by the time Rashid wrote the book I had been working in Kumasi for almost two years. But it was also part of a great tradition of Islamic scholarship that I only barely understood at the time and that I am still not entirely competent to write about. This paper is a very preliminary discussion of what Rashid Shaaban wrote; the original text, along with a complete and accurate translation and a more extensive discussion will be published at a later date.[13]

Rashid Shaaban was about thirty-five years old[14] when he presented me with the manuscript. Before I had it translated we sat down and went over it page by page, although I could not read the Arabic, so that along with the work itself, I have notes about the content given to me at the time the work was written by the author himself. In going over these notes, I discovered that the handsome young arbiter in the dispute with al-Hajj Baba al-Wa'iz was Rashid himself (also confirmed in field notes), and that one poetic section about unrequited love for a woman named Cecilia Owusu is really a parable about me. I was not able to read the document until I reached Cambridge, where it was translated

Rashid Shaaban and Enid Schildkrout in a Kumasi photo studio in the mid-1960s. Collection of Enid Schildkrout.

Rashid Shaaban outside his home in Suame, Kumasi in 1994. Collection of Enid Schildkrout.

into English by a fellow graduate student from Kuwait, Saif Daher, who also made some notes about literary style.

I always had the intention of publishing this document, and I had Shaaban's permission to do so. The explanation for why I never did anything with the document is complex, but it has very much to do with the actual contents of the book. One section of the work titled "Portrait of Enid in Ghana and Upper Volta," was written in the embellished style of Arabic praise poetry. In this form, Saif Daher, the translator, wrote (in reference to another work):[15] "It was the custom of early Arabic poets to mention in the erotic prelude of his [*sic*] *qasida,* the names of his real or imaginative sweet-hearts." Given the ambiguity of the fieldwork/informant relationship, this declaration was something that I found I could not deal with. He wrote, for example:

> Enid who is a pretty girl in looks and spirit loved the black people. She was a bright star in their dark night; yet color is a problem in their country.
>
> Rashid is a dark slender man, with wide reputation in praising pretty young girls.

My embarassment with this part of the text partly explains why the document has remained in a box among my field notes for almost three decades.

It was with great trepidation that I opened the box in 1993, only to discover that almost thirty years later I can read this document in a new light. Besides Rashid Shaaban's account of me, the ethnographer, his manuscript also contains a fascinating history of Kumasi and Ghana. Admittedly, it should have been published many years ago. What stood in the way was my self-conscious reading of Rashid's description of my fieldwork. While this is of little interest for students of Ghanaian history, it is quite interesting from the point of view of the history of anthropology. I shall deal with this first, before turning to the less personal part of Rashid's manuscript.

The whole genre of ethnographic writing has been transformed in the past two decades under the influence of literary criticism and postmodernism.[16] "Objective" accounts of the "other" are now deemed to be fictions, or at least constructions framed by agendas extraneous to those of the actors themselves. However, starting with the publication of Malinowski's field notes, autobiographical accounts of encounters in the field are suddenly of great interest to reflective and self-conscious anthropologists and historians—which all of us must in some sense acknowledge being, particularly as we get older and review our careers. Yet I know of no published account by an informant in which the ethnographer becomes the invented and idealized "other." This is precisely the nature of Rashid's document, and this is why I could not publish it, in the past, as a straightforward history of Kumasi.

> **E2.** Enid goes from door to door asking, inquiring about the events. She photographs events and happenings among the crowd. She [tape]records what they say, a picture became clear and meaningful to her. She visited many chiefs asking them about the violent brave tribe as it angered.[17]
>
> I mean the Moshi [*sic*] Tribe that was known by its courage. Enid went investigating about Moshi people. Musa was her interpreter. He was of Mamprushi tribe. He went with Enid everywhere. Her car was in the country at times and in town at others. Barimuda was her writer and he deputized for her in meetings if she wasn't there.
>
> **E3.** Haji 'Abdu became a close friend of hers. She visited him often and she stayed in his house. Malek Adam[18] helped her in his affairs in Ghana. She visited Isa (Sultan Moshi)[19] and asked him about various tribal affairs. She visited my house too asking me about people and events. Enid knew that I was knowledgeable in matters of history and I told her about Kumasi affairs. She accompanied me to the country. She had patience and resolution. Enid went to Moshi land [Burkina Faso] by car. She visited the lands of the people accompanied by 'Abdu, Musa and the driver. She went to the huts. She saw Mogho Naba Kogri in this town and saw Ouagadougou, the capital of the free people.

Today, so many years later, even the somewhat embarrassing biographical references make interesting ethnography and give us another point of view (though not necessarily a more realistic one) of the informant/ethnographer relationship, one in which the roles of the parties are reversed: the "other" has become the author.

> Enid loves our people and she helped us. She helped men and women, she gave away cloths and money. We all thank her, and we grieved at her departure. We could not repay her. She attended the funerals of our dead. She brought cheer and happiness to our marriages. When the chief was wounded, she carried him immediately to the doctor. Her car was used for everyone. There was a dispute that created a problem. The news spread. The wounded Haji 'Abdu has wide relations with people's affairs and difficulties. Mumen and Buraim differed on something and it was a war between them. When Haji 'Abdu came to help solve the problem, he was wounded by a tool someone had thrown and knocked unconscious. The Western girl shouted at people, then she carried him to her place where he stayed a day resting. Such are her services to our people. We called her Zeinab and she was so known.

Because I felt uncomfortable about being described as an actor on the stage of Kumasi Zongo politics—however minor my role—I am not sure that I ever read the document very carefully before I put it away in 1968. It contains, in fact, only about 2,500 words (out of approximately 14,000) about me and my fieldwork, including a number of comments about the fact that I am Jewish. For example:

> I have written the history of Enid. She had a great mind which was apparent to those who knew her. I studied her character. . . . She was Jewish and dwelt in the West, but she did not come to Ghana for spying. While she dwelt among us no propaganda for Israel came from her. Rather she concentrated on her work. She had read about the Arabs and Islam. She was aware of the miracle of Islam.[20]

There were also things in the text that I regarded as extraneous because they were personal matters such as descriptions of my "significant other," my dog, and a visit by my parents to Ghana. At the time I felt all this was irrelevant for scholarly consideration. I certainly did not see myself as a historical figure in the Kumasi Zongo, and I was uncomfortable with the fact that in

Rashid's history I got almost equal billing, in terms of the number of words, with General Kotoka and the leaders of various political parties—second only, it seemed, to Kwame Nkrumah and Sheikh Ibrahima Niass of Kaolack, Senegal.

In the three decades since this document was written, the practice of writing ethnography and history, as well as the practice of writing itself,[21] has been reexamined. An account written by an informant of the anthropologist in the field now seems relevant to the whole question of the production of knowledge. For me, the section "Enid in Ghana" is now ancient enough to be seen as history, and having dared to reread the document I have discovered that most of it is not about me at all, but about the history of West Africa, colonialism, the politics of Ghanaian independence, and the fascinating and ongoing disputes among the inhabitants of Kumasi Zongo. It also contains a great deal of philosophy as well as commentary about world events, such as the East/West and Israeli/Arab conflicts, the influence of various Muslim sheikhs (particularly Sheikh Ibrahima Niass of Kaolack), and even the first trip by an astronaut to the moon.

In preparing this essay, and in anticipation of publishing the entire work, I wrote to the author, a man whom I have not seen since 1970. I had not, at the time of writing the first version of this paper, received an answer, although I did receive an answer to another letter I wrote to al-Hajj 'Abdu Rahman, the chief of the Kumasi Mossi community and a friend of Shaaban's.[22] That letter brought up all of the ambivalent and complicated feelings I still have about ethnographic fieldwork in Africa. After a decade-long lapse in correspondence, the letter pleaded for an urgent loan of an airline ticket and medicines for 'Abdu Rahman himself. I realized that despite the fashion of now publishing autobiographical and personal accounts of fieldwork, there are still chasms that are not easily bridged, inequalities that do not disappear even with new kinds of ethnographic writing. These chasms trouble me as much in the 1990s as they did in 1967, for the praise poem to Enid, which part of this document undeniably is, can only be read as an expression of inequality and a struggle against it, through its incorporation of the ethnographer into the world of the "informant"/author. These feelings are not mitigated by the fact that I am aware that in this document I serve mainly as a metaphor for—and an idealized, and highly gendered, representative of—the West. Through me as "the other," the author deals with his attitudes toward whites, interracial love and marriage,[23] Jews and Israel, global conflict, and the place of the Kumasi Zongo community in a wider world. Rereading the poem now, I am also struck with the breadth of Shaaban's view of the events in Kumasi. Whereas my work in the 1960s situated Kumasi politics in the context of British colonial history and emerging Ghanaian nationalism, Shaaban's intellectual purview was decidely global.

The Poem: Genre and Dedication

Thomas Hodgkin summarized the Islamic literary traditions of Ghana by distinguishing a number of genres: history, *ta'rikh;* poetry, *shi'r;* and poems in praise of the prophet, *madh.* Rashid's work is a combination of all of these. In discussing al-Hajj 'Umar ibn Abi Bakr ibn Uthman al-Kabawi al-Kanawi al-Salghawi of Keti-Kratchi (c. A.D. 1850–1934), Hodgkin notes that besides al-Hajj 'Umar's works of a classical model, "his major contribution to the development of the Islamic literary tradition in the region was of quite another kind. It might be described as making poetry the vehicle of social commentary, social criticism, and reflections on the history of his time."[24] Al-Hajj 'Umar is in fact the direct intellectual predecessor of Rashid Shaaban, for Shaaban's father was a student of al-Hajj 'Umar in Kete Kratche. Rashid learned from his own father who was a teacher, first in Kete Kratche and then in Kumasi.

In the first five sections of the poem, which are basically the introduction and dedication, Shaaban acknowledges a debt to a number of Islamic poets, most prominently Ibrahim Joub. This is probably a transliteration in Arabic of Ibrahim Diop, one of a number of Senegalese Tijani leaders. Behrman[25] mentions Ibrahima Diop, "an important Tijani leader in Dakar" who was active in the 1950s.[26] Later in the text, Shaaban speaks of Sheikh Ibrahima Niass of Kaolack who visited Kumasi as he toured West Africa recruiting followers in the 1950s. The Ibrahim "Joub" referred to in the text was, in fact, a disciple of Ibrahim Niass. I recall a great deal of discussion in the 1960s about a visit to Ghana by Sheikh Ibrahim of Kaolack. The dedication of this poem, as well as parts of the narrative history, suggest that the sheikh served as a political and spiritual beacon for Shaaban and probably for other Kumasi Muslims. The influence of Ibrahim and other leaders is expressed in terms of radiance and physical beauty used as a metaphor. Their ability to write and recite poetry and to inspire through oratory are equated with their political stature:

> 1.4[27] When Enid asked me for a copy of my humble poem I couldn't but comply. This poem was written in praise of the Nikromian [?] Poet Ibrahima Mahmoud Joub [Diop?].
> 2.3 I have tried to describe past events in the Gold Coast—this part of the world, playing its role in world politics has achieved great success. Its people called it blissfully "Ghana," in anticipation of [its being] a great country amongst its neighbors. I mentioned reasons for its rising, after so deep a sleep, the reason being the great revolutionary spirit which radiated throughout the world, and which only Africa was honored to claim. He, in Kaolack, stays and to his Senegal the whole nation aspires.
> 3.1 Am I dreaming, I wonder, or have I truly seen a tall slender bright looking young man whose black coloring reflected proudly onto him? . . . In beauty and purity he resembled Ayat of Qur'an.
> 3.3 In Sufism and politics he was a poet, and literature and culture were well in hand.

The next section of the poem, still written in praise of Sheikh Ibrahim, is called *Portrait of Ibrahim Mohammed Joub's thoughts (the thought being a daughter).* Here Shaaban describes Ibrahim's thought as a woman, and is impassioned by the inspiration of "her" beauty. Poetics and politics merge, as the "daughter" inspires revolutionary ardor:

> 4.2 That very beauty, with her sister, came upon me one night. The moon was full in the skies. I sat myself between these two beauties and I could not stop glancing on them, I then was captured so com-

pletely. I vanished in that beauty, my senses became numb. Then I heard the voice of truth which seemed to make me see clearly and wake from my coma. I saw myself on a train reading Ibrahim's book yet again.[28] As I arrived in Kumasi, I had that strong desire to write following his style.
4.3 I stayed at home feeling the fire raging in me. The fire then seemed to spread throughout and engulf my country, till a reactionary group volunteered to put it out. That group failed and was burnt in the fire. Then Youth and Progress came marching, activated, headed, and represented by Haji Ibrahim.

Historical Narrative

The dedication takes the reader straight into an account of events that contribute to the revolutionary "rising" of Ghana. The independence movement is compared to the "fire" of poetry that rages in the author and in his mentor. The author first describes a visit by Sheikh Ibrahim to Kumasi (probably the visit in 1953–54) and suggests that this was the beginning of the involvement of Kumasi Muslims in preindependence pan-African politics.[29]

5.1 The Radiance of Guidance itself has settled in Ghana as Ibrahim returned here from Almadina.
5.2 The guest house was surrounded by delegates and he himself appeared on the balcony. He looked glamorous. His smile added to his beauty, made purer still by God. We stood on tiptoes to glance at him in his splendor. Before disappearing into his solitude, he blessed us all.
5.3 His residence had the monumental beauty of a Presidential palace. In our Sheikh's Presence, two opposites have met, and two sexes have mixed, and all to meet him—earthly desires fainted—we all busied ourselves to see this man—high above men. There holding a gun is a uniformed policeman that our government ordered to guard our Sheikh. His servants guarded the gates in his absence. But our Sheikh was protected by God and the presence of the guards was merely to maintain law and order. Then he, our teacher, came upon us with his book, recited a poem melodically, then another. He urged the Youth for political understanding and prayed for Ghana's rulers who had departed to Addis Ababa to put things right. May prayers be accepted for them as they are representing the wisdom of our Sheikh.

Section 6, "Internal and external (two portraits—one of spiritual mysticism and the other of materialistic philosophy)," continues the description of Ibrahim as the material and worldly embodiment of the Prophet. He is "the flood" and a magnet; magnetism is the mediating force between the material and the spiritual world [the Prophet].

> 6.2 Ibrahim (the flood) is but a spiritual magnet, he attracts from within. Hearts are made of iron and to him they [are] bound to be attracted.

Shaaban then goes on to discuss the limitations to the perceptual functions of the brain, and how perception and the senses often deceive. Knowledge derived from the five senses is contrasted with spiritual knowledge. This gets him to the issue of the *miraj,* the flight of the Prophet.

> By Spirit, I realized truth, as I see happenings even after they physically disappear. The brain denies what we see in this life after it is gone. But as for flying objects, you (The Prophet) offered hope for that which the brain rejects as impossible.[30]

Shaaban is always grounded in the affairs of this world, and this discussion takes him to a consideration of space travel:

> 6.5 Miraj of the Prophet—The Most Blessed—is indisputable. Yet, in Red Russia, an astronaut has made the news to a specified purpose [target?]. He went into the atmosphere, and back he came, to tell his people what he saw to and fro. Brain believed his story, yet denied the Selected (Prophet) in his Miraj. There are Ayat for the brain to believe. I mean Qur'an.

Shaaban comments on the fact that unbelievers accept the idea of space travel, whereas they reject the earlier version of such events as described in the Qur'an.

Section 7, "Portrait of the causes of Africa rising and independence," again describes Ibrahim as the motivating force behind the liberation of Africa from colonialism.

> 7.1 The events and their causes became evident in Africa. Africa has been long waiting for liberation with no avail. Western nations sought the opportunity to colonize it and so they did, while Africa's

> hopes were in the faraway horizons. The hope has come and the sun has risen throwing light all over Africa's dark corners. This light materialized into a being, gracious and beautiful among people. I mean Ibrahim.

Section 8 continues praise of Ibrahim's book, here described as a book he wrote "jointly" with his, or his friend's, eldest daughter. It then recognizes the literary abilities of the northern Nigerian writers and reformers. Section 9, "Portrait of a young African rebel from Upper Volta," is again in praise of "a young revolutionary leader" who is never named: "He hopes to write his country's history as he wishes to establish truth . . . in the new Parliament he was given a front seat." This too refers to Ibrahim Joub and the influence of the Muslims in Senegalese politics.[31]

The Politics of Independence

Section 10 begins a section on Kwame Nkrumah, referred to as Osagyefo. The key to Nkrumah's complicated legacy, Shaaban writes, is in his personality, which is "like the sea full of ships." There follows an allegorical discussion invoking the sea, wind, and seafood. Islamic legislation is compared to the pure water: "its water resembles the vein of life." The turbulence of the sea is the metaphor used for the fights between political parties. There is a description of a plot to kill Nkrumah and the jailing of his opponents. Then another poetic passage follows: section 11, "Portrait of the Ghanaian people at Kwame Nkrumah's dinner party," in which Nkrumah's socialism is condemned:

> 11.2 He, Nkrumah, is a socialist, and he wanted his people to be accustomed to a one man rule. People digested that deadly snake which the President had so skillfully cooked. People ate this day by day and criticism was forbidden. Bolshevism is the deadly snake. Atheism is its lethal poison.

We then come to a discussion of global conflict between the atheistic and "bolshevik" East and the West, which is also condemned for its support of Israel. Africa must reject them all: "let them go to the moon, there they will find colonies" (sect. 12.2).

Four paragraphs praising Egypt and condemning Israel follow. The political geography of the Middle East is discussed, with each country mentioned in terms of its relationship to Egypt and Israel.[32]

The text then turns to a detailed description of French colonization of Africa and of African resistance, including mention of the arrest of the author's father when he was traveling in Upper Volta, and a suggestion that he was a successor to Ibrahim. In section 13.3 we read:

> They forbade him to teach his people the knowledge of the learned (the Sheikhs). They saw the similarity between him and Ibrahim, so the star rose in West Africa. I visualized Ibrahim's spirit through Shaaban [the author's father]. This much feared Sheikh left with his family and came to Kumasi."

Because we are used to thinking of history in terms of linear chronology or narrative time, the logic of the poem is sometimes difficult to follow. This is, as Fabian puts it in his analysis of a not dissimilar Swahili text,[33] an event-driven history rather than a chronology. One of the most important tasks to accomplish in analyzing this poem will be to try to ascertain the logic of the sequence of sections. Rashid's cognitive map, the itinerary of his narrative journey, skips from local events to global ones and even encompasses events on Mars and the moon. In some parts of the poem it seems that the vision goes even further as the author attempts to analyze the relationship between the physical world of matter and the world of spirit. His field of vision shifts continually from Kumasi Zongo to Ghana to West Africa to the globe to the universe. The most provocative question in analyzing the narrative is how these fields are linked.

After the discussion of French colonialism and Rashid's father's arrest, the text shifts back in time to a description of the senior Shaaban's arrival in Kumasi and his relationship with Prince Hussain Salaw, who was Sarkin Zongo in Kumasi from 1919 to 1932 and was a student of the senior Shaaban. Section 13 then describes how Salaw flees (1932) and Prempeh II "becomes a King in his tribe" with the restoration of the Asante Confederacy in 1935. The narrative then moves back to Portuguese colonization in the fifteenth century; British conquest in the late nineteenth century; the conquest of Asante and deportation of Prempeh I (1896), finally to the Seychelles; the revolt of Yaa Asante (1900); the division of Asante into districts by the British and the policy of indirect rule; the return of Prempeh from exile (1924); the succession of Prempeh II as Kumasihene (1926); and ends with a description of a time of two wars, either in Asante (1874 and 1900) or, more likely, the two world wars.

The next fifteen sections, translated into an English text of almost 7000 words, are about preindependence politics with a detailed account of the rise of Kwame Nkrumah and the Convention Peoples Party (CPP), negotiations with the British over independence, the rise of other parties including the Muslim Association Party (MAP), the complicated relationships between political parties, and a series of scenes involving the main political actors in this great drama. Both J. B. Danquah and Kwame Nkrumah are praised as orators, as were the important Islamic leaders, but the rhetoric of the CPP politicians is parodied:

> 16.2 Sheikhs have their palaces and the people live in huts. Those people who are living in the shadow will have the power one day. Chiefs will run for their lives when the people rule. Empty envelopes should be thrown away. Your father is the envelope and you are the message. You are the hope. Denounce your father if he appeared to be an enemy of the chief. If the English leave, you'll have enough wealth to live happily. There will be no poverty. Clothing will be cheap, every one will have a palace.

Section 21, "Portrait of the Accra people and their position in regard of monarchy," is an interesting account of the differences between the Accra and Kumasi Muslims and their attitude toward monarchy. Here, Shaaban attributes the adherence of some Accra Muslims to the CPP and a majority of Kumasi Muslims to the MAP (and the National Liberation Movement [NLM]) to their different relationships to monarchy, specifically to the influence of the Asantehene in Kumasi.[34]

21.1 The Accra dispute was a simple one, when examined. They are republicans and among them there were no Royalists. You would see the prince walking alone getting his food by himself. There were very few problems and people had power over their rulers. But people of Kumasi are people of Princehood, there, people fear the prince. So, their problems were more and their disputes became dangerous.

In Kumasi the disputes between the parties could be explained in terms of the activities of opportunistic politicians, as well as the manipulation of chiefs, and leaders' exploitation of intergenerational cleavages:

21.2 Islam came to their land and they became happy. The Zongo tribe followed the MAP Party that preached justice. Ahmadu Baba (the Prince of Kumasi) became the leader of the party. He headed the eleven-man teachers society which was the leading body of the party in its risings. Their president was Haji Lardan, leader of the Moslems.[35] Their Imam was the gracious learned Chiroma. He issued a decree that stated that the CPP Party was unfaithful to the Islamic Religion. The CPP reacted angrily and asked for the Imam's dismissal. They had a poet leader who was loved, he was Mutawakilu. This CPP orator urged the young to rebel against the chiefs whom he attacked strongly. The young responded to his speeches and hurried to please him—they were a minority in Zongo headed by the government party. Imam Ahmadu Baba's son was a leader among them. Their women had a poetess whose voice was heard above that of the enemy. She attacked the enemies and praised her party system. Moslem women of Kumasi are a cornerstone in the party. Their women poets were eloquent in praise, vigorous in attack. A poetess' poem was an arrow that hits deep into the hearts of the enemy. Such was the poet Fati Bemous, as she was the party poet in its ascendance. Another woman poet was Sa'a.

The discussion of party politics in Kumasi again leads to a discussion of the role of the Asantehene as a mediator and peace keeper in the Zongo.

21.4 The Asante King called for good will and urged the MAP and the CPP to forget their differences. The learned tried to heal the wounds, but the young refused. They forbade their leader from making peace, as the King directed.

Shaaban then goes on to recount the history of disputes among Muslims in Kumasi Zongo and the role of the Asantehene in mediating them in the past.

> 22.1 The disputes among the people of Kumasi are old ones.[36] Malam 'Ali, past prince of Zongo, was dismissed as his people revolted against him. He was a great Sultan, a man of knowledge; and the Asante King loved him for his brightness. It was rumored that Haji Yahaya[37] had exceeded the limit with his women so the Prince of Zongo went to investigate the matter one afternoon. Haji Yahaya came to the Prince's residence and denied strongly what was rumored, he blamed people for the rumor. The Prince of Zongo took the matter to his King Prempeh, as he was his favorite. The King had the habit of entrusting a visiting Prince[38] of taking his place and giving judgments. The authorized prince called on people to attend the court at the King's palace.

Shaaban's account then deals with the history of the dispute between Ahmadu Baba and Mutawakilu and the relationship of the latter to politicians in Accra. Mutawakilu's ascendancy is attributed to his cunning and oratorical prowess, while his downfall is attributed to greed, jealousy, and eventually mental illness: "He developed a complex" is how the translator phrased it. "Mutawakilu was reduced to a desperate heart-wounded man among his wives" (22.16).[39] Plots and court cases are recounted and a long list of influential leaders is given. The text includes the comment: "These events took place in Kumasi and affected the whole country. Renner [Bankole Awooner Renner] came to Kumasi and founded the Islamic party [MAP]" (22.22).

Section 23 deals with the rise of the National Liberation Movement (NLM) and its internal disputes. This leads into a discussion of the building of the Kumasi Central Mosque, the Asantehene's role as grantor of the land for the Mosque, and disputes over the funds for the Mosque.[40] This concludes the first part of the poem but continues in what I have labeled sections 23–30 to deal with personalities and events up until independence. The next four sections deal with the Nkrumah government, the coup by the National Liberation Council against Nkrumah, followed by a return to local events in Kumasi Zongo, and then again a return to national events.

In the section on local events Shaaban continues to discuss the disputes between Mutawakilu and his opponents. He also discusses the disputes within the Mossi community, including the dispute with al-Hajj Baba al-Waʿiz mentioned above. In the text, Shaaban refers to himself only as "a young man." When the history arrives at the point of discussing the return of al-Hajj Ahmadu Baba from exile and his reappointment as Sarkin Zongo, the Asantehene, Prempeh II once again enters the picture: "King Prempeh showed his love and consideration to the Prince Haji Baba and treated him well. He then attacked the Imam and came strongly on the Prince's side and praised him" (39.1).

The conclusion of the poem, quoted below, speaks for itself and shows again that there clearly is an Islamic way of interpreting political events in Ghana in the twentieth century, as in the nineteenth as described by Ivor Wilks. Despite the way the text skips back and forth over space and time, there is a consistent worldview throughout the poem. The downfall of Nkrumah was not that he aspired to be a king, but that he eschewed religion and was idolized as no man should be. This is something that in the view of the Muslims the Asantehene never did, which is why they have lived in peace with their hosts in *dar al-harb* for so long.

> 49 At first, the good deeds of the publican [*sic*] party were apparent. Then its ills became clearer as it drew towards its end. Its leaders raised Ghana high in position and built good houses there. They tried to unite the African Continent. So they spied and plotted in secret. That was the Party's mistake. They disbelieved in religion and idolized the President. . . .
>
> Prayers. Fini.
>
> By Mohammed Rashid Shaaban.
>
> The General Secretary of the Mossi Youth Society and Islamic Society in Ghana—Ashanti land.

Notes

1. See I. Wilks, "The Transmission of Islamic Learning in the Western Sudan," in *Literacy in Traditional Societies,* ed. J. R. Goody (Cambridge, 1968), 161–97; J. R. Goody "Restricted Literacy in Northern Ghana," in *Literacy in Traditional Societies,* 198–264; T. Hodgkin, "The Islamic Literary Tradition in Ghana," in *Islam in Tropical Africa,* ed. I. M. Lewis (Oxford, 1966), 442–60.

2. See J. Allman "'Hewers of Wood, Carriers of Water': Islam, Class, and Politics on the Eve of Ghana's Independence," *African Studies Review* 34, no. 2 (September 1991): 1–26.

3. Ibid.

4. See I. Wilks, "The Position of Muslims in Metropolitan Ashanti in the Early Nineteenth Century," in *Islam in Tropical Africa,* ed. I. M. Lewis (Oxford, 1966), 318–41; and I. Wilks, *Asante in the Nineteenth Century* (Cambridge, 1975).

5. I am very grateful to John Hunwick for looking over a portion of the original Arabic text. Based on the sample that John Hunwick translated, it seems that the translation used here has sometimes abbreviated the original, leaving out words and summarizing ideas. A second translation for verification is now under way.

6. The Yarse are the Muslims among the Mossi. See N. Levtzion, *Muslims and Chiefs in West Africa* (Oxford, 1968), chap. 9; and E. Schildkrout, *People of the Zongo: The Transformation of Ethnic Identities in Ghana* (Cambridge, 1978).

7. See R. Sanjek, "Anthropology's Hidden Colonialism: Assistants and Their Ethnographers," *Anthropology Today* 9, no. 2 (April 1993): 13–18, for a discussion of the denial of authorship to informants. Sanjek interprets this as one more manifestation of anthropology's status as a colonial discipline.

8. These are used in E. Schildkrout, *People of the Zongo;* E. Schildkrout, "Government and Chiefs in Kumasi Zongo," in *West Africa Chiefs: Their Changing Status Under Colonial Rule and Independence,* ed. M. Crowder and O. Ikime (Nigeria: University of Ife, 1970), 370–93.

9. For example, 5 May 1966: "Today Rashid brings an Arabic book that al-Hajj Abdu' Rahman reads—very engrossed. *Rohu Deen al Islami*—Muslim life book, by Abduul Fari da Bar. It tells you what to do if, for example, someone says *salamu aleikum* and the person inside the door replys *Aleikum salam.* You don't enter until they say *bissimilla.* . . . He then began talking about Adam and Eve and Jesus, and Rashid asked me 'what comes first, chicken or egg, and where was the start of a circle?'"

10. Al-Hajj Baba al-Waʿiz, *Kanz al-Mufid li'l-murīd al-ṣādiq* (Cairo, 1950). This work is cited in the list in J. R. Goody, ed., *Literacy in Traditional Societies,* 253, and in B. G. Martin, *Research Review, Bulletin of the Institute of African Studies,* University of Ghana, 2, no. 2 (1965): 76–77.

11. E. Schildkrout, *People of the Zongo.*

12. Shaaban had a very complicated relationship with Baba al-Waʿiz. My field notes from 15 April 1966 describe an argument that ended up with police in-

tervention. Rashid told me: "*Kanz-al Mufid* tells how in the time of Mallam Sallow there were many thiefs in Kumasi but that they were all Mossi. . . . This history that Alhaji Baba wrote made the Mossi people angry. Baba [who was also a Mossi] wrote that Arabic schools were for the Hausa, and all other groups, except he didn't say that the Mossi had a school in this country. . . . Alhaji Baba wanted to give Mossi people a bad name in the book." Malik, Alhaji Baba al-Wa'iz's younger brother, had a different version of the dispute and claimed that Rashid had tried to take over the leadership of the mosque [the Muslim community] from al-Hajj Baba al-Wa'iz and used the excuse that al-Wa'iz was not only pro-CPP but also, citing his published book, pro-Hausa and anti-Mossi. This appears in Rashid's history, in section 34: *Portrait of the rebellion of Moshi youth against Haji Baba Al-Wa'iz.*

13. There are several works that may serve as models of this sort of endeavor: J. A. Braimah and J. R. Goody, *Salaga: The Struggle for Power* (London, 1967), and J. Fabian, *History from Below, The 'Vocabulary of Elisabethville' by Andre Yav; Text, Translation and Interpretive Essay* (Amsterdam, 1990).

14. Although he figures prominently in *People of the Zongo,* most people's names were changed in that book, and in my thesis, making him difficult to identify. The name changes were done not to deny people their individuality or identity, but to protect the confidentiality of some highly personal and political information.

15. He was referring to IASAR 239i, a poem by al-Hajj Umar, that he also translated.

16. See, for example, J. Clifford and G. E. Marcus, eds., *Writing Culture: The Poetics and Politics of Ethnography* (Berkeley and Los Angeles, 1986); J. Fabian, *Time and the Other: How Anthropology Makes Its Object* (New York, 1983); R. Sanjek, ed., *Fieldnotes: The Makings of Anthropology* (Ithaca, N.Y., 1990); M. M. J. Fischer and M. Abedi, *Debating Muslims: Cultural Dialogues in Post-modernity and Tradition* (Madison, Wis., 1990).

17. This probably refers to political activity including the organization of the Mossi within Kumasi Zongo.

18. 'Abdul Rahman's younger brother.

19. Chief Yisa or Isa, then the elderly chief of the Kumasi Mossi community. He was succeeded by 'Abdu Rahman, who still holds this office.

20. This paragraph was translated by John Hunwick. I am very grateful for his assistance.

21. See J. R. Goody, ed. *Literacy in Traditional Societies,* and J. R. Goody, *The Domestication of the Savage Mind* (Cambridge, 1977); J. Fabian, *History from Below.*

22. In the summer of 1994 I returned to Kumasi and spent many hours going over the manuscript with Shabaan, who is now Na'ib (assistant imam) of the Kumasi Mossi community. Mossi chief 'Abdu Rahman died subsequently, in December 1994.

23. The rest of the paragraph translated by John Hunwick and noted above reads: "Farewell Enid, your stay with us has been long. She disappeared from sight but she remains in our heart. I was absorbed in her, but it had no perma-

nancy. My soul was connected to that soul. By God, blackness of skin is a problem that is solved in the presence of love if the heart is agreeable."

24. Hodgkin, "The Islamic Literary Tradition," 454.

25. L. C. Behrman, *Muslim Brotherhoods and Politics in Senegal* (Cambridge, Mass., 1970), 70.

26. See D. B. Cruise O'Brien, *The Mourides of Senegal: The Political and Economic Organization of an Islamic Brotherhood* (Oxford, 1971).

27. The numbers refer to paragraph numbers that I have added to Shabaan's text. See the Appendix for the titles of sections.

28. Even though I have a list—undoubtedly incomplete—of books in Rashid's library, there is none by Sheikh Ibrahim Joub, or Diop, or even Niass. Later on in the document (sect. 8.1) Shaaban writes, "Ibrahim's book deals with philosophy and thoughts of the President. If you ever read that book you'll be a follower." Shabaan's library also included translation of Western novels including *Cyrano de Bergerac, Ghāniyat Bārīs* (Pleasure Women of Paris) by Emile Zola, and *al-Muṣāri' al-jarī'* (The daring wrestler) by Blasco Ibáñez.

29. See Allman, "Hewers of Wood," note 13, for a mention of this visit.

30. The translator wrote here: "The ref. here is to Mohammed's night travel from his bed in Mecca to Jerusalem—*isra*—as stated in Qur'an—and from there to Heavens (Miraj). As stated in other sources, the journey took place in one night." This interpretation was confirmed by Rashid Shaaban in 1994 (personal communication).

31. Rashid Shabaan, personal communication, July 1994.

32. Note that a large proportion of the books in Rashid's library are from Egypt.

33. Fabian, *History from Below.*

34. See also the parallel discussion in Allman, "Hewers of Wood," 19.

35. al-Hajj Othman Lardan, a Yoruba who had been educated in Cairo. See Schildkrout, *People of the Zongo* and Allman, "Hewers of Wood," who refers to him as Mallam Alfa Lardan (8ff.).

36. This section refers to the period between 1932 and 1945 when Malam Ali was Sarkin Zongo. The dissension in the Zongo that led to the downfall of his predecessor, Malam Salaw, along with the strengthening of the power of the Asantehene in this decade, led to a close relationship between the Sarkin Zongo and the Asantehene. Both Ahmadu Baba and Mutawakilu figured in the dispute that ended with the "destoolment" of Malam Ali, but they were still too young to assume the position of Sarkin Zongo. See Schildkrout, "Government and Chiefs in Kumasi Zongo," 370–92.

37. The leader of the Zabarama community. See Schildkrout, *People of the Zongo,* 169.

38. This refers to one of the Omanhene.

39. "Alone among his wives" means, here, out of public, male, view; that is, cut off from political influence.

40. See E. Schildkrout, "Islam and Politics in Kumasi: An Analysis of Disputes over the Kumasi Central Mosque," *Anthropological Papers of the American Museum of Natural History* 52, no. 2 (1974): 113–37.

Appendix

Rashid Shaaban's "History of Ghana"
Table of Contents (parentheses show wordcount)

1. Preface to a poem. (258)
2. The poem. (218)
3. Portrait of Ibrahim Mohammed Joub, being and mannerism. (200)
4. Portrait of Ibrahim's thoughts (the thought being a daughter). (367)
5. Portrait of the Tijanian crowd reception to Ibrahim in Ghana. (325)
6. Internal and external. Two portraits—one of spiritual mysticism and the other of materialistic philosophy. (538)
7. Portrait of the causes of Africa rising and independence. (236)
8. Portrait. (Some thoughts of Ibrahim together with Mohammed al-Habib (figuratively, the eldest daughter). (214)
9. Portrait of a young African rebel from Upper Volta. (215)
10. Portrait of the personality of President Nkrumah. (347)
11. Portrait of the Ghanaian people at Kwame Nkrumah's dinner party. (107)
12. Portrait of the big countries in regard to independent Africa. (351)
13. Portrait of the colonials and colonized Africa. Listen to history telling the hidden story. (563)
14. Portrait of the Gold Coast as it sought independence. (577)
15. Portrait of the MAP and its ally the CPP. (173)
16. Portrait of the attack of the CPP on the democratic party. (165)
17. Portrait of Danquah as he defends his party in front of the people. (217)
18. Portrait of the first elections to Accra municipal council. (299)

19. Portrait of the positive stand of Great Britain in the Gold Coast. (339)
20. Portrait of the dispute between the MAP and CPP. (472)
21. Portrait of the Accra people and their position in regard of monarchy. (425)
22. Portrait of the disputes in Kumasi preceding the appearance of parties. (2522)
23. Portrait of the MAP and NLM in the Gold Coast. (788)
24. Portrait of the fight between Mutawakilu and 'Abdu Rahman. (146)
25. Portrait of the assault on Yusuf Yadiga by Mossi youth. (80)
26. Portrait of the acquittal of the accused. (107)
27. Portrait of the United Party before its dissolution. (195)
28. Portrait of the errors of the opposition party in Ghana before its dissolution. (258)
29. Portrait of the general elections before independence. (112)
30. Portrait of the independence of the Gold Coast under the name Ghana. (48)
31. Portrait of the tyranny of the President against the opposition. (111)
32. Portrait of the negative stand of the Islamic party towards the government in Kumasi. (368)
33. Portrait of the conspiracy of police officers on the life of Osagyefo. (80)
34. Portrait of the rebellion of Moshi youth against Haji Baba al-Wa'iz. (160)
35. Portrait of the standing dispute among the Moslems of CPP in Kumasi. (118)
36. Portrait of the army coup against the ex-President Nkrumah and his government. (107)
37. Portrait of the singing dancing crowds after the military coup. (89)
38. Portrait of the end of Prince Muhammed Mutawakilu. (87)
39. Portrait of the dispute between the Prince Haji Baba and

History of Enid in Ghana and Upper Volta
Table of Contents

Bibliography of the Writings of Ivor Wilks

Books, Monographs, and Pamphlets

1961 *The Northern Factor in Ashanti History.* Institute of African Studies, Legon, 46.

1971 *Political Bi-polarity in Nineteenth Century Asante.* Edinburgh University, 22.

1975 *Asante in the Nineteenth Century: The Structure and Evolution of a Political Order.* Cambridge University Press, xvii and 800.

1984 *South Wales and the Rising of 1839: Class Struggle as Armed Struggle.* Croom Helm and University of Illinois Press, 270.

1986 *Chronicles from Gonja: A West African Tradition of Muslim Historiography* (with Nehemia Levtzion and Bruce Haight). Cambridge University Press, xii and 258.

1989 *Wa and the Wala: Islam and Polity in Northwestern Ghana,* Cambridge University Press, xvi and 256.

1989 *Asante in the Nineteenth Century: The Structure and Evolution of a Political Order.* 2d ed. Cambridge University Press, lv and 800.

1989 *South Wales and the Rising of 1839: Class Struggle as Armed Struggle.* 2d ed. Gomer Press, 270.

1993 *Forests of Gold: Essays on the Akan and the Kingdom of Asante.* Ohio University Press, xvii and 388. [Paperback ed., 1995]

1995 *A Portrait of Otumfuo Opoku Ware II as a Young Man.* Anansesem Publications, Ghana, v and 35.

1996 *One Nation, Many Histories. Ghana Past and Present, The Aggrey-Fraser-Guggisberg Memorial Lectures for 1995.* Anansesem Publications, Ghana.

Chapters Contributed to Edited Works

1964 "The Growth of the Akwapim State: A Study in the Control of Evidence." In *The Historian in Tropical Africa,* ed. J. Vansina, R. Mauny, and L. Thomas. Oxford University Press, 390–411.

1966 "The Position of Muslims in Metropolitan Ashanti in the Early Nineteenth Century." In *Islam in Tropical Africa,* ed. I. Lewis. Oxford University Press, 318–41.

1966 "Aspects of Bureaucratization in Ashanti in the Nineteenth Century." In *Perspectives on the African Past,* ed. M. Klein and G. Johnson. Little, Brown, 107–25. [Reprinted from *Journal of African History* 7, no. 2 (1966)]

1967 "Salih Bilali of Massina," "Abu Bakr al-Siddiq of Timbuktu," "Wargee of Astrakhan." Part 2 of *Africa Remembered,* ed. P. Curtin. University of Wisconsin Press, 143–89. [Reprinted and paperbound, 1968, 1977]

1967 "Ashanti Government." In *West African Kingdoms in the Nineteenth Century,* ed. D. Forde and P. Kaberry. Oxford University Press, 206–38. [Reprinted 1969, paperbound ed., 1971]

1968 "The Transmission of Islamic Learning in the Western Sudan." In *Literacy in Traditional Society,* ed. J. Goody. Cambridge University Press, 161–97. [Paperbound ed., 1975]

1968 "Writings in Gonja" [with J. Goody]. In *Literacy in Traditional Society,* ed. J. Goody. Cambridge University Press, 241–61. [Paperbound ed., 1975]

1968 "A Medieval Trade-route from the Niger to the Gulf of Guinea." In *Problems in African History,* ed. R. O. Collins. Prentice-Hall, 312–16. [Reprinted from *Journal of African History* 3, no. 2, (1962)]

1969 "A Note on Sovereignty." In *In Defense of Sovereignty,* ed. W. J. Stankiewicz. Oxford University Press, 197–205. [Reprinted from *Philosophical Quarterly* 5, no. 21, (October 1955)]

1970 "In Vindication of Sidi al-Hajj 'Abd al-Salam Shabayni" [with P. Ferguson]. In *African Perspectives,* ed. C. Allen and R. W. Johnson. Cambridge University Press, 35–52.

1970 "African Historiographical Traditions, Old and New." In *Africa Discovers Her Past,* ed. J. Fage. Oxford University Press, 7–17.

1970 "Documentary Sources for African History." In *Africa Discovers Her Past,* ed. J. Fage. Oxford University Press, 39–52.

1970 "Chiefs, Constitutions, and the British" [with P. Ferguson] In *West African Chiefs,* ed. M. Crowder and O. Ikime. University of Ife Press and Africana Publishing, 326–69.

1971 "Asante Policy towards the Hausa Trade in the 19th Century." in *The Development of Indigenous Trade and Markets in West Africa,* ed. C. Meillassoux. Oxford University Press, 124–41.

1971 "The Mossi and Akan States 1500–1800." In *History of West Africa,* ed. J. F. A. Ajayi and Michael Crowder. Longman and Columbia University Press, 1:chap. 10, 344–86.

1975 "Dissidence in Asante Politics: Two Tracts from the Late Nineteenth Century." In *African Themes: Northwestern University Studies in Honor of Gwendolen M. Carter,* ed. Ibrahim Abu-Lughod. Program of African Studies, Evanston, Ill., 47–63.

1976 "The Mossi and Akan States, 1500–1800." In *History of West Africa,* ed. J. F. A. Ajayi and Michael Crowder. 2d ed. Longman and Columbia University Press, 1:chap. 11, 413–55.

1977 "Land, Labour, Capital and the Forest Kingdom of Asante." In *The Evolution of Social Systems,* ed. J. Friedman and M. J. Rowlands. Duckworth and University of Pittsburgh Press, 487–534. [Paperbound ed., 1983]

1979 "The Golden Stool and the Elephant Tail: An Essay on Wealth in Asante." In *Research in Economic Anthropology* 2, ed. G. Dalton. JAI Press, 1–36.

1986 "The Mossi and the Akan States, 1400 to 1800." In *History of West Africa,* ed. J. F. Ade Ajayi and Michael Crowder. 3d ed. Longman and Columbia University Press, 1:chap. 11, 465–502.

1987 "What Manner of Persons Were These? Some Reflections on Asante Officialdom." In *The Golden Stool: Studies of the Asante Center and Periphery,* ed. E. Schildkrout. Anthropological Papers of the American Museum of Natural History 65, pt. 1, New York, 109–30.

1988 "She Who Blazed a Trail: Akyaawa Yikwan of Asante." In *Life Histories of African Women,* ed. Pat Romero. Ashfield Press, 113–139.

In press "The History of the Sunjata Epic: A Review of the Evidence." In *In Search of Sunjata: The Mande Oral Epic as History, Literature, and Performance,* ed. Ralph Austen. Indiana University Press.

Journal Articles

1955 "A Note on Sovereignty." *Philosophical Quarterly* 5, no. 21, 342–47.

1957 "The Rise of the Akwamu Empire, 1650–1710." *Transactions of the Historical Society of Ghana* 3, no. 2, 99–136.

1959 "Akwamu and Otublohum: An Eighteenth-Century Akan Marriage Arrangement." *Africa* 24, no. 4:391–404.

1960 "The Ashanti Kings in the Eighteenth Century: A Revised Chronology" [with Margaret Priestley]. *Journal of African History* 1, no. 1:83–96. [Reprinted, Bobbs-Merrill Reprint Series in Black Studies, BC-226]

1961 "The Northern Factor in Ashanti History: Begho and the Mande." *Journal of African History* 2, no 1:25–34. [Reprinted, Bobbs-Merrill Reprint Series, BC-318]

1961–62 "Qissatu Salga Tarikhu Gonja: The Story of Salaga and the History of Gonja" [with Mahmoud El-Wakkad]. *Ghana Notes and Queries* 3:8–13, and 4:6–25.

1962 "A Medieval Trade-route from the Niger to the Gulf of Guinea." *Journal of African History* 3, no. 2:337–41.

1962 "Islam in Ghana History: An Outline." *Ghana Bulletin of Theology* 2, no. 3:20–28.

1963 "The Growth of Islamic Learning in Ghana." *Journal of the Historical Society of Nigeria* 2, no. 4:409–17.

1966 "Aspects of Bureaucratization in Ashanti in the Nineteenth Century." *Journal of African History* 7, no. 2:215–32. [Reprinted, Bobbs-Merrill Reprint Series, BC-317]

1966 "A Note on the Early Spread of Islam in Dagomba." *Transactions of the Historical Society of Ghana* 8:87–98. [Reproduced, with corrections, Northwestern University Program of African Studies, Reprint Series No. 13]

1975 "Do Africans Have a Sense of Time?" *International Journal of African Historical Studies* 8, no. 2:279–87.

1982 "Portuguese, Wangara and Akan in the Fifteenth and Sixteenth Centuries: The Matter of Bitu." *Journal of African History* 23, no. 3:333–49.

1982 "Portuguese, Wangara and Akan in the Fifteenth and Sixteenth Centuries: The Struggle for Trade." *Journal of African History* 23, no. 4:463–72.

1982 "Insurrections in Wales and Texas: The Careers of John Rees." *Welsh History Review* 11, no. 2:67–91.
1982 "The State of the Akan and the Akan States: A Discursion." *Cahiers d'études africaines* 22, nos. 3–4:231–49.
1984 "Wales and the Black Country: The Wrexham Connection." *Blackcountryman* 17, no. 3:49–55.
1988 "Asante: Human Sacrifice or Capital Punishment? A Rejoinder." *International Journal of African Historical Studies* 21, no. 3:443–52.
1992 "On Mentally Mapping Greater Asante: A Study of Time and Motion." *Journal of African History* 33, no. 2:175–190.
1994 "'Slavery and Akan Origins?' A Reply." *Ethnohistory* 41, no. 4:657–65.
1995 "Consul Dupuis and Wangara: A Window on Islam in Early Nineteenth Century Asante." *Sudanic Africa* 6:55–72.

Shorter Pieces

1950 "The Welsh Advisory Council on Rural Depopulation." *Welsh Nation* 19, no. 3:1–2.
1951 "Resolutions, Resolution, Revolution." *Welsh Republican* 2, no. 2:3.
1952 "Aggression in Llyn." *Welsh Republican* 2, no. 4:3.
1953 "The Rebecca Revolt." *Welsh Republican* 3, no. 3:2.
1953 "Idris Davies: Poet of the People, Prophet of Revolt." *National Weekly* 5, 240:2 May, 3.
1954–55 Seven articles on the South Wales Uprising of 1839: "Revolt"; "'A Noble Cause': The Background of a Rebellion"; "Ripe to Rebel: Preparations for a Rising"; "Ballot or Bullet: Reformers and Radicals"; "Rebels in Arms: The Bid for Power"; "Rebel Assault: An End to Arms"; "A New Wales: Emigration and Revolution." *Welsh Republican,* Feb.–March 1954:2; June–July 1954:2; Aug.–Sept. 1954:2; Oct.–Nov. 1954:2; Dec. 1954–Jan. 1955:2; Feb.–Mar. 1955:2; April–May 1955:2.
1956 "Tribal History and Myth—I." *Universitas* (Legon), 84–86.
1956 "Tribal History and Myth—II." *Universitas* (Legon), 116–18.
1956 "Northern Territories Palaver." *West Africa,* 16 June:387.
1957 "Portrait. The Tolon Na." *West Africa,* 16 March:245.
1958 "A Note on Twifo and Akwamu." *Transactions of the Historical Society of Ghana* 4, no. 1:215–17.
1960 "A Burial Mound near Tamale, Ghana" [with P. Shinnie]. *Journal of the West African Science Association* 4, no. 1:47–48.
1960 "A Note on the Traditional History of Mampong." *Transactions of the Historical Society of Ghana* 4, no. 2:26–29.
1961 "Festival at Jenne." *West African Review,* June:48–50.
1961 "Burukung." *Ghana Notes and Queries* 1:11–12.
1962 "The Mande Loan Element in Twi." *Ghana Notes and Queries* 4:26–28.
1964 "Africa: History." *Collier's Encyclopedia,* rev. ed., 225–34.
1964 "The Institute of African Studies Collection of Arabic Manuscripts from Ghana; A Note on Material Relevant to Ashanti History." In *Ashanti Research Project. First Conference,* Institute of African Studies, Legon, 17–18.

1964 "The Ashanti of Rattray and the Ashanti of Reality." In *Ashanti Research Project. First Conference,* Institute of African Studies, Legon, 21–24.

1965 "Ghana." *Encyclopedia of Islam,* 2d ed., 1003–4.

1966 "A Note on the Chronology, and Origins, of the Gonja Kings." *Ghana Notes and Queries* 8:26–28.

1966 "The Saghanughu and the Spread of Maliki Law." *Research Bulletin, Centre of Arabic Documentation* (Ibadan) 2, no. 2:11–17.

1966 "A Note on the Arabic MS IASAR/298, and others, from Wa." *Research Review, Institute of African Studies, Ghana* 2, no. 2:63–68.

1971 "Ashanti." *Encyclopaedia Britannica,* 14th ed., 2:567–69.

1974 "Nkrumah, Kwame." *Encyclopaedia Britannica,* 15th ed., 13:136–37.

1975 "Asante Officialdom: A Note on Scaling by Rank, for Purposes of Multiple Career Line Analysis." *Asante Seminar '75* 2:18–20.

1976 "A Photograph of Asantehene Kwaku Dua II." *Asante Seminar '76* 4:39–40.

1976 "A Letter of 1819 from J. Ebelt to Asantehene Nana Agyeman Prempe." *Asante Seminar '76* 5:29–31.

1976 "A Letter of 1888 from Abū Bakr b. 'Uthmān Kamaghatay to Asantehene Nana Agyeman Prempe." *Asante Seminar '76* 4:42–44.

1977 "Boakye, Kwasi," "Boakye Tenten," "Kofi Kakari," "Kwaku Dua I," "Kwaku Dua II," "Mensa Bonsu," "Muhammad ibn al-Mustafa and 'Umar Kunandi ibn 'Umar," *Encyclopaedia Africana: Dictionary of African Biography,* vol. 1, *Ethiopia-Ghana,* 217–18, 218–19, 260, 265–66, 266, 268–69, 270–71.

1977 "Asante Officialdom: A Further Note on Rank." *Asantesem* 7:19–21.

1978 "The Population of Asante, 1817–1921: A Rejoinder." *Asantesem* 8:28–35.

1978 "The Chronology of the Asante Kings: a further revision," [with L. Yarak]. *Asantesem,* 8:39–40.

1978 "A Further Note on the Death of Asantehene Osei Yaw Akoto and on the Enstoolment of Kwaku Dua Panin," [with L. Yarak]. *Asantesem* 9:56–57.

1982–83 "Chronicles from Gonja." *Fontes Historiae Africanae,* nos. 7–8:5–8.

1984–85 "Samoriana" [with J. Hunwick]. *Fontes Historiae Africanae,* nos. 9–10:70–76.

1986 "R. A. Sargent: From a Redistribution to an Imperial Social Formation: Benin c. 1293–1536." *Canadian Journal of African Studies* 20, no. 3:437–38.

1987 "The Keeper of the Tales: The Bard and Oral Tradition." *Avalon to Camelot* 2, no. 4:10–12

1990 "Harri's Web: Ivor Wilks on the Welsh Republican Years." in *Planet: The Welsh Internationalist* 83:12–17.

1993 "A Note on the Asante Resident as 'Magistrate.'" *Akan Studies Council: Newsletter* 6:13–14.

1994 "Omanaso, and the Mines of the Great Elephant." *Ghana Studies Council: Newsletter* 7:6–7, and 8:3.

Reviews

1951 *The Social Consequences of Pneumoconiosis among Coalminers in South Wales,* HMSO, London, 1951. In *Welsh Republican,* Feb–Mar.:2.

1954 Hans Kohn, ed., *German History: Some New German Views,* Allen and Unwin, 1954. In *Universitas* (Legon), 1, no. 4.

1955 Henry Steele Commager, *Freedom, Loyalty, Dissent,* Oxford University Press, 1954. In *Universitas* (Legon), 1, no. 5:21–22.

1956 Thomas Hodgkin, *Nationalism in Colonial Africa,* Muller, 1956. In *Universitas* (Legon), 2, no. 4:127–28.

1958 Eva L. R. Meyerowitz, *The Akan of Ghana,* Faber and Faber, 1958. In *Universitas* (Legon), 3, no. 4:119–20.

1960 J. D. Fage, *Ghana: A Historical Interpretation,* University of Wisconsin Press, 1959. In *Journal of African History* 1, no. 2:323–25.

1961 Roland Oliver, ed., *The Dawn of African History,* Oxford University Press, 1961. In *West African Review,* Sept.:70–71.

1962 Eva L. R. Meyerowitz, *The Divine Kingship in Ghana and Ancient Egypt,* Faber and Faber, 1960. In *Ghana Bulletin of Theology* 2, no. 2:45–46.

1962 David Tait, *The Konkomba of Northern Ghana,* Oxford University Press, 1961. In *Universitas* (Legon), 5, no. 2:56–58.

1966 A. W. Lawrence, *Trade Castles and Forts of West Africa,* Jonathan Cape, 1963. In *Africa* 36, no. 4:460.

1967 Hugo Huber, *The Krobo: Traditional Social and Religious Life of a West African People,* The Anthropos Institute, 1963. In *Africa* 37, no. 3:553–54.

1968 Georg Norregard, *Danish Settlements in West Africa, 1658–1850,* Boston University Press, 1966. In *Journal of African History* 9, no. 1:162–64.

1968 William Bosman, *A New and Accurate Description of the Coast of Guinea,* Frank Cass, 1967. In *Journal of African History* 9, no. 1:164–66.

1969 J. A. Braimah and J. R. Goody, *Salaga: The Struggle for Power,* Humanities Press, 1967. In *African Historical Studies* 2, no. 2:338–39.

1977 Eva L. R. Meyerowitz, *The Early History of the Akan States of Ghana,* Red Candle Press, 1974. In *Africa* 47, no. 1:108–9.

1978 J. D. Fage, *A History of Africa,* Knopf, 1978. In *Chicago Sun-Times,* 31 December:9.

1979 Robin Law, *The Oyo Empire, c.1600–c.1836. A West African Imperialism in the Era of the Atlantic Slave Trade,* Clarendon Press, Oxford, 1977. In *African Affairs* 78, no. 311:272–74.

1979 Adda Bozeman, *Conflict in Africa. Concepts and Realities,* Princeton University Press, 1976. In *Journal of African History* 20, no. 2:309–10.

1979 Thomas J. Lewin, *Asante Before the British: The Prempean Years, 1875–1900,* Lawrence: The Regents Press of Kansas, 1978. In *Albion* 11, no. 1:99–101.

1980 Hywel Francis and David Smith, *The Fed: A History of the South Wales Miners in the Twentieth Century,* Lawrence and Wishart, 1980. In *Albion* 12, no. 3:308–10.

1980 Henrika Kuklick, *The Imperial Bureaucrat: The Colonial Administrative Service in the Gold Coast, 1920–1939.* In *Africana Journal* 11, nos. 1 and 2:163–64.

1981 Kwame Arhin, *West African Traders in Ghana in the Nineteenth and Twentieth Centuries,* Longman, 1980. In *Journal of African History* 22, no. 1:117–18.

1981 Timothy F. Garrard, *Akan Weights and the Gold Trade,* Longman, 1980. In *African Affairs.* 80, no. 320:417–18.

1982 J. Ki-Zerbo, ed., *General History of Africa,* vol. 1, "Methodology and African Prehistory"; and G. Mokhtar, ed., *General History of Africa,* vol. 2, "Ancient Civilizations of Africa," Heinmann, University of California Press, and UNESCO, 1981. In *International Journal of African History* 15, no. 2:283–85.

1982 M. D. McLeod, *The Asante,* British Museum Publications, 1981. In *Journal of African History* 23, no. 2:249–50.

1985 R. R. Davies, Ralph A. Griffiths, Ieuan Gwynedd Jones, Kenneth O. Morgan, eds., *Welsh Society and Nationhood,* University of Wales Press, 1984. In *Ninnau,* 1 February.

1985 Peter Beresford Ellis, *The Celtic Revolution. A Study in Anti-Imperialism,* Y Lolfa, 1985. In *Ninnau,* 15 August.

1985 John Rowlands, *In the Valley Long Ago,* trans. Graham Hughes, Washington, D.C., 1985. In *Ninnau,* 1 October.

1985 David Rees, *The Son of Prophecy: Henry Tudor's Road to Bosworth,* Black Raven Press, 1985. In *Ninnau,* 1 December:13.

1986 A. I. Asiwaju, ed., *Partitioned Africans: Ethnic Relations Across Africa's International Boundaries, 1884–1984,* St. Martin's Press, 1985. In *International Journal of African Historical Studies* 19, no. 1:171–73.

1986 Emyr Humphreys, *The Taliesin Tradition: A Quest for the Welsh Identity,* Black Raven Press, 1986. In *Ninnau,* 1 January:14.

1986 Chris Barber, *Cordell Country,* Blorenge Books, 1985. In *Ninnau,* 1 April:16.

1986 Olivier Zunz, ed., *Reliving the Past: The Worlds of Social History,* University of North Carolina Press, 1985. In *International Journal of African Historical Studies* 19, no. 3:575–77.

1986 Gwyn A. Williams, *When Was Wales? A History of the Welsh,* Black Raven Press, 1985. In *Ninnau,* 1 May:10.

1986 Emyr Humphreys, *The Taliesin Tradition: A Quest for the Welsh Identity,* Black Raven Press, 1983; and Gwyn A. Williams, *When Was Wales? A History of the Welsh,* Black Raven Press, 1985. In *Albion* 18, no. 3:551–54.

1986 B. Blackett and A. Wilson, *Artorius Rex Discovered,* King Arthur Research Publications, 1985. In *Ninnau,* 1 Oct.:16.

1986 Richard Faber, *High Road to England,* Faber and Faber, 1985. In *Albion* 18, no. 3:714–15.

1986 Gwyn Thomas, *A Few Selected Exits,* Seren Books, Bridgend, 1985. In *Ninnau,* 1 Dec.:16.

1989 A. H. Dodd, *A Short History of Wales,* Batsford, 1987; T. Herbert and G. E. Jones, eds., *Tudor Wales,* University of Wales Press, 1987; T. Herbert and G. E. Jones, eds., *Wales 1880–1914,* University of Wales Press, 1987. In *Albion* 21, no. 1:182–84.

1989 A. van Dantzig and A. Jones, eds., *Pieter de Marees. Description and Historical Account of the Gold Kingdom of Guinea (1602),* Oxford University Press, 1987; A. Jones, *Brandenburg Sources for West African History, 1680–1700,* Stuttgart, 1985. In *Africa* 59, no. 3:402–4.

1989 R. Roberts, *Warriors, Merchants, and Slaves: The State and the Economy in the Middle Niger Valley, 1700–1914,* Stanford University Press, 1987. In *Slavery and Abolition: A Journal of Comparative Studies* 10, no. 1:87–88.

1993 S. Pilaszewicz, *The Zabarma Conquest of North-west Ghana and Upper*

Volta. A Hausa Narrative "Histories of Samory and Babatu and others" by Mallam Abu, Polish Scientific Publishers, 1992. In *Sudanic Africa* 4:213–22.

1993 G. Williams, *The Welsh Church from Conquest to Reformation,* University of Arkansas Press, 1993; H. Thomas, *A History of Wales, 1485–1660,* University of Wales Press, 1991. In *Ninnau,* 1 Dec.:10.

1994 S. A. Winsnes, trans. and ed., *Letters on West Africa and the Slave Trade: Paul Erdmann Isert's "Journey to Guinea and the Caribbean Islands in Columbia,"* Oxford University Press, 1992. In *Sudanic Africa* 5:276–78.

1995 R. Rathbone, *Murder and Politics in Colonial Ghana,* Yale University Press, 1993. In *Journal of Interdisciplinary History* 26, no. 1:171–72.

1995 T. C. McCaskie, *State and Society in Pre-Colonial Asante,* Cambridge University Press. In *Journal of African History* 32. no. 1 (1996):138–40.

In press Jan Vansina, *Living with Africa,* University of Wisconsin Press, 1994. In *Ethnohistory.*

In press R. B. Edgerton, *The Fall of the Asante Empire,* Free Press, 1995. In *The Historian.*

In press Kenneth O. Morgan, *Modern Wales: Politics, Places, and People,* University of Wales Press, 1995. In *Albion,* 28, no. 3.

Poems

1947 "Poem for Epynt." *Welsh Nationalist,* April.

1948 "Sonnet." *Omnibus: Magazine of U.C.N.W., Bangor* 57, no. 1:28.

1949 "Sonnet." *Omnibus: Magazine of U.C.N.W., Bangor* 57, no. 2:17. [Joint winning sonnet, Inter-College Eisteddfod, 1949]

1983 "The March on Newport 1839." *Welsh Nation* 55, no. 11:5.

Notes on Contributors

Jean Allman is associate professor of African history at the University of Minnesota and chair of the Ghana Studies Council. She is the author of *The Quills of the Porcupine: Asante Nationalism in an Emergent Ghana* (1993) and related articles on the social history of Ghanaian politics. Her current research, focusing on gender and social change in colonial Asante, has appeared in the *Journal of African History, Gender and History,* and *History Workshop Journal.*

Ralph A. Austen is professor of African history, University of Chicago. His recent work includes *The Elusive Epic: The Narrative of Jeki la Njambe in the Historical Culture of the Cameroon Coast;* a coauthored book with Jonathan Derrick, *Middlemen of the Cameroon Rivers: The Duala and Their Hinterland, ca. 1600–ca. 1960;* and an edited volume, *In Search of Sunjata: The Mande Epic as History, Literature and Performance,* all published in 1996.

Basil Davidson, journalist and author, is probably the most widely read contemporary writer on African history, politics, and liberation movements. Among his many books are *Old Africa Rediscovered* (1959), *Africa in History* (1969), *The Eye of the Storm: Angola's People* (1972), *Modern Africa* (1983), *The Black Man's Burden: Africa and the Curse of the Nation State* (1992), and *The Search for Africa: History, Culture and Politics* (1994).

Esther Goody is lecturer in social anthropology at Cambridge University and a fellow of New Hall. She is the author of *Contexts of Kinship: An Essay in the Family Sociology of the Gonja of Northern Ghana* (1973) and *Parenthood and Social Reproduction: Fostering and Occupational Roles in West Africa* (1982); and editor of *Questions and Politeness: Strategies in Social Interaction* (1978),

From Craft to Industry: The Ethnography of Proto-industrial Cloth Production (1982), and *Social Intelligence and Interaction: Expressions and Implications of the Social Bias in Human Intelligence* (1995).

JACK GOODY is professor emeritus of social anthropology, Cambridge University, and fellow of St. John's College. He is the author of numerous books, including *The Interface between the Written and the Oral* (1987), *The Culture of Flowers* (1993), *The Expansive Moment: The Rise of Social Anthropology in Britain and Africa, 1918–1970* (1995), and, most recently, *The East in the West* (1996).

SANDRA E. GREENE is an associate professor of history at Cornell University. Her most recent publication is *Gender, Ethnicity and Social Change on the Upper Slave Coast* (1996). She is currently engaged in research on the changes that have occurred in the meanings that the Anlo attach to particular sites in the Keta District.

POLLY HILL is emeritus Smuts Reader in Commonwealth studies, Cambridge University. Her writings include *The Migrant Cocoa Farmers of Southern Ghana: A Study in Rural Capitalism* (1963), *Studies in Rural Capitalism in West Africa* (1970), *Rural Hausa: A Village and a Setting* (1972), and *Economics on Trial* (1986).

RAY A. KEA is professor of history at the University of California, Riverside. He formerly taught at Carleton and St. Olaf Colleges. His research interests are precolonial Ghanaian and West African history. He is the author of *Settlements, Trade, and Polities in the Seventeenth-Century Gold Coast* (1982) and many papers.

ROBERT S. KRAMER, a Northwestern Ph.D., is an assistant professor of history at St. Norbert College in De Pere, Wisconsin, specializing in the precolonial Sudan. He is the author of several articles on Islamic society in sub-Saharan Africa and a forthcoming study of Omdurman, the Mahdist capital.

ROBERT LAUNAY is professor of anthropology at Northwestern University. He has conducted extensive fieldwork among the Dyula of Ivory Coast. He is the author of *Traders Without Trade:*

Responses to Change in Two Dyula Communities (1982) and *Beyond the Stream: Islam and Society in a West African Town* (1992).

DONNA J. E. MAIER is a professor of African history at the University of Northern Iowa. She has published *Priests and Power: The Case of the Dente Shrine in Nineteenth-Century Ghana* (1983) as well as articles on the social and economic history of Asante's eastern periphery. She is currently an editor of *African Economic History*.

PAULO FERNANDO DE MORAES FARIAS currently teaches at the University of Birmingham (U.K.) and has previously held positions at the Centro de Estudos Afro-Orientais, Federal University of Bahia (Brazil), IFAN (Dakar, Senegal), and Ahmadu Bello University (Zaria, Nigeria). His current research interest is Arabic epigraphy in Mali and Borgu history. He is coeditor, with Karin Barber, of *Discourse and Its Disguises: The Interpretation of African Oral Texts* (1989) and *Self-Assertion and Brokerage: Early Cultural Nationalism in West Africa* (1990).

R. S. O'FAHEY is professor of history at the University of Bergen, Norway. He is the author of *State and Society in Dar Fur* (1980), *Land in Dar Fur* (1983), *Enigmatic Saint: Ahmad ibn Idris and the Idrisi Tradition* (1990), and *Arabic Literature of Africa,* Volume 1, *The Writings of Eastern Sudanic Africa* (1994).

DAVID OWUSU-ANSAH, formerly a visiting fellow at the Harry S. Truman Institute for International Peace at the Hebrew University of Jerusalem, is now an associate professor of African history at James Madison University. In addition to several scholarly articles, he is the author of *Islamic Talismanic Tradition in Nineteenth Century Asante* (1991), and coauthor, with Daniel M. McFarland, of *Historical Dictionary of Ghana* (2nd ed., 1995).

ENID SCHILDKROUT is curator of anthropology at the American Museum of Natural History and an adjunct professor at Columbia University. She does research in Ghana and Nigeria on ethnicity, women and children, and art. She is also concerned with representations of Africa in museums. Her most recent book, with Curtis A. Keim, is *African Reflections: Art from Northeastern Zaire* (1990).

Peter Shinnie is emeritus professor of archaeology, University of Calgary. He has taught at the University of Khartoum and the University of Ghana. He is author, among other works, of *Meroe: A Civilization of the Sudan* (1967), *The African Iron Age* (1971), and, with F. J. Kense, *Archaeology of Gonja, Ghana: Excavations at Daboya* (1989). His book *Ancient Nubia* will be published in 1996.

Victoria B. Tashjian is an assistant professor of history at St. Norbert College in De Pere, Wisconsin. She received her Ph.D. from Northwestern University in 1995. Her research interests include social change in rural Asante and Asante law during the colonial period.

Larry W. Yarak is an associate professor in the Department of History at Texas A&M University. His 1983 dissertation was published as *Asante and the Dutch, 1744—1873* (1990). His current research focuses on the social history of the Akan coastal districts in the nineteenth century.